Theory and the Evasion of History

Theory and the Evasion of History

David Ferris

The Johns Hopkins University Press
Baltimore and London

This book has been brought to publication with the generous assistance of the Frederick W. Hilles Publication Fund of Yale University.

Printed in the United States of America on acid-free paper

The Johns Hopkins University Press
2715 North Charles Street
Baltimore, Maryland 21218-4319
The Johns Hopkins Press Ltd., London

Library of Congress Cataloging-in-Publication Data

Ferris, David.
Theory and the evasion of history / David Ferris.
p. cm.
Includes bibliographical references and index.
ISBN 0-8018-4504-1
1. English literature—19th century—History and criticism—Theory, etc. 2. Literature and history—Great Britain—History—19th century. 3. Classical literature—History and criticism—Theory, etc. 4. Criticism—Great Britain—History—19th century. 5. Romanticism—Great Britain. 6. Rhetoric, Ancient. 7. Deconstruction. I. Title.
PR468.H57F47 1993
809—dc20 92-22951

A catalog record for this book is available from the British Library.

For Gordon, Adrienne, and Alison

ἐτεῇ οὐδὲν ἴσμεν περὶ οὐδενός,
ἀλλ' ἐπιρρυσμίη ἑκάστοισιν ἡ δόξις.

—Democritus, fr. 7

Contents

Preface

Is literary history a discipline of history? The question is Walter Benjamin's, and it is posed in a context of crisis about the name and nature of literary history. But, as Benjamin remarks, "if literary history is in the midst of a crisis, this crisis is only a partial aspect of a much more general crisis" since, "literary history is not only a discipline, but is, in its own development, a moment of general history."[1] Given the current revival of interest in the subject of literary history, these remarks and the question they lead to are still pertinent some sixty years after they were first written.[2] These remarks bear repeating precisely because the current interest in literary history may be read as the symptom of a crisis frequently attributed to the theoretical direction taken by literary study since the 1970s. If literary study is indeed in the midst of a crisis about what it is, never mind what it does, then the turn to literary history can be viewed as an attempt to face this crisis.[3] This turn does, however, run the risk of transforming this crisis into the origin of a history of literary history. In this respect, literary history would move closer to becoming a discipline of history since such a conclusion would demand that this crisis be regarded as a historical event in its own right—as if it could be attributed to something as specific as a conference or the publication of a book.[4] But can such a crisis be defined by the very historical understanding meant to be in crisis?

As Benjamin comments, if there is a crisis, it is a general crisis that cannot be localized in any particular event. Nor can it be localized within a particular branch of literary study such as literary history. The crisis is general because interpretation can never cease being a mode of historical understanding: to be able to account for how one interprets a particular literary text is to account for one's historical relation to that text.[5] It is this relation that constitutes the essential theoretical question of literary study. The question is theoretical because our relation to the past as well as to any event is not historical but rather linguistic in origin. It should be obvious that this question, despite its theoretical character, is directed at literary theory as much as it is directed at literary history: if it is a question about the ability of literary history to produce a historical knowledge of literature, it is also a question about literary theory's ability to produce a theoretical knowledge. In this way, the historical and theoretical study of literature are linked by their common need to account for the same relation. In terms of the question posed by Benjamin, this accounting, if successfully completed, would have the result of turning literary history as well as literary theory into a discipline of history. But is such an accounting possible?

In this context, Benjamin's response to his question about whether or not literary history is a discipline of history should be considered. Benjamin writes that this question has to receive a negative answer. Among the reasons cited for this answer is the origin of literary history. As Benjamin puts it, "Literary history did not at all emerge in the beginning within the framework of history . . . it was located, during the eighteenth century, between the handbook of aesthetics and the bookseller's catalog."[6] Yet there is a more general reason why literary history and, ipso facto, literary theory could never become a discipline of history. The object of literary history as well as literary theory is ultimately literature. Consequently, if the justification of literary history and literary theory may only be had through a historical relation to literature, then the object of their study is ill-suited to answering their needs. Unable to overcome this mismatch, it is not surprising that theory and history should try to resemble the literary more and more.

In each of the works discussed in the course of this book, the relation of literature to history is present as a subject of both theoretical and thematic importance: theoretically, in the case of the two critical texts that form the basis for the first part of this book, namely, Aristotle's *Poetics* and Coleridge's *Biographia Literaria,* and, thematically, in the case of the literary episodes discussed in the second part, namely, the Simplon Pass episode from Wordsworth's *The Prelude* and chapter 15 of George Eliot's *Middlemarch.* In each instance, the explicit focus is an evasion which literary history and literary theory cannot help but perform if they are to maintain themselves as a discipline.

The evasion to be discussed here may be quite readily discerned in those shifts which are traditionally evoked by literary history in order to distinguish, as in M. H. Abrams's example, an Aristotelian from a Romantic model of literature or even a shift from Romanticism's preoccupations with imagination, language, and literary tradition to the social and historical concerns that tend to dominate the interpretation of a narrative such as George Eliot's *Middlemarch.* In the readings that follow, such shifts are implicated as moments in which the distinction of both a historical and a theoretical project as well as the ability of one to define the other is at stake. However, as Abrams's appropriation of Yeats's metaphor would already indicate, the significance of such shifts cannot be restricted to the history they encapsulate so effectively. Here, the recasting of Yeats's "mirror turn lamp" into "mirror *and* lamp" underscores a recurrent pattern in Coleridge, Wordsworth, and Eliot.[7] The pattern involves the recourse to a grammatical paradigm as a means of deriving the relation of literature to history, literature to theory, as well as theory to history. As the recasting of Yeats's phrase indicates, the resulting history usurps its guiding paradigm. Such a usurpation and the grammatical form it relies upon is hardly enough to support so ingrained a shift in literary history. If this shift is to be sustained and achieve historical credence, then, what is shifted away from, namely mimesis, must be as unambiguous as the singularity of a historical event or act. In the end, such a shift is unsustainable (except as the expression of a desire for modernity) unless it is taken for granted that the concept of mimesis bequeathed to us by Aristotle is simply unproblematic. If such a shift is to gain historical credibility, mimesis can no longer be an issue of literary debate. Mimesis must be "for us a thing of the past," to use the words that Hegel reserved for the art of the historical period in which the shift from a mimetic to a formative model is said to take place.[8] It is in order to open the question of these shifts within literary history that the study undertaken in this book begins with Aristotle's attempt to elaborate a theory of mimetic language in the *Poetics.*[9]

Specifically, the first chapter examines how the definition of mimesis in Aristotle's *Poetics* turns upon a need to account for the historical relation demanded by its most essential preposition: about. Not only is the *Poetics* a text about the structure of tragedy but, first and foremost, it is a text about the possibility of a discourse on literature. As such, the *Poetics* is an account of its ability to be about literature. Here, the historical relation demanded by this preposition (what something is about would always be what it is preceded by even if this were not made manifest until the future) is inseparable from a theoretical project which would bring theory and history to their common completion in literature. Yet, this completion would entail the indistinguishability of history and theory from not just one another but also, in this case, from the historical object of their knowledge: literature. To avoid this eventuality, the *Poetics* adopts a concept of possibility as a means of establishing a relation between history and theory, on the one hand, and literature, on the other. Defined by their possibility, history and theory need never face what Aristotle could still call the art without a name but which, thanks to the adoption of the notion of possibility through which Aristotle invents critical discourse, this nameless art establishes a relation between history and theory in the form of literature. While this relation is given the name mimesis in Aristotle's *Poetics,* its mimetic effect is derived from an understanding of ῥυθμός, or rhythm, as a self-reflexive act. To trace mimesis to such an act is to admit the necessity of a purely formal moment as the source of an argument that advances a historical understanding of literature. Given the necessity of such a source, it is entirely predictable that the concept of mimesis presented in the *Poetics* should be viewed as essentially unproblematic. But, what could be less unproblematic or less contradictory than the definition of literature as a mode of imitation that owes its power of reflection to a self-reflexive origin? In this context, the history of criticism may be defined as the attempt to overcome or ignore this contradiction and it is such an attempt that may already be read in the *Poetics.*

While Coleridge's *Biographia Literaria* may be viewed as the reflection of a shift away from a concept of mimesis derived from the *Poetics,* the *Biographia* is, in the end, less a turning away from Aristotle than the attempt to redefine the historical relation left suspended by Aristotle in the form of a concept of possibility. In the case of Coleridge, this attempt focuses on the production and subsequent authority of a subject within critical discourse. As such, Coleridge makes explicit what may already be perceived within the *Poetics:* the inability of mimesis to account for the relation of Aristotle's argument to the object of its study. In short, what this amounts to is an inability of a critical or theoretical text to authorize itself (as if it possessed the means to arrive at a historical knowledge of itself and thereby decide its own historical importance). Since it is precisely this inability that informs what has become known as the crisis of the subject in Kant, the critical surpassing of Aristotelian mimesis may be linked to the overcoming of such a crisis. Yet, as the *Biographia* attempts to attain this goal it interrupts itself. This interruption becomes necessary because the structure and philosophical content of this work cannot be sustained by the grammatical paradigm of subject and predicate in which its central critical principle is expressed. The paradigm is interrupted so that the result to be derived from it will always be a possibility. At this point, the overcoming of Aristotle becomes a reenactment of the *Poetics* in the form of a crisis of the subject. From a model of history based on mimesis, one moves to a model based on crisis and interruption as history comes to reflect the inability of a subject to know its own history. Suffice it to add at this point that this understanding of history as a movement toward crisis defines the literary history that would now know itself in terms of a crisis. Here, the threat to historical authority becomes the source of a new authority for history as interruption becomes the form in which Coleridge transfigures the ῥυθμός of Aristotle into modernity.[10]

As mentioned earlier, the second part of this book turns to two quite discrete episodes in the poetry of Wordsworth and the fiction of George Eliot. This turn to literature is not intended to privilege literature at the end—as if literature were a panacea for the problems and questions that arise in the readings of Aristotle and Coleridge. Rather, the intention is to demonstrate how the question that informs two of the most crucial moments in critical and literary history is, in fact, an issue within literature. In the case of these two episodes, this issue can be most economically described as a question about how a literary text positions and reflects upon historical knowledge.

The position of historical knowledge within a literary text is examined first in the Simplon Pass episode of Wordsworth's *Prelude*. This episode turns upon an inability to see a conjunction of paths which subsequently allows Wordsworth to arrive at a theoretical recognition of a historical moment: the crossing of the Alps. The recognition is theoretical because the crossing is not experienced as a historical event. As such, this crossing is not only dependent on a theoretical conjunction but, through this dependency, it repeats the theoretical path followed by the subject of Sophocles' tragedy as he takes on the name of Oedipus. In this respect, the Simplon Pass episode reiterates the extent to which any resolution of the question of the subject and its authority insists upon an ability to know history as an intersection of name and place (which in this episode is a place of difference, the border). In the case of Wordsworth, it transpires that such a knowledge must also be derived from a grammatical paradigm. In this episode, however, the paradigm is missing its subject, the grammatical model remains incomplete. Only a predicate and perhaps only part of the predicate is given in the translated phrase on which so much turns in this episode: "that we had crossed the Alps." This phrase not only lacks a main clause but the only possible subject for that clause is someone who could never have spoken these words. The recourse to a grammatical paradigm as a means to derive both a subject and a knowledge of history also becomes in Wordsworth, as its does in Coleridge's *Biographia,* the necessary prelude to the rising of the imagination. Here, the interruption practiced by Coleridge occurs in the form of a translation. This translation is not just another version of what takes place in the *Biographia* but, rather, it defines Aristotle's reliance on form and Coleridge's on interruption as the translation of a difference—not between theory and history, on the one hand, and literature, on the other, but within literary history.[11] In this context, Wordsworth's account of historical knowledge in this episode defines the pass that such a translation must pass through. Whereas Aristotle and Coleridge approach such a pass, the *Prelude* is alone in reflecting upon the incompletable paradigm that now stands in the place of literary history.

If the legacy of the *Poetics* invites the recourse to a grammatical paradigm as a source for historical understanding, it is because Aristotle invents literary history as a metaphor for the discipline of history. In Coleridge and Wordsworth, the grammatical paradigm also becomes a metaphor for the historical relation of a subject to itself. Although the choice of Coleridge and Wordsworth would suggest that the problematic nature of this relation could be historically restricted to Romanticism, its recurrence, albeit in a different form, within chapter 15 of *Middlemarch* suggests, as Benjamin has already indicated, the presence of a general difficulty that transgresses historical as well as literary fields.

The title of *Middlemarch* already implies what has been at issue in Aristotle, Coleridge, and Wordsworth: the question of a relation to history, the question of a middle term. In the case of Eliot's novel the grammatical and rhetorical aspects of this question become clear if one recalls George Puttenham's *The Arte of English Poesie* (1589) in which the Greek figure mezozeugma is called a "middlemarcher."[12] Mezozeugma is the rhetorical term describing a grammatical structure wherein a single word, usually the verb, not only belongs to two separate phrases but occurs as the middle term through which they are joined. This rhetorical figure marks the incomplete repetition of a grammatical pattern which, once recognized, would not be deficient in grammar at all. In this case, the rhetorical performs the completion of grammar by identifying a repressed repetition which, as a result of this identification, would no longer need to be produced. (The relevance of this repressed repetition to the missing deduction of the *Biographia* and the missed crossing of the Simplon Pass episode should be obvious.) The narrative of this chapter from *Middlemarch* explores the production of such a middle term in three parts: first, through the narrator and the metaphor of weaving; second, through the scientific researcher whose experiments would have immediate historical significance if successful; and, third, through the actress who murders her husband in the course of a dramatic production. The first two parts of this narrative make explicit use of the metaphor of weaving and its web as an index of historical relations. It is this web and this weaving that both the narrator and the scientist are implicated in as they attempt to unravel such a metaphor in the pursuit of historical veracity. But, more than anything else, it is the thematic insistence on this metaphor that forms the subject of this study. The significance of this episode to the difficulty encountered by Aristotle, Coleridge, and Wordsworth is realized in the third part of the narrative recounted in chapter 15 of *Middlemarch* when Eliot relates an incident that addresses the necessity of not just this metaphor but the recourse to grammar as a model for historical knowledge. This incident tells the story of an actress who murders her husband in a melodrama in which she is supposed to murder the character played by her husband. Here, the combination of act and text poses several questions about a difference which the mimesis of Aristotle, the interruption of Coleridge, the translation of Wordsworth and the thematization of this difference in weaving would all evade. Is the murder a literary or a historical act? Can a text, for example Eliot's, be the source of a distinction between history and literature? If so, is this text theory or history? Is it literary history?

The questions posed by Eliot's actress cannot be restricted to *Middlemarch.* The questions themselves call for the intervention of metaphor and, in so doing, they reproduce the difficulty of articulating the historical relation that determines the course of Aristotle's *Poetics,* Coleridge's *Biographia,* and the Simplon Pass episode from Wordsworth's *Prelude.* Nonetheless, when weaving is the metaphor, a thematic history that extends from Plato to beyond Eliot is invoked. The middle term to which the weaving and unraveling in *Middlemarch* owe so much goes by the name of a "primitive tissue." Despite the reference to nineteenth-century science, this phrase also translates what Plato refers to as πρώτη συμπλωκή or "primary interlacing" in the *Sophist.* For Plato this phrase describes the simplest and most essential grammatical paradigm (subject and verb). Here, the recourse to metaphor would be woven into a history that goes hand in hand with grammar. It is such a weaving that the final part of this chapter from *Middlemarch* confronts with an example whose unraveling does not lead to historical knowledge but only to the sense that *something* happened. While it is always tempting to read this moment as the failure of mimesis (and thereby assert our modernity or, more precisely, our Romanticism), it should not be forgotten that mimesis is a player in the production of this same moment. Without the possibility of history associated with mimesis, there would have been a murder but, then, this murder would have been nothing less than the murder of mimesis.

A murder of this kind also takes place when the exclusion of mimesis becomes the basis of a shift in literary history. When such an exclusion becomes a historical act in its own right, one can be sure of the thoroughly dialectical nature of the literary treatment of history. For such a treatment, philosophy must be thanked for it was Plato who taught history how to murder mimesis. In this context, the exclusion of mimesis takes on the character of a political act reminiscent of that exclusion that would assure the health of the republic. In this case, such an exclusion allows a republic of letters to find its definition in the form of literature. Yet, if the examples of Aristotle, Coleridge, Wordsworth, and Eliot are remembered here, it is only by excluding the arguments that lead to such a definition that the definition can avoid facing history. This is why, in each of the readings presented here, there arises an unavoidable tendency within literary study to produce a formal understanding of history—neither new historicism nor the politicization of literary study can forgo this tendency. The recourse to this formal understanding is unavoidable, since, in the words of Democritus which stand as the epigraph to this book, "We know nothing real about nothing, but everyone gives a form to their opinion."[13] What we really know about history may be the question of literature, and, if it is, it is a question about form, about formal arrangement, about the ῥυθμός Aristotle will adopt as a definition of mimesis in the *Poetics*. Such a reliance on form leads to literary history and literary theory as disciplines but not a discipline of history. In this light, the theoretical critique of literary history is nothing less than literary history critiquing itself in the form of a crisis, and, such a critique amounts to an evasion of its inability to become a discipline of history.

Despite the chronological ordering of the authors discussed in this book, the pattern followed by these chapters is less one of historical development than the necessity of returning to those questions which any such development must first ask of itself. In returning to the question of literary history, the readings undertaken in this book have been written in almost constant reference to Aristotle's *Poetics*. This reference is not only a reflection of the significance of the *Poetics* to literary history and theory but it underlines the philosophical provenance of literary study as well as, in the case of Coleridge, the necessity of a divorce from this same provenance. By returning to such a historical provenance, this study aims at nothing more than the retracing of the intellectual debts of literary interpretation. This movement does, however, involve a risk, the risk of entering into, as Arthur Lovejoy, writing in 1940, so aptly described as a dangerous liaison: "The liaison between literary and philosophical study . . . is no doubt regarded by some students of literature and its history as a *liaison dangereuse*."[14] The liaison is dangerous if only because it is so frequently misunderstood and thereby set aside. It would be a great mistake to set aside the debt of literary history to philosophy, and, in particular, the decisive role of

Aristotle in defining the form of this debt. At the same time, if we flip the coin of literary history and read its other side, it is plain that any attempt to turn philosophy into literature would be just as great a mistake and just as dangerous a liaison. Between the two, there is the question of a difference that history has already made. From the evasion of this difference there arises the transfiguration that makes literary theory literary history.

Acknowledgments

Among those who have read and commented on this book both as a dissertation and in its present form, a special debt of gratitude is owed to Carol Jacobs, Rodolphe Gasché, and Irving Massey.

Special thanks are due to Anna, whose careful eye brought a sense of grammar to a syntax not always convinced of its need and also to Gordon, Adrienne, and Alison, without whose interruptions this would not have been half as pleasurable as it was.

For the diligent preparation of the manuscript, thanks are due to Adrienne Mayor.

Parts of chapter 2, now extensively revised, first appeared as "Ventriloquus Interruptus: The Abduction from the *Biographia,*" in *Studies in Romanticism* 24 (1985):41–84 (copyright holder, the Trustees of Boston University). A version of chapter 3 first appeared as "Where Three Paths Meet: History, Wordsworth, and the Simplon Pass," in *Studies in Romanticism* 30 (1991):391–438 (copyright holder, the Trustees of Boston University).

CHAPTER ONE

The Possibility of Literary History ❧ *Aristotle*

> *Wiederholung des Möglichen bedeutet gerade nicht das Aufgreifen dessen, was "gang und gäbe" ist, wovon "begründete Aussicht besteht," daß sich daraus "etwas machen läßt." Dieses Mögliche ist allemal nur das allzu Wirkliche, das im je herrschenden Betrieb jedermann handhabt. Das Mögliche in dieser Bedeutung verhindert gerade eine echte Wiederholung und damit überhaupt ein Verhältnis zur Geschichte.*
>
> —Heidegger, *Kant und das Problem der Metaphysik*

. . . περὶ ποιητικῆς αὐτῆς . . . of, about, around, concerning what is capable of production (in) itself . . . to these opening words of Aristotle's *Poetics* literary criticism cannot fail to recognize an indebtedness. Acceptance of this debt does not, however, prevent the *Poetics* from being assigned the role of an archaeological remain whose critical significance may be compared to a curiosity that fleshes out the stage on which the insights of succeeding criticism perform their denouements. Yet, the tendency to assign the *Poetics* such a role cannot be attributed solely to the hubris of subsequent critical history. Rather, this tendency belongs to a critical practice whose investment in the possibility of a poetics of literature was already defined through Aristotle's *Poetics*. By reducing the *Poetics* to an archaeological remain, this critical practice would effectively set aside the text in which the possibility of its historical existence is first defined. As a result, the *Poetics* takes its place in a history that will always begin περὶ *τῆς* Ποιητικῆς . . . [About *the* Poetics . . .] as if the question of literary production had been settled long ago.

Despite the critical reduction of the *Poetics* to a fact of history, the significance of Aristotle's *Poetics* is neither archaeological nor simply historical.[1] No matter how outmoded Aristotle's terms may now seem, what remains crucial within the argument of the *Poetics* is its explicit derivation of meaning in literature from a formal concept of history. The unavoidable role of such a concept at the very origin of literary interpretation should not be overlooked even though modern critical and literary history has been reluctant to discover the conditions governing its own history within antiquity (not to mention any consideration of how antiquity already formulated this reluctance as the necessary first step in the development of criticism). More specifically, it appears to be necessary for modern critical and literary history to avoid the question of how the argument of Aristotle's text moves from the produced to a knowledge of production, that is, it must avoid the question of how Aristotle strives to produce this work as a poetics of literature. Ultimately, such an avoidance is hardly an accidental or isolated event in literary history. Indeed, an avoidance of this kind appears to be absolutely necessary if literary criticism is to possess a history of its own. Unquestioned, this history would effectively foreclose any inquiry into the relation between the *Poetics* and the history which has decided its critical place. But if this foreclosure is to be possible, and if the *Poetics* is to be considered a genuinely critical work, then it must also be capable of producing a model of history that denies any such inquiry.[2] In other words, the *Poetics* must be capable of determining the necessity of an avoidance which will always allow the critical significance of the *Poetics* to be understood as the effect of a literary history it helped produce.

Within literary history, the significance of the *Poetics* has focused all too often on the meaning of certain terms that have attained a dominant place in the interpretation of this work, for example, fault (ἁμαρτία), plot (μῦθος), imitation (μίμησις), and above all, catharsis.[3] The continuing resistance of these terms to any definitive critical understanding indicates, at least thematically, their role in establishing a debt that can never be paid off. As a result of this resistance, both the *Poetics* and the history it engenders seem doomed to the endless reinterpretation of these terms. In this case, the model of history produced by the *Poetics* could only be synonymous with this endless task. Yet, to the extent that such an endless history is driven by the task of recovering a specificity of meaning now lost, this history is governed by the possibility of denying the goal that defines it. Consequently, if the critical history initiated by the *Poetics* is to avoid this denial, it must already possess the means to set aside but not forgo such a goal.[4]

The reading of the *Poetics* as an example of formalist criticism plays an important role in securing a history that fosters its own denial. Indeed, this reading of the *Poetics* sustains such a model of history by emphasizing formal attributes in the place vacated by a presumed loss of meaning. Through this emphasis, it becomes clear that the historical cannot be disassociated from the formal particularly since the definition of the *Poetics* as a work of formalist criticism (if not *the* work of this kind of criticism) arises within a critical history that has always adopted ahistorical or formal techniques of analysis—even when a quite different political or social interpretation is anticipated.[5] In this instance, historically oriented approaches must admit, at some level, an unavoidable formal moment. This intervention of the formal is not a weakness in historical thought but rather the condition of its continued significance. By this recourse to the formal, history no longer needs to be defined by the attainment of a definite end, rather, it will be defined and protected by the *possibility* of such an end.

Both the historical reduction of the *Poetics* to an archaeological remain and the formalist reading of this work thus reveal a crucial interrelation. Why this interrelation should be present as well as necessary in two approaches whose results would seem to be so utterly different from one another raises several questions. If this interrelation of the historical and the formal constitutes literary history, then, what is the relation between, on the one hand, the formal structure of Aristotle's argument in the *Poetics* and, on the other, the critical history inaugurated by this work? What is at stake in the argument of the *Poetics* that it needs to be determined by history as bequeathing only a formalist understanding of literature? Moreover, if the *Poetics* can inaugurate the history of criticism through which it is subsequently defined and, at the same time, be part of that history, then, to what is it indebted? The analysis of these questions will involve an inquiry into the structure of the history that the thematic and formalist reading of this text would not willingly disclose or, at best, would argue that it cannot be known except as the disclosure which speaks (apocalyptically) about the end of all history. As will already be obvious, no empirical sense of history (the singularity of an event) is at stake in this structure or, more generally, in critical reflection. Nor can this structure be unfolded in the form of a history that merely assigns such a structure a place within the evolution of critical thought and procedure. To do so is to write the same critical history in the form of the history of history—precisely the form of history that Hegel was to call critical and which was nothing more than a "criticism of historical narratives and an inquiry into their truth and credibility."[6] Rather, what is involved here is the nature of a fundamentally unavoidable structuring which the more common sense of history seeks to bring within its sphere of indebtedness and thereby transfigure it into the offspring of its authority.

To select Aristotle's *Poetics* as the exemplary ground for an inquiry into a structure that lies at the basis of critical reflection would appear to repeat how subsequent critical history has defined this work as its primary text. There is, however, a difference between the exemplarity examined here and the primacy bequeathed to the *Poetics* by the history of criticism. The exemplariness analyzed here is concerned with nothing less than the possibility of producing a primacy that would determine both the discourse of the *Poetics* as well as the critical discourse on the *Poetics*. Within the *Poetics,* the production of such a primacy would establish beyond all question that mimesis, as a mode of analogical substitution and repetition, may indeed yield knowledge according to Aristotle's example in chapter 4 of the *Poetics*.[7] Similarly, the primacy bestowed on the *Poetics* by subsequent critical reflection is unthinkable without the substitutive model of mimesis that permits the *Poetics* to discourse on literature in the first place. Yet, what enables the discourse *of* the *Poetics* as well as the discourse *on* the *Poetics* cannot be reduced to a simple matter of substitution or repetition—as if the power of substitution and repetition associated with mimesis were a natural rather than a critical necessity. Within literary criticism such substitution and repetition will, however, always be unavoidable, since each sustains a mode of exemplification without which literature could not appear as the object of critical reflection. As a result of this necessity, the production of such an exemplification will be the task of the critical history that is said to begin with the *Poetics*—this text being taken first *as* the example of such a beginning.

To read the unavoidable structure that marks the possibility of critical reflection it is thus necessary to analyze how the *Poetics* inaugurates criticism by producing a theory of exemplification—a theory that will guarantee the exemplary status of this same text within critical history. Hence, to read the production of exemplariness in the *Poetics* is far from affirming it as a historical origin for subsequent critical reflection. To read the *Poetics* as an exemplary text is rather to examine criticism articulating its historical nature in the form of an exemplary problematic which allows this history to continue by ensuring the primacy of *its* problematic origin.[8]

The Path of Example

Example, my good friend, needs in turn an example of its own.

—Plato, *Statesman*

As if to repeat its treatment by the history it is about to inaugurate, the argument of the *Poetics* begins with an example when it refers to nature as the source of its method. With this recourse to nature, a larger question is already posed even though it will be quickly forgotten as the study of the capacity to produce (ἡ ποιητική) narrows and defines its focus through literature: the question of the relation between philosophy and that discourse on the poetic which will later be known as literary criticism. In the *Poetics,* such a relation would be forged in the name of nature since the argument of this text unfolds according to its example (κατὰ φύσιν [47^a12]). As such, the *Poetics* would be written under the guidance of a nature that would already define the method of its argument in terms of the substitutive and repetitive definition of mimesis. This manner of proceeding leads directly to the determination of the capacity to produce which occurs in poetry and music as being essentially mimetic—as if it were the nature of poetry and music to be mimetic by virtue of being poetry and music. However, mimesis must already be at work since this assumption about poetry and music is only possible if the *Poetics* is inscribed within an inherently but unstated mimetic relation between the argument of this text and the nature it follows. Moreover, the *Poetics* must sustain its own argument within this relation if it is to remain, from the beginning, a discourse about the poetic, that is, if it is to possess the title to a discourse about the poetic—περὶ ποιητικῆς. . . . It is the referential relation announced by this preposition, by this "about" (περί) which poses the central question of the *Poetics*. In effect, the *Poetics* is about a preposition that both this work and the history *of* criticism cannot help but overlook in their preoccupation, even obsession, with theories of mimesis, representation, figuration.

Already the method of argument adopted by the *Poetics* suggests an inquiry into mimesis conducted by mimesis, a procedure that would indicate that the object to be inquired into has already determined the means as well as the outcome of such an inquiry. Immediately prior to evoking the example of nature, Aristotle refers to this procedure by the word μέθοδος in a phrase whose repetition of the preposition (περί) with which the *Poetics* begins indicates that method and the poetic cannot be addressed separately: "About the poetic itself and its forms . . . and likewise about other things insofar as they belong in the same inquiry (ὁμοίς δὲ καὶ περὶ τῶν ἄλλων ὅσα τῆς αὐτῆς ἐστι μεθόδου), let us speak . . ." ($47^{a}8$–12).[9] Although inquiry or research are more accurate renderings of μέθοδος than a straight transliteration of the Greek word, they belong, nonetheless, to the logic of method, to the logic of the path (ὁδός) that follows after, among, and across (all implicitly present in the preposition μετά), to the logic of a path that re-searches for itself.[10] As such, the method of the *Poetics* would be the means to regulate the relation between the mimesis of the inquiry and the mimesis examined as a result of this inquiry. What then becomes absolutely necessary is a method that permits mimesis to inquire into itself in such a way that there should be no asking after how this mimesis is produced even though the concept of method presented here could not be thought unless such a production had already taken place. But, if method is to inquire into what it is preceded by (mimesis), then, method must follow a path already determined by the object of its research. Consequently, this method is nothing less than the work of a mimesis which has substituted method for itself: hardly a disinterested act since the substitution of the name of method for mimesis disguises the work of mimesis while affirming its substitutive power. As a result, any reading of the place occupied by the *Poetics* in the history of criticism must first be directed at how the necessity of this substitution is produced. In order to inquire into such a necessity, this reading must first be directed at the way in which method produces the path it will follow. Properly speaking, the question of method is a question about its *re*production. In this light, the opening words of the *Poetics* should rather be περὶ μεταποιητικῆς τῆς ὁδοῦ [about the after-production of the path]. The question that the *Poetics* turns around is therefore not only a question about mimesis in literature but rather a question of the mimesis necessary to the method of its argument—the very mimesis at work in the relation between the example of nature and the inquiry which, by acting in accordance to this same nature, determines the poetic as literature. What is then at stake in the method of the *Poetics* is nothing less than the ability to be about literature, in short, nothing less than the ability to become critical.

In the opening sentence of the *Poetics*—and before the phrase which announces that the method is to take nature as its example—the difficulty to be confronted by the mimesis of this text appears when the concept of possibility or potentiality (δύναμις) is introduced: "About the poetic itself and its forms (εἴδων), the potentiality (δύναμιν) which each [form] possesses . . . let us speak (λέγωμεν) . . ." ($47^{a}8$–12).[11] Here, the concept of potentiality is adopted as the means of establishing an analogy between the discourse of the *Poetics* and what this discourse takes as its subject. In this respect, the role given to potentiality in the *Poetics* follows the definition of this term in Aristotle's *Metaphysics*.[12] According to the definition presented in the *Metaphysics,* a poetic form may come into existence because it is preceded by something that is both actual and different from this form.[13] Although potentiality provides the link that bridges this difference, it is unthinkable unless it can be derived from a form.

In temporal terms potentiality can only be known and only be recognized as possessing a prior existence after the form has been realized. As such, form is already understood as the production of not simply its own past but as the production of what would be more accurately described as its potential past. Yet, if the *Poetics* is to affirm its right to speak about production in literature, it must regard this potential past as if it had all the status of a historical event. Since form provides the definition through which literature is to be approached in the *Poetics,* this work must then account for the difference between form and potentiality as a historical difference.

Here, it is evident that the relation between interpretation and text as it is defined by the *Poetics* involves, first and foremost, a formal concept of history. Without this concept there could be nothing for the *Poetics* to be about since the art of production which it takes as its subject would have no historical record of its activity or even of its existence. Yet, before the *Poetics* can apply this difference to the production of literature, it must first justify its adoption as an organizing principle within the argument of the *Poetics.* This is why the *Poetics* must be read as a text about the potentiality of its own production; it is a text that attempts to produce a potential history as the basis of the discourse on the poetic. Consequently, through the adoption of this concept of potentiality, what governs the production of a poetic form is nothing less than a history that has been derived from a concept of formal difference.[14] What is truly crucial to the *Poetics* is less an analysis of the form of Greek tragedy than the production of a potentiality for criticism. In the *Poetics,* literature is to be determined as the form, that is, as the visual product (εἶδος: "what is seen") of the potentiality of criticism.

Already in the adoption of such a concept of potentiality, the difficulty of this text's discourse would be concealed by the unannounced, unwitnessed, yet necessary operation of a mimesis. Through mimesis the potentiality of the εἶδος, or form, becomes known. Mimesis thus serves as the means of bringing to sight a potentiality that can never be known separately from its future use. Potentiality can neither be seen nor even be known as itself but only as the effect of a history (that is, a use) which it cannot predict. In this respect, mimesis permits potentiality to be known while at the same time avoiding the situation in which potentiality, by becoming *known in itself,* would no longer be potential since it would have become, in effect, actual.[15] If mimesis is to govern the relation between potentiality and form, then, mimesis is not primarily concerned with the reproduction of some actual or possible object (that is only its consequence) but rather with producing a difference that allows such a reproduction to become knowable, at least potentially, in terms of a history. Potentiality thus owes its existence to a mimesis that transfigures a formal difference into a historical and thus temporally measured difference. Primacy, exemplification, and method, all depend on this transfiguration. In other words, the *Poetics* represents the attempt to reproduce a formal difference that will regulate critical reflection and its history. As such, mimesis invents literary history as the repetition of a difference in form whose potentiality will be subsequently called literature.

In the *Poetics,* the attempt to define literature as the potentiality of history may be traced from the differentiation of forms of mimesis which Aristotle introduces immediately after referring to nature as the example that guides the inquiry of this text. In the sentence that occurs immediately after the opening statement of the *Poetics,* Aristotle lists the various artistic productions that belong to mimetic production: "Epic and tragic poetry, and also comedy, dithyrambic poetry, and most flute-playing and lyre-playing, happen to be in general all mimetic" (47ª13–16). This passage marks the first attempt to relate difference to a form of analogy in the *Poetics* and as such it would provide the basis for the production of differences within the arts of mimesis. Within this list, it is stated that "most flute-playing and lyre-playing" are mimetic. This distinction, which divides one single activity within itself, marks the point at which Aristotle's list of mimetic forms moves from distinctions between different means of producing mimesis to a distinction between the mimetic and the non-mimetic within one of those means. As is the case with the concept of potentiality, this mimesis is to be known in a form. Thus, at this stage of Aristotle's argument, the production of mimesis would already be indistinguishable from the production of forms (which is to say, it is indistinguishable from what differentiates one form from another). Since the sentence that follows this distinction of one kind of flute-playing and lyre-playing from another is concerned only with differences within this already delimited field and not at all with how or why the difference between mimetic and non-mimetic playing is established (never mind why the playing of music is the site of this distinction) there would appear to be no means of intervening in the argument derived from this distinction. Nevertheless, Aristotle's elaboration of these differences and, in particular, how they relate to one another, permits the analysis of this distinction within an argument that clearly points to the necessity of such a distinction whether or not it is made with respect to music: "They [mimetic productions] differ from one another in three ways; either they imitate by different mediums (ἐν ἑτέροις) or they imitate different objects (ἕτερα) or they imitate differently and not by the same manner (ἑτέρως καὶ μὴ τὸν αὐτὸν τρόπον)" (47^a16–18). Each step in this elaboration of differences depends upon an internal distinction in the preceding step. The sequence begins with an essentially external and empirical difference through which, for example, imitative music, and imitative language could be distinguished from one another solely by virtue of their medium of production. Second, each of these media may be differentiated internally as a result of the object to be imitated. Third, it is possible to imitate this same object according to a different mode or manner, for example, the same person could be the subject of an epic or an elegy. This sequence of distinctions is both exhaustive and self-generating to the extent that any work is potentially mimetic as long as it uses a medium that belongs, by nature, to mimesis. Furthermore, mimesis emerges as an activity unaffected by differences either in what is imitated or in the mode of imitation. Yet, no object could arise for mimesis unless the assumption made in the first step of this trifold sequence is accepted, namely, the assumption of a natural relation between mimesis and a given medium such as language (to refer to the example of 47^a13–16).

The sequence of differentiations analyzed to this point take place immediately following the distinction between mimetic and non-mimetic music. This distinction circumscribes and organizes the subsequent series of differences within the field of mimesis since it alone marks a border within which mimesis and, consequently, the concept of potentiality may be operative. However, the distinction that defines this field must again be different in kind from the internal distinctions it gives rise to otherwise it could not sustain itself as the boundary between the mimetic and the non-mimetic. On what ground is this distinction made?

According to the ordering of the argument of the *Poetics,* the only approach to this question takes place by considering those media where mimesis is already said to be at work. The lack of any explicit return to the question of the non-mimetic in the subsequent sentences of the *Poetics* would suggest that it is not a problem within this text's argument. Nonetheless, in the sentence immediately following the reference to "most flute-playing and lyre-playing" and the statement of differences between imitations, Aristotle introduces three terms intended to affirm and guide the production of mimesis within differing media:

> Just as some, whether by art or habit, make use of colors and figures (σχήμασι) to imitate many things by making images (ἀπεικάζοντες), others make use of sound (φωνῆς); even so, with the arts already mentioned, all produce mimesis in rhythm (ῥυθμῷ), language (λόγῳ), and harmony (ἁρμονίᾳ), either separately or in combination. (47ª18–23)

Again, an initial distinction is made which, in this case, isolates those arts whose mimetic effect is derived from merely visual productions. In contrast to, but also in analogy to these arts, there is a mimesis that occurs through sound. The use of φωνή (voice) to characterize this sound would also define this other mimesis in terms of speech—φωνή refers to articulated sound and, in particular, the sound of the human voice, rather than sound in general.[16] Since mimetic music is not referred to as an example of sound in general (ψόφος) but as a mode of speech, the initial occurrence of the distinction between mimetic and non-mimetic music should be considered less a distinction between, on the one hand, undifferentiated noise and, on the other, articulated sound. Rather, it is a distinction between what can be figured as speech (because human in origin) and other articulated sounds (some flute-playing and lyre-playing) which are excluded from this figuration. Hence, the appearance of a distinction between a mimesis based on colors and figures and a mimesis based on sound disguises a more important distinction yet unresolved between mimetic and non-mimetic sound. At the same time, the recourse to human sound as the basis of this unresolved distinction already indicates the extent to which any relation between an object and its interpretation tends to return to language even if such a return cannot fully account for the distinction made in its name. The occurrence of this recourse so early in the *Poetics* poses two questions. Why does language need, on the one hand, to recognize the articulations of flute-playing and lyre-playing according to human sound, and, on the other, set aside everything which cannot be figured as such? And why must a distinction based upon the articulation of speech take place within the production of musical sound?

The Dance of Rhythm

> *Un art tient la scène, historique avec le Drame; avec le Ballet, autre, emblématique. Allier, mais ne confondre; ce n'est point d'emblée et par traitement commun qu'il faut joindre deux attitudes jalouses de leur silence respectif, la mimique et la danse, tout à coup hostile si l'on force l'approchement. Exemple qui illustre ce propos . . .*
>
> —Mallarmé, "Ballets," *Crayonné au théâtre*

Having made the distinction between a mimetic and a non-mimetic music, the *Poetics* continues by emphasizing the elements of harmony and rhythm. The introduction of these elements should provide, at least conceptually, the means to account for the mimesis of music and thereby permit music to be separated from a sequence in which the articulation of human language (φωνή) provides the privileged model. Indeed, when rhythm and harmony are spoken of in relation to music, no direct reference to language takes place. At the same time, there is no longer any question about the ability of harmony and rhythm to divide flute- and lyre-playing into mimetic and non-mimetic parts. Aristotle states quite simply:

> Harmony and rhythm alone are used by flute-playing and lyre-playing as well as any other art which has the same potential (δύναμιν) such as the art of the pipes. (47^a23–26)

Although the introduction of harmony and rhythm into this argument would explain why music is mimetic, nothing explains why harmony and rhythm should be synonymous with mimesis. The question initially posed by the division of flute- and lyre-playing into mimetic and non-mimetic parts thus remains: can harmony and rhythm be denied all flute- and lyre-playing? The persistence of this question leads to the more general issue of why the *Poetics* should rely upon non-linguistic examples in an argument whose primary concern will be the mimesis produced by literary works. This issue is brought sharply into focus when it is realized that the example of flute- and lyre-playing marks the first application of the three elements (rhythm, language, and harmony) to which Aristotle traces the production of mimesis. Why does Aristotle give no example of a mimesis produced by (rather than in) language either by itself or in conjunction with rhythm or harmony at this point in the argument? A first response to this question would be to state that the division between mimetic and non-mimetic flute- and lyre-playing must be accounted for first. If this is the case, then, the initial difficulty faced by the *Poetics* will be to account for a formal difference from which the presence of mimesis may be derived within one medium such as music or language.

As Aristotle states in the passage just cited, the determination of mimesis in flute- and lyre-playing is derived from the presence of harmony and rhythm. Here, it is essential to resist the temptation to substitute the modern sense of these words, for example, musical harmony for ἁρμονία and the recognition of a recurrent beat for ῥυθμός. In the case of the former, such a substitution would be like saying that grammar produces mimesis in language. The word ἁρμονία refers to a "fitting together," "joining," "arranging."[17] This sense might single out harmony as the crucial synthetic element in the production of mimesis through music, but such a production occurs by the same means in both harmony and rhythm. Indeed, the distinction of harmony and rhythm is not so clear-cut in this respect particularly when it is remembered that the sense of arrangement associated with ἁρμονία is closer to the meaning possessed by the word ῥυθμός prior to its use as a term measuring repetition and intervals within a temporal movement.[18] Before becoming a term of temporal measurement, ῥυθμός designates the figure, pattern, or form that has been produced by something moving. This sense of ῥυθμός is less a measurement of repetition within movement than the result of that movement. Consequently, and despite the fact that the figure described by ῥυθμός appears as the historical record of a sequence of movements, its significance may only be recognized when it is considered without regard for the temporal or even narrative development from which it is produced. In this usage, ῥυθμός describes an arrangement or figure produced by a whole sequence of movements; it is the figure that "fits together" the movements comprising this sequence.

Following the duplicatory function of harmony and rhythm in the example of flute- and lyre-playing, it is hardly surprising that Aristotle should exclude one of these elements in his next example of mimesis. In the example of dance, the primacy of rhythm as a single determinant of mimesis is strongly asserted as Aristotle emphatically excludes harmony:

> Rhythm alone, without harmony, is the means by which dancers (ὀρχηστῶν) are mimetic: through rhythmic figures (διὰ τῶν σχηματιζομένων ῥυθμῶν [through figuring rhythms]) the mimesis of character, what is done to one (πάθη) and what one does (πραξεις) are produced. (47^a26–28)

According to this passage, the mimesis of the dance takes place through figures (σχήματα) produced by rhythm alone. The emphasis which the introduction of the example of dancing gives to rhythm not only underlines the importance of articulation to the possibility of mimesis but it explicitly equates rhythm with mimesis in the same way that harmony was equated with mimesis in the example of music, that is, through the production of a figure. This equation suggests that rhythm should be regarded as the sole crucial element in the production of mimesis since the sense of arrangement associated with harmony is precisely what comes to the fore when the rhythm of dance is said to produce a figure. Consequently, if rhythm is to be the central element in the production of mimesis, the argument of the *Poetics* must establish a distinction between rhythm and the articulation which defines all the playing of the flute and the lyre. It is in order to make such a distinction that the argument now turns to the example of the dance.

The sequence of the argument traced so far moves toward the detachment of rhythm from harmony. This detachment occurs after both these elements have served as the means to define the mimesis of "most flute-playing and lyre-playing" according to human speech (φωνή) rather than a more general category of articulation.[19] Through this sequence, the argument comes to focus on a mode of mimesis that uses neither language nor any other sound. This movement away from language is hardly accidental. Nor can it be accounted for by arguing that the medium of the dance anticipates precisely what will be described later as the object of tragic mimesis: action. The example of the dance occurs as Aristotle attempts to account for the difference from which the *Poetics* will derive its ability to speak on behalf of literature: the difference between literature and language in general. But if this movement away from language and its example, the dance, is not an accident, why then must this account of a distinction between the mimetic and the non-mimetic articulation turn to an example of determined muteness, to a determined voicelessness (αφωνή), before it returns or even turns to the language (of epic and tragic poetry, etc.) in whose name the whole sequence is articulated? Furthermore, if the example of the dance does not anticipate dramatic mimesis through language, in what way does it facilitate the passage from the imitations of most music to the imitations of language that dominate the rest of the first chapter of the *Poetics?*

The movement toward dance in the *Poetics* is a movement toward an example that will define mimesis according to a model of self-articulation. As a medium, dance does not exist apart from the movements through which it produces its mimetic figure. For this reason, the rhythm of the dance should not require any supplementary concept such as the arrangement or "fitting together" that ἁρμονία brings to the flute and the lyre. Rather, the dance would be fitted together by the rhythm that articulates its mimesis. In short, because the dance cannot exist apart from the articulation of its rhythm, it articulates mimesis as an act or performance of articulation. As such, the dance would be, in the first instance, the figure of mimesis. Yet, for this to occur, rhythm must be regarded as synonymous to mimesis. The necessity of this identity between mimesis and rhythm (which is to say, the necessity of the example of dance) is central to Aristotle's argument, as becomes evident in the section on language that closes the first chapter of the *Poetics* and which again takes up the topic of rhythm within the context of literary production.

The section on language and rhythm begins by observing: "[the art] using bare language only or meters (whether in meters mixing with one another or with one kind of meter) happens to be, up to the present, without name (ἀνώνυμος)" (47^a28–b9). The namelessness of this general use of language suggests that the difference between mimetic and non-mimetic uses of language is not clearly enough defined to authorize already what will subsequently be called a "common name" by Aristotle. However, the word ἀνώνυμος already assumes such a differentiation since it defines the field that any substitute, for example, "literature," would also define.[20] The necessity of so defining a field may be realized from the following passage which records the inability of rhythmical language to assure the presence of mimesis:

> For we are unable to call by a common name (ὀνομάσι κοινὸν) the mimes of Sophron, Xenarchus, and the Socratic dialogues nor yet if someone should produce mimesis through trimeters, elegiac meters, or any other meters of this kind—except that people combine the word poet with the name of the meter and speak of epic poets and elegiac poets; they are called poets not on account of mimesis but collectively (κοινῇ) on account of their use of meter—just as it is customary to call poets those who write in meter about medicine and natural order (φυσικόν). Yet, Homer and Empedocles have nothing in common except meter, consequently, it would be fitting to call one a poet and the other an inquirer into natural causes (φυσιολόγον) rather than a poet. (47^b9–20)

After citing two examples which are immediately set aside (mimes and Socratic dialogues) the focus of this passage turns exclusively toward those productions that can be called the work of a poet. The available means of definition for these productions depends less on their potentiality than on the audible fact of their having been written in meter. This emphasis on meter is again an emphasis on rhythm—meter is clearly related to rhythm in a subsequent passage when Aristotle states, "It is obvious that meters are constituent parts (μόρια) of rhythms" (48^b21–22). Yet it becomes clear in the course of this passage that, as far as language is concerned, rhythm in the form of meter is unable to produce mimesis despite its stated ability to do so in the example of the dance. In order to distinguish a language that is properly mimetic, a division is made between the writing of the poet and, in the example of Empedocles, the writing of the inquirer into natural causes. Thus, rhythm, the most important of the elements responsible for mimesis to the extent that it figures in each of the arts named as examples of mimesis, is now subjected to an internal division through the agency of another kind of language (exemplified by Empedocles), or to be more accurate, a different configuration of the same language which, by virtue of this difference, stands over and against the work of the mimetic poet. Not only does this division repeat the earlier distinction which would restrict mimesis to most flute-playing and lyre-playing but, as before, what accounts for this division is not given.

Unlike the earlier example of flute- and lyre-playing, the discussion of mimesis in language requires a distinction between uses of mimesis rather than a distinction between mimetic and non-mimetic music (or language). In this respect, Aristotle's argument moves toward but does not pursue a recognition more frequently present and more frequently attacked in Plato: mimesis names a general activity. Even as it avoids such a recognition, Aristotle's discussion of writing in meter does, however, implicitly admit two distinct modes of expressing meaning through language (that of the poet and that of the inquirer into nature). It is for good reason that the path uncovered by this distinction is not followed: such a distinction requires that the difference between the poet and the naturalist be traced to a difference that language cannot decide precisely because it does not possess the means to distinguish between a poet and the inquirer into nature. In other words, language does not reflect the formal difference so crucial to the unfolding of a literary history whose understanding of mimesis, representation, and reference is derived from such a difference.

At this point, the necessity of a concept of potentiality for the argument of the *Poetics* cannot be emphasized enough (and not only because of its links to the discernment of formal difference in literary genres). Here, the concept of potentiality that defines the mimesis of one literary form from another in chapter 1 of the *Poetics* reappears as an ability to speak about difference within language. As was the case when different genres were defined according to their potentiality at the very beginning of the *Poetics,* this ability to speak about difference in language is derived from precisely what it is supposed to account for: language as a medium of mimesis. Literature must be regarded as already an example of mimesis, otherwise criticism would have no justification for its own reliance on mimesis: literature would justify critical method. But, how can criticism establish literature as a model of mimesis if its critical power can only be derived from a literature whose distinction from language in general already reflects the exercise of this power? Mimesis or the ability of criticism to be about literature thus poses the question of what literature is about.

The opening sentence of the *Poetics* clearly anticipates such a question when it states that the method of its argument will follow the example of nature. As becomes quickly apparent, the example of nature makes no distinction between mimetic production and a general mode of production that would include mimesis. For this reason, the distinction between mimetic and non-mimetic production is introduced in the example of flute-playing and lyre-playing as well as in the example of language. Both require such a distinction in order to avoid the situation in which mimesis would be understood as just another word for production in general. Indeed, if mimesis is to become a term of critical value it must name a mode of production defined by what it is meant to produce (what it is meant to produce being another way of describing its potentiality), that is, literature. In order to sustain this distinction, the argument of the *Poetics* turns to and then follows the example of the dance. Through this example, any inability of rhythm (or even harmony) to distinguish between mimetic and non-mimetic flute- and lyre-playing would be overcome. At the same time, once the dance has instituted rhythm as the crucial factor in producing mimesis, the stage is set for rhythm to become the means of establishing a difference between mimetic and non-mimetic language. Nevertheless, the path taken to language through music and dance requires that language be separated from those elements which Aristotle first describes as capable of producing mimesis, namely, rhythm, language, and harmony. As a result of this separation, language now becomes equivalent to flute- and lyre-playing. By the same token, metrical language ought to become equivalent to the rhythmical playing that forms the basis for the harmony of mimetic music. However, the model provided by music and dance does not work in the case of language precisely because language is equivalent to all flute- and lyre-playing. Although language may be a different medium from music and dance, this distinction does not define language as a different form or even a different mode of producing mimesis. The grouping of rhythm, language, and harmony may be read as a reflection of the analogy through which language ought to become a form of mimesis (the analogy between music and dance, on the one hand, and literature on the other). The grouping thus reflects an essential aspect of Aristotle's attempt to account for literature as a mode of mimesis: the definition of one artistic form in terms of another, and, in particular, the definition of the poetic in terms of a form whose mimetic potentiality would be most self-evident as well as most visible.[21] This is why the dance is singled out as a form of mimesis; dance alone supplies the single example in which the medium would be inseparable from the figure that *forms* the object of mimetic production.

While dance offers the crucial pivot in the initial movement of the argument from the mimesis of "most flute-playing and lyre-playing" to the mimesis present in language, the turn to language marks the beginning of a development in which rhythm will be ultimately subjected to the very necessity that caused language to be distinguished from harmony and rhythm. To trace the reasons for this second displacement, it will be first necessary to recall the argumentative steps that make such a development possible as well as unavoidable. Initially, Aristotle speaks of rhythm, language, and harmony as being the three elements capable of producing mimesis. Second, harmony and language are called upon to define musical mimesis. Third, rhythm is used alone. The argument proceeds from three elements, then to two elements, and then, finally, to one. Up to this point, Aristotle does not deviate from the three elements which were first introduced as if they, either separately or in combination, could account for the production of mimesis in any form. As a result of this consistency, rhythm emerges as the essential factor in the production of mimesis. At this stage of the argument, however, Aristotle introduces two new terms, song (μέλος) and meter (μέτρον), which now take the place of both language and harmony: "There are those who use [in their productions] everything we have spoken of, I mean rhythm, song, and meter" ($47^{b}24$–27).[22] Despite the introduction of these two terms, rhythm remains the most consistent term. But what dictates the removal of language and harmony from the first set of three terms and their subsequent replacement by song and meter? Is it merely a reflection of the form being described or is it the reflection of a necessity in the argument?

As we have already seen, the combination of rhythm, language, and harmony takes place in reference to specific artistic productions that have been defined as mimetic ("Epic and tragic poetry, and also comedy, dithyrambic poetry, and most flute-playing and lyre-playing, happen to be in general all mimetic" [$47^{a}13$–16]). To invoke rhythm, language, and harmony at this stage of the argument marks an attempt to provide a first accounting for the production of mimesis according to elements that may be severally or individually present in each of these arts. Nevertheless, the breaking down of essentially linguistic and musical arts into these elements demands that the argument correct the generic inconsistency of grouping language with rhythm and harmony. Why then is language initially included within this group? Or, to put this another way, why does the *Poetics* make this analogy at the beginning of its discussion of mimetic production? As the movement of the argument toward the dance makes clear, the least vexed example of how mimesis is produced is the one in which a single element defines the distinction of a particular form: without rhythm, which is to say, without movement, there is no dance, and, accordingly, no mimetic figure. As this movement also reveals in the crucial example of the dance, the argument of the *Poetics* demands an analogy without which there could be no theory of mimesis: language and rhythm must be synonymous at some level. Consequently, the central difficulty confronted by the *Poetics* involves the more general issue of analogy, and, in particular, the question of an analogy between language and the figure of the dance.

In terms of Aristotle's later remarks on language in the *Poetics,* any justification of such an analogy between the rhythm of the dance and language must at the same time be an account of metaphor as a mode of argument. The definition of metaphor in chapter 21 of the *Poetics* describes precisely the kind of substitution which must now be accounted for if the analogy of dance to language, and, ultimately, the definition of metaphor is to be justified:

> Metaphor is the transfer of the name [of one thing] to something else, either from the genus to the species, or, from the species to the genus, or, from species to species, or according to analogy. ($57^{b}7$–9)

While Aristotle offers four ways in which the transfer of a name may take place, the last is the most significant because it expresses the principle of likeness that regulates the other three. If Aristotle's examples ($57^{b}9$–16) are followed, it becomes clear that the transfer between species and genus occurs because of their homogeneity. Similarly, the transfer between species and species occurs because of their analogous positions within two separate genera or contexts. When grouped with harmony and rhythm, language is placed within a group of terms whose organizing principle would be their analogous function of producing mimesis within different media.

In other words, this group is formed according to the last mode of metaphor described by Aristotle but, as such, it is formed according to the principle without which no exposition of metaphor could be undertaken in the *Poetics*. When language is displaced from this group, it is because the analogy can no longer be sustained—at least not between the mimesis of literature and the whole of language. However, this does not mean that the argument has turned away from the metaphorical (in Aristotle's definition) procedure it has adopted. The subsequent relation of rhythm to language adopts another mode of metaphor: the substitution of the species for the genus in the example of rhythmic language. This substitution becomes necessary because rhythm and harmony, and especially the latter, refer to an internal arrangement governing the production of mimesis within a particular medium, whereas language would simply refer to a medium whose production of mimesis would rely upon the additional shaping influence of elements such as rhythm and harmony. Thus, if language is to be maintained as a medium for the production of mimesis, the kind of metaphorical relation Aristotle describes between genus and species is now demanded if the argument is to proceed.

The movement from one mode of metaphor to another does not change the essential problem which lies behind the shifts and displacements that occur as Aristotle describes the mimesis of music, dance, and language. This problem may be traced to the difficulty Aristotle encounters in an argument whose emphasis demands that the mimesis of language be derived from rhythm. In this respect, the movement of the argument in the *Poetics* would suggest that the defining critical gesture of this text is to be found in the substitution of one genus or species for another (to the extent that music and dance provide the practical examples for the mimesis of language). Yet this substitution which assumes an analogy between music, dance, and language can only be derived from the formal difference that defines each of these mediums. In other words, a formal difference that has nothing to do with the presence or absence of mimesis in language is called upon to account for its mimetic production.

The displacement of language from the three elements initially associated with the production of mimesis reflects the difficulty posed by the practical elaboration of the analogy between language and mimesis. Nonetheless, as Aristotle's argument proceeds, language is not totally displaced. Rather, song and meter take its place. While song may be read more readily as a substitution for harmony, and meter for language, these are not exact equivalents. Song is also a form of language, albeit a language whose mimesis would now be dependent on the presence of rhythm and harmony rather than on any specific aspect of language itself. This substitution would avoid the difficulty that arises when language is placed in analogy to both rhythm and harmony as one of three determinants of mimesis. Through this substitution, language is concealed by the two elements that are said to determine the mimesis of "most flute-playing and lyre-playing." Harmony, as a term more closely associated with music, reappears in song (as would rhythm)[23] while rhythm reappears in meter (the more narrowly rhythmical definition of language). The introduction of song and meter is thus a transformation of language according to the two mediums (dance and music) that have already been determined as mimetic through their prior figuration as spoken sound (φωνή). Through this transformation, the *Poetics* unfolds an argument which, having moved to the dance in order to isolate a medium of mimesis synonymous with rhythm, subsequently seeks to return the mute voice of the dance to sound by retracing its initial movement through music. Thanks to this movement, the question of how "*most* flute-playing and lyre-playing" is mimetic may no longer be raised.

Given the path taken by Aristotle's argument, it becomes evident that the presence of language in the first combination (rhythm, language, and harmony) must not only be displaced but that the element (rhythm) dominating the term substituted for language (meter) must also undergo a distinction into mimetic and non-mimetic components. This distinction occurs because the rhythmical element so privileged in the example of the dance can neither sustain nor determine language as a form of mimesis. In other words, the dance is not about the mimesis of language but a *praxis* that attempts to decide the theoretical question of how mimesis is possible.[24] This is why the rhythm associated with the dance cannot produce the figure of mimesis in language: since language cannot dance, rhythm, in the form of meter, can make no meaningfully mimetic difference with respect to language—where it matters most if the *Poetics* is to be able to speak about the production of mimesis through poetic language, let alone retain such a mimesis within its own language so that it may speak about that production. Without such a mimesis in its own language, the *Poetics* cannot have a method, cannot follow what goes before, cannot follow the path method lays before itself, in short, cannot account for the mimesis it needs in order to conduct a mimetic inquiry into mimesis. For such an inquiry to be possible, the *Poetics* must produce a rhythmic figure that is proper to itself. In other words, the *Poetics* must dance.

Criticism and the Cuisine of History

> *Gab es für die alte abergläubische Art des Menschen überhaupt etwas* Nützlicheres *als den Rhythmus? Mit ihm konnte man alles: eine Arbeit magisch fördern; . . . die Zukunft sich nach seinem Willen zurechtmachen. . . . wird auch der Weiseste von uns gelegentlich zum Narren des Rhythmus, sei es auch nur darin, daß er einen Gedanken als* wahrer empfindet, *wenn er eine metrische Form hat.*
>
> —Nietzsche, *Die fröhliche Wissenschaft*

The difficulty that already arises with regard to language in the first chapter of the *Poetics* is the direct result of the analogy of language to rhythm and harmony, an analogy that is crucial if the analysis of tragedy that the *Poetics* aims at is to be at all possible. Even though this analogy has to be made, it cannot be sustained by the argument even after the substitution of language for meter. At the same time, this failure implies that rhythm can no longer be regarded as an unequivocally mimetic element despite its singular presence in the mimesis attributed to dance. By the time the argument of the *Poetics* arrives at the third combination of terms centered on rhythm, the difficulty produced by this substitution necessitates the discounting of rhythm and its associated terms insofar as they are applied to language. The passage in which this deemphasizing occurs requires to be cited in full if the concerns that demand this deemphasis are to be seen in the context where they are most clearly stated.

> Let us speak about tragedy setting apart (ἀπολαβόντες) the definition of its essence which arises out of what we have said (ἐκ τῶν εἰρημένων τὸν γινόμενον ὅρον τῆς οὐσίας). Tragedy is the mimesis of an action that is serious, complete in itself, and of a certain

> greatness, in an enriched language (ἐδυσμένῳ λόγῳ) each of whose elements are used separately according to the parts of the work (ἐν τοῖς μορίοις). . . . by enriched language I mean rhythm, harmony, and song (ῥυθμὸν καὶ ἁρμονίαν καὶ μέλος), and, by elements used separately, the fact that certain parts are accomplished in meter only and others through song (μέλους). (49^b22–26, 28–31)

The word used here to describe language as "enriched" is related to the verb ἡδύνω which, in a general sense, refers to the act of making something agreeable. The noun form of this verb occurs once again in this same chapter when Aristotle turns to the last of the six constituent parts of tragedy: "Of the remaining parts, song (μελοποιία) is the most important of the agreeable additions (ἑδυσμάτων) to tragedy" (50^b15–16). In both instances, the translation all but erases the degree of figuration at work in this description of the language of tragedy—ἥδυσμα is the word employed to describe whatever seasoning is added to a dish in order to make it more agreeable (in the plural [ἡδύσματα], this word refers to spices).[25] Through this figuration, the path produced through rhythm becomes a seasoning after having led, so to speak, to the meat, the definition of tragedy. Indeed, what is now determined to be seasoning was formerly the very substance of the argument inasmuch as rhythm and its associated terms were analogous to the production of mimesis.

This change in the status of the original determinants of mimesis indicates that when the shift to tragedy (for Aristotle, the privileged form of mimesis in language) takes place, the sequence of analogies that sustains the argument as it passes from "most flute-playing and lyre-playing" to a language variously transformed by rhythm and harmony into song and meter can be continued no longer. The very elements that made the definition of tragedy possible now become seasonings whose presence confirms that language can never be synonymous with mimesis unless it is formalized into the measured rhythm of meter or else transmuted into the condition of music in the form of song. Here, the setting aside that relegates song to a seasoning is also the setting aside of the mimetic basis of the flute-playing and lyre-playing from which this whole sequence is derived. Thus, song is unable to produce mimesis despite being the embodiment of all the means through which the mimetic forms referred to at the beginning of the *Poetics* are said to achieve their mimesis (song is the combination of rhythm, language, and harmony but a combination that effectively withdraws language as a determinant of mimesis). The movement of the argument from its first determination of the means through which mimesis is realized is consequently a movement that attempts to make the definition of tragedy palatable in order to ensure that it will not only be swallowed but that what is swallowed along with it (mimesis) will appear to be more than a mere seasoning in the discourse of the *Poetics*.

At this juncture, the very act of definition—or at least the performance of this act—plays a crucial role in distinguishing something substantial within the seasonings (ἡδύσματα) that were formerly the principal elements in the production of mimesis. The definition of tragedy is introduced as "setting apart the definition of its essence which arises out of what we have said." This "setting apart," which has all too frequently been ignored not to mention concealed by the acceptance of Bernays's emendation of ἀπολαβόντες to ἀναλαβόντες ("taking up again," "recollecting," "resuming"),[26] marks a necessary structure in the argument of the *Poetics*. Without such a "setting apart," the language of tragedy risks subjection to those means of realizing mimesis which demand that language be formalized to the point where it can possess no semantic function except that of self-formalization.[27] To the extent that the argument of the *Poetics* is derived from such a formal relation, its treatment of language prior to the definition of tragedy demands the kind of self-relation offered by the example of the dance when Aristotle attempts to account for the passage from the mimesis of "most flute-playing and lyre-playing" to the mimesis of language. The *Poetics* sets itself apart from the possibility of such a return both in the definition of tragedy and immediately afterward when the combinations of rhythm, harmony, and song are admitted only as a seasoning. Yet, what occurs at this point in Aristotle's argument is no simple "setting apart."

The introduction to the definition of tragedy states that a precedent is involved even as this definition sets apart the prior argument. The definition, we are told, is made with regard to an "essence arising out of what we have said (ἐκ τῶν εἰρημένων [out of our saying])" ($49^{b}23$–24). The essence of tragedy will be spoken as a result of this "setting apart," however, this definition must also retain a relation to what has been said. To fulfill this condition, the prior argument is to be set apart and then picked up as if such a setting apart were merely a formal device and not an indication of a separation or argumentative lapse. In this passage, the use of εἴρω points to the difficulty that must be overcome in an argument that has been unable to give an adequate account of its central concept: the question of whether the setting apart performed by ἀπολαβόντες can avoid becoming a merely formal and non-mimetic link between the preceding chapters of the *Poetics* and the definition of tragedy that follows.

The verb used by Aristotle to speak about what has been said to this point in the *Poetics* means, like the verb used to state the argument in the first chapter of this work, "to say." In this context, εἴρω speaks about the speaking (λέγωμεν) from which the definition of tragedy is supposed to arise. As such, εἴρω speaks about a passage from language to meaning that, thanks to the example of the dance, ought to have been accomplished already. It is as if one ought to be able to say that such a passage were already history by the time one comes to the definition of tragedy in the *Poetics*. In this case, εἴρω would speak of the argument that has been made as if it were the source of a potentiality that the definition of tragedy will now realize. It is here that a mimetic passage would be enacted within the argument of the *Poetics* as this work attempts to realize the mimetic potentiality (δύναμις) of literature in an exemplary form (εἶδος), namely, tragedy. Yet, when the *Poetics* comes to enact this passage, it relies upon a setting apart that would separate the essence of what has already been said from what has been already said. Through this attempted separation, the *Poetics* reveals its most essential critical gesture as it speaks about its ability to speak about literature. The occurrence of this attempt within the argument of the *Poetics* may be read as one more example of how a critical text's most essential question addresses its ability to speak about literature.

Aristotle's *Poetics* poses such a question when it sets apart what precedes the definition of tragedy and attempts to draw out the essence which had not yet been given form. While Aristotle's use of ἀπολαβόντες poses this question, the use of εἴρω becomes the means to forget that any such question persists: what is first introduced by λέγωμεν is now referred to by the verb εἴρω. Over and above the claims of stylistic variation, the substitution of εἴρω for λέγω follows a critical necessity within the argument: the reflexive turn of language upon itself at the very moment where language must be able to speak *and* bind together what it says. It is with respect to this necessity that the use of εἴρω is most crucial. Unlike λέγω, the verb εἴρω used by Aristotle to speak about the argument preceding the definition of tragedy does not have the double sense of "saying" and "binding together."[28] Εἴρω would thus turn away from the binding or interlacing (λέγω) that sought to define language according to an ordered (mimetic) relationship. Here, εἴρω separates the two senses of λέγω: speaking and the binding together which, in the case of the *Poetics,* is associated with mimesis.[29] What has been said is no longer spoken about as if it were at the same time a binding together. This moment in the argument of the *Poetics* repeats the necessary turn away from an argument whose account of mimesis in language relies upon a self-reflexive relation (exemplified in the dance) that may only possess a formal existence. To the extent that this relation (as well as any attempt to tell the dancer from the dance) demands a separation that would subsequently be accounted for by a theory of form (again, εἶδος: what is seen). What the *Poetics* turns away from at this juncture in its argument is its inability to derive a formal account of mimetic language from the example of the dance. Yet, this turn away from a relation that may only be known through the intervention of a formal understanding is what occasions the formal separation that introduces the definition of tragedy in the *Poetics*. What the *Poetics* sets apart or rather, would set apart, when it states λέγωμεν ἀπολαβόντες [let us speak setting apart] is consequently its inability to account for language as a form of mimesis.

Such a failure is not, however, the end of literary or critical history since, as will be seen, this history is defined by the repeated enactment of this very failure. When εἴρω redefines how the *Poetics* has spoken by separating the speaking and the binding together that defines the speech associated with λέγω, this same failure is not only present but is repeated as the *Poetics* turns away from this failure and seeks, once again, to make language capable of both speaking and binding together what it says. In the present case, such a binding would already be reasserted through this "setting apart." This binding occurs in the form of a speaking which ought to take the place of what has already been said: περὶ δὲ τραγῳδίας λέγωμεν ἀπολαβόντες . . . ["About tragedy *let us speak* setting apart . . ."] ($49^{b}22$–23; emphasis mine). Here, λέγω now returns to speak in the place of the separation produced by εἴρω. Thus, in the name of language (λόγος the substantive of λέγω), this speaking would enact a binding together which will be exemplified by the definition of tragedy. But, in so doing, this speaking reiterates the very gesture of "speaking about" with which the *Poetics* begins and which had been redefined by the speaking of εἴρω: περὶ ποιητικῆς αὐτῆς . . . λέγωμεν. . . . περὶ δὲ τραγῳδίας λέγωμεν αὐτῆς ἐκ τῶν εἰρημένων. . . .

When the definition of tragedy is given, the speaking of language is set apart in order to become the subject of εἴρω. By virtue of this "setting apart," what speaks through the voice of εἴρω is a voice that belongs, formally, to the past. The necessity of this "setting apart" is the necessity of an act of definition that would have something to define rather than reiterate the separation which makes such an act possible. Also, it is from such a necessity and not anything else (εἴρω included) that the formalization of this setting apart arises. Formalization intercedes in order to produce a discursive connection between what is set apart and what follows. Since this setting apart must be interpreted formally if the definition of tragedy is to arise from what has been said already, then what is at stake in the *Poetics* is less a definition of tragedy or even mimesis but rather the formal relation that would make such definitions possible. The speaking (τὸ λέγειν) of the definition of tragedy may give meaning to what has been said only by assuming that a determination of mimesis has in fact been attained. This assumption is necessary to justify the path taken by an argument that sets language apart from rhythm and then rejoins them in the form of meter and song as if nothing had happened, as if the narrow relation between rhythm and mimesis in the dance had assured this movement. Yet, just as this movement serves to define the rhythm of dance as a mimetic attribute of language albeit in a medium heterogeneous to language, the return of language as meter and song will be governed by this definition. As a result, when language returns in the form of meter or song, it runs the risk of appearing as a language without significance or, at best, as a language whose meaning is subordinate, on the one hand, to rhythm and, on the other, to music. It is the formal pattern established by this "setting apart" that returns the articulation of language to meaningfulness by installing a historical relation between what has been said and what is now being said.

The necessity of a formal relation between what is said in the definition of tragedy and what has been said prior to this definition is the necessity of preserving a minimal mimetic structure between parts of the discourse of the *Poetics,* parts that are not in themselves mimetic nor are they capable of determining mimesis by themselves. The relation established by this formalization produces the possibility of mimesis within the *Poetics.* Accordingly, this formalization is as much a structural necessity within the argument of the *Poetics* as it is within the tendency to read this work as an example of formalist criticism. Indeed, such a formalist interpretation is the only way that this text may be read within a history of poetics, that is, within a *literary* history. But, as the product of a necessity generated by the unfolding of the argument, this relation is threatened by the "setting apart" out of which it is produced. If this structural necessity is regarded in terms of the initial analysis of how mimesis is realized, such a "setting apart" repeats the rhythm, that is, it repeats the articulations that govern the pattern of analogy, exclusion, and substitution which runs from rhythm, language, and harmony, through rhythm, song, and meter, and then issues into rhythm, harmony, and song. Just as this pattern is articulated around a mimesis which, in the form of dance, uses rhythm only, the passage connecting this pattern to the definition of tragedy repeats a difficulty already present in the argument developed by the preceding chapters of the *Poetics.* Where the analysis of rhythmic language results in a setting aside of the purely rhythmical determination of mimesis in dance, the definition of tragedy results in the setting aside of the purely rhythmical determination of language as meter. Both the dance and this "setting apart" enact the minimal relation necessary for mimesis to take place: each would involve the articulation of its own act of articulating. The possibility of such an enactment is not only necessary to the possibility of regarding dance as a mimetic form but, in the case of the definition of tragedy, it would also provide the precondition necessary to any relation between the saying of that definition and what has been said in the preceding chapters. Here, the possibility of mimesis is inseparable from the possibility of meaning and definition in the *Poetics:* both demand the same formal relation. As a result, the mimesis at work in the "setting apart" of the definition of tragedy repeats the dance which had previously instituted the possibility of a mimesis not afflicted by the distinction which reserves mimesis for "most flute-playing and lyre-playing."

The crucial role of the example of the dance is revealed most clearly at this point in the *Poetics*. The self-articulation embodied in this example is now repeated on the level of the argument as the formal possibility of the definition of tragedy. Through this repetition, the difficulties and inconsistencies encountered in the chapters preceding the definition of tragedy take on the appearance of having been overcome. However, the recourse to a formal repetition cannot cut itself off entirely from these difficulties and inconsistencies and precisely because these difficulties and inconsistencies arise from the unavoidable reliance on a formal rather than a mimetic method in the *Poetics*. At the very point where a formal definition of mimesis in language would be turned away from, the argument of the *Poetics* relies upon an analogy which, like the grouping of language, rhythm, and harmony, is derived from formal categories. Accordingly, the turn away from the argument of the opening chapters does not escape the difficulty that articulates these chapters. Indeed, as the definition of tragedy enacts this turning away, it can only repeat the formal relation from which it would set itself apart. What now emerges from the argument of the *Poetics* is the necessity of this formal relation as the condition of a definition of tragedy, which is to say, the possibility of a form is the decisive factor without which there could be no literary interpretation and, consequently, no literary history.

Ultimately, the possibility of a concept of form in the *Poetics* is derived from the example of the dance—a repetition that imitates the self-articulating, that is, the self-figuring rhythms of the dance. What orchestrates this pivotal passage which makes possible the analysis of tragedy as a form of mimesis is, in effect, a figure of self-articulation. The dance, however, can only fulfill this role by means of a relation whose meaning is derived from its form. Here, Aristotle's attempt to embody such a relation in the self-articulating mimesis of the dance indicates the necessity faced by the *Poetics:* if the argument of this text is to succeed, then, mimesis must be located within an act (the dance) whose performance of articulation remains external to language. This necessity finds its most concise expression in a relation that takes the form of what may be best described as an articulation of articulation—what amounts to a determination of articulation as bearing a relation to itself which is at one and the same time a relation of meaning and a relation of mimesis (to the extent that each are understood as forms of repetition and substitutive definition). Such a model of self-relation not only grounds the argument of the *Poetics* but also it produces the model of mimesis that has been attributed to this text throughout the history of criticism. In this respect, the Aristotelian model of mimesis requires precisely that kind of self-reflexive relation which literary history has always attributed to modernity rather than antiquity. In the argument presented by Aristotle in chapter 1, this relation, in the figure of the dance, determines the possibility of the discourse on literature undertaken by the *Poetics*. Without this self-reflexive model, the *Poetics* could not speak of language as a form of mimesis. However, with this model, the ability of the *Poetics* to speak about literature is indebted to a formal relation that cannot be accounted for mimetically. It is just such an account that the *Poetics* strives to avoid when the elements that govern the line of argument developed in the first chapter are displaced and transmuted into the "seasonings" of tragedy—a displacement which, as already mentioned, is repeated once more at the end of chapter 6 when song, in the form of μελοποιία, is referred to as the "most important of the seasonings (μέγιστον τῶν ἡδυσμάτων)" ($50^{b}16$). Such a displacement, and, in particular, the culinary metaphor through which it is expressed, would point to the presence of a certain cuisine at work in the *Poetics,* a cuisine written in accordance with the recipe of a language unable to figure itself out from a rhythm (in the sense of ῥυθμός) it can neither separate itself from nor separate from itself. The *Poetics* can only perform the possibility of this separation in the mimetic interpretation of dance. Here, the *Poetics* would tell the dancer from the dance. But to do so, the *Poetics* would have to repeat the difference to which meaning and all the differences made in the name of meaning owe their possibility. For this reason, to assume that the difficulty encountered by Aristotle could be resumed and thereby defined in the phrase "the articulation of articulation" is to persist with the concept of meaning that such a phrase would seem to have undermined.

While the "cuisine" of language practiced by the *Poetics* is aimed at the displacement of the semantic reflexiveness of phrases such as "the articulation of articulation," and so on, this same "cuisine" can only effect such a displacement by virtue of the very conditions of its own existence *as* a language. In doing so, the cuisine of language reiterates in both this displacement and in its own name precisely what no difference can stand in the place of, since to do so is to have already displaced and redoubled the difference that constitutes any possession of language. At the same time, this difference cannot be chased from one place to another as if it were a carrot, receding as one approaches with the recipe of a tragic language in hand—such a recession would be, properly speaking, the structure of a *mise en abyme,* the structure of a meaning driven to another meaning by the concept of meaning, not to mention the concept of mimesis affirmed through the production of this effect.[30] The difference in question can neither be divorced from the meaning it makes possible nor can it be defined by that meaning for it is a difference that cannot be set apart from the name through which such meaning would be carried—the word *difference* is no privileged exception here, yet it is precisely such an exception that arises whenever the phrases "the difference of difference" or "the articulation of articulation" are invoked. The very genitivization at work in these "exceptions" is the sign of a minimally historical and minimally semantic preposition that would geneticize and thereby determine the difference in question by semantically establishing its relation to yet another conceived difference. This latter difference would then stand as the possibility and totality of all difference. Whether the genitive be subjective or objective, it obeys the same logic, it is decisively and semantically productive in the place of its reproduction: it would know the place of its difference, it would know the place of its engendering as the site of its mimesis and it would know this site as its past. It would, however, be an aberration of language to assume that the possibility of the semantic is to be escaped from—an assumption that envisages the possibility of knowing difference in itself. A pure difference in itself is, as Hegel has analyzed it, a mere abstraction unable to fulfill even what its form requires.[31] Moreover, since such an escape would be meaningful *for itself,* it would repeat the concept of meaning it appears to be beyond—this repetition (as well as the rhythm it engenders) being the possibility of meaning.

At this point, the concept with which the *Poetics* begins may be returned to: the possibility, the potentiality of formal difference. The role played by a concept of formal difference is crucial; it is in fact the one way in which the question of difference will always be elided since such a concept is the possibility of this elision. The importance of this concept may be recognized in a passage from Hegel's *Lectures on the History of Philosophy* in which a difference of form is evoked as a means of accounting for the relation between difference in itself and what it is different from. For Hegel, everything depends on this difference of form ("*auf diesen Unterschied [der Form] kommt alles an*").[32] Formal difference is the difference that belongs to meaning inasmuch as it marks the development of a form in relation to what it contains: the passage from potentiality (δύναμις) to a form (εἶδος) is the development of a content and, as such, formal difference is the possibility of content. As a result, formal difference will always contradict or speak against itself (*widersprechen*) and it is this speaking against itself that articulates difference in language as a difference between saying and what has been said: λέγωμεν . . . ἐκ τῶν εἰρημένων [let us speak . . . out of what we have said].

The difference that the concept of potentiality would make, on the one hand, between genres and, on the other, between itself and those genres, would now *appear as* a contradiction both necessary to and at the service of Aristotle's argument in the *Poetics*. But such a concept can only exist if it is differentiated from the differences it gives rise to. In other words, the distinction that produces the possibility of form *ought not* to be the same as the difference that distinguishes the various genres of mimesis. It *ought* to be the possibility of the difference of form. However, it is only through the owing which lies within this imperative (this "ought") that the concept of potentiality produces the difference whereby it becomes meaningful. Without this owing, no significant difference could be produced and without this difference there would be no possibility of generic distinction—which reiterates the extent to which this contradiction is already the work of both the concept of meaning and the concept of mimesis. Such a concept of potentiality already obeys the logic of the "setting apart" as the possibility of differentiating itself through formal differences. These differences, so defined, become the basis of producing the effect that allows them to be distinguished in the first place. For this reason, the structure at work in the opening sentence of the *Poetics* is precisely what must be repeated when the definition of tragedy is given: while the potentiality of a particular form is said through the very speaking of that form, the concept of potentiality on which it relies would retain a mute "voice" which is set apart. If this were not the case, the concept of potentiality would be indistinguishable from the forms in which it is supposed to be realized. The concept of potentiality would therefore not be able to play the role assigned to it in the *Poetics*. The repetition of a self-relating structure in the dance and the definition of tragedy is therefore determined by the possibility of formal difference which initiates the discourse of the *Poetics*. Only through this concept of formal difference can the *Poetics* establish the possibility of having been *about* something. According to the self-articulating relation at the center of the argument presented by the *Poetics,* this would even include the possibility of being about the word that initiates the *Poetics,* the possibility of being about about: περὶ περὶ . . .[33]

The reliance of the concept of potentiality on the mode of self-relation which the *Poetics* first articulates and then seeks to set apart not only has repercussions for the formalist reading of the *Poetics* but it also indicates how a notion of a semantic loss becomes a necessary element in the production of meaning. This loss is, in fact, another name for a pure formalism which, in the end, can never relinquish its intention to signify. Such a loss and the purity it implies is produced by meaning in the very place where it has determined the possibility as well as the necessity of its own production. This loss is, in effect, meaning's debt to itself. Here, the rhythmic difference that the *Poetics* would orchestrate itself by is most marked at the point where the argument of this text would set aside what it needs most to imitate. This rhythm, clearly articulated by the setting apart of its formal consequences, is how the argument of the *Poetics* constantly attempts to figure itself out even to the extent of figuring itself out from the dance to which the argument owes more than it can ever hope or even want to pay. This setting aside constitutes Aristotelian mimesis as an indebtedness to the formal relation it can never know except in terms of its possibility. Mimesis is, consequently, not just the articulation of a loss but the means of repeating this articulation. Without this loss, mimesis would have nothing to reproduce. As a result, the reproduction associated with mimesis is not predicated upon a prior object but rather upon the appearance of a loss which is figured most powerfully through the loss of meaning associated with a purely formal self-reflexive relation. Such a formalization and such an apparent loss become the means through which mimesis sustains itself *as* mimesis.

In this context, the loss *of* meaning is the means by which meaning is enabled as meaning. This loss constitutes the ironic voice of meaning (ironic in the senses of εἴρω noted earlier). This ironic voice is, in effect, the invention of a meaning that guarantees its continuation through loss and, in so doing, opens the possibility for not only method, but also history as the incessant producer of such a "setting apart." This self-determined inability of method to coincide with its own future is the opening for and the necessity of mimesis as a model for the historical recovery of meaning. Since this non-coincidence is so fundamental to the discursive practice of history, it is no accident that it can account for the structure of literary history. Indeed, literary history is effectively the thematization of this non-coincidence inasmuch as literary history is the history of mimesis and its derivatives, including their absence or negation.

Such a thematization is even more pronounced within the history of criticism and emphatically so when the *Poetics* is determined as an essentially formalist text. This determination is nothing less than the invention *of* literary and critical history, an invention that continually safeguards the possibility of mimesis, because this formalization permits the persistence of the very mimesis that would seem to meet its impasse in a purely formal relation. While it would be tempting to figure such a formalization of the *Poetics* as a misreading of the *Poetics,* such a determination would preserve the possibility of a formalization that may still be set apart (it would then be argued that the *Poetics* is only about such formalization). Such a misreading already belongs to the "setting apart" of the *Poetics;* such a misreading is already determined by the *Poetics* as the necessary condition for the act of critical reflection recorded in both literary and critical history. In this respect, the legacy of the *Poetics* is both a receipt and a recipe for a debt which neither the *Poetics* nor the literary history it inaugurates can ever pay off or, indeed, would ever want to pay off since, literary history is, in effect, the invention of such a debt. As a result, the *Poetics* (and therefore literary history) will only be about production as the setting apart in which this debt is produced . . . περὶ ποιητικῆς. . . . λέγωμεν ἀπολαβόντες. . . .

CHAPTER TWO

The Ghost of Aristotle

❧ *Coleridge*

> *The author, having occasion for the character of a poet and a philosopher in the fable of his narration, had chosen to make him a* chimney-sweeper; *and then in order to remove all doubts on the subject, had* invented *an account of his birth, parentage and education, with all the strange and fortunate accidents which had concurred in making him at once poet, philosopher, and sweep! Nothing but biography can justify this.*
>
> —Coleridge, *Biographia Literaria*

The place habitually granted Coleridge's *Biographia Literaria* in the history of literary criticism suggests that this work reflects a break with the mimetic understanding of literature traditionally associated with Aristotle's *Poetics*. Within this history, the *Biographia* would have the status of a theoretical work whose overriding concern is the establishment of new critical principles rather than the more modest biographical concern announced in its title.[1] If the *Biographia* is to establish such principles, then, it may be expected to have found a way to avoid any recourse to the formal model adopted then set aside by Aristotle's *Poetics*. What will then be crucial to any confirmation of this break (as well as the literary history it informs) will be the extent to which the *Biographia*'s theory of the imagination provides an understanding of a literary work that can also double as a model for the relation of literary criticism to literature. In pursuing such a relation, the *Biographia* effectively substitutes imagination for mimesis but does not alter the critical role that mimesis must play in Aristotle's *Poetics*. Despite the change in terminology, the essential question posed by Aristotle remains. In this respect, the *Biographia* not only continues the critical project initiated by the *Poetics* but, by its recourse to the philosophy of German Idealism, it also returns criticism to its roots in philosophical speculation.

Through this return to philosophy, the *Biographia* takes up the question of a paradigm from which criticism may derive its ability to speak on behalf of another text. To resort to philosophy in order to develop a discourse on literature indicates that such a paradigm must achieve nothing less than an interrelation of philosophy and literature. In other words, this interrelation of philosophy and literature is not exactly a paradigm for criticism, rather, it must already be literary criticism. Given this condition, the attempt to relate philosophy to literature begins to look like an attempt to make philosophy become literary criticism (as if one could say, for example, that Kant wrote literary criticism or even literature). Yet, for such a transfiguration to occur, the difference between philosophy and criticism would have to be dissolved. Such a dissolution can only take place if criticism remains indifferent to its philosophical provenance. Indeed, the transfiguration of philosophy into literary criticism can only be derived from an indifference which allows one to occupy the place of the other. Despite its thematic persistence within deconstructive criticism, this dissolving of the difference between philosophy and literary criticism is hardly the undoing but rather the continuation of philosophy by another name. Consequently, Coleridge's turn to philosophy is not simply a reflection of criticism's search for a paradigm in philosophy, but rather, a reflection of criticism's attempt to determine itself as a paradigm of relation for philosophy.

As a mode of relation, criticism vies with philosophy for the status traditionally accorded the latter, namely, the discourse possessing a privileged relation between language and knowledge. It is irrelevant whether this relation is to be understood, in the end, as either the possibility or impossibility of knowledge: to *know* this relation as an impossibility (whether necessary or not) is to privilege language with a certainty no different from that granted an unproblematic access to knowledge. Thus, literary criticism, as an interpretative mode of discourse, is initially (and ultimately) contingent upon its ability to assert or deduce a knowledge of relation, possible or impossible, negative or not, between itself and literature. In its desire to know this relation, literary criticism follows a path to self-knowledge that has for long been the property of philosophy—as the prominence in Coleridge's writing (including the *Biographia*) of the Socratic dictum "Know thyself" affirms. The failure to articulate such a relation provides no escape from this shared provenance. Indeed, without having posited or assumed some concept of relation, literary criticism would be faced with an inability to account for what it says about the object of its study. Whether this concept of relation is called imagination, as is the case in the *Biographia*, or by a more current term such as culture, politics, psychoanalysis, or deconstruction, or even by the easy assumption of a rhetorical term such as catachresis is irrelevant, its structural role does not change. Since Aristotle's mimesis, such terms have been called upon to direct and ground the *purpose* of a critical activity.

In the case of the *Biographia*, the attempt to establish a mode of interrelation would be especially paradigmatic, but not merely because of the status Coleridge accords philosophy vis-à-vis literary criticism. Indeed, the relation of literary criticism to, for example, what is regarded as deconstruction, would be equally paradigmatic since what is under consideration here is the very relation that gives rise to and justifies a critical reflection while allowing it to be restricted to a particular kind. To consider the question of this relation only within the confines of a particular approach to literature is to practice an evasion that would be yet another sign of the dilemma facing literary criticism at its very inception in Aristotle's *Poetics*. Similarly, it would be an evasion to attribute this dilemma to what is called the "literary" text. This attribution only invites the phenomenalization of literature as something that resists critical reflection. More important, to assume that the dilemma of criticism may be exemplified in literature is to assert exemplarity as the mode of interrelation that allows literature to be interpreted and avoided by virtue of its very exemplariness. Through such a mode of relation, criticism would see a dilemma that arises from within its own activity as if it were a difficulty residing in the object of its study. This objectification ensures that theory will remain a mode of thematic criticism.

The operation of this exemplarity is not restricted, however, to literature and its language but also, as is evident from the case of Aristotle's *Poetics*, it appears in the relation literary criticism bears to its own history. In particular, the *Biographia* has fallen prey to this mode of exemplary interrelation as literary criticism turns upon one of its formative texts while evading the question of its own practice. In the case of the *Biographia,* such an evasion occurs most obviously in the effusive comments made in the name of this work. Despite their hyperbole, these comments cannot be dismissed out of hand since this reaction would also dismiss any intervention into what such comments conceal in the name of a history and its critical practice. As the editors to the 1983 edition of the *Biographia* would remind us in sentences that could hardly be more exemplary, to read this text is to take on the task of reading not just "one of the classics of English Literature" but of reading a text that has become "established as one of the supreme works in the history of literary criticism, perennially germinal in providing premises, values, and aims to other writers and critics from the later nineteenth century until the present."[2] To the extent that these sentences reiterate the critical mythology surrounding this so frequently unread and untaught "classic," they also form a barrier to any reflection on the question of why this work *must* be accorded such an exemplary status within the history of literary criticism. Two interrelated aspects of the *Biographia* would seem to explain the necessity of this status.

To a large extent, the *Biographia*'s status may be accounted for by its ability to do anything other than state a concept of imagination as if such a statement were able to guide literary understanding unaided. This inability may be easily ignored by going along with Coleridge's own judgment of the *Biographia* as "so immethodical a miscellany" (1:88). Yet, to assert that this text's difficulties may be attributed to Coleridge's inability to properly organize this work is to suggest that the problem of the *Biographia* may be simply a question of formal organization—as if, in terms of Aristotle's *Poetics,* the *Biographia* had attained a ῥυθμός or figure indistinguishable from its argument. This immethodical aspect clearly appeals to a critical practice that resists any attempt to be reduced to a set of formal rules (precisely the kind of reduction one would associate with what Coleridge calls the "Fancy"). At the same time, the unquestioned acceptance of Coleridge's judgment on the *Biographia* is hardly a disinterested one for either Coleridge or subsequent criticism of this work. Indeed, a notebook entry from March 1818 points to the constructive role of a confessed incoherency:

> ⟨S.T.C. =⟩ who with long and large arm still collected precious Armfuls in what ever direction he pressed forward, yet still took up so much more than he could keep together that those who followed him gleaned more from his continual droppings than he himself brought home—Nay, ~~farther~~ made stately Corn-ricks therewith, while the Reaper himself was still seen only with a strutting Armful of newly cut Sheaves.—But I should misinform you grossly, if I left you to infer that his Collections were a ~~med~~ heap of incoherent Miscellanea—No!—the very Contrary—Their variety conjoined with too great Coherency, the too great both desire & power of referring them in systematic, nay, genetic subordination was that which rendered his schemes gigantic & impracticable, as an Author—& his Conversation less instructive, as a man—Inopes sua *Copia* fecit [his *abundance* made them poor], too much was given, all so weighty & brilliant as to preclude choice, & too many to be all received—so that it passed over the Hearers mind like a roar of waters—[3]

Not only would subsequent criticism "glean" more from Coleridge than Coleridge ever brought home but this gleaning will always prevent the *Biographia* from being read. Above all, it will prevent any attempt to examine a fundamental difficulty rather than forget it in the name of a "too great Coherency" against which all else would be a "roar of waters." While the abundance of material could well be read as so great that it permits no entry to the specificity of Coleridge's thought, it must also be noted that this reflexive gesture simultaneously protects coherency and incoherency from all inquiry. Incoherency may not be inquired into because it is incoherent, consequently, the coherency said to be contained in this incoherent material must be equally resistant to inquiry. In this context, Coleridge's confession of incoherency may be seen as a rhetorical gesture that preempts any questioning about where the imagination may derive its coherency. Here, the *Biographia*'s inability to account for the imagination as a source of literary and artistic activity in the philosophical chapters would reaffirm the tendency to view the imagination as a principle of interrelation not to be inquired into—as if it were actually, in Wordsworth's words, an "unfathered vapour" (this phrase will be discussed at length in chapter 3). Indeed, for literary criticism and its history, the inability to account for the imagination is perhaps the most attractive aspect of this text since it effectively isolates what is invariably regarded as the *Biographia*'s most significant contribution to the history of criticism: the theory of the imagination and its accompanying principle of organic unity. In the end, this isolation is less concerned with what the *Biographia* says about the imagination than with the exclusion of the argument that precedes Coleridge's theory of the imagination.[4] The philosophical nature of this argument would not only account for the relative lack of attention accorded to the first volume of the *Biographia*, but it would also suggest why literary criticism should prefer, for example, a passage such as the Simplon Pass episode to Wordsworth's more discursive critical writings on the imagination even though the former may prove to be considerably more complicated than it appears at first. Clearly, the appeal of these two moments in Romanticism may be attributed to the fact that both would assert the existence of an imagination unrelated to any precedent. One wonders what ghost this incoherency exorcises in the interest of an all too great and coherent imagination.

The ghost that has come to haunt Coleridge's *Biographia* more than anything else has been the charge of plagiarism. Like the gesture toward incoherency, this charge has been an extremely efficient and paradoxical means of isolating the imagination, since it effectively lessens the relation of the philosophical chapters to its announcement in chapter 13 of the *Biographia*. The accusation of plagiarism thus serves the same end as a criticism less charged with an ethic of originality. Both strive for conclusions that are equally dependent on formal attributes (any charge of plagiarism must arise from a recognition of formal similarity before one can even ask if the relation of word to meaning remains unchanged from one discursive instance to another). Too frequently, this charge expresses an unwillingness to recognize that the *Biographia*, over and above the question of plagiarism, is concerned with a fundamental problem in not just criticism but the whole history of literary interpretation since at least Aristotle. The ghost that haunts criticism in the *Biographia* is hardly plagiarism; if it were, the difficulties inherent to literary criticism would be only too easy to define.

If restricting the problem posed by the *Biographia* to a question of plagiarism serves as an excuse to avoid and thereby overcome the difficulties that define the task of literary criticism, it would seem reasonable to expect that the defense of Coleridge against this charge implies a willingness to account for these difficulties as they arise in the philosophical chapters of the *Biographia*. Despite this expectation, the defenses against plagiarism have tended either to discover in Coleridge's writing those qualities of originality, novelty, and creativity associated with this text's central critical concept or else to displace these characteristics onto the *Biographia*'s textual practice. In each case, the defense against the charge of plagiarism tries to rescue critical reflection from the dilemma imposed by the task it has set itself, a dilemma that remains even as criticism attempts to apply guiding principles derived from another artistic medium or interpretative discourse.[5] Significantly, this defense focuses literary criticism on two essential and related elements that define the possibility of its discourse: analogy and method. In this respect, any defense of Coleridge against the charge of plagiarism must repeat the discursive structure of the *Poetics* or else presume to have overcome the question of analogy that Aristotle bequeathed to literary history as its decisive question. By presuming the latter, the defense against plagiarism goes beyond the analogy assumed by Coleridge and Aristotle at the outset of both the *Biographia* and the *Poetics*. Furthermore, by deriving a method from this analogy, such a defense will have done considerably more than the first volume of the *Biographia* ever achieved or, in the end, ever attempted to achieve. In terms of the *Biographia*'s critical achievement, the defense against plagiarism may turn out to be an impossible, distracting task which clouds the real critical issues that surface in the *Biographia*.

The incoherency of an immethodical textual practice when combined with the question of plagiarism produces a critical subject of such attraction that it would seem to render irrelevant the relation of philosophy to critical principle in a work that starts out to deduce the latter from the former. Acting on the strength of such a desire, the tendency of literary criticism to distinguish itself from philosophy would find itself justified in the failure of the *Biographia* to achieve such a deduction—hence the exemplariness of this work to a critical practice that would so distinguish itself. However, to assume that such an inability does more than confirm the prejudices of literary criticism is to avoid any consideration of the precise nature of Coleridge's inability to account for such a principle of interrelation theoretically. In so doing, any reflection on how theory relates to criticism would also be refused precisely because no reflection on the nature of this relation can take place without considering how, in the case of the *Biographia,* philosophy is to produce criticism. Ironically, this avoidance of philosophy would require that the *Biographia* be read according to a highly traditional and philosophical distinction between the practice of literary criticism, on the one hand, and philosophy, on the other. Here, literary criticism and its history would distance itself from philosophy by disguising the nature and provenance of the distinction it employs.

The persistence with which such a distinction has established itself as a crucial element in literary criticism's attempt to avoid reflecting upon its own possibility already points to the evasion that allows literary criticism to appropriate to itself all questions that pertain to the discussion of literature and its language. By so distancing itself from philosophy, literary criticism gives the appearance of separating itself from not just the difficulty that literature has always posed for philosophy but also it determines philosophy as if it were the discourse to which such a problem properly belongs—as if philosophy created the problem of literature for its own enjoyment. Such a separation is persistent enough to indicate its necessity in any project that would be authentically critical even though philosophy would not always be the object evoked in the course of this separation. Indeed, a separation of this kind operates as a founding act whenever one critical approach seeks to preserve or establish itself by purging the "ideological" taint of another; such a purging is nothing less than a polemical contest for the control of not merely an ideology but the very determination of ideology itself. Yet, while a desire to separate philosophy and literature has informed the critical reception of the *Biographia* (whether laudatory or not), it should not be forgotten that such a repetition does nothing more than repeat a constitutive act within a discourse that sought to relate philosophy and literature in the name of literary criticism. Accordingly, by separating philosophy from critical reflection in the *Biographia,* literary criticism would separate this work from itself—separates the *Biographia* from itself and from literary criticism. In so doing, literary criticism would authorize a mode of interrelation for the *Biographia* and itself but only at the price of repeating the very difficulty that should have been overcome through this same authorization.

The Autobiographical Imperative

> *Denken ist* Reden *mit sich selbst (die Indianer auf Otaheite nennen das Denken: die Sprache im Bauch)*
>
> —Kant, *Anthropologie*

> *Man lügt wohl mit dem Munde, aber mit dem Maule, das man dabei macht, sagt man doch noch die Wahrheit.*
>
> —Nietzsche, *Jenseits von Gut und Böse*

To the extent that Coleridge's *Biographia* sets out to provide an "application of the rules, deduced from philosophical principles, to poetry and criticism" (1:5) but, in the end, is unable to do so, it would indeed be an exemplary text in which to examine what is at stake when literary criticism attempts to authorize its interpretive power by separating itself from the source of that power. The case of this work is all the more significant since Coleridge's aim (to ground poetic and critical practice in rules derived from philosophical principles) indicates a project that would seek to avoid the kind of critical evasion that has been exercised subsequently upon the *Biographia*. Yet, if this evasion is to be avoided, it would seem to be absolutely necessary to turn to a discipline whose concern with the grounds of knowledge would provide an example for a critical activity prone to regard the literary text as the ground of its knowledge. This recourse to philosophical principles not only underlines the role that philosophy will play as an authority with respect to both poetry and criticism in the *Biographia,* but it also affirms the traditional role of philosophy as the *scientia scientarum,* as the discipline that would truly ground all other disciplines.

For philosophy to assume this grounding role, it must presume the ability of one discourse to speak in and through another while at the same time retaining its proper identity—otherwise the attempt to ground literary criticism would only produce more philosophy. At the very point where the *Biographia* records its obligations to philosophy, Coleridge not only provides an awareness that such a relation must be accounted for, but recognizes that this accounting is concerned with nothing less than the speaking of truth. Thus, any account of how philosophy may determine literary criticism without turning it into a species of philosophy becomes at the same time an account of how truth may be spoken without being contradicted by the very speech in which it is expressed. In the *Biographia,* this speaking of truth is said to occur by means of a ventriloquy, however, Coleridge's description of this mode of address is far from overcoming the difficulties that prompted the recourse to this metaphor. The description is as follows: "I regard truth as a divine ventriloquist: I care not from whose mouth the words are supposed to proceed, if only the words are audible and intelligible" (1:164).[6] Although this declaration and the statements made immediately before it suggest (and have frequently been read as) a defense against the charge of plagiarism, such a narrow reading obscures how they will define the dilemma that Coleridge must face in the project undertaken by the *Biographia.* If this statement is to have any role apart from a mere defense of plagiarism, however, it would be first necessary to reflect upon Coleridge's indifference ("I care not") as well as consider the consequences of a truth whose origin is understood as nothing more and nothing less than its audibility and intelligibility.

Although Coleridge's determination of how truth is made known requires two conditions, the absence of one, audibility, would effectively make the other, intelligibility, impossible to maintain. In the case of ventriloquy, intelligibility is dependent on the audibility of words: without hearing the words there could be no possibility of ascertaining what is said, never mind decide its intelligibility.[7] Yet, even if sounds are heard and recognized *as* language, this does not mean that what is spoken is necessarily intelligible. What defines a word (as a word) is simply the differentiation of sound. Hence, what makes language audible as language is a difference that cannot be heard or seen. This differentiation is necessary to Coleridge's description of truth since it is the precondition of a word as a discrete unit of sound. Without this differentiation there would be no sign, acoustic or otherwise, to which an intelligible meaning may be attached. Yet, when he speaks of the audibility of a word, Coleridge adopts a model of intelligibility that derives the meaning of a word from a differentiation which can only make a word recognizable as a word. Such a model is inevitable if truth is to be spoken by means of ventriloquy. Without this model, truth would remain heterogeneous to language no matter how audible and intelligible. With this model, however, a relation is forged between, on the one hand, a difference that cannot be heard but which makes a word audible and, on the other, the intelligibility or meaning of a word. This model, which amounts to a theory of language, indicates the necessity of such a relation to the possibility of truth.[8] The ventriloquistic truth described by Coleridge is structured according to this relation: what does not speak (truth, difference) is made intelligible by being given an audible form in language. This relation is necessary because truth, as the unconditional, cannot speak since, if it did, it would be conditional upon what it said.

In Coleridge's description of a ventriloquistic truth, this relation between what is heard and what cannot be heard occurs as a confusion of what is seen and what is heard. What cannot be heard is *regarded* ("I regard truth . . .") and what speaks (the mouth) is not observed but listened to. This confusion of visual and aural aspects is not a result of chance but a necessary structural moment in elaborating a relation that ought to guarantee that truth will be protected from the self-compromise that attends its utterance. According to this structure, truth is silent or, more accurately, truth has the appearance of muteness and this appearance is the guarantee that whatever is heard is indeed true.[9] Here, the critical project of the *Biographia* relies upon a metaphor that, as the example of ventriloquy makes clear, is understood as if it were capable of determining the relation of a figure (the ventriloquist's dummy) to a source (truth) that it makes audible and intelligible despite never being seen to speak. Yet, if this metaphor and the relation it originates are to be sustained, then the truth articulated here will be not simply dependent upon the concealment of its source but also upon the awareness that this concealing is taking place. Without this awareness, there would be no way of knowing that what the dummy says is not what the dummy thinks. Thus, the relation between truth and the mouth from which it issues must involve the recognition of a difference between a truly dumb figure who appears to be capable of speech and a source capable of speaking truth even though it must appear to be truly dumb. Recognition of this difference is essential if what is audible and intelligible is to be identified as originating in a source other than the one from which it appears to proceed. Otherwise, it would be presumed that whoever is speaking is the author of what is said and, consequently, whatever is said would be necessarily untrue despite its intentionality. Such a difference ensures that the source of truth cannot be confused with the mouth into which it is projected. At the same time, this difference would also make it impossible to question the source of truth. Any such questioning would have to be made in the voice of a dummy. As a result, this questioning is either truth addressing itself (and thereby affirming the truth of this ventriloquy even as it questions itself) or else it is a questioning divorced from truth (and is thereby irrelevant).

One further consequence of this ventriloquistic structure is that it would clearly deny any concept of intention as it is traditionally understood in literary study, because it requires that whatever is said can be recognized as coming from a source other than the source usually attributed to the mouth (or work) from which it is seen to proceed. Here, it is easy to see why Coleridge should be so attractive to New Criticism and its espousal of an intentional fallacy: such a ventriloquy frees the reference of a work from a narrow focus on biographical concerns. It would be presumptive, however, to equate this ventriloquy so quickly and so emphatically with such a fallacy since to do so would be to confirm a history and an origin for New Criticism at the expense of a work where the possibility of a history and an origin for literary criticism is still at stake. Moreover, Coleridge's disregard of an intention no longer traceable to its speaker does not deny intention per se, but rather affirms its continued operation in a way that would include (but not be restricted to) the merely biographical. In this respect, Coleridge's ventriloquy explicitly underlines what a disregard of intention seeks to establish whether or not it is expressed in the form of an intentional fallacy: the derivation of what is said to what was to be said. Here, a disregard for intention precedes what is, in effect, a relation of language to meaning (what was to be said) that would be untainted by any question about intentionality *in* language precisely because it would refer all questions of intentionality to an external and non-linguistic source—a state of affairs that would be comparable to asserting that the referentiality *of* language (without which there could not be language as such) may be understood if one examines the objects or things language is *said* to name.

To propose an understanding of truth that effectively makes the author of a work irrelevant to what is written or said in that work would place any aspiring author (especially an author writing his own literary biography) in an extremely difficult position. Indeed, given his understanding of truth as a "divine ventriloquist," Coleridge would seem to be inviting disaster by proceeding with a philosophic work in the form of a biography: not only would the philosophical part appear to be compromised by being written in the form of a biography, but the biographical would be compromised to the extent that its source could never be recognized if the *Biographia* were to remain a true account of Coleridge. Yet, as early as a notebook entry from 1803, Coleridge insists that the philosophical concerns of the *Biographia* are to be written as the reflection of his life: "Seem to have made up my mind to write my metaphysical works, as *my Life, & in my Life*—intermixed with all the other events or history of the mind & fortunes of S. T. Coleridge."[10] The use of the biographical as a mode of philosophical disquisition is again repeated in September 1815, when Coleridge writes that

> instead of Poems *and* a Preface I resolved to publish "Biographical Sketches of my LITERARY LIFE, Principles and Opinions, chiefly on the Subjects of Poetry and Philosophy, and the Differences at present prevailing concerning both: by S. T. COLERIDGE. To which are *added,* SIBYLLINE LEAVES, or a Collection of Poems, by the same Author,"—the *Autobiography* I regard as the *main* work . . . both because I think that my *Life* &c will be more generally interesting, and because it will be an important Pioneer to the great Work on the *Logos,* Divine and Human, on which I have set my Heart and hope to ground my ultimate reputation.[11]

Since the metaphysical chapters of the *Biographia* (chapters 5–12) were already written at the time of this letter, Coleridge's emphasis on a "Life" as a mode of exposition clearly indicates that these chapters should be understood as part of a biographical narrative. This being the case, the project of deducing the principles of literary criticism from philosophy should also be understood as proceeding from a biographical necessity. Indeed, if Coleridge is taken at his word when he writes in July 1815 of the "necessity of extending, what I first intended as a preface, to an Autobiographia literaria, or Sketches of my literary Life & opinions, as far as Poetry and *poetical* Criticism is [are] concerned," then the biographical arises here out of the theoretical intent latent in any writing of a preface.[12] In its most essential form, this intent concerns the ability to say what one has written, to say the truth of what is past. That a theoretical intention is modeled on what is essentially a historical structure may be discerned from the very function of a preface.[13]

Structurally, the preface functions as a means of determining what is written according to historical categories (past, present, future). By transposing these categories it becomes possible to speak about a text as if it had not yet been read. This transposition defines the figurative or theoretical mode of speech that characterizes a preface as well as the model of language necessary for such a speaking to occur. In this respect, the preface plays the role of speaking on behalf of a work that it keeps from sight and hearing. Here, the work and the preface reflect the model of ventriloquy already described by Coleridge: the preface speaks on behalf of a work that cannot speak for itself. (In the case of the preface from which the *Biographia* evolved, this work was to be composed of the collection of poems published as "Sybilline Leaves" in 1817.) If one follows Coleridge's letter of September 1815, then, it becomes evident that what starts out as a fairly straightforward critical endeavor cannot be sustained. In the terms of this letter, what starts out as a text speaking on behalf of literature (here the preface is no different than criticism in its relation to literature) becomes, of *necessity,* what Coleridge refers to as an autobiographical work. In this respect, the recourse to a biographical concern, when allied to this adoption of a ventriloquistic model of truth, can be seen as Coleridge's attempt to authorize the theoretical intention of a preface on firmer critical ground. Since this authorization will occur through the autobiographical, then, according to Coleridge, the interpretive intent of the preface can only be fulfilled through the attainment of a mode of self-relation. But, if this relation is to be justified, it must accord with Coleridge's model of a ventriloquistic truth. Such a condition is not easy for an autobiography to meet, because an autobiography that makes any claim to truth (as regarded by Coleridge) must deny all biographical knowledge of its source. At the same time, it must deny any knowledge of a relation between the voice that is seen to speak and the face that claims to be its author. The dilemma this situation presents to Coleridge threatens the possibility of literary criticism because it is, first and foremost, a threat to the very possibility of the critic: if truth is to be a "divine ventriloquist," then a criticism that is true would be in the unenviable position of forgoing *any* apparent relation to the source of its production. What is ultimately at stake in the *Biographia* is therefore the relation that Coleridge calls a necessity ("the necessity of extending"), the relation of literary criticism to a subject's biographical account of itself: the possibility of auto-biography. In Coleridge, autobiography becomes the extended preface of critical principle.

As if to give voice to the difficulty of a critical project entwined with the autobiographical and, at the same time, extricate himself from it, Coleridge follows his description of truth as a "divine ventriloquist" with a citation that seems to perform the kind of textual ventriloquy demanded by both autobiographical and critical writing. The performative aspect of this moment is telling, since, like the example of the dance in Aristotle, it indicates the critical need to make a text in a way that remains foreign to its very nature. In the *Biographia,* this citation would indicate the intrusion of the voice of another who would speak through Coleridge and say precisely what Coleridge wishes to say yet would not be identified as Coleridge:

> "Albeit, I must confess to be half in doubt, whether I should bring it forth or no, it being so contrary to the eye of the world, and the world so potent in most men's hearts, that I shall endanger either not to be regarded or not to be understood."
>
> MILTON: *Reason of Church Government* (1:164)

To consider these lines as solely an indication of indecision or even as a mere preemptive defense against a later charge of plagiarism would be to disregard their reflection on the difficulty Coleridge will face in attempting to express a truth that cannot be spoken by its author. For Coleridge to give a true account of himself, he must speak in the voice of another. In this instance, Milton, as a surrogate voice, bears witness to the anxiety that this ventriloquism will produce: the anxiety that the voice which is heard must either conceal the identity of its author and thereby nullify a critical project whose exposition is modeled on a "life," or else disclose that identity and thereby lose all authority for what has been said. For Coleridge to say the truth, Milton must speak. But then, if Milton speaks, the source, the subject from which such a truth proceeds and is to return to, namely Coleridge, cannot be recognized.

As if to exacerbate the situation in which Coleridge finds himself, this dilemma of self-recognition is already present in the lines from Milton. To bring forth a truth endangers the "I" that would bring it forth and it does so in two mutually exclusive ways. Either the subject will not be regarded or else this subject will not be understood. In the first case, the subject would be identified as what is seen to speak, thereby causing Coleridge to be disregarded. In the second, Coleridge, even if regarded, would not be understood precisely because such an identification is inconceivable without there first being an allegorical relation between what is heard and who is said to speak—allegorical in the sense of a speaking that does not permit deduction of a subject even though it posits the possibility (and only the possibility) of such a deduction. As a result of this bind, the example of ventriloquy involves a difficulty that questions a later formulation of ventriloquy given by Coleridge in the second volume of the *Biographia:* "Ventriloquism, where two are represented as talking, while in truth one man only speaks" (2:135). Although the difference between subject and language that articulates this bind may enable the possibility of a ventriloquy, it will at the same time always prevent the grounding of two in a single identity—a relation that Coleridge defines in another context as "*taut*egorical, that is, expressing the *same* subject but with a *difference*."[14] Indeed, Coleridge's subsequent definition of ventriloquy in the *Biographia* would assume that an adequate theory of representation had been accounted for between chapter 9 and chapter 22. Only then could one speak of two being grounded in one—or, as in the present example, identify Coleridge in the voice of Milton. This being the case, the whole critical project of the *Biographia*—which is nothing less than the repetition of the project of literary criticism itself—would belong to the possibility of a theory of representation. Such a theory is essential to criticism if it is to account for its interpretative acts but, also, if it is to undertake this accounting in the first place. The difficulty this theory contends with is so general that it is unavoidably present in what ought to be criticism's most innocent and formal of practices: citation. As the foregoing passage from Milton (Coleridge?) demonstrates, citation is suspended between two discursive instances. In this position, the difficulty posed by the mere fact of citation is whether it can even be decided if what is seen or heard to speak is allegorical or tautegorical in nature—that is, in the name of which subject does it speak, Coleridge or Milton? The example of this citation articulates a question unavoidable at the inception of any critical project: the question of not just its subject but the possibility of a subject.

To the extent that such a question is posed by the *Biographia,* it is hardly surprising that this work ultimately distances itself from the tautegorical claims of autobiography by refusing to be recognized as an example of this genre. Toward the end of the second volume of the *Biographia,* Coleridge clearly states that this work should not be considered an autobiography even though it is written as if it were a first person narrative. In this passage, Coleridge refers to his autobiography and, in the same breath, postpones it to some indefinite date: "Write it I assuredly shall, should life and leisure be granted me" (2:237).[15] If Coleridge's autobiography is yet to be written, then, there arises the question of what function the "I" performs in the *Biographia.* Deprived of generic determination as an autobiography, the *Biographia* would no longer simply assume an identity between the "I" and a proper name. In such a case, can this "I" be, in fact, Coleridge? The statement of intent given by Coleridge on the first page of the *Biographia* suggests that the "I" is functional and that the difference between Coleridge and this "I" is not a difference that belongs to the same subject—as it must be if the *Biographia* were tautegorical in the sense of Coleridge's definition cited earlier, namely, "expressing the *same* subject but with a difference." The statement of intent is as follows:

> It will be found, that the least of what I have written concerns myself personally. I have used the narration chiefly for the purpose of giving a continuity to the work, in part for the sake of the miscellaneous reflections suggested to me by particular events, but still more as introductory to the statement of my principles in Politics, Religion, and Philosophy, and an application of the rules, deduced from philosophical principles, to poetry and criticism. (1:5)

Here, the kind of personal history normally associated autobiography would be disavowed. The first person narrative is only, or so it seems, a formal resource that derives the possibility of continuity and coherence from the grammatical priority granted to the concept of a subject.[16] Coleridge's deferral of an autobiography, when combined with this functional subject, would indicate that criticism, as "an application of the rules, deduced from philosophical principles, to poetry and criticism," veers away from the very autobiographical project in which it originates and which guides its subsequent development—development in the sense of a movement toward an even greater self-knowledge about its practice, methodology, and possibility. Moreover, given the title of this work, such a deferral would indicate that a distinction should be made between the autobiographical and the biographical despite the fact that these terms are used interchangeably by Coleridge in much of his correspondence describing his work on the *Biographia*.[17] As a result of this distinction, Coleridge would seem to be turning away from any attempt to identify himself as the author of the truth that would be spoken in the course of this work. But is it a question of simply turning away, indeed, can criticism turn away from the relation named by the generic term *autobiography?*[18]

From "Me" to "I"

> *Je, vraiment, c'est personne, c'est l'anonyme . . .*
>
> —Merleau-Ponty, *Le visible et l'invisible*

> *Il y a "derrière moi" ce que moi dissimule pour être à soi.*
>
> —Blanchot, "La solitude essentielle et la solitude dans le monde"

To distinguish the *Biographia* from autobiography would offer Coleridge the appearance of fulfilling the ventriloquistic condition of speaking truth while, at the same time, preventing the autobiographical identification of its authority from denying that truth is indeed being spoken in this work. Coleridge's denial that the *Biographia* is an autobiographical work cannot occur unless a difference is established between two generic terms, biography and autobiography, which were otherwise interchangeable during the Romantic period. Although this difference is essential to a critical project that finds itself led to ventriloquy and autobiography, no direct attempt is made to account for it. Are we then to accept the narrative structure of the *Biographia* as a ventriloquistic practice that posits an unseen subject (Coleridge) as the speaker of its truth?

Although Coleridge makes no direct attempt to distinguish autobiography and biography, the principle from which such a distinction would be derived holds a place of considerable importance in the argument of the *Biographia*. This principle appears when Coleridge first speaks of differentiating imagination and fancy according to a principle of desynonymization:

> Repeated meditations led me first to suspect . . . that fancy and imagination were two distinct and widely different faculties, instead of being, according to general belief, either two names with one meaning, or, at furthest, the lower and higher degree of one and the same power. It is not, I own, easy to conceive of a more apposite translation of the Greek *Phantasia,* than the Latin Imaginatio; but it is equally true that in all societies there exists an instinct of growth, a certain collective, unconscious good sense working progressively to desynonymize those words originally of the same meaning. . . . The first and most important point to be proved is, that two conceptions perfectly distinct are confused under one and the same word, and (this done) to appropriate that word exclusively to one meaning, and the synonyme [*sic*] (should there be one) to the other. . . . Now were it once fully ascertained that this division is no less grounded in nature . . . the theory of fine arts, and of poetry in particular, could not, I thought, but derive some additional and important light. It would in its immediate effects furnish a torch of guidance to the philosophical critic; and ultimately to the poet himself. (1:82–85)

Not only would the work of desynonymization play an essential role in distinguishing imagination and fancy but, more significantly, it is crucial to sustaining the difference between a speaker and the mouth through which an act of ventriloquy may be recognized (thereby authorizing the truth of what is heard). Yet, the sudden appearance of desynonymization as "a certain collective, unconscious good sense working progressively" and existing "in all societies" marks a decisive disjuncture in a sentence that begins with the appositeness of substituting *imaginatio* for *phantasia*. From the essentially substitutive exercise of translation, the sentence moves abruptly to an understanding of language that is both societal and unconscious. Although this movement clearly defines desynonymization as a form of social expression, any inquiry into the source and, indeed, the authority of that tendency is refused by its concealment in unconsciousness. This authority may be heard and may even be seen in the written form of a language but where or what it issues from is denied sight. Here, a ventriloquistic model of truth is called upon to sustain a theory of meaning in language. At the same time, acceptance of this ventriloquy (which is to say, acceptance of the truth of desynonymization) would be the means through which language is made dependent upon a model of historical development.

This recourse to the historical (which turns away from the substitutions of translation) plainly indicates the extent to which any model of relation, whether between truth and its speaking or between philosophy and criticism, is inconceivable unless it produces a theory of language based on an essentially progressive and genetic understanding of history.[19] Consequently, what is at stake in the passage from the *Biographia* just cited is not so much the distinction between the imagination and the fancy but the necessity that the relation of language to meaning should always be regulated by a historical model. That necessity is in fact what relates language to history in the form of desynonymization is stated by Coleridge when he describes this desynonymizing tendency in the course of his lectures on the history of philosophy in 1818: "The whole process of society, as far as it is human society, depends upon . . . the progress of desynonymizing, that is, the feeling that there is a necessity for two distinct subjects which have hitherto been comprehended in one."[20] The necessity spoken of here is the necessity of a temporality within which distinctions of meaning may arise as if they were the effect of history. According to this necessity, meaning, and, above all, the meaning of difference can only be understood in temporal terms. To regard difference as a form of temporality is the necessary condition of a criticism whose authority is vested in its historical persistence. Only such a concept of difference could account for the tautegorical relation ("expressing the same subject but with a difference") so necessary to critical authority in the *Biographia*.

Given the tautegorical, and hence autobiographical, relation that underlies a project seeking to ground critical reflection, it is hardly coincidental that Coleridge's examples of desynonymization should end by turning to the terms "I" and "me." In a note to the verb "desynonymize" in the passage last cited, Coleridge writes,

> This [desynonymization] is effected either by giving to the one word a general, and to the other an exclusive use; as "to put on the back" and "to indorse"; or by an actual distinction of meanings as "naturalist," and "physician"; or by difference of relation as "I" and "Me." (1:82–83)

Of the three examples Coleridge employs to explain how desynonymization occurs, the first two are to be distinguished from the third since they each involve the attempt to attain precision in meaning by distinguishing a word or phrase from what it translates: as nature translates the Greek word φύσις so "put on the back" translates the medieval Latin verb *indorsare.* At the same time, the translated term is recalled as a means of establishing this distinction. Thus, the English form, *physic,* derived from φύσις, φυσικός, returns with a significance wholly distinct from their meaning in Greek which indicates nature in the sense of outward appearance. Likewise, *indorsare* returns to distinguish, for example, the act of putting a coat on one's back from the act of signing the back of a document. In both cases, desynonymization occurs through an initial (and formal) recognition of identity (φυσικός, physician) which is superseded by a differentiation that allows the English form to be distinguished from its Greek or Latin equivalent (φυσικός, naturalist). In each of Coleridge's examples, this process of desynonymization can occur if translation is accepted as an essentially tautegorical exercise. This understanding of translation is also essential to the recognition of synonyms—if it were not, there could be no such thing as a synonym since a synonym operates exactly the same way within one language as translation would (or ought to) operate between two languages. Consequently, what remains unaccounted for in both the process of desynonymization and the historical model it relies upon (and which translation from Greek or Latin also involves) may be described more generally as a synonymy of language.[21]

It is symptomatic of the difficulty confronted by the *Biographia* that these first two examples (which each aim at a distinction of meaning) should make no attempt to account for the synonymy assumed as their starting point. To attempt such an account must admit that two words regarded as equivalent in meaning (e.g. nature, φύσις) can only be regarded as equivalent if we reject the historical difference that defines desynonymization as a process progressing toward a state in which a meaning and a sign would be historically fixed. The synonymy of nature and φύσις demands the possibility of other signs standing in the same place. Despite its appearance, the problem to be confronted here does not involve the specter of an infinity of substitutions but rather the repeated question of whether there is or is not any historical relation between a sign and what it is said to mean. Coleridge's third example of desynonymization would appear to avoid this question and, at the same time, confirm the central role of a process of desynonymization in a critical work whose authority turns upon the contradictory demands of a ventriloquistic truth on the one hand, and autobiography on the other.

The third example concerns the words "I" and "me." To be more precise, this example is concerned with those words that signal an autobiographical expression of the self in the case of the former, and, in the case of the latter, it expresses what is essentially a biographical relation of a subject to itself to the extent that "me" is the objective form of "I." In terms of Coleridge's ventriloquy, "me" must be considered the mouth through which the "I" not only speaks but is recognized as the speaker. The formal congruence between this example and the situation of Coleridge in the *Biographia* will appear overdetermined, precisely because the resolution sought by Coleridge will not be produced by the process of desynonymization described by the first two examples. For this reason, Coleridge shifts from a desynonymization based on translation to a desynonymization based on grammar. Why Coleridge should make this shift to a grammatical explanation may be explained by the movement toward nominalism latent in the first two examples. What this shift also recognizes is that there are words that cannot be desynonymized by restricting them to one object rather than another. As Coleridge admits, "I" and "me" refer to the same subject. Consequently, if the historical process of desynonymization is to avoid being halted in its tracks, it must account for a difference in meaning (such as that between naturalist and physician) as if it were equivalent to two ways of regarding the same subject (φυσικός), or, as in the present case, the identity of "I" and "me."

The importance of Coleridge's introduction of grammatical relation at this point in the argument of the *Biographia* may be realized in an earlier passage from the same chapter which first presents Coleridge's description of a process of desynonymization. In this passage, Coleridge attempts to account for an example in which the identity of "I" and "me" cannot be deduced from the very grammar it depends on:

> Thus in the well known bull, "*I was a fine child, but they changed me*"; the first conception expressed in the word "*I*" is that of personal identity—*Ego contemplans:* the second expressed in the word "*me,*" is the visual image or object by which the mind represents to itself its past condition, or rather, its personal identity under the form in which it imagined itself previously to have existed—*Ego contemplatus.* Now the change of one visual image for another involves in itself no absurdity, and becomes absurd only by its immediate juxtaposition with the first thought, which is rendered possible by the whole attention being successively absorbed in each singly, so as not to notice the interjacent notion, "changed," which by its incongruity with the first thought, "*I,*" constitutes the bull. (1:72–73)[22]

Immediately before elaborating this example, Coleridge had noted that a bull consists in "bringing together two incompatible thoughts, with the sensation, but without the sense of their connection" (1:72). Such an incompatibility arises because of an intermediary term which only gives the appearance of making a meaningful connection. In the example just cited, Coleridge examines this incompatibility in a sentence whose grammatical correctness cannot be questioned. Yet, the grammar of this same sentence permits a divergence between what is said and the conceptual understanding that governs the relation of its key terms. As Coleridge explains, both "I" and "me" are to be understood in relation to personal identity, the former in its present and the latter in its past form. Normally, to change one of these representations of self for the other would involve no incongruity since they are both assumed to derive from the same source—in grammatical terms they would be defined as subject and object. Incongruity would not arise here precisely because a third element (the subject of "I" and "me") has intervened to define the two exchangeable terms as the exclusive property of a single identity. What Coleridge refers to as the "bull" arises because this sentence interposes a notion of change as the relation between "I" and "me." If "I" relates to "me" through change, then, according to Coleridge's argument, there can be no "sense" of connection because the "I" can never be congruous with its representation of itself ("me"). Thus, the example cited by Coleridge would affront the tautegorical understanding in which "I" and "me" would always refer to the same subject albeit under a different form: the difference that constitutes the tautegorical cannot be a difference made by a change in (the) subject. This affront to the tautegorical can only arise as long as it is assumed, first of all, that the relation of "I" to "me" can never be one of change and, second, that the notion of change is in fact the source of what Coleridge refers to here as an absurdity.

In the case of Coleridge's example, the determination of absurdity is inconceivable without a notion of alteration or change. The argument hangs upon this notion if Coleridge is to distinguish a connection of sense from connections of sensation. Yet, how might the relation of "I" to "me" be known as a relation of change? A third and external term is invoked; it is "they" who account for such a change. Through this third term, the notion of change not only allows absurdity to be recognized but, in so doing, it affirms the tautegorical structure behind which the same subject always lies: change and absurdity are always measured against a difference between "I" and "me" that cannot be a difference brought about by change (if it were, one would never know if "I" and "me" could ever refer to the same subject). Consequently, the concept of personal identity that underlies Coleridge's understanding of the relation of "I" to "me" depends upon the notion of change that would appear to contradict it. Yet Coleridge, in this example, dissociates change and personal identity as the condition of maintaining the indifference of the subject expressed in either of the forms "I" or "me." Not only does this dissociation protect such indifference but it also serves as a means of defining any incongruity it may contain as if it were always the result of an external source of change. But are "they" the real difficulty here? What role does the paranoid's favorite pronoun play in this argument? Does this external source merely serve to enable two concepts of change, one of which remains unquestioned because concealed by a questionable relation?

In a later part of Coleridge's footnote describing desynonymization, there is an example of how the splitting of one word into two may occur. The example is particularly significant to Coleridge's discussion of "I" and "me" since it relies upon neither temporal change nor translation to explain desynonymization: "Even the mere difference, or corruption, in the *pronunciation* of the same word, if it have become general, will produce a new word with a distinct signification; thus 'property' and 'propriety'; the latter of which even to the time of Charles II was the written word for all the senses of both" (1:83). Through a slip of the tongue that distorts the pronunciation of a known word, there arise another word which may subsequently carry a meaning previously associated with the distorted word. In itself, there is nothing strange about this process as a type of desynonymization, however, it cannot be overlooked that the "mere difference" of pronunciation is placed immediately after the series of examples in which a tendency toward nominalism is countered by a reliance on grammatical relation. While the recovery of a translated term provided the basis for desynonymization in the first two examples, the third (and most important since it would arrest the nominalism of the first two) provides no linguistic account of an initial identity between these terms except for a parenthetical reference to "rustics of our provinces [who] still use ["I" and "me"] in all cases singular of the first personal pronoun" (1:83). In the place of the account missing from the example of "I" and "me," Coleridge embarks upon a lengthy description of mispronunciation as a way of accounting for the merest of differences, that is, the difference between what is seen or written ("propriety") and what is heard ("property"). The ventriloquistic structure so crucial to the *Biographia* is not at all removed from the example of mispronunciation since what is heard would again be clearly different from its source. Here, what could so easily be obscured by a metaphor of deception (ventriloquy) may be read: desynonymization or the distinction of meaning in language is indistinguishable from mispronunciation (the examples involving translated terms provide no exception since the anglicization which makes physician available can also be defined as a long developing shift in the pronunciation of φύσις, φυσικός).

At the same time, it is not simply a question of mispronunciation but rather a question of the "merest difference," that is, a difference between a word whose meaning would be known and another sound whose very existence estranges it from the meaning attributed to the distorted word. Why Coleridge should describe this difference as being the "merest" becomes evident from his immediate recourse to an analogy from nature which indicates that the relation expressed by the "merest difference" should be understood as the most like:

> There is a sort of *minim immortal* [hardly there immortality] among the animalcula infusoria [single cell organisms found amongst decaying animal or vegetable matter] which has not naturally either birth, or death, absolute beginning, or absolute end: for at a certain period a small point appears on its back, which deepens and lengthens till the creature divides into two, and the same process recommences in each of the halves now become integral. This may be a fanciful, but it is by no means a bad emblem of the formation of words, and may facilitate the conception, how immense a nomenclature may be organized from a few simple sounds by rational beings in a social state. For each new application, or excitement of the same sound, will call forth a different sensation, which cannot but affect the pronunciation. The after recollection of the sound, without the same vivid sensation, will modify it still further; till at length all trace of the original likeness is worn away. (1:83)

Does language grow by dividing itself according to an inheritable genetic law? No more than breaking a stick into several pieces and then arranging these pieces into their various different combinations. Yet, not only must Coleridge resort to such a genetic example if he is to account for the "growth" of language but, as the preceding passage also makes clear, "rational beings in a social state" must account for language in this way if there is to be anything that answers to the name of a social state. In each case, the difference made by mispronunciation is a difference directed toward a social and regulatory need (regulatory since desynonymization represents a process that describes the attempt to control more effectively the relation of language to meaning). To safeguard this need, the example of cell division would demand not only likeness between itself and the formation of language but it would also answer this demand by positing a likeness in the place where there can only have been a difference. For Coleridge such an originary difference cannot be admitted; difference must arise later and within an organic model. Such an originary difference is, however, unavoidable despite Coleridge's attempt to estrange it from the analogy made in this passage ("has *not naturally* either birth, or death, absolute beginning, or absolute end" [emphasis mine]). Consequently, the analogy made by Coleridge enters as the after-recollection of an accident (mispronunciation). This "accident" is subsequently understood within the process of desynonymization as if it were always meant to be intentional. Only after this recollection is described does Coleridge permit a difference to intrude but, at this juncture, what intrudes is a difference produced by a wearing away ("till at length all trace of the original likeness is worn away"). To portray this difference as the result of a wearing away lays the ground for a historical understanding of difference as well as an "essentially progressive" understanding of language.

For this historical understanding to arise, the assumption of an original likeness is absolutely crucial since, without it, there could have been no wearing away, and, above all, no history in which such a wearing away could occur. But can the difference that makes this likeness possible in the first place be equivalent to a history in which a wearing away takes place? Here, the examples of desynonymization derived from translation and mispronunciation combine to support the most crucial example, "I" and "me," even though the historical understanding that allows them to be read as examples of desynonymization is only asserted but never accounted for when Coleridge describes the difference of "I" and "me" as a difference of relation. Indeed, the relation involved here and which also underlies the grammatical distinction of "I" and "me" is, in Coleridge's own words, nothing less than historical. As Coleridge states in his explanation of the "bull," "I" is to be understood as the sign of personal identity whereas "me" is to be understood as the sign of "personal identity under the form in which it imagined itself *to have previously existed*" (1:72; emphasis mine). Yet the historical knowledge that makes this relation possible has no legitimate claim on the linguistic difference that distinguishes "I" from "me." Despite the inability of history to account fully for its explanation of the difference between "I" and "me," its claim is aided by language's own inability to prevent history from asserting that the difference of one word from another reflected a difference between past and present. At the same time, it must be admitted that this linguistic difference (between "I" and "me" or even "property" and "propriety") cannot be ascribed to chance or the accidents of history. To account for it as chance would again demand a post facto recognition of what something ought to have been like so that what is called an accident may in fact be known as an accident or deviation from the expected. In this respect, to assert that what is at stake here is an accident is to enter the path clearly marked by desynonymization as a path in which a history of language is exclusively a history of meaning. Indeed, to regard mispronunciation as an accident is immediately to submit this alteration of language to the same relation adopted by Coleridge, namely, likeness. As such, the accidental retains a complicitous relation to the intentional since it safeguards the audibility and intelligibility of an intention precisely because it is always understood as a swerve away from what was intended or what is subsequently regarded as having been the intention.

Coleridge's recourse to desynonymization not only indicates that the narrative structure of the *Biographia* is the site where the possibility of this text's critical project must eventually be played out but it does so in a way that points unequivocally to autobiography or the relation of "I" to "me" as the constitutive difficulty with which the distinction between the imagination and the fancy must contend. The example of the "bull," in which any disjuncture in the relation of "I" to "me" is to be recognized as an absurdity, already sets the pattern that this projected distinction will follow. Where the "bull" would bring together "I" and "me" in a way that threatens personal identity, so the "fancy" is to act as the agent of those arbitrary connections that may not be confused with the work of the imagination.[23] This congruity between the "bull" and "fancy" measures a merely linguistic juxtaposition solely from within the viewpoint of meaning. Determined according to this measure, any such juxtaposition must be unjustified since "I" and "me" would not only be interchangeable but the historical and tautegorical relation in which they are *meant* to find their distinction would be unable to halt this interchangeability. In this way, meaning would evade what it cannot account for by regarding this juxtaposition as an absurdity without meaningful relevance to itself. If this juxtaposition may be termed a blind metonymy then such a blind metonymy is the mirror in which history and desynonymization view themselves.

The sequence of examples through which an understanding of desynonymization is offered would now indicate that Coleridge's distinction (or desynonymization) of the autobiographical and the biographical is not generic but rather linguistic in origin. Consequently, to read it as the turn of one genre away from another is to conceal a difficulty common to both. Since this difficulty is essentially linguistic, it may also be discerned within the realm of intentionality. Structurally, autobiographer and biographer would possess the same relation to a written text: like the biographer, the autobiographer can only write the history of a self as the history of another. Accordingly, the difference that articulates the biographer's relation to a written text is the same as the one that occurs between an autobiography and its declared author. Yet, to the "I" that writes the autobiography, the "I" that is written would always be a "me" even though it may be expressed in the form of an "I." This interchangeability would be a necessary requirement if there were to be any determinable, which is to say, historical relation between autobiography and the subject about which it writes. But then, what articulates autobiography becomes a substitutability that may occur quite apart from any third term, such as a subject, which would subsequently regulate this substitution by means of its indifference.[24] This substitution cannot, however, be confined to autobiography. Indeed, the minimal condition for such a substitution is a difference of language that cannot be restricted to "I" and "me" but would be equally present in the relation of "I" to whatever personal pronoun is used in a narrative written in the third person. Consequently, any attempt to evade a constitutive difficulty within autobiography by turning away from it can only repeat the difficulty that prompted such a turn in the first place. This is not, however, a difficulty that can be restricted to the *Biographia;* to do so is to forget that criticism is an auto-biographical project in which criticism attempts to account for its right to discourse upon literature by describing how a given literary work produces its (criticism's? literature's?) meaning.[25] Literary interpretation, by its very nature, has no choice but to tell a story of identity in the place of what is other. Yet, the story it tells would not be complete without the indifference that regulates the relation of "I" and "me" in the examples cited previously. According to these examples, an authentically critical project demands such an indifference so that literature may be seen to state the claims made in its name. Such a criticism is indifferent to what it takes as its proper object and, like Coleridge's ventriloquistic truth, "care[s] not from whose mouth the words are supposed to proceed, if only the words are audible and intelligible." But is criticism really a project that wants to attain the indifference it requires or is it also indifferent to even this?

Obviously, it is preferable that critical interpretation should be audible, intelligible, and thereby understood. Otherwise, there would not be much point in the concept of a criticism (never mind a truth) whether ventriloquistic or not. Such a preference is, however, bought at the price of the indifference that surfaces within Coleridge's argument. Like the issue of plagiarism in the *Biographia,* this preference would halt (or else prevent by indifference) any inquiry into how such truth can be said to originate. Here, again, the affinity of New Criticism to Coleridge indicates what is at stake. Just as the notion of ventriloquistic truth forbids all inquiry into the source of truth (if it is to remain truth) so would New Criticism's doctrine of an intentional fallacy forbid any examination of intentionality in language, let alone the intentionality that determines a given work's autonomy. Moreover, this doctrine, through the notion of autonomy, would also be a guarantee of intelligibility to the extent that it would promise the coherence of a literary text in itself over and against other external determinations of what it means.

Not surprisingly, such an autonomy also guarantees the intelligibility of the critical text and its relation to a literary work. The disregard of the biographical in both Coleridge and New Criticism would be, therefore, a gesture made in the name of intelligibility as well as a gesture that would seem to distinguish criticism from any biographical project, auto- or otherwise. Yet, it is not the role or place of the life of a particular author that is at stake in these exclusionary gestures. Indeed, the dismissive gesture only serves notice that the difference between what the author says (intent) and what the work says is not a difference of form—as if the literary work were merely tautegorical and represented the same subject but with a difference in expression. Rather, one relation to a source or meaning has been dismissed in order to facilitate another which is essentially the same in structure not to mention intent. For example, in the case of the New Criticism's espousal of the intentional fallacy, the relation of an author to a work is replaced by the authoritative and autonomous relation of a work to itself. To assert this autonomy, the work, however, can only repeat the intentional relation it appears to have relinquished (the relation which holds that intention may be regarded as synonymous with the biographical). Coleridge's disregard of the personal is no different from New Criticism in this respect. The relinquishing of personal recognition would facilitate the speaking of truth, yet this speaking is derived from the model of relation already assumed within biographical interpretation. This derivation can take place only as long as the metaphor of ventriloquy can be sustained. For it is only through this metaphor, and, above all, through the either-or structure it establishes that the speaking of truth becomes possible: either the source of what is said is not recognizable and what is said may be the truth, or, the source of what is said is recognizable and the truth cannot have been spoken in those words. Either the author spoke or truth did.

What the exclusionary logic of this either-or structure conceals is the substitution of truth in the place of a biographical source. Hence, the real theoretical question of this work (as well as of New Criticism) lies in the possibility of a self-reflexive truth (or autonomy), that is, a truth that would require no precedent except itself. The *Biographia* (and New Criticism) would therefore become, a tautegory in search of *its* tautology—although the *Biographia* would have to be distinguished from New Criticism in one respect. Only the *Biographia* attempted to unfold such a logic. In this case, the critical project of the *Biographia* (as a project that aims at a tautology, that is, a logic of identity, as the ground of its practice) would have to be read as the attempt to account for its inability to *authorize* truth—such an inability thereby becoming the authority of truth. It is the question of this inability that is at the center of the *Biographia*, and, above all, at the center of the philosophical chapters. In contrast, the deduction of the imagination only possesses importance to the extent that it is one of the forms in which (the evasion of) this question takes place.

e cælo descendit

> *If I die, and the Booksellers will give you anything for my Life, be sure to say—"Wordsworth descended on him like the* Γνῶθι σεαυτόν *from Heaven; by shewing to him what true Poetry was, he made him know, that he himself was no Poet."*
>
> —Coleridge, Letter to W. Godwin, March 25, 1801

> *Man betrachtet die kritische Philosophie immer so, als ob sie vom Himmel gefalle wäre.*
>
> —Friedrich Schlegel, *Fragmente*

> *Die gesamte uns bekannte und sie ein Himmelsgeschenk behandelte Logik in einer ganz bestimmten Antwort auf die Frage nach dem Seienden gründet.*
>
> —Martin Heidegger, *Einführung in die Metaphysik*

In chapter 9 of the *Biographia,* Coleridge introduces the philosophic argument whose stated aim is to establish a ground for the transfiguring power of the imagination. The establishment of such a ground is clearly essential not only to the possibility of a criticism guided by the "torch" of philosophy but also to the ability of philosophy to act as a "torch," since without this ground there could be no interrelation between philosophy and literary criticism and, hence, no theoretical basis for a faculty such as the imagination. Given this situation, the philosophic ground on which the imagination rests must be, in the first instance, a mode of self-determination since it demands that philosophy be capable of articulating its relation to itself. If this ground is to attain such a self-relation and, at the same time, avoid privileging one of the opposed schools of thought described at the beginning of chapter 5 of the *Biographia* (on one side, the idealistic or subjective, and, on the other, the materialistic or objective), a radical shift in how the relation of these opposed terms is thought would be required. The origin of such a shift may be traced to Kant, and, in particular, to a critical project which sought, in Kant's words, "[eine] Entscheidung der Möglichkeit oder Unmöglichkeit einer Metaphysik überhaupt und die Bestimmung so wohl der Quellen, als des Umfanges und er Grenzen derselben, alles aber aus Prinzipien" [a decision about the possibility or impossibility of metaphysics in general and the determination of its sources as well as its scope and limits, and all according to principles].[26] However, it is to the work of Kant's immediate successors that Coleridge turns in order to avoid the repetition of a merely idealistic or materialistic misunderstanding. With this turn, Coleridge follows the so frequently adopted philosophical history that runs from Kant, through Fichte and Schelling, to Hegel. The very fact of this adoption would assume the overcoming of the limitations analyzed by Kant's critical philosophy. Nevertheless, Coleridge makes no sustained attempt to account for this assumption, still less give any awareness of the dialectical nature of the history it inaugurates—despite the fact that this history and the sense of philosophical development that accompanies it had been articulated by Hegel as early as 1801.[27] Nor is there any understanding of the extent to which even the partial tracing of this history would already participate in the kind of dialectic that has always privileged Hegel as its synthesis, and, in so doing, made Hegel the crucial figure to be contended with. Yet, even ignoring this relative inattention to Hegel, the path Coleridge embarks upon rehearses the philosophical development that requires such a synthetic figure.

While the history of philosophy sketched by Coleridge in chapter 9 is unthinkable without such a dialectical development, it is also unthinkable without the adoption of a species of ventriloquy. According to this dialectic and the ventriloquy through which it operates, Kant, Fichte, Schelling, and Hegel are related in such a way that the latter would always speak the truth unspoken by the former. This recourse to ventriloquy is, however, more complicated than the mere manipulation of a puppet would suggest. Over and above the projection of a voice from a source never seen to speak, there must occur the return of this voice to a source so that what was intended but never witnessed as the source of that speech would now be known. Without such a return, this philosophical development could not be known in the form of a history. Here, the tautegorical imperative that casts literary criticism and autobiography in the same mold would now include history. And, as this chapter from the *Biographia* implies, what is at stake in this history is Kant, but a Kant whose writings do not yet say what they mean or even meant to say. Accordingly, the story of this ventriloquy and the history it sustains will again be the story of the veiling of authority. In this case, the veil will be known as the "cloak" of Kant. Coleridge writes: "KANT's followers, however, on whom (for the greater part) their master's *cloak* had fallen without, or with a very scanty portion of, his *spirit,* had adopted his dynamic ideas, only as a more refined species of mechanics. With the exception of one or two fundamental ideas, which cannot be withheld from FICHTE, to SCHELLING we owe the completion, and the most important victories of this revolution in philosophy" (1:163). Through Fichte and Schelling, Kant will say what he means, yet the price to be paid for such a meaning is that it will always be spoken by the voice of another—an eventuality that defines the theoretical question of the *Biographia* as the question of how one meaning may be said in two different ways but only known after its second articulation. Given the nature of this problem, it is hardly an accident that the paragraph in which these sentences occur should turn to Kant's determination of the thing-in-itself since such a determination would seem to resist any other articulation, never mind a second articulation of what it is. It is also hardly an accident that the paragraph following the one in which Coleridge speaks of the thing-in-itself should advocate a symbolic understanding of what Kant writes:

> In spite therefore of his own declarations, I could never believe, it was possible for him to have meant no more by *Noumenon,* or THING IN ITSELF, than his mere words express. . . . (1:155)
>
> An IDEA, in the *highest* sense of that word, cannot be conveyed but by a *symbol;* and, except in geometry, all symbols of necessity involve an apparent contradiction. Φώνησε συνετοῖσιν [he spoke to the wise]: and for those who could not pierce through the symbolic husk, his writings were not intended. Questions which can not be answered without exposing the respondent to personal danger, are not entitled to fair answer; and yet to say this openly, would in many cases furnish the very advantage, which the adversary is insidiously seeking after. Veracity does not consist in *saying,* but in the intention of *communicating* the truth; and the philosopher who can not utter the whole truth without conveying falsehood, and, at the same time, perhaps, exciting the most malignant passions, is constrained to express himself either *mythically* or equivocally. (1:156–57)

Here, the symbol would be the guarantee that what one means to say may not be exactly what one has said. Yet, if the "cloak" is to be removed and this meaning revealed, then the language from which it can only be derived must always be what Coleridge terms mythical or equivocal. If this were not the case, there could be no symbolic understanding, since Kant would already have said what he meant to say (and, consequently, there would be no need to say what Kant meant to say). Where, then, does this need come from?

According to Coleridge, such a need may be located in a "personal danger." Thus, in order to preserve what is called Kant, Kant does not say what Kant means. By the same logic, to preserve something literal, one cannot speak literally and it is for this reason that Coleridge must determine as more than mere words what Kant refers to as the thing-in-itself. Yet, what is at stake in this determination is not simply the mere preservation of a body and a life or spirit to inhabit it. Indeed, the recourse to a body is only a cloak for a model of language that would locate intentionality in anything but language (without which there could never be intentionality—never mind a questioning of it). Through this recourse, writing necessarily becomes a "husk" which conceals an intention, and, it is this concealing to which the symbol is supposed to point while inviting its penetration. In this respect, the symbol becomes a mnemonic device that serves to remember that something other than what is *said* is to be recalled. For Coleridge, this consists in the veracity that resides in "the intention of communicating the truth" rather than in saying it. However, the question remains, how does one know that what is being recalled is what is meant to be recalled? This question is hardly recognized by Coleridge who states confidently that Kant's writings "were not intended" for anyone "who could not pierce through the symbolic husk." Evidently, Kant's intentions may only be known by those who already know Kant's intentions, that is, by those who will already have recalled all there is to recall and thus would have no need to recall at all.

The question about whether recollection can ever know intention cannot be confined to Coleridge. Indeed, some recognition of this question is all but mandatory wherever there is the attempt to overcome the limitations imposed on philosophy by Kant. It would seem that there can be no progress without a return to what Kant meant to say rather than what Kant actually did say. In the *Biographia,* Coleridge makes little direct attempt of his own to return to what Kant writes but instead turns to the work of Fichte and Schelling for the systematic expression of Kant's intention. In Fichte, Coleridge sees not only the crucial importance of the act of self-positing as what allows a step beyond Kant to be claimed but also recognizes the development of systematicity as the mark of this step when he goes on to state that such an act "supplied the *idea* of a system truly metaphysical, and of a *metaphysique* truly systematic: (i.e. having its spring and principle within itself)" (1:158). As this statement implies, and as Fichte repeatedly makes clear, what has to be settled in the step beyond Kant is the very possibility of systematicity in philosophy—a step that repeats the decision Kant sought about the possibility or impossibility of metaphysics in general. Yet, not only does a system of philosophy hang upon this step, but, the possibility of saying what Kant meant to say is also unavoidably tied to it since nothing less than a systematic exposition is understood as corresponding to Kant's intention. Intentionality and systematicity therefore become, respectively, the posing and the resolution of the question of Kant's critical philosophy. As a resolution, such a system would be, as Coleridge's description alone implies, the culmination rather than the reflection of metaphysics. Nevertheless, two questions persist: the first concerns why Kant achieves no systematic exposition (and neither old age nor personal danger are satisfactory responses); the second concerns whether what is at stake in developing the system implied by Kant is really systematicity at all.

Both of these questions may be addressed in Fichte's own remarks about his relation to Kant in the preface which belongs to the first of the two introductions (1797) to the *Science of Knowledge:*

> Ich habe von jeher gesagt, und sage es hier wieder, daß mein System kein anderes sei als das *Kantische;* daß heißt: es enthält dieselbe Ansicht der Sache, ist aber in seinem Verfahren ganz unabhängig von der *Kantischen* Darstellung. Ich habe dies gesagt, nicht um durch eine große Autorität mich zu decken, oder meiner Lehre eine Stütze außer ihr zu selbst suchen; sondern um die Wahrheit zu sagen und gerecht zu sein. . . . Meine Schriften wollen *Kant* nicht erklären, oder aus ihm erklärt sein; sie selbst müssen für sich stehen, und *Kant* bleibt ganz aus dem Spiele.[28]

> I have long said, and say once more, that my system is no other than the *Kantian;* that is, it contains the same view of things, but in

> its method is quite independent of the *Kantian* presentation. I have said this not to hide myself behind a great authority, nor to seek an external support for my teaching, but rather to speak the truth and be just. . . . My writings seek neither to explain *Kant* nor be explained by him; they must stand for themselves, and *Kant* takes no part in them at all.

According to Fichte, his presentation of the Kantian system would be the speaking of the truth embedded within Kant's work, but nowhere explicitly formulated by Kant. In this presentation, Fichte would be no mere mouthpiece dependent on the authority of Kantian thought but would rather be seen as seeking the exposition of a self-authorizing system that authorizes what Kant meant but may never have said. To attain this authorization, Fichte resorts to the very distinction that will be repeated later by Coleridge in his advocacy of a symbolic understanding of Kant. But, as Fichte states in the second introduction, this recourse cannot be restricted to those who would surpass Kant:

> Nach dem *Geiste* zu erklären ist man wohl genötigt, wenn es mit der Erklärung nach dem *Buchstaben* nicht recht fort will. Kant selbst legt in dem bescheidenen Bekenntnisse, daß er sich der Gabe der Deutlichkeit nicht sonderlich bewußt sei, keinen großen Werth auf seinen Buchstaben, und in der Vorrede zur zweiten Auflage der *Kritik der reinen Vernunft* [B] xliv empfiehlt er selbst, seine Schriften nach dem *Zusammenhange,* und nach der *Idee* im Ganzen, also nach dem *Geiste, und der Absicht,* die einzelne Stellen haben können, zu erklären. (*WL* 1:479n.)

> We are surely obliged to read by the *spirit* if reading by the *letter* gets us no further. Kant himself, in the modest admission that he was not specially conscious of a gift for clarity, attaches no great value to the letter of his doctrine, and in the Preface to the Second Edition of the *Critique of Pure Reason,* B xliv, himself recommends that his writings be interpreted by their *interconnection* and according to the *idea* of the whole, and thus by the *spirit and intention* that individual passages may display.

All that would be required in order to know what Kant says, and even for Kant to know what Kant says, is to know the difference between the spirit and the letter.

The need to read Kant according to such a difference becomes a chorus in the work of the main figures of German Idealism. Both Schelling and Hegel, from whom so many of our aesthetic concepts are derived, will reiterate it.[29] The systematic exposition of Kant depends on a knowledge of figurative language even though such a knowledge cannot be accounted for until this exposition has achieved systematic completion. As such, the condition of a system is a difference between literal and figurative language that can never be known until the system becomes complete. Systematicity may be defined as the attempt to account for a distinction that, ultimately, it will no longer need to know. Here, the so-called new beginning that Romantic philosophy finds in Kant is less the beginning of something new than the attempt to justify a formal and self-reflexive relation as a model of knowledge. Coleridge's turn to German Idealism after Kant may be more properly seen as an attempt to produce principles for a literary criticism which takes as its central concept the very relation that Aristotle set aside at the very moment that the *Poetics* moves from theory to practice.

If Coleridge's own critical goals are to be attainable, then those goals must now be dependent on a system whose exposition requires a concept of difference that is immediately understood as leading back to its starting point: to use Coleridge's language, this could be referred to as the return of the already tautegorical. For Fichte, this difference would lie in method (*Verfahren*) thus indicating the reliance on a path that discovers its direction in repetition. As a repetition, such method falls within recollection since, for repetition to occur, something must be remembered. If the conditions of this method are applied to what Fichte says of his relation to Kant, then, Fichte's method does not just set out to recall what already exists previously but could never be known beforehand. Fichte's method would also remember what came before it could remember. Under these circumstances, the title distinguishing Fichte's prefatory remarks in the first introduction, "Vorerinnerung," is not simply a formal requirement since memory (*Erinnerung*) is the work of a system that would remember what it says in the place of what it sets out to recall. Such a recollection does not return to Kant, rather, it acts as a means to forget Kant. This forgetting takes the form of remembering Kant better than Kant—and re-membering is precisely what would occur here since for Fichte "alles, er [Kant] wirklich vorträgt, Bruchstücke und Resultate dieses Systemes sind" [everything (Kant) actually propounds consists of fragments and consequences of . . . a system] (*WL* 1:478).

As Fichte will go on to state, this remembering (which is predicated upon a loss that belongs to memory) cannot be conceived without a primary principle which Fichte describes as an act.[30] This principle is subsequently defined by a formula, self = self (Ich = Ich), whose possibility requires that "das Setzen des Ich durch sich selbst ist die reine Tätigkeit desselben. Das Ich *sezt sich selbst,* und es *ist,* vermöge seines bloßen Setzens durch sich selbst; und umgekehrt: Das Ich *ist,* und es *sezt* sein Sein, vermöge seines bloßen Seins" [the self's own positing of itself is its own pure activity. The *self posits itself,* and by virtue of this mere self-assertion it *exists;* and conversely, the self *exists* and *posits* its own existence by virtue of merely existing] (*WL* 1:96).[31] However, in Fichte's analysis of the proposition "*I am I,*" this activity of positing comes to rely less on an act than on the grammatical distinction between subject and predicate. Fichte writes:

> Man nehme an, daß das im obigen Satze [*Ich bin Ich*] in der Stelle des formalen Subjekts stehende Ich das *schlechthin gesezte;* das in der Stelle der Prädikats aber das *seiende* bedeute; so wird durch das schlechthin gültige Urteil, daß beide völlig Eins seien, ausgesagt, oder schlechthin gesezt: das *Ich* sei, *weil* es sich gesezt habe. (*WL* 1:96)

> Let it be assumed that what is *absolutely posited* is the I occupying the place of formal subject in the above proposition [*I am I*] while that in the predicate position represents that which *exists;* hence, the absolutely valid judgment that both are completely identical, states, or absolutely asserts, that the *self* exists *because* it has posited itself.

The recourse to a linguistic paradigm is even more pronounced in a note to this passage, where Fichte states that "*Ist* drükt den Übergang des Ich vom Setzen zur Reflexion über das gesezte aus" [*Is* expresses the passage of the *self* from positing to reflection on what has been posited] (*WL* 1:96n.). From this note, it becomes clear that only through the predicate may the subject be remembered and this recalling is authorized by a difference derived from the grammatical category occupied by a finite verb. Consequently, if predication is ever to occur then grammar must always be an art of memory as well as a theory of the subject since, by remembering its subject, it would speak for what came before (*prædicere*) and thereby posit the formal subject necessary to the predicative nature of theoretical reflection. Furthermore, this use of grammatical structure as a means of explanation indicates that what is at stake in the step beyond Kant is an understanding in which grammatical structure is to be derived from an act of self-reversion—only then can "is" express the prelinguistic state demanded by an absolute positing.

Given the emphasis Fichte places on an absolute activity of the self and its relation to consciousness in the proposition "I am I," it is easy to see how the direction followed by German Idealism after Kant would be taken up by the *Biographia* and especially by an autobiographical design which demands that what is written be the truth of an author whose relation to that writing must be unknown if it is to remain true. In addition, the critical activity that the *Biographia* seeks to establish would be inconceivable without resolving the difficulty posed by this design. The literary-critical project defined by the *Biographia* requires a surpassing of Kant which would always take the form of a "return" to Kant. The importance of this project is such that the relation of Fichte to the *Biographia* cannot be reduced to the formal structure of a given work since what is at stake in both is a relation that would avoid what Kant saw as an unavoidable and recurrent deceptiveness.[32] If the absolute activity of the self is to ground all relation, it would also be the relation that enables, without deception, the passage to the imagination as well as the determination of the imagination. Consequently, a preoccupation with the imagination within literary criticism would also be predicated upon the self-positing activity at work in Fichte's principle of self = self.[33]

Despite the direct relevance of the Fichtean act which posits the possibility of a self-authorizing subject, Coleridge dismisses Fichte's presentation on account of a "crude egoismus, a boastful and hyperstoic hostility to NATURE, as lifeless, godless, and altogether unholy" (1:158–59) and turns instead to Schelling for the actual true completion of a "system truly metaphysical and of a *metaphysique* truly systematic." Coleridge's rejection of Fichte is barely understandable in these terms. Fichte clearly states that his *Science of Knowledge* is neither atheistic nor stoic.[34] In this case, why should the literary-critical project undertaken by the *Biographia* turn from Fichte to Schelling? On the strength of the just-quoted comment, this turn seems to result from the absence of any philosophy of nature in Fichte. But even this is untenable if Fichte's system is considered fully, since a philosophy of nature is already deduced within what Fichte calls the "not-self."[35] Given the existence of such a philosophy of nature in Fichte, Coleridge's turn to Schelling would merely exchange one exposition of the primary act through which this philosophy arises for another: Fichte's subjective for Schelling's objective exposition. In so doing, Coleridge would reject what Hegel called a "subjective Subject-Object" principle in order to replace it with an "objective Subject-Object" principle.[36] In this case, the turn to Schelling would be made as a turn away from Fichte which unwittingly follows a dialectical development plotted by Hegel. Not only does this turn indicate a limited knowledge of the full extent of German Idealism (not to mention a limited understanding of what is known) but, also, it points to the way in which Coleridge confuses the place of a philosophy of nature in German Idealism with the derivation of a philosophy and system from nature. That the latter is the case may already be seen in the statements about desynonymization and the distinction of imagination and fancy in chapter 4 of the *Biographia* ("were it once fully ascertained that this division is no less *grounded in nature*. . . . it would in its immediate effects furnish a torch of guidance to the philosophical critic" [1:84–85; emphasis mine]). By itself, this confusion indicates that the presence of Schelling in the *Biographia* responds to a necessity that is regarded as essential to a criticism that would possess guiding principles, yet, it also poses the question of whether Schelling is necessary to this criticism or whether Schelling is only the form, or cloak, in which this necessity appears in the *Biographia.*

Although introduced as early as chapter 9 of the *Biographia,* Schelling does not begin to play a significant role until chapter 12. Yet, despite the weight given to the imagination in a work such as Schelling's *System of Transcendental Idealism* (as well as in Fichte), Coleridge does not emphasize the crucial role played by what Schelling refers to as "an aesthetic act of the imagination" in either this work or the *Abhandlungen zur Erläuterung des Idealismus der Wissenschaftslehre* [Treatise Demonstrating the Idealism of the Science of Knowledge] (1796/97), which also figures significantly in the *Biogra-*

phia.[37] Coleridge concentrates on specific elements whose systematic relation is made possible by this aesthetic act.

In the *Biographia,* the elaboration of these elements begins with a concern for evidence and, in particular, evidence that would not be "a part of the problem to be solved" (1:247). Here, Coleridge is referring to a concern for a "system, which aims to deduce the memory with all the other functions of the intelligence," a system which must "place its first position from beyond the memory and anterior to it" (1:247) if it is to provide a solution. This first position, which Schelling terms "the absolutely unconscious and non-objective," is precisely what the aesthetic act of imagination is intended to bring into reflection: "Dieses Reflektirtwerden des absolut Unbewußten und nicht-Objektiven nur durch einen *ästhetischen* Akt der Einbildungskraft möglich ist" [This coming-to-be-reflected of the absolutely unconsciousness and non-objective is only possible through an aesthetic act of the imagination] (*System, SW* 3:351). To the extent that this first position guides Coleridge's argument, it must and can only be affirmed retroactively, that is, it must always be a fore-remembering (*Vor-erinnerung*), that is, anterior to recollection. Yet, this first position is also what a systematic exposition is to recall once it has accounted for its power of recollection. Since this recollection cannot be derived from any external source it must be produced within that same systematic exposition. These conditions lead Coleridge to a question posed by Schelling in his *Abhandlungen:*

> Philosophy is employed on objects of INNER SENSE, and cannot, like geometry, appropriate to every construction a correspondent *outward* intuition. Nevertheless, philosophy, if it is to arrive at evidence, must proceed from the most original construction, and the question then is, what is the most original construction or first productive act for the INNER SENSE. (1:250)[38]

As a result of this first productive act, philosophy will attain the evidence necessary to justify its employment upon the objects of inner sense precisely because it would account for the production of those same objects. To account for this act of production is ultimately to account for not only the inner sense itself, but, also, for philosophy (since without this accounting philosophy could never have an object for reflection that was proper to it).

In answer to the question of how this account may proceed,

Coleridge first states that it "depends on the direction which is given to the INNER SENSE" (1:250). Subsequently, Coleridge writes that "the inner sense has its direction determined for the greater part only by an act of freedom" (1:251). Whereas Schelling's text only speaks of freedom and not an act of freedom in the sentence corresponding to Coleridge's, this freedom is clearly referred to as an act in the earlier *System* when Schelling speaks of how an unconditional principle may become an object of knowledge: "Was *Princip* alles Wissens ist, gar nicht ursprünglich, oder an sich, sondern nur *durch einen besonderen Akt der Freiheit* Objekt des Wissens werden kann" [By no means can that which is the *principle* of all knowledge become, originally, or in itself, an object of knowledge, rather, it can only become an object of knowledge *through a particular act of freedom*] (*System, SW* 3:368). As Coleridge's language makes clear, what is to be accounted for if the inner sense is to furnish any object at all (and therefore enable philosophy) is an act but an act that is absolutely free and unconditioned. Since a free and unconditioned act would become dependent upon any account of its freedom or unconditionality, the relation between this unconditioned act and its accounting could not be free. Schelling recognizes this difficulty in a passage that suggests that what is really at stake is not simply an act but a form of repetition which does not simultaneously compromise this act:

> Wenn nun aber der Philosoph auch jenes Akts als Akts versichert, wie versichert er sich seines bestimmten Gehalts? Ohne Zweifel durch die *freie Nachahmung* dieses Akts, mit welcher alle Philosophie beginnt. Woher weiß denn aber der Philosoph, daß jener secundbäre, willkürliche Akt identisch sei mit jenem ursprünglichen und *absolut* freien? (*System, SW* 3:396)

> Now that the philosopher thus assures himself of this act as act, how does he assure himself of its distinct content? Without doubt, through the *free imitation* of this act with which all philosophy begins. But then, how does the philosopher know that this secondary, arbitrary act is identical to the original and *absolutely* free one?

According to what Schelling states here, the relation of an original and absolutely free act to the account of that act must be, on the one hand, arbitrary if it is to be free and, on the other, imitative if it is to have any relation to such an act. This requirement indicates that the unconditioned act spoken of by Schelling and subsequently by Coleridge is irrelevant unless a relation of this nature is established.

The relation envisaged in this "free imitation" is directly relevant to the ventriloquistic structure within which the *Biographia* operates, since this "free imitation" would present but not disclose the source of its authority. In both Schelling's *Abhandlungen* and *System,* as well as Coleridge's *Biographia,* the ability to perform this imitation depends absolutely on the inner sense. Here, the direct relation of literature and its interpretation becomes evident, since, as Schelling argues, the inner sense is also inseparable from an aesthetic sense: "Die Philosophie beruht . . . ebenso gut wie die Kunst auf dem produktiven Vermögen. . . . Der eigentliche Sinn, mit dem diese Art der Philosophie ausgefaßt werden muß, ist also der *ästhetische,* und eben darum die Philosophie der Kunst das wahre Organon der Philosophie" [Philosophy is founded just as much as art on a productive faculty. . . . The proper sense with which this kind of philosophy must be apprehended is thus an *aesthetic* sense and, for this reason, the philosophy of art is the true organ of philosophy] (*System, SW* 3:351). From this, it is evident that any claim to systematic understanding must include an aesthetic theory if its claim to knowledge is to appear justified. Consequently, what determines the systematicity of a philosophy is less the unconditionality of its principle of knowledge than an aesthetics which allows such an unconditionality to be known in an act. What is ultimately at stake in a systematic exposition is therefore an aesthetics of the act, that is, an account of how the aesthetic is at the same time an act.

With such a stake, the failure of Coleridge's *Biographia* to perform what it set out to do could be attributed to an inability to see that what must be grounded in the critical project envisaged by this text is not the imagination but the ability to ground the imagination. Coleridge's attempt to control this necessity may be read in a series of modifications that begin immediately following the section of the *Biographia* dealing with inner sense (largely drawn from the *Abhandlungen*) and which precede those sections drawn from Schelling's *System.* Although these modifications effectively transform the character of Schelling's exposition, they are far from acquitting Coleridge of dependency on Schelling since they reflect an attempt to adopt not just Schelling's *System* but also employ it as a means of adoption. This adoption surfaces as Coleridge seeks to establish the principle of Schelling's *System* in relation to an ultimate transfiguring authority: "The postulate of philosophy and at the same time the test of philosophic capacity, is no other than the heaven-descended KNOW THYSELF! (*E cælo descendit,* Γνῶθι σεαυτόν)" (1:252).[39] Such a command occurs nowhere in Schelling's *System,* however, given that this work takes the self as its unconditioned principle of knowledge, it is not difficult to see how this could be subsumed within an understanding focused exclusively on a knowledge of the self.[40] As the following passage makes clear, this understanding is radically different from Schelling's description of the self as a principle of knowledge: "Das Ich ist reiner Akt, reines Tun, was schlechthin nichtobjektiv sein muß in Wissen, eben deßwegen, weil es *Princip* alles Wissens ist. Soll es also Objekt des Wissens werden, so muß dieß durch eine vom gemeinen Wissen ganz verschiedene Art zu wissen geschehen" [The self is pure act, pure doing, which, because of this, must plainly be non-objective in knowledge since it is the *principle* of all knowledge. Consequently, should it become an object of knowledge, this must happen through a kind of knowing quite different from ordinary knowledge] (*System, SW* 3:368–69). By incorporating what Schelling calls "pure act, pure doing" within this command, Coleridge adopts what has become, since its association with Socrates, a virtual philosopheme. Moreover, this adoption reveals the extent to which Coleridge understands Schelling's principle of self (whose activity allows self-consciousness to occur) as if this principle were no different from the self recognized by self-consciousness.[41] In addition, Coleridge, through the citation of Juvenal, speaks of this command as something descended from the sky, thereby underlining that Coleridge not only postulates an external source as the possibility of a system "having its spring and principle within itself" but also requires that this postulate should take the form of an act of ventriloquy.

The tracing of authority to a ventriloquistic source will take on added importance as chapter 12 of the *Biographia* proceeds; however, the primary example in which authority would be established through ventriloquy cannot be overlooked at this point especially when it is remembered that the adoption of Schelling is as much at stake as the authority to adopt. Although the command "Know Thyself" may be associated with the Delphic oracle and the god Apollo, any discussion of the voice descending from heaven would also have to include that scene of transfiguration in which a father first claims a son and does so for an aesthetic reason:

> And after six days, Jesus takes Peter, James, and John his brother and leads them privately up to a high mountain. And he was transfigured (μετεμορφώθη) before them and his face shone as the sun (ἔλαμψεν τό πρόσωπον αὐτοῦ ὡς ὁ ἥλιος) and his garments became white as the light. And, lo, there was seen by them Moses and Elias conversing with him. And answering, Peter said to Jesus: Lord, it is good for us to be here; if you wish, I will make three tents here, one for you, and one for Moses, and one for Elias. While he was still speaking, lo, a bright cloud overshadowed them, and, lo, a voice out of the cloud, saying: This is my beloved son, in whom I was well pleased; hear you him (φωνὴ ἐκ τῆς νεφέλης λέγουσα· οὗτός ἐστιν ὁ υἱό μου ὁ ἀγαπητός, ἐν ᾧ εὐδόκησα· ἀκούετε αὐτοῦ). And hearing, the disciples fell on their faces and feared exceedingly. And Jesus approached and, touching them, said: Rise and do not fear. And lifting up their eyes, they saw no-one except only Jesus himself. (Matt. 17.1–8)

Not only is this passage significant because of its exemplary use of a topos which Coleridge evokes as the origin of philosophy, the voice descending from heaven, but also, because the authority of its exemplariness is established through a repeated metaphoricity or transfiguration which conceals the source of its authority: an unseen voice claims as its own a face which would be as unseeable as the sun and does so in an expression of pleasure which is immediately followed by the granting of an authoritative voice in the command "hear you him." By establishing authority through a sequence that proceeds from metaphor to a filial recognition which results from the pleasure taken in an individual's life, this passage repeats the dependence of authority on an essentially aesthetic act. Indeed, would the father have recognized the son if he were not well pleased? What passes for an act in this passage would be the voice of the father speaking from a cloud. This act is aesthetic since the recognition that the voice is indeed the voice of the father causes the cloud to be understood as the veil (or external appearance) of an authority that cannot present itself but can only possess a form not its own. Through this aesthetic reading of the voice, it becomes possible to distinguish between a cloud that conceals something and a cloud that gives no sign whether it conceals or does not conceal something. But, if this recognition may be assumed so readily, why is this aesthetic component so necessary? An answer is indicated by the precise moment at which the act of speaking takes place in this passage.

The act of speaking, which would stand as the source of authority, only occurs in this passage between the transfiguration of Christ into something like the sun and the passage in which Christ commands the disciples to rise. The passage from *pater incertus* to the knowledge of authority is thus enabled by an intervention in which a claim to pleasure stands as the only support for the words which say, "This is my beloved son." Thanks to this intervention, Christ passes from aesthetic object ("as the sun") to figure of authority by repeating the sequence established by the intervention of the father. In this instance, the authorizing of Christ depends on a repetition whereby the relation of the father to both the disciples and the son is embodied by the relation of the son to the disciples. Even though the son would repeat the father, the possibility of this repetition only arises once the father appears veiled by a cloud, this presentation of the father repeats the prior veiling of Christ as the sun. Consequently, the initial transfiguration of the son helps establish the pattern that enables the aesthetic reading of this passage. Within this pattern, the second veiling (the father behind a cloud) would assume epistemological authority through the sheer force of its repetition of the already accepted figure of Christ as the sun. And, as always within such a sequence, the second instance considers the first a reflection of its authority (since the second authorizes the sequence to which the first veiling subsequently belongs). Prior to such an assumption, there would be no ground to support a passage from an aesthetic transfiguration to a sign of authority since there would only be the repetition of a transfiguration in which the presence or absence of authority always remains unknown. Unless this transfiguration, that is, unless the aesthetic were always understood as an act, there would be no authority to recognize. But, if authority is derived from an aesthetic act, can this act be anything other than aesthetic, and, if it is aesthetic, can it ever be an act? Indeed, can language, even the word *act,* ever be an act?[42]

The question posed in the account of Christ's transfiguration may be directed at the command "Know Thyself," since this command must also be known as a pure act, a pure doing, otherwise, it could not stand as the postulate of all philosophy in an argument so indebted to Schelling's philosophy. The adoption of Schelling's philosophy (as if it were the offspring of the heaven-descended command "Know Thyself") suggests that Coleridge fails to grasp how Schelling understands the principle of self as an unconditioned activity. But here, failure to understand would be too easy an answer, an answer that would only serve to conceal a larger question. In the end, failure to understand is not an issue, since it is a matter of indifference how one characterizes a postulate whenever this same postulate can only derive its power of authorization from a history that both embodies and is predicated upon an act of aesthetic self-reflection ("my beloved son, in whom I was well pleased" [ἐν ᾧ εὐδόκησα]). To mark the difference between Coleridge and Schelling as one of inferiority (or even superiority if literary history's aversion to its philosophical roots is at issue) is to direct attention away from a question central to the possibility of a systematic exposition for philosophy in Schelling, the question of how a repetition could ever have had the authority of knowledge—a question about repetition itself.

Repetition and the Theft of Schelling

Car Samuel Taylor Coleridge avait fini par tout oublier.

—Artaud, "Coleridge le traître"

Although the question of repetition may be traced directly in a reading of Schelling's *System,* such a reading runs the risk of being seen as exposing only a philosophical difficulty rather than a difficulty whose generality is impossible to avoid even in Coleridge's rendering of Schelling. What the *Biographia* makes explicit in its attempt to ground the practice of literary criticism in philosophical principle is that even the thematic or literary appropriation of philosophy cannot overcome a difference which constitutes philosophy. To the extent that this appropriation is literary or thematic, it will be led to repeat the formal and schematic models employed by philosophy to account for its claim to a knowledge of difference.

In the *Biographia,* the attempt to account for such a claim begins as Coleridge states the preliminary propositions of Schelling's *System.* In Coleridge's account this work is chosen as the example of a system that does not exclude nature from its consideration. Yet, more significant to Coleridge's goals in the *Biographia* is the movement toward aesthetics which takes place in the final pages of Schelling's *System.* This movement would make literature (as an aesthetic activity) become the form to which philosophy aspires. While such a movement may explain Coleridge's attraction to Schelling's *System,* it should be already clear that Coleridge's adoption of Schelling takes place within an argument that envisages a synthesis of philosophy and literature in the form of critical knowledge.

Coleridge's conclusion may be different from Schelling's, however, it is developed from the same propositions that Schelling uses as the basis of his systematic exposition. The first of these propositions makes the assertion that "all knowledge rests on the coincidence of an object with a subject" (1:252). In Coleridge and Schelling, this proposition leads to the description of the two possible ways through which knowledge may be arrived at. In this instance, knowledge is formed by the coincidence of the subjective and the objective (these terms being abstract equivalents for the words "I" and "me" discussed in the previous section). Coleridge writes:

> For if all knowledge has as it were two poles reciprocally required and presupposed, all sciences must proceed from the one or the other, and must *tend toward the opposite as far as the equatorial point in which both are reconciled and become identical.* (1:255; emphasis mine)

The language of Coleridge's account betrays the extent to which he overstates what Schelling says and, in so doing, asserts an understanding that responds immediately to the critical goals of the *Biographia.* Schelling writes:

> Wenn alles *Wissen* gleichsam zwei Pole hat, die sich wechselseitig voraussetzen und fordern, so müssen sie in allen Wissenschaften

> sich suchen; es muß daher notwendig *zwei* Grundwissenschaften geben und es muß unmöglich sein, von dem einen Pol auszugehen, ohne auf den andern getrieben zu werden. (*System, SW* 3:340)
>
> If all *knowing* has, as it were, two poles, which mutually presuppose and demand one another, then, they must seek each other in all the sciences; hence, it [knowing] must necessarily produce *two* basic sciences, and it must be impossible to set out from one pole without being driven toward the other.

As becomes evident from Schelling's account of how the two poles are related to one another, Coleridge has suppressed the notion of a drive (*Trieb*) which causes one pole to seek the other. Coleridge's emphasis on an "equatorial point" not only reflects an understanding that demands a more static relation but also it stresses that the coincidence of subjective and objective exists as a point independent of both. In contrast to Schelling, Coleridge makes identity a point rather than a relation. Adopted in this way, Schelling's initial proposition would appear to authorize the intermediary power anticipated in the *Biographia* as a power partaking of the two poles between which it exists. Despite this adoption, Coleridge must still face the same problem of authorization which Schelling defines two pages later as being "ohne Zweifel die *Hauptaufgabe der Philosophie*" [without doubt the *main task of philosophy*] (*System, SW* 3:342).

By ascribing an intermediary function to the essential principle of Schelling's *System,* Coleridge grants this principle a role it cannot yet exercise since, as Schelling repeatedly points out, it is only through the aesthetic that this principle could ever possess such a function. In this respect, Schelling's *System* reflects more accurately the difficulty to be surmounted in any attempt to ground knowledge in any such principle. As Schelling insists, this principle must be free, that is, whatever direction it takes must be undetermined but, at the same time, it must be capable of determining the direction taken by either of Schelling's two starting points of knowledge, the subjective or objective. The ability to produce such a determination is a necessity ("*muß* . . . notwendig geben und *muß* unmöglich sein" [emphasis mine]), otherwise there could be no relation between knowledge and the principle that makes it possible: neither the subjective nor the objective would know where to go nor could they be opposed to one another. Since the aesthetic is to embody this relation, then, the problem to be faced by both Schelling and Coleridge is to ground the aesthetic as a mode of knowledge. However, Coleridge's emphasis on an equatorial point already assumes this grounding by modeling his point of departure according to the desired result (this assumption explains why Coleridge, contrary to Schelling, finds it unnecessary to retain the activity of a drive [*Trieb*]). To the extent that the *System* aims at the demonstration of a coincidence between the two poles of knowledge, it indicates that what must also be accounted for is the possibility of a relation through which criticism would both produce an authoritative voice and distinguish that voice from among its own transfigurations.

In the *Biographia,* this relation is to be articulated through the sequence of ten theses that dominate chapter 12. As if to resolve the difficulties posed by any systematic deduction of these ten theses, Coleridge undertakes to define their relation to a systematic exposition before they are even presented. This preemptive move reflects a difficulty that persists even through Coleridge's adaptation of Schelling—the difficulty posed by an exposition whose systematicity can only be known by being brought to an end. Coleridge's avoidance of the difficulty posed by a systematic exposition first surfaces in his reference to a projected work, the "Logosophia." In this work, Coleridge asserts that he will "give (deo volente) the demonstrations and constructions of the Dynamic Philosophy scientifically arranged" (1:263). In anticipation of this exposition, the Ten Theses stand as a summary conclusion which amounts to the postponement of a fully philosophic exposition by what it is meant to achieve. An arithmetical analogy is offered to justify this procedure: "The science of arithmetic furnishes instances, that a rule may be useful in practical application, and for the particular purpose may be sufficiently authenticated by the result, before it has been fully demonstrated. It is enough, if only it be rendered intelligible" (1:263). Here, Coleridge speaks before he has the authority to say what he means. Consequently, this avoidance of an expository demonstration of how one arrives at the ten theses follows the model of authority described by Coleridge in the form of a divine ventriloquy—"if only the words are audible and intelligible" now becomes "if only it be rendered intelligible."

According to this model of authority, the onus of authentication will always rest upon the intelligibility of a result that would in effect annul the need for any demonstration. In this instance, authenticity or truth of the demonstration resides in the mouth of a puppet who speaks the words of an unseen authority. As before, when Coleridge cited Milton after describing the ventriloquy of truth, the recurrence of the need to recognize an authority that may never appear as such (if it is to remain authoritative) produces a significant anxiety. This anxiety is expressed clearly at the beginning of chapter 12. This expression of anxiety is one of several occurrences but here it is all the more important since it is stated immediately before Coleridge's attempted presentation of the philosophic ground of the imagination. Coleridge writes:

> In lieu of the various requests which the anxiety of authorship addresses to the unknown reader, I advance but this one; that he will either pass over the following chapter altogether, or read the whole connectedly. The fairest part of the most beautiful body will appear deformed and monstrous, if dissevered from its place in the organic Whole . . . even a *faithful* display of the main and supporting ideas, if yet they are separated from the forms by which they are at once cloathed and modified, may perchance present a skeleton indeed; but a skeleton to alarm and deter. (1:233–34)

Here, it is a question of reading aesthetically so that the whole may be rendered without appearing deformed or skeletal. The onus of authentication is thus placed, in the last instance, upon a reader who, at this point in the disquisition, is presented with that very kind of skeleton but who is required, nevertheless, to clothe it. However, this has been the least "cloathed" section of the *Biographia* (whenever Coleridge's literary "theory" is discussed, all too frequently it is only the last page of volume one, and volume two up to the "Sibylline Leaves," which are considered—an omission that either serves to conclude the establishment of a philosophical ground by leaping over its problematics or else refuses to recognize the presence of these problematics within its own assumptions). Notwithstanding, Coleridge explicitly points to this section of the *Biographia* as providing the possibility of, first, authentication and, second, intelligibility:

> This [authentication] will, I trust, have been effected in the following Theses for those of my readers, who are willing to accompany

> me through the following Chapter, in which the results will be applied to the deduction of the imagination, and with it the principles of production and of genial criticism in the fine arts. (1:264)

Not only do the Ten Theses take the place of demonstration, but, this substitution would establish the basis of the deduction of imagination and, ipso facto, artistic production and its criticism. Criticism and the production of its proper object are thus linked once again to the same source, the "awful power" of imagination which, in this instance, establishes the possibility of authentic, intelligible reflection upon the work of art.

Although the Ten Theses are indebted to Schelling, Coleridge's arrangement indicates the necessity imposed by the critical principles sought in the *Biographia.* The first thesis already suggests the necessity which the remaining nine are intended to support: "If we know, there must be somewhat known by us" (1:264). Within this frame, knowing is directed toward the unfolding of a "correspondent reality" (1:264). In Thesis II, this knowing requires a reflection upon truth if this correspondence is itself to be accounted for:

> All truth is either mediate, that is, derived from some other truth or truths; or immediate and original. The latter is absolute, and its formula A. A; the former is of dependent or conditional certainty, and represented in the formula B. A. The certainty, which inheres in A, is attributable to B. (1:265)

While immediate truth would be absolutely identical to itself, mediate truth can only refer to another truth which lacks the self-grounded nature essential to what is unconditionally true. Nevertheless, Coleridge argues in the Scholium to Thesis II that truths of conditional certainty may also contain a central principle through which they are related to an original truth—a claim which suggests that what the *Biographia* eventually seeks to ground will have an instrumental role in attaining that ground:

> Equally *inconceivable* is a cycle of equal truths without a common and central principle, which prescribes to each its proper sphere in the system of science. That the absurdity does not immediately strike us, that it does not seem equally *unimaginable,* is owing to a surreptitious act of the imagination, which, instinctively and without our noticing the same, not only fills up the intervening spaces

> . . . but likewise supplies, by a sort of *subintelligitur,* the one central power, which renders the movement harmonious and cyclical. (1:267)

The absurdity of equal truths is described in an earlier version of this thesis as "an endless Cycle, a perpetual Interfusion of all particular Positions, each with each & each with all, in a common Chaos."[43] It is against such a chaos that the imagination acts surreptitiously and, in so doing, supplies the "one central power." Yet, the imagination is not quite the absolute truth upon which Coleridge will seek to base either the *Biographia* or his critical principles—if this were the case, then the *Biographia* would be pursuing an imagination that would and could have no relation to anything other than itself (if even that). This is not the issue; the issue is how an absolute and self-reflexive principle can also be reflected in something other than itself and still be known in that reflection. The reflection of this principle into something other than itself would then stand as the affirmation of its reflection into itself. As is already apparent from the preceding citation, the imagination fulfills a particular role on the level of mediate truth by providing a sense of what relates such mediate truths.

Over and above the imagination, however, there is the principle itself, the principle of absolute truth described in Thesis III:

> We are to seek therefore for some absolute truth capable of communicating to other positions a certainty, which it has not itself borrowed; a truth self-grounded, unconditional and known by its own light. In short we have to find a somewhat which *is,* simply because it *is*. In order to be such, it must be one which is its own predicate, so far at least that all other nominal predicates must be modes and repetitions of itself. (1:268)

If equal truths are to have their "proper sphere in the system of science," then, this certainty must be capable of being transmitted by a truth that does not enter into the process of communication. This kind of truth and its principle thus seek to ground mediate truths without becoming one with them and therefore losing the authority to grant any certainty. To explain this capability, Coleridge resorts to a grammatical term: all mediate truths are to be grounded in the same way that all predicates are grounded in a primary predicate, that is, in a subject that would be its own predicate. The occurrence of this predicate in the same thesis that demands an unconditioned principle (the actual principle is not named until Thesis VI) indicates that grammar may be the model rather than an analogy called upon to explain such a principle. This recourse to grammatical paradigm offers a precise definition of the difficulty facing both Coleridge and Schelling: each seeks to account for reference by positing an absolute that must be set apart from all reference in order to fulfill the claims made in its name. The contradictory relation that lies at the heart of any such account of reference will be more familiar in its most recent service as a critique of deconstruction. This critique frequently takes the following form: deconstruction denies all reference except when it makes this denial. Surprisingly, what is at stake in this critique is not reference at all but the possibility of a formally closed point of reference—precisely the absolute demanded by Coleridge. Without this formal possibility, there could be no critique of deconstruction as a denial of reference (still less could deconstruction even confess to denying reference). What is already taking place in the *Biographia* may be subsequently read as the attempt to justify such an overdetermination by articulating a relation that mediates between reference and its denial. In Coleridge's words, this relation is to be known as a mode of repetition through which an absolute principle may appear as the subject of a mode of reference ("its own predicate, so far at least that all other nominal predicates must be modes and repetitions of itself" [1:268]). But, once again, why does Coleridge resort to a grammatical term at the very point where he touches upon the essential question of how the same subject may be repeated but with a difference?

Thesis V takes up the question of such a repetition as it tries to clarify what may serve as a principle of knowledge. Thesis V states that this principle cannot be "any THING OR OBJECT" (1:270) because things and objects owe their existence as things and objects to a perceiver and not a principle. But neither can the principle be a subject since it would then be no more than a form of Berkeleian idealism, which, like the critique of Hartleian association in chapters 5–8 of the *Biographia,* cannot transcend or "alter the natural difference of *things* and *thoughts*" (1:90). At the end of Thesis V, an alternative is described: "It [the principle] is to be found in neither subject nor object taken separately, and consequently, as no other third is conceivable, it must be found in that which is neither subject nor object exclusively, but which is the identity of both" (1:271). Here, it is assumed that, since there is no other alternative (no third) to the subjective or objective, the principle or third element must be conceived in the identity of these two opposed positions. For Schelling, the only possibility for such a solution is the self ("Ich" [*System, SW* 3:368]). Coleridge follows Schelling at this point, but, in doing so, he substitutes the Latin "SUM." Quite apart from the scholastic and Cartesian inclination present in his translation, what is most significant about this substitution is Coleridge's use of a single word which possesses both a subject and a predicate: "This principle . . . manifests itself in the SUM or I AM; which I shall hereafter indiscriminately express by the words spirit, self, and self-consciousness. In this, and in this alone, object and subject, being and knowing are identical, each involving, and supposing the other" (Thesis VI; 1:272–73). Not only is this principle made manifest in the SUM or I AM," but it is in this manifestation ("and in this alone") that being and knowledge are said to be identical. Yet, to what extent can the grammatical condensation of subject and predicate into one word carry an argument that has avoided all demonstration?

In the Scholium to Thesis VI, the grammatical paradigm represented in the Latin "SUM" is reinforced as Coleridge articulates his understanding of Schelling's concept of the self in a phrase that enacts the repetition of a subject and its predicate on two levels. Coleridge asserts that the phrase "sum quia sum" [I am because I am] (1:274) may be taken as expressing the ground *of a knowledge* of existence. In distinction, Coleridge goes on, the ground of existence would be expressed by the phrase "sum quia Deus est [I am because God is] or still more philosophically, sum quia Deo sum [I am because I am in God]" (1:274). Through these repetitions of "SUM," Coleridge would derive his own ability to say "I am" from, in his own words, the "absolute self, the great external I AM . . . [in which] the ground of existence, and the ground of the knowledge of existence are absolutely identical, Sum quia sum; I am because I affirm myself to be; I affirm myself to be, because I am" (1:275). Coleridge's reasoning may be summarized in the phrase *Deus quia sum est* since, in this espousal of the "I am," Coleridge would authorize the possibility of critical knowledge through what amounts to an act of speaking ("I am") that would be known as an act of God ("I AM"). What emerges as crucially important here is this knowledge of an act. Indeed, it is only by recognizing this speaking as an act that the ability to say "I am" can perform its function as the source or ultimate principle of every science. Otherwise, it could only be a grammatical example dressed in the clothes of knowledge. In this case, Coleridge's God would be merely a name acting as a veil rather than what is veiled.

The priority of such an act is insisted upon in Thesis IX when Coleridge tries to account for this act as a mode of repetition traceable to the exercise of a will:

> This principium commune essendi et cognoscendi [common principle of being and knowing], as subsisting in a WILL, or primary ACT of self-duplication, is the mediate or indirect principle of every science; but it is the immediate and direct principle of the ultimate science alone, i.e. of transcendental philosophy alone. (1:281)

This primacy of the will marks the culmination of a series of references in the *Biographia*.[44] Here, the will is to account for a repetition without which there can be neither system, knowledge, nor the ability to say "I am." Consequently, the will must account for not just the ability to say "I am," it must account for the first utterance of language as an act of existential repetition. Through such a repetition, language would not only repeat an act in which existence is supposed to be grounded, but that repetition would also be read as the act it repeats. Only in this way can a knowledge of the ground of existence even enter into a relation, never mind an identity, with what is called the ground of existence.

This necessity of a repetition which would also be the source of the act it repeats becomes absolutely clear in Thesis IX when such a repetition is equated with the formation of self-consciousness: "The highest principle of knowing . . . at once the source and accompanying form in all particular acts of intellect and perception . . . can be found only in the act and evolution of self-consciousness" (1:282). In Thesis VIII, this same act and evolution was declared to be "impossible, except by and in a will" (1:280)—implying that Coleridge makes the will an agent of causality with respect to self-consciousness. Even though the will has this causative function, it cannot be separated from or given priority in relation to self-consciousness. Coleridge states, "The self-conscious spirit therefore is a will" (1:280)—"therefore" appearing to validate the substitution of cause and effect as well as the synonymity of will and self-consciousness. Despite the presence of "therefore" in this place, no logical account of how such a transition occurs is offered: the will is a cause ("impossible, except by . . . a will") whose effect (self-consciousness) only exists within this same causal activity ("impossible, except . . . in a will").

What the foregoing determination of the will offers Coleridge is a relation that ought to account for how a cause and an effect are possible through the same act. The will must therefore operate as the conjunction that allows "I am" to be read as both an utterance and an act which gives the self knowledge of its existence. The most concise commentary on this conjunction is given by Nietzsche who, in a passage from *Beyond Good and Evil,* attributes the knowledge derived from such an act as being authorized by a "grammatical habit," that is, a habit that legitimizes thought according to the grammatical definition of syntax: the verb is the sign of an acting which will always be preceded by a subject who acts. In Coleridge, the will would be sustained by this same habit:

> Ein Gedanke kommt, wenn "er" will, und nicht wenn "ich" will; so daß es eine *Fälschung* des Tatbestandes ist zu sagen: das Subjekt "ich" ist die Bedingung des Prädikates "denke." *Es* denkt: aber daß dies "es" gerade jenes alte berühmte "Ich" sei, ist, milde geredet, nur eine Annahme, eine Behauptung, vor allem keine "unmittelbare Gewißheit." Zuletzt ist schon mit diesem "es denkt" zuviel getan: schon dies "es" enthält eine *Auslegung* des Vorgangs und gehört nicht zum Vorgange selbst. Man schließt hier nach der grammatischen Gewohnheit "Denken ist eine Tätigkeit, zu jeder Tätigkeit gehört einer, der tätig ist, folglich—"[45]

> A thought comes when "it" wills not when "I" wills; consequently it is a falsification of the facts to say that the subject "I" is the condition of the predicate "think." *It* thinks; but that this "it" should be precisely the old celebrated "I" is, to put it mildly, only a supposition, an assertion, and above all not an "immediate certainty." In the end, there is even too much performed with this "it thinks"—even the "it" contains an *interpretation* of the process, and does not

> belong to the process itself. One infers here according to grammatical habit: "Thinking is an activity, to every activity there belongs someone who is active, consequently—"

For the "I think," "it thinks," or "I am" to be accounted for in and by a will would also require that language be understood as an act. Only then could it be used to recognize its origin in an activity that never appears in language as such. Coleridge's synonymy of will and self-consciousness is therefore a will to action as the ground of language. This amounts to saying that language's simplest and most pervasive grammatical paradigm (subject and predicate) ought to account for the origin of language in an act. But, if the structure of grammar is to be defined by an act, then, the very existence of any inscription whatsoever would serve to recollect an act while forgetting the grammatical habit from which it is derived. This understanding of grammar leads to the grammatically correct but logically absurd conclusion: *it* (the grammatical category of the subject) wills therefore I am. To avoid this logical absurdity, Coleridge must rely upon a formal identity if grammar is ever to reflect the activity of a will. Only through this formal identity can one become interchangeable with the other.

In a notebook entry from 1810, Coleridge describes such an identity as a synonymy: "Will, strictly synonimous with individualizing Principle, the *'I'* of every rational Being."[46] The use of this word clearly indicates the extent to which the more philosophical chapters of the *Biographia* continue Coleridge's concern with the kind of tautegorical understanding so emphatically present in the final example of desynonymization already discussed, the example of "I" and "me." In this context, the principle at the center of Coleridge's philosophical discussion can be read as the attempt to justify what the historical process of desynonymization demanded as its starting point but did not account for: an equally historical synonymy of language. Thus, despite being written somewhat earlier than the *Biographia,* Coleridge's use of "synonimous" in the notebook entry accurately defines the relation on which his biographical, critical, and philosophical concerns all rest: a synonymy of act and word. Only through this synonymy can "I" and "will" possess the same relation to meaning expressed in the word "SUM." Here, as before, this synonymy only becomes thinkable because of a formal category which defines the grammatical function of the subject accorded to the word "I."

Although grammar enables such a synonymy, its consequences reach far beyond the grammatical. The will, once related to the "I," no longer remains its equivalent but assumes a historical relation when it emerges as the activity that commands and controls the self expressed through the word "I." In the terms used by Nietzsche in the following passage, also from *Beyond Good and Evil,* the will not only demands the ear of grammar but commands that grammar will obey, that is, repeat its dictates as if it were a ventriloquist's dummy:

> Ist der Wille nicht nur ein Komplex von Fühlen und Denken, sondern vor allem noch ein *Affekt:* und zwar jener Affekt des Kommandos. Das, was "Freiheit des Willens" genannt wird, ist wesentlich der Überlegenheits-Affekt in Hinsicht auf den, der gehorchen muß: "ich bin frei, 'er' muß gehorchen"—dies Bewußtsein steckt in jedem Willen, und ebenso jene Spannung der Aufmerksamkeit, jener gerade Blick, der ausschließlich *eins* fixiert, jene unbedingte Wertschätzung "jetzt tut dies und nichts andres not," jene innere Gewißheit darüber, daß gehorcht werden wird, und was alles noch zum Zustande des Befehlenden gehört. Ein Mensch, der *will*—, befiehlt einem Etwas in sich, das gehorcht oder von dem er glaubt, daß er gehorcht.[47]

> The will is not only a complex of feeling and thought but above all it is an *affect:* namely, the affect of the command. What is termed "freedom of the will" is essentially the affect of dominance in relation to him who must obey [listen]: "I am free, 'he' must obey [listen]"—this consciousness lies hidden in every will; likewise the straining of the attention, the straight look which fixes exclusively on *one* aim, the unconditioned evaluation that "this and nothing else is necessary now," the inner certainty that it will be obeyed [listened to]—and whatever else belongs to the position of commander. A man who wills, he commands something in himself which obeys [listens], or which he believes obeys [listens].

Rather than repeating the act of freedom required by both Coleridge and Schelling, the ability to say "I am" is determined by the obedience of language to the will. Without this obedience, no original act of freedom could ever be described. Consequently, the original act of will demanded by Coleridge and Schelling arises, in Nietzsche's terms, from an affect or "feeling" of obedience: the mouth of language obeying the will when it says "I AM." Within this understanding of freedom, there will always be an "I am" that precedes all others so that every subsequent saying of "I am" will be known as its repetition, as its obedient mouthpiece. In this respect, what Coleridge posits as primary must always be an utterance that is its own act. But, for this self-reflexive relation of language and act to "occur," what is primary can only be derived from the utterance in which it is said to be repeated. A repetition that expresses the same subject but with a difference is thus what lies behind a system as well as a critical project which takes self-consciousness as its point of departure. Within such a project, all must obey the dictates of self-consciousness and the self-reflexive sum of act and word through which it is thought.

The Interruption of Coleridge and Schelling

> *L'interruption permet l'échange. S'interrompre pour s'entendre, s'entendre pour parler.*
>
> —Maurice Blanchot, "L'interruption"

The assertion of a self-reflexive act as an origin within the *Biographia* finds an easy critical counterpart wherever Romanticism is interpreted as marking a shift to a model of literary production that takes the self as its source. As Aristotle's *Poetics* also demonstrates, this turn to a self defined according to a reflexive principle does not make any difference to the essential conditions of literary interpretation unless the evasion of those conditions is accepted as the sign of such a difference. Indeed, if self-reflexivity or self-consciousness (or even a lamp) is taken as a source of critical light as well as a mark with which to measure the progress of literary history, then, that history and its promise of critical insight rests upon a distinction made by and through mimesis.[48] The concept of mimesis which derives the significance of a literary work from an already existent historical world cannot be given up so easily—precisely because what is at stake in the concept of mimesis is a relation between history and language. Yet, as Aristotle's *Poetics* already reflects, any account of this relation is fraught with a difficulty, namely, how to account for such a relation without already adopting its result as the sole instrument capable of producing this result. Given this difficulty and bearing in mind the experience of the *Poetics,* it may be expected that this concept of mimesis would continue to pose considerable difficulty for the critical turn associated with Romanticism. Is this why Romanticism is so often interpreted as the end of a literary history based on mimesis? And why is mimesis so unequivocally set aside when the moment from which we would trace our critical modernity is defined reflexively?

As will become even more apparent in the next chapter, the self-reflexivity associated with Romanticism cannot live up to its name without the concept of mimesis that it must also expel. This interdependence indicates that the tendency to see Romantic critical thought (and this thought is not restricted to the historical period of Romanticism) in terms of a self-reflexive principle is a reversal of the *Poetics* and not a development beyond it. Where the *Poetics* sets aside the self-reflexive mode of articulation attributed to the dance in order to preserve mimesis, the *Biographia* sets aside mimesis in order to preserve the relation that Aristotle turns away from. In each case, the problem does not stem from the traditional understanding of mimesis but the difficulty that emerges whenever one tries to account for that understanding. The depth of this difficulty may be gauged from the persistent and mistaken banishment of mimesis to a historically naive past: the rage of Caliban seeing his face in a glass would be, in this instance, the rage of a modernity finding itself trapped within antiquity. Indeed, without possessing the power of repetition traditionally accorded to the concept of mimesis, a self-reflexive principle can only promise to authorize a system. The logic adopted by this promise would require that a child give birth to its parents and then await its own birth. The affront to history present in this logic suggests why the central concept of literary criticism should be, as Aristotle rightly proposes, the concept of possibility (δύναμις). A self-reflexive principle is more palatable when it remains in the realm of possibility than when its actuality has to be faced. Given this natural aversion to the actual consequences of adopting a self-reflexive principle, it is wholly predictable that literary history should bury mimesis beneath the weight of a conceptual definition that this same history produced:

the repetition of what already exists. By burying mimesis, Romantic critical thought would not have to account for its central principle. Accordingly, it would be impossible to decide if it is the concept of mimesis or an inability to account for this concept that has been rejected in the name of critical modernity. This inability to decide is infinitely more acceptable than the consequences of rejecting the latter.

Having discarded a literary history defined by a concept of mimesis, Coleridge's adoption of a self-reflexive principle is left with the question of how to preserve a principle whose historical effectiveness is threatened by the rejection of what it most needs. In the *Biographia,* Coleridge maintains such a principle by means of an injunction which, on the one hand, would thwart all inquiry into the common ground of a literary criticism derived from mimetic or self-reflexive principles and, on the other, banishes any answer that might arise from this inquiry to the endless imitations of a *mise en abyme:*

> We . . . can never pass beyond the principle of self-consciousness. Should we attempt it, we must be driven back from ground to ground, each of which would cease to be a Ground the moment we pressed on it. We must be whirl'd down the gulph of an infinite series. But this would make our reason baffle the end and purpose of all reason, namely, unity and system. (1:285)

If, for Coleridge, the root of unity and system is to be found in the will, and, if this will must avoid the infinite regress from ground to ground, then, the imitative and essentially historical logic that governs this regression and makes it knowable must be avoided. In order to avoid this regression, self-consciousness (or its synonym, in Coleridge, the will) is called upon to mark a limit beyond which it is impossible to know any kind of cause—to make such an assertion would be to enter into an infinite series of antecedents. But can this impossibility grant the will the authority to say "I am"? If it can, the will will always owe its existence to the limit created by such an impossibility. According to this argument, the will or self-consciousness can never know anything other than *what it calls the self* since what is called the self must always hear, understand, and obey what the "I" (that is, the will) says *it* is. The grammatical habit: the self obeys, listens to, answers to the will as the object the subject. For

Coleridge, the price of ignoring this habit would be the necessity ("We *must* be . . .") of whirling down "the gulph of an infinite series," that is, a series without system, a series without the ability to know or account for its own repetitions, in short, a mimesis fated to produce its self without any end in sight. Yet, if the limit that establishes the authority of Coleridge's argument is to be maintained, it is imperative that the mimesis of such a *mise en abyme* be seen as a real threat to unity and system. Since this mimetically driven "infinite series" will then be defined by its ability to baffle or veil the self-reflexive, it will always point to the self-reflexive as the legitimate ground that remains beyond the reach of the "gulph" in which mimesis goes to meet its end.

While "the gulph of an infinite series" is crucial to the development of Coleridge's argument, the pertinence of this strategic metaphor to one of the themes of the contemporary critique of theory should not go unnoticed. In both this critique and the *Biographia,* the specter of an infinite regression provides the example of a willful and misconceived threat whose existence remains essential to the authority of both. Indeed, the uncritical acceptance (by Coleridge, theory, and the critique of theory) of this regression raises the question of what is being evaded in its name.

That an evasion is at stake becomes clear as Coleridge seeks the authority to sanction its necessity through the occurrence of an interruption. Coleridge's account of this interruption is as follows:

> We must break off the series arbitrarily and affirm an absolute something that is in and of itself at once cause and effect (*causa sui*), subject and object, or rather the absolute identity of both. But . . . this is inconceivable except in a self-consciousness . . . in which the *principium essendi* does not stand to the *principium cognoscendi* in the relation of cause to effect, but both one and the other are co-inherent and identical. . . . Thus the true system of natural philosophy places the sole reality of things in an ABSOLUTE, which is at once *causa sui et effectus,* πατὴρ αὐτοπάτωρ, υἱὸς ἑαυτοῦ [father self-fathering, son of himself]—in the absolute identity of subject and object, which it calls nature, and which in its highest power is nothing else than self-conscious will or intelligence. (1:285)[49]

The infinite series is conceived in order to be set aside. As the movement of argument in this quotation makes clear, the infinite series derives its existence as a real danger from the necessity of setting it aside ("we *must* break off . . . and affirm") forcefully stated in the first sentence (this setting aside also dispenses with any need to account for the concept of mimesis present in the "infinite series," it is defined in opposition to the *causa sui.* Having "established" the reality of this potential danger, Coleridge may refer to it by a negation which points to what must be affirmed in the place of an infinite series ("*in*conceivable except in," and "does *not* stand"). The logical "thus" which begins the third sentence introduces a result whose only justification is the unaccounted necessity of setting aside a potential infinite regression. The principle present in what Coleridge calls the "absolute identity of subject and object" is thus affirmed by what it is not: the infinite series authorizes the system from which it must be excluded. In this way, mimesis and the self-reflexive principle espoused by Coleridge are kept separate, even though any systematic exposition or critical application of this principle must still account for its repetition, that is, for the reflection of its authority in language and history.

At this point, the relation between Coleridge and Schelling's systematic thought undergoes an interruption which decides the subsequent course of the *Biographia,* and, in particular, its project of providing "an application of the rules, deduced from philosophical principles, to poetry and criticism" (1:5). Through this interruption, Coleridge would emancipate criticism from philosophy. Yet, the attainment of this freedom will have the paradoxical result of confining criticism to a model of history that derives its authority from a formal structure whose pretense to historical knowledge owes more to its thematic repetition than any other source. Indeed, if we follow Coleridge at this telling juncture in the *Biographia,* it can be seen that Coleridge's interruption of Schelling is made in the name of an "absolute something" which lacks any historical existence, never mind a knowledge of history. The principle associated with this "absolute something" is its own cause and effect, or, as Coleridge describes it in words taken from Synesius of Cyrene's Third Hymn, this principle takes the form of a perfectly self-referring and self-affirming genealogy: "father self-fathering, son of himself."[50] Consequently, in place of a series where causes are endless antecedents, a formally closed antecedent is called upon. This recourse to a formal structure is the defining critical moment of the *Biographia*. Through this recourse, Coleridge turns away from a path that Schelling continues to follow (and to which we will have occasion to return shortly). At the same time, this recourse to formalization, by repeating a crucial moment in the argument of Aristotle's *Poetics,* indicates that criticism—or theory for that matter—is led to a formal arrangement whenever it must account for what Coleridge describes as a relation between knowledge and existence. In less abstract terms, this may also be referred to as a relation between the language in which knowledge is given and the history in which existence is recorded. In the more practical sphere of literary criticism, this relation would be located between literature and meaning. Yet, as the path followed by Schelling demonstrates, the question of a history that does not owe its existence to formal relation is a vexed one.

While Coleridge transfigures Schelling's central principle so that it becomes a mode or relation defined by the chiasmatic form (the father who is the son, and the son who is the father) in which it is given, Schelling seeks to account for the origin of history from this same principle. In so doing, Schelling will also resort to the device of interruption. In Schelling's case, this device is used to interrupt the formal closure in which Coleridge tries to ground the argument of the *Biographia* when he asserts that "we must break off the series arbitrarily." Contrary to what Coleridge says in the *Biographia,* this interruption is not solely a necessity of the objective realm of natural philosophy (see 1:285), but, as Schelling points out in a passage whose consequences Coleridge chose to ignore or else did not realize their critical importance, interruption stands as the possibility of philosophy and thus of the principles from which the *Biographia* seeks to derive a philosophically sound method for the study of literature:

> Das Ich, einmal in die Zeit versetzt, ist ein steter Übergang von Vorstellung zu Vorstellung; nun steht es allerdings in seiner Gewalt, diese Reihe durch Reflexion zu unterbrechen, mit der absoluten Unterbrechung jener Succession beginnt alles Philosophiren, von jetzt an wird dieselbe Succession willkürlich, die vorher unwillkürlich war. (*System, SW* 3:396)

> The self, once transposed into time, consists in a steady passage from representation to representation; yet it remains after all,

> within its power to interrupt this series by reflection. With the absolute interruption of that succession all philosophizing begins and, from now on, the same succession becomes voluntary where it was previously involuntary.

Not only does all philosophizing begin with interruption in Schelling, but this interruption is synonymous with a reflexive act which would possess no relation to the series from which it separates itself (absolutely). What is interrupted is a self not yet capable of knowing itself as a self—the ability to attain such knowledge relies upon the ability to decide whether "the same succession" is voluntary or not. Consequently, what inaugurates philosophy for Schelling is an interruption that gives rise to a difference between voluntary and involuntary acts.

To the extent that Schelling's account of the origin of philosophy requires that an original self be repeated but with a difference, it requires what has always been called mimesis. Accordingly, it should be no surprise that Schelling should also speak about the difference between voluntary and involuntary succession as if it could be defined by the vocabulary of imitation:

> Solange das Ich in der ursprünglichen Evolution der absoluten Synthesis begriffen ist, ist nur Eine Reihe von Handlungen, die der ursprünglichen und notwendigen; sobald ich diese Evolution unterbreche, und mich freiwillig in den Anfangspunkt der Evolution zurückversetze, entsteht mir eine neue Reihe, in welcher *frei* ist, was in der ersten *notwendig* war. Jene ist das Original, diese die Copie oder Nachahmung. Ist in der zweiten Reihe nicht mehr und nicht weniger als in der ersten, so ist die Nachahmung vollkommen, es entsteht eine wahre und vollständige Philosophie. Im entgegengesetzten Falle entsteht eine falsche und unvollständige.
>
> Philosophie überhaupt ist also nichts anderes als freie Nachahmung, freie Wiederholung der ursprünglichen Reihe von Handlungen, in welchen der Eine Akt des Selbstbewußtseins sich evolvirt. (*System, SW* 3:397)

> So long as the self is apprehended in its original evolution of the absolute synthesis, there is only one series of acts, that of original and necessary acts; as soon as I interrupt this evolution, and freely place myself back in its starting point, there arises for me a new

series, in which what was *necessary* in the first series, is now *free*. The former is the original, the latter the copy or imitation. If there is nothing more and nothing less in the second series than there is in the first, the imitation is perfect, and there arises a true and complete philosophy. In the opposite case, there arises a false and incomplete philosophy.

Philosophy as such is therefore nothing other than the free imitation, the free repetition of the original series of acts in which the one act of self-consciousness evolves itself.

That Coleridge does not refer to an original series which philosophy imitates or copies in freedom could be considered as further testimony of Coleridge's inability to comprehend the essential difficulty faced by Schelling: how to imitate an origin whose only evidence is linguistic or, at best, grammatical. In the passage just cited, Schelling articulates this difference in the form of an imitation that must repeat its original perfectly if there is to be a true philosophy. Yet, if this repetition cannot support any deviation from its original, then, as Socrates already recognizes in Plato's *Cratylus,* such a perfect imitation is no longer an imitation.[51] Accordingly, what Schelling calls a true and complete philosophy is only true and complete because it is no longer imitative: an imitation without repetition.

Schelling's recourse to such a paradoxical formula indicates the point where the systematic presentation undertaken in the *System* not only depends upon imitation but at the same time must transform and exclude this dependency. As Schelling states, freedom would be the result of this exclusive transformation, yet, to the extent that this result is built upon a difference between two series (one necessary, the other free) which are otherwise indistinguishable from one another ("nothing more and nothing less in the second series than there is in the first"), then, this transformation demands that their difference be known as what allows one to belong to the other. What Schelling gives expression to in the second (free) series is an account of freedom that is unthinkable without the necessity of an unending series. In other words, necessity must be limited to an original series, that is, it must refer to what, like nature, merely exists. Accordingly, if what is free is the interruption of the first series then the necessity attributed to this series is what grounds the possibility of such interruption. Here, necessity would serve as a refusal of all inquiry into what Schelling calls "the steady passage from representation to representation" (and indeed the more recent tendency to speak of literature as merely representation would also conceal such a necessity in the guise of attributing an essential freedom to literature). To advocate this passage as the modality of literature would be to advocate what Hegel quite rightly called "the superstition of the understanding" (der Aberglaube des Verstandes)—as if this superstition could ever make any difference with respect to a totalizing system in which an endless series is a necessary element.[52]

And yet, even as such a system is thought there occurs a difference which one cannot fail to make even though it may never be produced as if it were something made. To account for philosophy, Schelling must distinguish between the necessary and the free, the original and the (perfect) imitation. The difference Schelling makes between the two series can have no relation to what is free or necessary; it is a difference that is neither necessary nor free, still less is it free to be otherwise. Such a difference is what Schelling would interrupt, and precisely because it does not belong to the necessity of freedom.[53] Consequently, what occurs is a substitution through which interruption takes the place of a difference that has no place to take, let alone a place of its own in which to hide. Indeed, the difference usurped by interruption has no formal existence of its own. Interruption thus transfigures difference into a distinction between the free and the necessary, as well as into a difference between knowledge and what is to be known yet never present except in the perfection of its ventriloquizing imitation.

The Evasion of History and the Return of Kant

The specific object of the present attempt is to enable the spectator to judge in the same spirit in which the Artist produced, or ought to have produced.

—Coleridge, "On the Principles of Genial Criticism"

Der Unterleib ist der Grund dafür, daß der Mensch sich nicht so leicht für einen Gott hält.

—Nietzsche, *Jenseits von Gut und Böse*

In the course of its philosophical argument, Coleridge's *Biographia* admits the necessity of interruption but does not develop it any further. To undertake this development demands that Coleridge try to account for a free and perfect imitation that lacks the means to justify its own imitative status. Yet why should Coleridge turn away from such an account at this point in the *Biographia?* The question is even more compelling if we consider that Coleridge implies something close to the perfect imitation described by Schelling four chapters prior to the point we have reached in the philosophical argument of chapter 12 of the *Biographia.*

In the last of the chapters dealing with the theory of association in the *Biographia,* there occurs a remark which suggests that the passage from interruption to perfect imitation already has a place within the argument of the *Biographia.* The following sentence from chapter 8 of the *Biographia* speaks about the work of a copyist in a way that seems to invoke Schelling's perfect imitation:

> The formation of a copy is not solved by the mere pre-existence of an original; the copyist of Raphael's Transfiguration must repeat more or less perfectly the process of Raphael. (1:137)

This sentence brings to a close Coleridge's critique of the assumptions employed by materialist philosophy. This critique is aimed at the tendency of materialist philosophy to justify its perceptions about the nature of matter by appealing to the mere preexistence of that matter. Given that such a preexistence can in no way support a perception that would know its object in its entirety, Coleridge argues that the only way to possess this knowledge requires, not a return to the object through perception, but the production of that object—just as scientific experiment would duplicate in the laboratory what occurs in nature. Unless this return to the object occurs, then, according to Coleridge, all that materialist philosophy can produce is "nothing but its ghost! the *apparition* of a defunct substance!" (1.136). By stipulating that the only true way to know and therefore produce the original is to repeat the process of its production, Coleridge seeks to invalidate any ground of knowledge for materialist philosophy. According to the critique expressed in the *Biographia,* such a ground demands a condition ("the copyist . . . *must* repeat") which materialist philosophy cannot fulfill without inheriting the ontological stability of a stone. In the case of Coleridge's example, any reenactment of the process employed by Raphael demands a historical repetition of uncompromising exactitude (in Schelling's words, "nothing more and nothing less in the second than there is in the first"). If such an exactitude were ever to be realized, it would be very difficult to tell the difference between a historical event and its repetition—or even decide which is which. A materialist philosophy capable of copying Raphael's *Transfiguration* would therefore be a threat to history as well as to any knowledge of history. The threat, however, is muted from the very beginning since Coleridge's critique is predicated upon the impossibility of repeating Raphael. But, is this a critique of Schelling's perfect imitation?

As Coleridge's reference to Raphael's *Transfiguration* implies, his critique of materialism requires not only the impossibility of repeating the process of Raphael but, it presupposes the ability to distinguish between, on the one hand, a copy of the *Transfiguration,* and, on the other, a *Transfiguration* whose doubleness poses the threat associated with a simulacrum. Given the ability to make this distinction, the impossibility of a perfect copy would be confirmed. At the same time, this distinction would return the idea of a perfect copy to the realm of a possibility. Such is the design of Coleridge's critique: the perfect copy Coleridge associates with materialist philosophy must be returned to the realm of historical possibility if it is to have any force as a critique of materialism. This critique, however, involves an overdetermination that exposes Coleridge to the charge he levels at materialist philosophy. Coleridge's critique of the materialist explanation of matter is equally applicable to Coleridge's attempt to sustain this same critique. Coleridge must, on some level, actualize the claims of materialist philosophy so that they can be regarded as a real threat. In this light, it becomes evident that Coleridge's criticism is not derivable from the mere preexistence of its object but rather it arises in response to the necessity of evading the inability to decide whether its claims are historical or imaginary. In the *Biographia,* this evasion would be accounted for, at least initially, by Coleridge's recourse to a distinction between copy and imitation. Through this distinction, Coleridge's critique of materialist philosophy points toward an understanding of imitation that closely resembles what Schelling calls a perfect imitation. Consequently, it would appear that the impossibility of a copy is not determined by the mere preexistence of an original but by the need to preserve a concept of imitation that the copy (in Coleridge's sense) would deny if it were ever to attain historical existence.

In chapter 18 of the *Biographia,* Coleridge distinguishes copy and imitation as follows: "Imitation, as opposed to copying, consists either in the interfusion of the SAME throughout the radically DIFFERENT, or of the different throughout a base radically the same" (2:72).[54] In both instances, imitation would be tautegorical whereas the copy would be regarded as without difference (the interfusion of the same throughout the same—if such a supposition were even imaginable). However, as is the case with the ventriloquy that enables the critical project of the *Biographia* to project an authoritative voice, the tautegorical is no heaven-descended concept. If materialist philosophy is impossible because of its inability to know whether history has in fact been repeated and if, in contrast, imitation (*qua* tautegorical) is to be capable of knowing such a difference, then, the distinction between copy and imitation appeals to a historically or temporally defined concept of difference for its justification.

Whereas this difference (which belongs to imitation) remains implicit in Coleridge's critique of materialist philosophy, it is quite explicit in an essay Schelling wrote on the relation of the plastic arts to nature. In this essay, Schelling not only refers to the same artist as Coleridge but also uses the same temporal difference that makes possible Coleridge's critique of materialism. In Schelling's hands, the temporal obstacle to producing a copy of Raphael's *Transfiguration* authorizes a conclusion whose genetic form appears, at first sight, to be diametrically opposed to Coleridge's argument. Schelling argues for the possibility of not another *Transfiguration* but another Raphael. That the relevance of this passage by Schelling should never have been cited in any of the editions of the *Biographia* is a curious omission particularly since the essay in which it occurs was also published in the 1809 volume of Schelling's writings in which Coleridge read the *Abhandlungen*.[55] Schelling writes: "Ein solcher Raphael wird nicht wieder sein, aber ein anderer, der auf eine gleich eigentümliche Weise zum Höchsten der Kunst gelangt ist" [One such as Raphael will never exist again, however, there will be another who has reached the highest level of art in an equally singular way].[56] As Schelling makes clear in this passage, there may only be another Raphael on condition of a historical difference that assures the originality of this second "Raphael." The temporal difference that makes the copy impossible not only permits the original to be distinguished from a copy but it also permits another Raphael to be recognized as both an original and a copy, that is, as an imitation. According to this argument, originality goes hand in hand with a difference that has been defined in temporal terms. In other words (and here is the logical bind of such an argument), originality cannot be separated from the *possibility* of history repeating itself. Consequently, the difference of form that distinguishes plagiarism from originality would be justified, in the last instance, by an empirical fact: the passage of time.

There is one aspect of this concept of imitation that still needs to be brought out, precisely because of its relevance to the role of interruption. In both of Coleridge's and Schelling's references to Raphael, imitation interrupts a copy whose existence would render irrelevant the passage of both history and time. In Coleridge's use of the example of Raphael, this interruption results from the impossibility of there ever being another *Transfiguration*.[57] But, as Schelling's example of Raphael indicates, what is really at stake in Coleridge's critique of materialist philosophy is the threat posed by the ontological stability of that philosophy's conclusions. What Coleridge's critique is aimed at is not materialist philosophy per se or even the reproduction of Raphael's *Transfiguration* but rather the preservation of imitation as the possibility of history. The point of Coleridge's critique is to ensure that the production of a copy that repeats "more or less perfectly the process of Raphael" will always remain in the realm of possibility and not attain historical existence. Paradoxically, it is from such a critique, as Schelling's reference to Raphael demonstrates, that history is recognized. Not a history reproducing what already exists (this would be merely the repetition of what Coleridge critiques in materialist philosophy) but rather history as a knowledge of possibility, in effect, the possibility of another Raphael.

From the combination of Schelling's and Coleridge's reference to Raphael, it is evident that interruption cannot be confined to the philosophic context in which it first appeared in this reading of the *Biographia*. Interruption is not merely the event, or more precisely, the advent of philosophy. Given the terms of Coleridge's and Schelling's discussion of Raphael, it now becomes clear that the interruption through which Schelling accounts for the possibility of philosophy is also the possibility of history: history and philosophy would thus be the identical twins generated in and through an interruption.[58] This double birth is as necessary to Coleridge's critical project in the *Biographia* as it is to the authority of philosophy in Schelling. However, what is necessary is also what poses the greatest difficulty. In Schelling's *System,* this difficulty persists in a history that repeats an origin whose existence can only be known through its interruption. What forms the subject of history is therefore the interruption of origin. What history repeats is this interruption. In the *Biographia,* this understanding of history is the unavoidable yet unstated consequence of Coleridge's critique of materialism. This unstated consequence indicates that the critical project undertaken by Coleridge must also be defined by an interruption. In Coleridge's hands, this interruption is directed at a philosophy whose historical authority resides in the endless recounting of its interruption (suffice it to say that such a recounting is itself an act of interruption). Consequently, the *Biographia* may interrupt Schelling, who represents the origin of its philosophic argument, but, in so doing, it will adhere to the condition that defines what it wishes to turn away from. As will be seen in the last section of this chapter, Coleridge will attempt to control the return of interruption by externalizing it at the very moment when the ground of a principled criticism is to be given. At this point, criticism itself will become a mode of interruption. But before proceeding to this final playing out of Coleridge's critical adventure with philosophy, the *Biographia*'s transfiguration of history requires discussion.

Having clarified the role of interruption in producing and preserving the decisive pairing of the concepts of possibility and imitation first recognized by Aristotle, there still remains the question of why the *Biographia* does not pursue the link between interruption and history once it has arrived at its philosophical conclusion. The question is pressing because the difficulty Schelling seeks to resolve through a historical development is precisely the difficulty Coleridge faces when he defines truth as an authorial origin that may be heard if only it speaks from a source other than its own. This ventriloquy demands, in effect, the perfect imitation of a truth that must remain historically and temporally distinct from its repetition (otherwise one could only conclude that the mouth which moves speaks for itself). While Coleridge and Schelling share a common difficulty, the form through which it is articulated differs significantly in the *Biographia.* To decide whether this difference results from a complete or inadequate understanding of Schelling would distract from what can be analyzed here since it would suggest that any failure in the *Biographia*'s attempt to ground criticism in philosophy would be either a failing on the part of Coleridge or Schelling. It is perhaps time to admit that the *Biographia* succeeds only too well as literary criticism when it adopts the authority of a philosophy that would already account for its own interruption through a history that repeats such an interruption. Nevertheless, the crucial question posed by Coleridge's ventriloquy and Schelling's perfect imitation focuses on how the authority of a philosophical system based on interruption may be established.

Schelling describes the authorization of his systematic thought as follows: "Eine System ist vollendet, wenn es in seinen Anfangspunkt zurückgeführt ist" [A system is completed when it is led back to its starting point] (*System, SW* 3:628). Only through such a return can the *System* produce a true and complete philosophy. Since the starting point of Schelling's *System* is nothing less than an interruption, the return described by Schelling would give rise to a system engendered from and by the necessity of interrupting its own birth. This system would thereby define itself according to a potentiality (or what Aristotle names δύναμις) to which it seeks to give the form of history. Such a definition preserves philosophy as the eternal project of its own (in)completion. As Schelling puts it in the concluding section of the *System,* philosophy may only become complete *as* philosophy and therefore it can never be universally valid (*allgemeingültig*)—only art and what Schelling calls the aesthetic intuition are granted this validity.[59] However, such a validity is essentially what Coleridge seeks by his recourse to philosophy in the *Biographia.* Through this recourse, the *Biographia* hoped to arrive at an adequate understanding of the aesthetic. But, in place of the interruption that guides philosophy along the path to completion *as* philosophy, Coleridge now assumes that the principle Schelling seeks to unfold may be completed in and by itself—an assumption that fails to acknowledge not only the function of systematicity in Schelling but also it effectively excludes any historical consideration. To make this assumption, Coleridge must regard Schelling's exposition as if it were in fact the original series and not already its potentially perfect imitation.

In the *Biographia,* Coleridge does not recognize the advantages of a philosophy that may only be known *as* philosophy but leaps beyond any such limitation and, in a single sweep, pronounces the kind of conclusion which, although ultimately envisaged by Schelling, is kept at a historical distance. The completion of philosophy in the *Biographia* does not lead back to an initial interruption but leads into religion. Significantly though, religion only appears in the *Biographia* after an interruption that takes the form of a loss, albeit a loss in which there would be, presumably, nothing to lose—as if religion were the lost and found of philosophy and as if the only difference at issue in philosophy were between itself and religion:

> The result of both the sciences [Subjective and Objective], or their equatorial point, would be the principle of a total and undivided philosophy. . . . In other words, philosophy would pass into religion, and religion become inclusive of philosophy. We begin with the I KNOW MYSELF in order to end with the absolute I AM. We proceed from the SELF, in order to lose and find all self in GOD. (1:282–83)

Philosophy once completed passes into religion, and religion, by virtue of this completion, encompasses philosophy. Coleridge's reply to the heaven-descended command, "Know Thyself," envisages a return to the source of that command. Here, the principle of Schelling's *System* is made to conclude in God—a conclusion that demands nothing less than the self-transfiguration of philosophy so that, at the moment it completes itself, it speaks as though a god had spoken. While Schelling does not exclude a movement to God within the *System,* such a conclusion is, however, deferred until the end of history: "Der Mensch führt durch seine Geschichte einen fortgehenden Beweis von dem Dasein Gottes, einen Beweis, der aber nur durch die ganze Geschichte vollendet sein kann" [Man, through his history provides a continuous demonstration of God's presence, a demonstration, however, which can only be completed through the whole of history] (*System, SW* 3:603). The distinction between Coleridge and Schelling is most marked here. As Schelling seeks to preserve a history within which it is possible to think the absolute, Coleridge would efface what makes such thinking even possible by asserting that the historical unfolding of the absolute principle of philosophy is superseded by a higher absolute in religion and God.[60] Yet, why should Coleridge call upon what is in effect the dissolution of history within an argument seeking to ground the practice of criticism? In short, to what extent is the dissolution of history necessary to the deduction of the imagination as well as the critical project named by this deduction?

The often-cited passage from chapter 13 of the *Biographia* would give an immediate answer to the questions just posed: "The primary IMAGINATION I hold to be the living Power and prime Agent of all human Perception, and as a repetition in the finite mind of the eternal act of creation in the infinite I AM" (1:304). In order to legitimize this repetition, there must be an unquestionable and infinite "I am" to repeat. For there to be such an infinite, the *Biographia*'s argument would require that philosophy attain its completion in the authority of God (the absolute I AM). Only then could the imagination even be thought of as the finite repetition of an absolute. Philosophy must, in effect, be brought to an end if Coleridge's imagination is to have anything to repeat. As a result, the so-called missing deduction which ought to have linked the philosophical chapters to the definition of the imagination, is, in fact, not at all the problem haunting the *Biographia,* or even the critical project to which it belongs. To assert that such a deduction is what the *Biographia* fails to provide is to accept that the philosophical argument of the *Biographia* has been brought to its conclusion when Coleridge writes, "We begin with the I KNOW MYSELF in order to end with the absolute I AM." This acceptance ignores the crucial question facing literary criticism as well as literary theory, namely, how to bring philosophy to an end so that literature may become the source as well as the repetition of its knowledge.[61] Since such an end is harder to attain than it is to evade, it should not be surprising that bringing philosophy to an end should be the form in which the evasion of the end of philosophy most frequently occurs. If the end of philosophy is no more than the evasion of philosophy, then it is in the best interests of the *Biographia* that the question facing literary criticism should be attributable to a missing deduction. A missing deduction is less embarrassing to deal with than a deduction that cannot take place because its premise has not yet been deduced. Not surprisingly, literary and critical history has tended to follow Coleridge's example and swallowed the missing deduction in order to evade this question. This evasion is why the *Biographia* has become an indispensable work in the history of criticism: it evades its own evasions. To the extent that such evasions are necessary to the critical project of the *Biographia,* they will define literary criticism as the unaccountable overcoming or dissolution of philosophy. Here, it can be seen how the *Biographia* would already establish the tendency to read this text according to a denial of philosophy discussed in the introduction to this chapter.[62]

Although the end of philosophy is implied by its transfiguration into religion in the *Biographia,* this conclusion cannot be restricted to Coleridge despite its particular form. Its contemporary counterpart may be found whenever philosophy is defined as the blind pursuit of a transcendental signified. This definition also attempts to bring philosophy to an end, and as such, it merely repeats in a negative manner the conclusion adopted by Coleridge. In both cases, the end of philosophy marks the point where literary criticism and literary theory are led to evasion as an act of self-preservation. Coleridge's *Biographia* makes clear that what is to be evaded is the relation that the *Biographia* displaces (and then misplaces) in the procession from self to God: the relation Schelling speaks of in the form of a free or perfect imitation. Thus, the result that appears as a derivative repetition in chapter 13 of the *Biographia* must be grounded in what cannot in any way rely upon a precedent for its justification: a derivative understanding of imitation (which alone supports Coleridge's definition of the imagination) is grounded in a principle that cannot in any way determine the course of its representation if that representation is, in Schelling's words, to remain a perfect imitation. The question posed by the freedom of this imitation would be avoided not only when Coleridge assumes a passage from philosophy to an absolute called God but also when it is assumed that such a passage is knowable (even to the extent of knowing that it cannot be known). This passage from self to God is in fact the missing deduction of the *Biographia.*[63] As Schelling states, this passage is nothing other than the unfolding of history. For Coleridge to have undertaken this deduction would have rendered its starting point meaningless, as this deduction may only become authoritative with the end of history (but not the end of philosophy).

Clearly then, it is better that this deduction be understood as simply missing. By being placed between philosophy and the stated result, it distracts attention away from the actual source of difficulty. A deduction that is simply missing raises no question about what its result is to be deduced from since it directs all attention toward that result. Consequently, the problem to be confronted in the *Biographia* does not concern the so-called missing deduction of the imagination but rather the question of repetition within transcendental philosophy.[64] It is this question that Coleridge cloaks through both the missing deduction and the procession from self to God. Accordingly, the dissolution of philosophy so crucial to not only the *Biographia*'s argument but also to the project of a literary criticism is nothing less than the dissolution of philosophy's most pressing question: its relation to history.

In a move that is less a return *to* Kant than the return *of* Kant, it becomes clear that what the cloak assumed by Coleridge is intended to conceal is a procession that may never move beyond philosophy (although whether this procession may therefore still be called philosophy remains to be seen).[65] In the section entitled "Natural Dialectic of Human Reason," from the *First Critique,* Kant writes:

> Denn, wenn dem größtmöglichen empirischen Gebrauche meiner Vernunft eine Idee (der systematischvollständigen Einheit . . .) zum Grunde liegt, die an sich selbst niemals adäquat in der Erfahrung kann dargestellet werden, ob sie gleich, um die empirische Einheit dem höchstmöglichen Grade zu nähern, unumgänglich notwendig ist, so werde ich nicht allein befugt, sondern auch genötigt sein, diese Idee zu realisieren, d. i. ihr einen wirklichen Gegenstand zu setzen, aber nur als ein Etwas überhaupt, das ich an sich selbst gar nicht kenne, und dem ich nur, als einem Grunde jener systematischen Einheit, in Beziehung auf diese letztere solche Eigenschaften gebe, als den Verstandesbegriffen im empirischen Gebrauche analogisch sind. Ich werde mir also nach der Analogie der Realitäten in der Welt, der Substanzen, der Kausalität und der Notwendigkeit, ein Wesen denken, das alles dieses in der höchsten Vollkommenheit besitzt, und, indem diese Idee bloß auf meiner Vernunft beruht, dieses Wesen als *selbständige Vernunft,* was durch Ideen der großten Harmonie und Einheit, Ursache vom Weltganzen ist, denken können, so daß ich alle, die Idee einschränkende,

> Bedingungen weglasse, lediglich um, unter dem Schutze eines solchen Urgrundes, systematische Einheit des Mannigfaltigen im Weltganzen, und, vermittelst derselben, den größtmöglichen empirischen Vernunftgebrauch möglich zu machen, indem ich alle Verbindungen so ansehe, *als ob* sie Anordnungen einer höchsten Vernunft wären, von der die unsrige ein schwaches Nachbild ist.[66]
>
> For if the greatest possible empirical employment of my reason rests upon the ground of an idea (systematically complete unity . . .) which in itself can never be adequately presented in experience although it is unavoidably necessary in order to bring empirical unity closer to the highest possible degree, I will not only be authorized, but will also be compelled to realize this idea, that is, to posit for it a real object although only as a something which I do not at all know in itself, and to which, as a ground for that systematic unity, I grant, in relation to it, such properties as are analogous to the concepts of understanding in their empirical employment. Accordingly, in analogy with realities in the world, that is, with substances, with causality and with necessity, I will think a being which possesses all this in the highest perfection, and, as this idea is rooted only in my reason, this being, which through the ideas of greatest harmony and unity is the cause of the universe, can be thought as *self-subsistent reason*. I thus omit all conditions which might limit the idea, solely in order to produce, under the shelter of such a fundamental ground, the systematic unity of the manifold in the universe and represent thereby the greatest possible employment of reason in which I regard all connections *as if* they were the ordinances of a supreme reason, of which our reason is but a faint copy.

For Kant, the greatest harmony and unity is only realizable through an analogy which, on the one hand, establishes a necessary relation between the highest unity and the systematic unity fated to be its faint copy, and, on the other, guards this highest unity by determining that this relation must remain unknowable—a state akin to being permanently missing or lost. Here, analogy, as thought by Kant, would be philosophy's attempt to ground itself without in any way undermining the highest unity which makes that grounding conceivable. Analogy therefore becomes the means of projecting the highest unity while safeguarding the necessity that this unity never reveal itself but always be represented or transfigured in another. For this reason, Kant, in a consideration of purposive unity and the investigation of nature in "The Canon of Pure Reason" (a consideration strictly analogous to that concerning supreme reason), concludes that the most one can do is to posit an original author: "Folglich ist es eine Bedingung einer zwar zufälligen, aber doch nicht unerheblichen Absicht, nämlich, um eine Leitung in der Nachforschung der Natur zu haben, einen weisen Welturheber vorauszusetzen" [Consequently, to posit a wise author of the world is a condition of an assuredly contingent but still not unimportant purpose, namely, to have direction in the investigation of nature].[67] Furthermore, in an earlier passage from the "Ideal of Pure Reason," Kant states that, as an idea supplying the regulative principle necessary to human reason and understanding, this wise author, the would-be archetype of all authors, is to be found in the copy provided by systematic unity, "So wie die Idee die *Regel* gibt, so dient das Ideal in solchem Falle zum *Urbilde* der durchgängigen Bestimmung des Nachbildes" [As the idea gives the *rule,* so, in such a case, the ideal serves as the *archetype* for the complete determination of the copy].[68] To realize this ideal in the copy would confuse what is to be ruled with what gives the rule. In Kant's terms such a confusion would fictionalize the ideal: "Das Ideal . . . in einem Beispiele . . . realisieren wollen . . . ist untunlich, und hat überdem etwas Widersinnisches und wenig Erbauliches an sich, indem die natürlichen Schranken, welche der Vollständigkeit in der Idee kontinuierlich Abbruch tun, alle Illusion in solchem Versuche unmöglich und dadurch das Gute, das in der Idee liegt, selbst verdächtig und einer bloßen Erdichtung ähnlich machen" [To realize . . . the ideal . . . in an example . . . is impracticable and, moreover, has in itself something absurd and far from edifying in that the natural limits which continually damage the completeness of the idea, make all illusion impossible in such an attempt and thereby make the good, which lies in the idea itself, suspect and like a mere invention].[69] These limits rule the analogy which Kant posits as the limit and possibility of philosophy.

Schelling, like Fichte, persists in observing such limits while at the same time maintaining the possibility of systematic completeness. When Coleridge turns from Schelling and asserts the procession of self to God, however, he not only turns from Schelling but also from the question of systematicity bequeathed by Kant. Coleridge's turn away from philosophy is thus an interruption of the very limit that makes possible the critical project exemplified in the *Biographia.* As such, Coleridge's grounding of criticism demands a move beyond the limit imposed by analogy and, in this respect, the project of literary criticism goes hand in hand with the attempt to move beyond Kant. Yet this move can only entail the return of what is to be moved beyond. This return occurs because analogy can only be thought according to a difference which, like Kant's wise author, arises through positing, that is, it is a difference that belongs to positing rather than analogy, imitation, identity, or what is posited. This return is what Coleridge forgets, and what Coleridge forgets is what Schelling would always remember to interrupt. Given Coleridge's argument, only a god can save criticism, not to mention *the* text; only a god can speak or project its voice through language and only then by virtue of a grammatical habit . . . *e grammatica descendit.*

Ventriloquus Interruptus

> *Alles vorgebliche Nichtverstehen jenes Philosophirens hat seinen Grund nicht in seiner eignen Unverständlichkeit, sondern in dem Mangel des Organs, mit dem es aufgefaßt werden muß.*
>
> —Schelling, *System*

> *Es ist, wie man errät, nicht der Gegensatz von Subjekt und Objekt, der mich hier angeht: diese Unterscheidung überlasse ich den Erkenntnistheoretikern, welche in der Schlingen der Grammatik (der Volks-Metaphysik) hängengeblieben sind. Es ist erst recht nicht der Gegensatz von "Ding an sich" und Erscheinung: denn wir "erkennen" bei weitem nicht genug, um auch nur so* scheiden *zu dürfen. Wir haben eben gar kein Organ für das* Erkennen, *für die "Wahrheit."*
>
> —Nietzsche, *Die fröhliche Wissenschaft*

As the *Biographia*'s philosophical argument forgets the limit of analogy which Schelling will thematize under the name of interruption, it transgresses what, for Kant, regulates the highest unthinkable unity and its all too thinkable systematic counterpart. It is the question of this analogy which, in the last instance, holds philosophy back from any pretense to absolute self-completion while at the same time defining the project of philosophy as such a holding back. For this reason, philosophy (as its systematic completion is thought by Schelling) must always be the interruption of what arose from interruption. In this case, the origin of philosophy must always be figured as an interruption.[70] While the passage from self to God adopted by Coleridge attempts to suspend this interruption, such an attempt is driven to make use of what it would suspend. This predicament dictates the course of the *Biographia* in chapter 13 as it resorts to the infamous letter of the friend. Through this recourse the *Biographia* remains an essentially critical work rather than fulfilling the promise of its philosophical conclusion and becoming a theological work masquerading as criticism—the difference between the two being only the effect of such a masquerade. Indeed, the fate of the theological conclusion that Coleridge envisages as the end of philosophy in chapter 12 is determined by the return of the critical concerns announced in the first chapter of the *Biographia*. The return of criticism is in effect the return of the question of philosophy's relation to history.

The return of this question surfaces as Coleridge describes, in chapter 13, the presence of a problem still persisting within the argument of chapter 12. In chapter 13, this historical question reasserts itself in a statement of philosophical demands which occurs immediately before the infamous letter from Coleridge's fictive friend. Coleridge writes:

> Now, the transcendental philosophy demands; first, that two forces should be conceived which counteract each other by their essential nature . . . secondly, that these forces should be assumed to be alike infinite, both alike indestructible. The problem will then be to discover the result or product of two such forces. (1:299)

Through this statement, the *Biographia* asserts once again the primary propositions that made the possibility of a principled literary criticism conceivable. Despite their audibility, however, the result anticipated by Coleridge in his introduction to the Ten Theses in chapter 12 is now posed as a problem. Have the Ten Theses then failed to "render intelligible" the result that would authenticate their claims?

The authentication of the claims made in the Ten Theses would demand that the discovered result account for the historical origin of the difference which the argument of the *Biographia* has constantly resorted to as it attempts to combine ventriloquy, desynonymization, the tautegorical relation of "I" and "me," and the principle of Schelling's *System.* The insistent and repeated use of "must" in the final paragraph of the *Biographia*'s philosophical exposition indicates that such an account is a necessity, there being no other possibility:

> The counteraction then of the two assumed forces does not depend on their meeting from opposite directions; the power which acts in them is indestructible; it is therefore inexhaustibly re-ebullient; and as something *must* be the result of these two forces, both alike infinite, and both alike indestructible; and as rest or neutralization cannot be this result; no other conception is possible, but that the product *must* be a tertium aliquid, or finite generation. Consequently, this conception is *necessary.* Now this tertium aliquid can be *no other* than an inter-penetration of the counteracting powers, partaking of both. (1:300; emphasis mine)

The anticipated result of the *Biographia*'s Ten Theses now becomes a necessity produced by the interaction of two opposed forces. This result is described as a "tertium aliquid, or finite generation." The exchangeability of "tertium aliquid" [third something] and "finite generation" is symptomatic of the critical dilemma facing the *Biographia.* The "tertium aliquid" describes a formal logical category within Coleridge's argument, whereas "finite generation" belongs to the world of history. It is the "or" that links these two terms that Coleridge must account for: the conjunction of the formal and the historical, which is to say, Coleridge must first establish their absolute difference if the historical is to exist without recourse to the formal. The difficulty of this conjunction is already apparent in the passage just quoted and its appeal to necessity. We are told that the "product *must* be a tertium aliquid, or finite generation. Consequently, this conception is *necessary.*" The logic of this argument may be seen more clearly in the following formulation: the product must be X, consequently X is necessary; why is X necessary? because the result must be X. Such a necessity returns, in the last instance, to the assumption it proceeds from and, in so doing, affirms this assumption as if it were necessary to its resulting conception, the "tertium aliquid, or finite generation." In the end, this result owes its existence to the way in which a chiasmus schematizes an interpenetration of opposites through the formal reversal of one linguistic element upon another.

The emphasis on such a chiasmatic interpenetration indicates the kind of relation that *must* be resorted to if Coleridge's projected completion of philosophy in religion is to become possible. This chiasmatic relation is the formal possibility of the unity envisioned in such a completion. Yet a difficulty persists within this relation and it is to this difficulty that Coleridge responds when he reduces it to the problem of apprehending the actuality of this unity:

> When we have formed a scheme or outline of these two different kinds of force, and of their different results by the process of discursive reasoning, it will then remain for us to elevate the Thesis from notional to actual, by contemplating intuitively this one power with its two inherent yet counteracting forces, and the results or generations to which their interpenetration gives existence, in the living principle and in the process of our own self-consciousness. By what instrument this is possible the solution itself will discover. (1:299)

The difficulty to be confronted by Coleridge is, however, not simply one of actualizing what persists in the realm of possibility but rather of safeguarding a relation between a formal possibility and its actualization. As the first line of this quotation makes clear, the task of establishing such a relation falls upon the possibility of figuration itself ("When we have formed a *scheme* or *outline*"). The recourse to a scheme or outline marks the return of a ῥυθμός as Coleridge repeats the role of form or figure in the argument of Aristotle's *Poetics*. The contemplative intuition to which Coleridge turns as a means to effect the passage from notional to actual thesis (the passage from a figure of thought to the thought which ought to ground this figure) would appear to provide a way of avoiding Aristotle's inability to maintain the relation between rhythm and imitation exemplified by the dance in the *Poetics*. In Coleridge, intuition would account for the ability of self-consciousness to actualize itself, that is, recognize itself as its own object. However, the one thing the self cannot do is become its own representation: the actualization of self-consciousness demands that the self observe itself looking at itself if it is ever to know what it is. To be actual, self-consciousness requires a minimum of three selves. Since it is unlikely that any self could be in three different places at the same time, self-consciousness would appear to be confronted with an impossible task of its own making. To prevent this eventuality, while at the same time maintaining knowledge in the face of its impossibility, Coleridge must adopt intuition as the origin of figuration. The task of intuition is to authenticate the "scheme or outline" as the figure of what will be intuited. By accomplishing this task, intuition will make possible a history of the self.

This reference to intuition in chapter 13, along with earlier references in the *Biographia,* confirms the crucial role of intuition as an act that contains the possibility of the philosophical-critical project manifested in this work. When, in chapter 10, Coleridge refers to intuition as a word "designating the *immediateness* of any act or object of knowledge" (1:172), it becomes clear that intuition, as a word, manifests an act in terms of language. In a footnote at the end of chapter 12, Coleridge affirms this immediacy and then goes on to state that such intuition is concerned with truth—"the term [intuition] comprehends all truths known to us without a medium" (1:289). While these statements repeat the truth as described in Thesis III—a truth "capable of communicating to other positions a certainty, which it has not itself borrowed; a truth self-grounded, unconditional and known by its own light" (1:268)—Coleridge's intuition cannot, however, view this truth, precisely because the relation demanded by such a truth has not been resolved, that is, the problem posed by a relation that can only be an interruption of any attempt to certify truth in "other positions." As if to overcome this problem, Coleridge asserts what will again return in chapter 13 (in the form of a solution which will discover the instrument of its own possibility through that solution): "How and whence . . . the intuitive knowledge, may finally supervene, can be learnt only from the fact" (1:239–40). If this position is recast into the ventriloquy described in chapter 9, then, Coleridge is dangerously close to basing his notion of a ventriloquistic truth on the fact that a mouth can even speak. To avoid this conclusion, intuition intervenes in order to make the merely audible intelligible. Intelligibility is thus measured by an act through which it comes to know itself (as intuition) and, *at the same time,* recognizes itself within a process that has been granted historical existence ("in the *living* principle and *in the process* of our own self-consciousness" [emphasis mine]).

What is at stake in Coleridge's recourse to intuition is thus the possibility of an origin for historical knowledge in an act of self-figuration. Although this possibility is never explicitly articulated by Coleridge, it may be viewed when, in a footnote, Coleridge refers to both Plotinus and Synesius and describes an intuition that would give rise to a subject whose repetition is the event of its own production:

> "[For Plotinus] . . . whatever is produced is an intuition, I silent; and that, which is thus generated, is by its nature a theorem, or form of contemplation; and the birth, which results to me from this contemplation attains to have a contemplative nature." So Synesius: 'Ωδὶς ἱερά Ἄρρητα γονά [Sacred travail, ineffable generation]. The *after comparison* of the process of the natura naturans with that of the geometrician is drawn from the very heart of philosophy. (1:240n.; emphasis mine)[71]

Whatever is produced in intuition is a form of contemplation and whatever is, in turn, generated from this form "attains to have" the contemplative nature of its originary intuition. Thus, intuition is the production of a form in which the "I" gives birth to itself. If Coleridge's description of this production is translated into the terms earlier in the *Biographia,* namely, *ego contemplans* and *ego contemplatus,* it becomes apparent that Coleridge's whole philosophical argument has always been trying to account for a connection between "I" to "me" that would not involve its author in an absurdity, a bull.[72] As if to deny the absurdity latent in his own argument, Coleridge calls again upon the words of Synesius. The passage from form ("scheme or outline") to an event such as a birth is now presented as a "sacred travail and ineffable generation." It is no accident that this phrase occurs in the same hymn Coleridge cites when he describes the *causa sui et effectus* of the will ("Father of himself, son of himself"). When Coleridge introduces and then continues the passage from Plotinus which appears in the footnote just cited, it becomes clear that will and intuition rely upon the same figure, an act born(e) in the form of a chiasmus:

> Realizing intuition . . . exists by and in the act that affirms its existence, which is known, because it is, and is, because it is known. The words of Plotinus . . . hold true of the philosophic energy. . . . With me the act of contemplation makes the thing contemplated, as the geometricians contemplating describe lines correspondent; but I not describing lines, but simply contemplating, the representative forms of things rise up into existence. (1:251–52)[73]

As presented in the Ten Theses, the very heart of the philosophy adopted in the *Biographia* consists of an act that exists "by and in a will" (1:280), and this will is itself determined according to the interchangeability of cause and effect. This interchangeability, designated by the *causa sui et effectus,* is nothing less than the expression of chiasmatic reversal: the cause which is an effect, and the effect which is a cause. Intuition is defined according to precisely the same principle, because it is possible only "by and in" the assumption of the two forces whose counteraction produces a "tertium aliquid, or finite generation." Consequently, what is at stake in the concepts of act, will, and now, intuition, is the formal coherence of the reversal attributed to a chiasmus. In short, the possibility of such formalism is what must be accounted for if the *Biographia* is to be read as wishing to attain its stated goal. Only through this formalism would it be possible to think of a notional thesis capable of being actualized through an intuition that imprints, and is imprinted by, the figure presented by the notional thesis.

The *Biographia* does not attempt, however, to actualize the notional thesis and for good reason. To do so would not only demand that the *Biographia* (as a notional thesis) produce Coleridge as its author (thereby contradicting the notion of truth introduced at the end of chapter 9) but also it would deny the formalism that makes such a notion of truth conceivable in the first place. Moreover, by turning away from this attempt the *Biographia,* like the *Poetics,* both secures and accounts for its appeal to formalist criticism. This turn occurs as a break in an argument that appeared to have been concluded in Thesis IX—the contemplated philosophy that passes into religion. To explain this rupture, Coleridge gives the following notorious reason which has all too often been glossed over in the interpretation of the *Biographia* as a device of deferment or dissimulation, particularly since the letter referred to is written by Coleridge himself.[74]

> Thus far had the work been transcribed for the press, when I received the following letter from a friend, whose practical judgment I have had ample reason to estimate and revere, and whose taste and sensibility preclude all the excuses which my self-love might possibly have prompted me to set up in plea against the decision of advisers of equal good sense, but with less tact and good feeling. (1:300)

Taste and sensibility overcome self-love through the intervention of a friend who expels the conclusion of the philosophical argument. And it is not without reason that self-love would have demanded its presence, since Coleridge's identity as author depends upon this very conclusion inasmuch as the *Biographia* recounts a philosophy that reverts upon itself in a self-authorizing, self-recognizing manner. However, in addition to interrupting the excuses of self-love, the friend interrupts what is intimately bound up with the establishment of legitimate taste, that is, the critical principle, the "torch of guidance" to be derived from philosophy. Yet, the letter is more than a simple interruption that defers the chapter Coleridge has not written and thereby facilitates Coleridge's definition of the imagination.

The letter marks the point at which Coleridge adheres most closely to Schelling and, in so doing, its interruption reflects most closely the possibility of a critical knowledge after Kant. The interruption marked by the letter, is, in effect, the source of the authority necessary to the critical project which finds itself repeated in the *Biographia*. Because of the primacy of interruption, no simple notion of authority—such as the one literary criticism has been only too willing to criticize metaphysics for—is implicated here. To equate authority with interruption allows any attempt at authorization to exercise precisely what it is unable to attain for itself. In this respect, the authority of the *Biographia* derives less from what it intends than from the self-determined thwarting of its stated intention. This thwarting is clearly present in the letter whose critical infamy has served to conceal the way in which it actually repeats the origin and the consequences of the philosophical argument of chapter 12 even as it refuses to present those consequences.

The friend's letter begins by suggesting that Coleridge's *Biographia* may not suit the taste of a public who, "from the title of the work and from its forming a sort of introduction to a volume of poems, are likely to constitute the great majority of your readers" (1:301). Public, therefore general, taste is likely to find the legitimate taste that Coleridge wishes to establish disagreeable to its palate on account of this deception. The friend, or Coleridge, however, knows better than to refuse the *Biographia* out of hand as a mere deception and, accordingly, attempts to explain why the philosophical argument should be stopped at this point:

> *As to myself, and stating in the first place the effect on my understanding, your opinions and method of argument were not only so new to me, but so directly the reverse of all I had ever been accustomed to consider as truth, that even if I had comprehended sufficiently to have admitted them, and had seen the necessity of your conclusions, I should still have been in that state of mind, which in your note to p.* 72, 73, *you have so ingeniously evolved, as the antithesis to that in which a man is, when he makes a* bull. *In your own words, I should have felt as if I had been standing on my head.* (1:301)

As perceived by this arbiter of taste, the *Biographia*'s philosophy offers the reverse of truth. The friend then refers to Coleridge's earlier discussion of the bull, a reference that returns the *Biographia* to the autobiographical imperative that defines this text's search for a critical ground. In chapter 4 of the *Biographia,* Coleridge explains that the state in which the friend would have found himself (if the necessity of Coleridge's argument had been seen) is a reversal more apparent than real: "The man *feels,* as if he were standing on his head, though he cannot but *see,* that he is truly standing on his feet" (1:73).[75] But, in the continuation of this explanation, the deduction runs the risk of a reversal which deranges the reader with exactly the same effect as a painful recovery from derangement: "This, as a powerful sensation, will of course have a tendency to associate itself with the person who occasions it; even as persons, who have been by painful means restored from derangement, are known to feel an involuntary dislike towards their physician" (1:73). Apparently, chapter 13, including the hundred-page deduction referred to by the friend, would be the critical physic offered by Coleridge, the physician who, in the *Biographia,* wishes to make a reader, such as the friend, see the truth clearly even though this friend may exhibit an involuntary dislike to what the physician wishes him to swallow. But, what is the nature of a physic which must not only be omitted from the *Biographia* but which never can be taken, this physic which is comparable to the suspension of the will in an involuntary refusal of analogy ("dislike")?

The friend, apparently having read the "substance" of chapter 13, provides an answer to this question when he summarizes the effect of this physic on his feelings:

> *Those whom I had been taught to venerate as almost super-human in magnitude of intellect, I found perched in little fret-work niches, as grotesque dwarfs; while the grotesques, in my hitherto belief, stood guarding the high altar with all the characters of the Apotheosis. In short, what I had supposed substances were thinned away into shadows, while everywhere shadows were deepened into substance:*
>
> If substance may be call'd what shadow seem'd,
> For each seem'd either!
>
> MILTON
>
> (1:301)

The nature of the truth offered to the friend demands a reversal that accords precisely with the formal structure of the chiasmus in which one side is the inversion of the other. Why the friend—whose taste and sensibility, Coleridge says, is to be revered—should resist what is, after all, merely the reverse reflection of all he venerates may be discerned in the passage cited from Milton. These lines belong to the description of one of the shapes guarding the gates of Hell:

> The other shape,
> If shape it might be call'd that shape had none
> Distinguishable in member, joint, or limb,
> Or substance might be call'd that shadow seem'd
> For each seem'd either. . . .[76]

To the friend, Coleridge's (missing) argument unveils what may be called either substance or shadow but which would not respond to such a call. To read these lines as the definition or synthesis of something that is both substance and shadow not only insists on this figure as the embodiment of a chiasmatic reversal and interplay but, also, it is to forget that the formal symmetry demanded by this synthesis is attained at the expense of language's referentiality, in other words, at the expense of language itself. To the friend, such a symmetrical reversal and interplay is regarded as destroying a notion of truth built solely upon a substance that must always remain a substance. For Coleridge (and Schelling), however, such reversal would be the necessary ground of a more radical notion of truth that transcends opposition.[77] And nowhere is this notion more explicitly present than in chapter 12 when the will is defined as an absolute *causa sui et effectus.* If what the friend says is to be regarded as the voice of Coleridge, then the purpose of this letter would be to enact a return to the kind of dogmatic assertion from which the *Biographia* attempts to move away in the name of criticism. In this case, the letter would be no more than a simple annulling of all that has been said in the *Biographia*. Such an annulling would, however, discard totally the tautegorical difference so manifestly espoused by this text. Who then speaks in the name of the friend and to what end? Does this interruption occur simply to introduce the imagination? Can this even be called an interruption when the passage from philosophy to the letter of the friend may be no more, as Coleridge admits, than the need to dip a pen in an inkstand?

As the passage from Milton indicates, reversibility would be as much a threat to the deduction performed in its name as it would be to the friend's cherished substances. Given this situation, the chiasmatic relation that figures so prominently in Coleridge's argument must be turned away from, since the chiasmus cannot even fulfill the promise of its own formal structure. It would, however, be overhasty to conclude that this failing automatically signifies the subversion of Coleridge's critical undertaking merely because a rhetorical figure has appeared.

Chapter 12 demonstrates that the chiasmus provides the formal articulation of an argument that begins with the will as an absolute of self-reversion and ends with a philosophy whose completion effects a passage into religion. In this argument, the chiasmus would appear to stand as a figure of total self-reflexivity—before passing into religion, philosophy must complete itself and, on the ground of this completion, the reversibility and interchangeability present in this passage is made possible. It will be readily apparent that such an argument demands first, the positing of opposition; second, the annulling of such opposition in the interplay of a chiasmus which then becomes the cause and effect of such an opposition; and finally, the substitution of a third term in the place occupied by the chiasmus. In a passage from the lectures on Shakespeare and Milton of 1811–12, this mode of argument is not only directly related to the imagination but also, by its reference to Milton, to the letter that figures so prominently in chapter 13:

> I can understand and allow for an effort of the mind, when it would describe what it cannot satisfy itself with the description of, to reconcile opposites and qualify contradictions, leaving a middle state of mind more strictly appropriate to the imagination than any other, when it is, as it were, hovering between images. As soon as it is fixed on one image, it becomes understanding; but while it is unfixed and wavering between them, attaching itself permanently to none, it is imagination. Such is the fine description of Death in Milton:
>
> The other shape,
> If shape it might be call'd, that shape had none
> Distinguishable in member, joint, or limb,
> Or substance might be call'd, that shadow seem'd
> For each seem'd either: black it stood as night,
> Fierce as ten furies, terrible as hell
> And shook a dreadful dart: what seem'd his head
> The likeness of a kingly crown had on.[78]

In the context of this passage, the reference to Book 4 of *Paradise Lost* in the letter from the friend takes on a less than accidental purpose. Together, they indicate that any attempt to determine the imagination must be considered as strictly comparable to Milton's attempt to define, that is, give form to death.

In *Paradise Lost,* this attempt to give a form to death relies upon the establishment of a genealogy and, as such, it repeats the scene of Christ's transfiguration, the scene in which language would be defined by what remains an unseen act or, in terms of the *Biographia,* an unseen deduction. In the case of *Paradise Lost,* what is described as neither substance nor shadow is claimed to be the son of Satan.

Yet Satan, unlike God, cannot say, "This is my beloved son in whom I was well pleased"; rather, the scene described by Milton would demand that Satan say, "Is this my son who does not please me and in whom I do not know myself?" The claim that the "other shape" is Satan's only begotten son is made by yet another shape who interrupts and declares that Satan is the author of this "double-formed" creature: " 'O father, what intends thy hand,' she cried / 'Against thy only son?' "[79] By accepting the "other shape" as his own, Satan may affirm his existence as an author. For this reason, the son, Death, wears "the likeness of a kingly crown" and only seems to have a head. Satan, as father, thus becomes the figure who may have and be the actual head on which an authentic crown must rest. This actual head and this authentic crown are the merest effects of a relation whose only claim to genetic existence is linguistic. Here, the example of *Paradise Lost* would indicate that authority is derived from the control and determination of figuration and not from what the figure is said to represent. Furthermore, as this scene in *Paradise Lost* also shows, authority, in order to secure this control, resorts to a self-determining and self-enclosing set of relations: Satan's authority and crown rest upon a head from which emerged the shape which claims to be the mother of the "other shape."[80]

The *Biographia*'s imagination would also demand a genealogy similar to that of Milton's Death if it is ever to fulfill Coleridge's initial statement of intention. The necessity of this demand is affirmed by the words of the friend when he speaks of the self-reversal produced by the (missing) deduction. The letter, however, is hardly reducible to a means of excluding the monstrous genealogy of the Milton's "other shape"—as if the difficulties of literary criticism were reducible to some genetic offense. The friend (Coleridge) also states:

> *Imperfectly as I understand the present Chapter* [the complete chapter 13] *I see clearly that you have done too much and yet not enough. You have been obliged to omit as many links, from the necessity of compression, that what remains, looks . . . like the fragments of the winding steps of an old ruined tower.* (1:302–3)

The (missing) link of the *Biographia* is missing some links of its own or, more precisely, it repeats what is already missing from the *Biographia*. To know the difference between what is missing from the

Biographia and what is missing from the missing deduction of the *Biographia* is, however, to speak of a difference that one would not know how to know: one might as well ask death if it is the imagination and then determine its silence as an intentional response conveying affirmation or negation. The link must be deduced from the possibility of the link but this possibility cannot be deduced without such a link having been posited as its possibility.[81] This is why the reversibility of which the friend speaks in the (missing) deduction must be excluded (the friend excludes a reversal that never occurs).

The reversal enacted in the letter from the friend is hardly a source of critical weakness, as becomes clear when it is remembered that it is Coleridge who writes the letter. The letter thus performs an exclusion in order to preserve the possibility of what the argument could never have attained. Coleridge conceals an impossible reversal in the form (the friend's letter) of a resistance to reversibility and does so in order that the difficulty of the *Biographia* should be located in a missing deduction and not in an inability of the deduction to be missing.

The friend's substantialist prejudice thus serves to affirm the "completion" of the deduction of the imagination as a deduction from which linkage has been omitted. Such an omission is necessary to the chiasmatic form that Coleridge adopts as a means to define the imagination. This necessity finds a consistent thematic expression in the appearance of this image of hovering at the point where a synthesis is anticipated.[82] This hovering indicates that what is at stake is not at all the totality traditionally associated with the chiasmus but rather the anticipation of this association. To attain such a totality (and thereby ignore such anticipation) would be to offer what the friend expects thereby asserting the friend's understanding over and above the rest of the *Biographia*. What is at stake is that the chiasmus should fail to take the place of the (missing) deduction. Thus, for the imagination to become the site of privileged attention in the *Biographia*, the chiasmus must always be read as performing the role of interrelation even when it remains incapable of fulfilling this role except on a more restricted and merely formal level. This incapacity demands the formal moment essential to any reading that would rescue itself from the consequences of its own intentions.

To say that the chiasmus invites this formal moment is also to say that language extends this same invitation since the chiasmus is, first and foremost, a syntactic sequence rather than a spatial arrangement. Yet such a sequence cannot authorize or prevent its formalization into a double figure of self-mirroring, nor can it prevent the transfiguration of this formal coherence so that it may appear as the substantial property of whatever is substituted in its place, for example, the imagination. Such formalization preys upon the inability of the chiasmus to fulfill even the rhetorical function normally attributed to this figure. It is precisely this inability that invites and, indeed, would necessitate the formalization of the chiasmus as a closed symmetrical figure. Consequently, if one is to speak of a dissymmetry in the figure of the chiasmus it is not because of a fourth element that does not fit within its symmetrical arrangement. The spatial arrangement associated with the figure of the chiasmus requires a formalization if it is to be possible to know the place of an element that does or does not fit the scheme of reversibility drawn by this figure. Like the *Poetics,* the chiasmus must dance whether or not its legs have matching feet. In each case, the reversibility of a self-reflexive figure is called upon, a reversibility that is described in Maurice Merleau-Ponty's late reflections on the chiasmus as "an act with two faces."[83] As the symmetry of the chiasmus is inconceivable without such a reversibility, so is a dissymmetry derived solely from its form. No dissymmetry of this kind can prevent this formalization precisely because any such prevention performs a two-faced act as it simultaneously affirms what is to be discounted. Moreover, to claim such prevention would be akin to literary criticism's attempt to thematize the difference it cannot account for when it posits its origin *in the form* of a difference.

The letter is therefore not a deceptive solution to the problem of a deduction which would grant authority to what must exercise authority over it. Nor is the letter an example of an inevitable narrativization of philosophical discourse—as if such narrativization were the inevitable effect of the difficulty facing the *Biographia* at this point.[84] Rather, the reversal within which this letter would be inscribed marks the attempt to exorcize the ghost that Coleridge's deduction must find in place of the imagination—the "ghost of a defunct substance," the ghost of total self-reflexivity, the ghost of a will returning to haunt the absolute interruption which, in Schelling, marks the beginning and the "end" of philosophy. It is such a revenant that the Kantian analogy confines to the limits of systematic thought and which Schelling will also contain by limiting the validity of philosophy to that of a science which may only be complete *as* philosophy. The passage opened by Coleridge in the *Biographia* conceives of this completion within a progression initiated by the heaven-descended "Know Thyself" and ending once again with the author of this command. In this way, Coleridge enters upon a path of self-mastery that would know its own deceptions but cannot conclude his journey. The will that follows and engenders this command is the will to be a *causa sui*. Yet, to return once again to Nietzsche: "Die *causa sui* ist der beste Selbst-Widerspruch, der bisher ausgedacht worden ist, eine Art logischer Notzucht und Unnatur" [The *causa sui* is the best self-contradiction that has been devised so far, a kind of logical rape and monstrosity].[85] While the unfolding of the imagination is to follow the logic of deduction, the premise from which this unfolding becomes possible is precisely the self-contradiction which Nietzsche calls a "kind of logical rape and monstrosity." The deduction must violate itself in order to produce any result but to do so is to produce no result at all. In this respect, deduction may only become possible as a violation rather than a triumph of logic.

The violation of logic is not only the missing link of Coleridge's life and opinions but also the necessarily concealed and therefore figurative violation of a critical project that demands a self-begetting and totally self-reflexive principle. In the *Biographia,* such a violation is, in the last instance, evaded. This evasion amounts to Coleridge's withdrawal from the figure that produces the possibility of the ventriloquy through which the *Biographia* was to be engendered as the critical text—the *ventriloquus interruptus.* Not to interrupt the birth of the imagination at this point is to deny the place of a figurehead. Its deduction interrupted, the imagination may not only be born as the result of an act that could never have happened, but may become, *as* a result of the analogy established in this interruption, "a repetition in the finite mind of the eternal act of creation in the infinite I AM" (1:304).[86] It is in this determination that Coleridge returns to the fold of a Kantian necessity having faced the discovery that the deduction of the imagination does not provide a torch of philosophical guidance but rather a candle burning at both ends—a candle that must consume its own identity and power of identification.[87] Coleridge, author of his own auto-biographical identity, would undergo the same fate. The metaphor, however, is imprecise. The *Biographia* can produce neither a torch of philosophical guidance nor a candle burning at both ends, but Coleridge, the critic, reflected in the darkness of a mirror that no language will ever see or know how to break.

CHAPTER THREE

Where Three Paths Meet

❧ *Wordsworth*

> *. . . and should the chosen guide*
> *Be nothing better than a wandering cloud,*
> *I cannot miss my way.*
>
> —Wordsworth, *The Prelude*

It would be difficult to understate the importance of the Simplon Pass episode in Book 6 of *The Prelude*. Historically, the episode has been crucial to any understanding of the imagination and its role as a mode of interrelation both within Romanticism and within the critical discourse on Romanticism. The ease with which this passage becomes a source of critical knowledge does, however, pose a danger of considerable magnitude. This danger is expressed most forcefully whenever literary criticism confers an emblematic status on this passage and, in so doing, imparts all the attributes of a historical event to this decidedly literary episode. In defense, it may be argued that this emblematic treatment reflects the anthologizing and synecdochic tendency which, it would seem, necessarily dominates critical interpretation of *The Prelude*. While this tendency could be (and is) defended on the grounds of its inevitability (there is, in effect, no other way to go about interpreting a poem or indeed any text of this length), such a defense may only proceed by invoking the imperative which introduces this very episode: ". . . let one incident make known" (1850, 6:562).[1] To accept this defense is to assume that this passage reflects the procedure and methodology adopted by its interpretation. Accordingly, the occurrence of this imperative at the very beginning of the Simplon Pass episode clearly marks this passage as an exemplary site to inquire into an approach whose own imperative would read: "let one episode make known." Indeed, to forget how Wordsworth's introduction of this episode prefigures the critical discourse in which it has become emblematized is to anticipate, like Wordsworth and his companion, a promise of knowledge, and, above all, a promise of historical knowledge made in the name of the Simplon Pass.

In the interpretation of *The Prelude* only the lure of this promise would be able to account for the frequency with which this passage not only occurs in the reading of this work, but also, the frequency with which these readings grant this episode all the force of a climax.[2] At the same time, one cannot forget that the frequent recurrence of this passage may also indicate the extent to which it poses an unavoidable challenge to any serious attempt to read the discourse practiced in *The Prelude*. As the locus of a challenge, the Simplon Pass episode becomes a pass that must be passed through if any knowledge of the Wordsworthian imagination, not to mention Romanticism itself, is to be arrived at. Accordingly, when a knowledge of this kind becomes a guiding light, this episode may be all too easily read as holding forth its own "Conspicuous invitation to ascend / A lofty mountain" (1850, 6:572–73), an invitation that has been accepted too often without consideration of its consequences or else taken up with a studied indifference to its consequences despite their conspicuousness.[3] To accept this invitation and thereby grant the Simplon Pass episode such primacy, such exemplary status (and I speak only of the way in which this passage figures within the discourse on *The Prelude*), to grant such primacy already indicates the need for a watershed—precisely the place of a border—as a means of articulating the imaginative crossing that Romantic criticism has been only too willing to promote and never more so than when it arrives at one of its exemplary watersheds, the Simplon Pass. The stakes of such an articulation are high and not simply because, without it, there could be no knowledge of where the border lies in this episode (and thus no knowledge of the incident to be made known), but rather, because the whole possibility of literary criticism's claim to a historical knowledge of Romanticism is derived from it.

Recognitions

Yet is a path
More difficult before me . . .
—Wordsworth, *The Prelude*

Within the critical discussion of the Simplon Pass episode, the imagination has been given so much prominence as a power which rises "from the Mind's abyss / Like an unfathered vapour" (1850, 6:594–95) that it is easy, if not convenient, to forget that this imagination first arises as a mode of address which results from what Wordsworth calls the "sad incompetence of human speech" (1850, 6:593).[4] All too often, such a sad incompetence is leapt over in favor of the "unfathered vapour." There would seem to be something reassuring about a child without a father that appeals to critical interpretation—as if this effacement of an origin in the very act of origination were able to satisfy deep rooted desires for a reflexive, self-generative power unperplexed by the "sad incompetence of human speech." Such an effacement forgets the sad incompetence of these lines and it does so by forgetting the simile through which the imagination would become an unfathered vapor. Despite this tendency to forget, it is clear from the opening sentence of the apostrophe that the conjunction announcing this simile should not be forgotten—as the metrical emphasis on "like" would already indicate:

> Imagination—here the Power so called
> Through sad incompetence of human speech,
> That awful Power rose from the mind's abyss
> Like an unfathered vapour that enwraps,
> At once, some lonely traveller.
>
> (1850, 6:593–97)

In these lines, the unfathering of the imagination cannot be understood in terms of an actual or even literal occurrence. The imagination arises *like* an unfathering. To regard the imagination as if it were actually unfathered is to assume that the conjunction "like" has only one role to play in this sentence, namely, to disappear into the vaporous analogy it announces. Instead of clarifying what the imagination is like, such a reading demands an unfathering that negates the analogy through which the imagination is to be made known. But there will be nothing to know if this analogy is effaced. At the same time, the relation between the imagination and the vapor must be unfathered or otherwise negated if this simile is to produce any knowledge about the imagination. If the imagination is to be made known, it must then accept the unenviable task of negotiating these two competing claims. Within such a negation, the emblematic status frequently accorded this passage goes hand in hand with the necessity of articulating an essentially figurative mode of negation. Clearly, this necessity cannot be restricted to this episode or even to Romanticism since the negation in question would constitute the passage from language to knowledge. As such, this negation, or unfathering, describes a recurrent and necessary moment within the interpretation of literature.

The difficulty posed by this episode may be traced to the recurrent effects of sustaining a figurative mode of negation. This difficulty cannot be swept aside, however, by simply remembering the conjunction that has been so consistently unfathered. Indeed, the crucial question posed by this passage does not reside solely in this conjunction but in what Wordsworth calls the "sad incompetence of human speech" to which this conjunction must also belong. Unfathering, and the negation it performs, would bypass the question of this incompetence by promoting a self-generating, self-productive beginning as the logical yet negative origin of all knowledge. If this origin and the negation it involves cannot be separated from human speech and its sad incompetence, then, any attempt to take up the imperative of this episode must turn first to the question of this speech.

It should be readily clear from this episode that the sad incompetence of human speech is not to be found in a simile which, to use a formula from deconstructive criticism, can only give rise to the mere expression of likenesses (a figure giving rise to a figure, a sign giving rise to a sign, etc., etc.). Such a formula repeats the concealment that occurs when the rising of the imagination is understood as if it were really an unfathered vapor. In the case of this literalization, the "like" is effectively removed in order to assert that the imagination is actually "an unfathered vapour." In the present case, where the "like" is understood as the mere expression of likenesses, such a concealment is repeated even though this understanding is predicated upon the inability of language to describe how the imagination actually arises. By virtue of this inability, human speech also comes to possess the property of "an unfathered vapour." Unable to say what something is and only able to say what it is like, human speech will always be unable to state its source precisely because it can only *state* its source. Despite the deconstructive character of this inability, this definition of human speech is far from articulating any of the issues at stake within deconstruction. The inability expressed by this understanding of human speech is sustained by a very definite idea of what language ought to be about: despite the incompetency of its expression, what it wants to say is known (otherwise this incompetency could not be recognized). Consequently, when the conjunction "like" is condemned to the endless expression of likenesses, it affirms that human speech is understandable through a negative relation between itself and an object possessing prior independent existence. This relation is a negative one because it derives a knowledge of human speech from an object whose existence remains completely independent of language. In such an instance, this human speech, by remembering only its ability to express the likeness of what it speaks about, would believe that it has come to know itself, but, in so doing, it forgets once more its conjunction, that is, it forgets a conjunction *of* human speech in order to remember an incompetency between speech and what it is supposed to speak about. Through this incompetency, the self-generating understanding enabled by the forgetting of the conjunction "like" persists.[5]

According to this understanding, the "sad incompetence of human speech" would be nothing more than the mere inability of language to translate some transcendent power such as the imagination. To view the incompetence of human speech as such an inability is, in the end, to be far from sad. Indeed, such an incompetence has already translated the inadequacy of human speech into a sign that points to the possibility as well as the place of the imagination in a beyond whose existence is affirmed by the very attempt to name or even point to that beyond. Being so determined, human speech would produce the trans-scendent inasmuch as this speech offers a conspicuous invitation to cross and climb (*trans-scandere*) to where there is no "like." When read as a figure of such sad incompetence, that is, when read as merely figurative, the simile announced by "like" would be the invitation to this crossing, an invitation to cross a border into a land of the father who would never have had a father, to a land where the child is more than *like* the father, to a land where the child is the father.[6] Such a crossing produces not only the effacement of the "like" but also the effacement of the incompetent image that enabled this crossing in the first place. Armed with a like incompetence of human speech, there would appear to be no choice but to read the conspicuous invitation of this phrase as the result of a human speech whose inadequate expressions reflect and point to what it is unable to say.

If such an understanding of the "sad incompetence of human speech" is accepted, then, it would seem entirely appropriate to read the following lines from the apostrophe as offering the sense of an infinitude expressed through the assumed finiteness of language:

> Our destiny, our being's heart and home,
> Is with infinitude, and only there;
> With hope it is, hope that can never die,
> Effort, and expectation, and desire,
> And something evermore about to be.
> Under such banners militant, the soul
> Seeks for no trophies, struggles for no spoils
> That may attest her prowess, blest in thoughts
> That are their own perfection and reward . . .
>
> (1850, 6:604–12)

From the incompetency expressed in the lines beginning "Imagination—here so called," the apostrophe moves to the infinitude of a "there" whose own incompetency is the guarantee of a hope that can never die precisely because "there" is evermore about to be *there*. It is hardly surprising that the soul should seek for no trophies, it does not need to, it is enwrapped in an incompetency that produces its own reward, an incompetency whose inability to rise to a power that no language is like becomes the very means of representing that power. Such an incompetency provides "banners militant" which effectively militate on behalf of human speech so that this same speech would only be read as the address to a transcendent power and not be its address. To address the imagination under the sign of such a militancy is itself an apt figure for the critical passage through the Simplon Pass inasmuch as this passage is so militantly full of the effort and the desire to forget the price it must pay for the fulfillment of its imaginative expectations.[7] Not only must this crossing be forgotten if the imagination is to be apostrophized but this forgetting must also be forgotten if the rise of the imagination is to be equivalent to "an unfathered vapour that enwraps, / At once, some lonely traveller." To the extent that this unfathered vapor enwraps, it would be a veil thrown over the very passage it is preceded by. As such, this veil would permit a crossing out of the Simplon Pass. Not only does this crossing out presuppose a recognition of the border which allows the discourse of Romanticism as well as the discourse on Romanticism to say that it too "*had crossed the Alps*," but, this recognition is what allows both Romanticism and its critical discourse to apostrophize the imagination in their turn.

Before one can proceed to the place of this crossing, there still remains the question of how the phrase "—here the Power so called / Through sad incompetence of human speech" is to be read—a question that will not allow the lines which speak of "thoughts / That are their own perfection and reward" to remain so militantly self-assured. In the line that contains the address to the imagination, the occurrence of the word "here" would point to the naming of this faculty as if it were a prior event now being reflected upon. If this were so, the dash between "imagination" and "here" ought to mark a difference that allows the act of apostrophizing ("Imagination—") to be understood in both historical and rhetorical terms. Accordingly, Wordsworth's text ought to be capable of addressing historically its own figures. Yet, this capability assumes that the name of the imagination, and, indeed, the apostrophe itself, can be determined by the mode of address described in the lines following the apostrophe—as if this dash could confirm that what is addressed by "here" is only the calling in which the imagination is named.[8] Through this understanding of how "here" relates to the imagination, the phrase "here the Power so called" would assert that the status ascribed to the naming of the imagination is quite different from the status possessed by the reflection upon this naming. According to this difference, the naming of the imagination would be nothing less and nothing more than a rhetorical figure, an apostrophe through which the imagination is merely addressed.

But the reflection that follows this naming would know such a figure as an act or event. In short, this act of naming would come to possess all the attributes associated with a historical event rather than a written text. So understood, the apostrophe enables the subsequent reflection to occur and, at the same time, allows a history of the imagination to arise (in the sense that any recognition of an incompetency in the naming of the imagination is at the same time a grounding of language in a faculty that is understood to precede language historically).

For the relation between human speech and what is called the imagination to remain historical, language must always be understood as an incompetent mode of expression with respect to what it means—a meaning whose existence is confirmed by this incompetence. If human speech were not defined according to this incompetence, there would be no possibility of either reflection or a historical discourse ever taking place. This eventuality is inescapable if one considers the consequences of a competent mode of speech. According to such a mode, the word "Imagination—" would always be able to say what it means. But, if this were the case, human speech would be capable of the impossibility of saying that it is incompetent and meaning it—an eventuality that would effectively deny language any ability to reflect upon itself (such reflection cannot except itself from the incompetency it names). Consequently, what is persistently at stake is the incompetency of language to say what it means but to do so in such a way that the meaning of human speech will be known without that meaning ever being competently expressed. This incompetency of language is nothing less than the dialectical recovery of competence, in effect, a negative competence.[9] In this context, the event that precipitates the apostrophe to the imagination cannot be emphasized enough—when Wordsworth and his companion encounter the peasant are they not supposed to know the meaning of words spoken in a language they do not understand?

A reflection in which the apostrophe is recognized as an act demands an understanding that subordinates human speech to a meaning whose source is always said to reside outside of language. In this instance, what is called history does not simply arise from an understanding that views human speech as an incompetent mode of expression; such a history also requires that human speech be understood as a competent means of expressing such incompetency. Here, history would mirror transcendence to the extent that both derive meaning from a determination of language as inherently figurative. Yet, if such a determination is to be effective, it must be capable of accounting for the syntactic structure of the opening lines of the apostrophe in historical terms. Such an account must answer this question: by what right can the incompetency of the word "imagination" be differentiated from the competency of the reflection which follows it? By a dash? Can such a dash articulate a theory of figurative language and, at the same time, give rise to historical knowledge? "—"?

The determination of the apostrophe as an act followed by a reflection turns upon the question of how this dash is to be read. Does the dash stand for an elapse of time? Is what follows the dash to be construed in terms of a here and now reflecting upon a past which could only say what it means rather than mean what it says?

To read the dash as the sign of a historical difference would be inconceivable without asserting that the reflection upon the act of naming described in these lines belongs to some immediate here and now of a speaking subject. It is toward the affirmation of such a subject that the reading of the "sad incompetence of human speech" as an expression of language's inadequacy is directed. The sadness invoked in the name of this incompetence would permit the recognition of a subject by means of a pathos much like the sadness Wordsworth seems to elicit when, at the beginning of Book 5 of *The Prelude,* he asks, "Oh! why hath not the Mind / Some element to stamp her image on / In nature somewhat nearer to her own?" (1850, 5:45–47). Here, pathos would express the negative relation between language and meaning to which the "sad incompetence of human speech" is most easily reduced. In the case of the apostrophe to the imagination, such a pathos (or sadness) intervenes in order to overcome any question about the relation of a subject to human speech, never mind the question of the relation of meaning *to* human speech. The recognition of a subject by this means is invariably pathetic and its inaccuracy is clearly stated by Wordsworth in the syntactic sequencing of the apostrophe: the only human subject who appears in the first sentence of the apostrophe *would be* "some lonely traveller," would be, because this traveler only appears enwrapped within the simile that compares the rising of the imagination to the rising of "an unfathered vapour." Even on this grammatical level—the level that ought to control the production of meaning—it is clear that the apostrophe to the imagination cannot be so easily assimilated or fitted to the historical, transcendent concept of language whose incompetence props up a subject by means of a pathos that ignores the rhetorical basis of its affection as well as its incompetence.

The difficulty impeding a subject who would speak in such a here and now is taken up in the subsequent lines of the apostrophe when the abrupt rising of the imagination is described as a situation in which a subject is said to be "Halted without an effort to break *through*" (1850, 6:597; emphasis mine).[10] This halting follows from the recognition that the poet "was lost" at this moment—a recognition that appears to form a link between the description of the imagination's rising and the poet's statement about an inability to break through: "That awful Power rose from the mind's abyss / Like an unfathered vapour that enwraps / Some lonely traveller. I was lost; / Halted . . ." (1850, 6:594–97). According to the sequence detailed in these lines, to be halted results from being lost, and, being lost results from being enwrapped in the simile that also enwraps the rising of the imagination.[11] This simile (which produces the mystification of "some lonely traveller") is thus what provides the means for the first person subject to intervene. The "I" would find itself in the shoes of a lonely traveler whose mystification had provided a place in which a subject may be lost.[12]

The passage from the simile that enwraps "some lonely traveller" to the "I" of "I was lost" is also marked by a shift in tense (from "enwraps" to "was"). Through this shift, the subject's ability to know itself would appear to be affirmed. But, this subject may only attain such knowledge if the lonely traveler is now understood as the historical origin of the subject who speaks the words "I was lost." Accordingly, the simile that enwraps the lonely traveler takes on the added function of enabling a passage from the rising of the imagination to the consciousness of a subject. The simile which is to make the imagination known now becomes instrumental in making a subject known to itself. Since the phrase "Like an unfathered vapour" is interpreted in both instances as the recognition of a place of loss, it is clear that a central issue in this episode involves an ability to speak about loss in a way that will ground both experience and history. This ability forges the path that leads directly to a conscious subject because it recognizes that this place of loss is, in effect, the antecedent, the father which gives rise to such a subject.[13] Accordingly, it is a loss that belongs to the history as well as to the here and now asserted by a subject in order to know that it has a past. However, such a subject was never and is never truly lost, since being lost now becomes nothing less than the assertion of its self-consciousness (the assertion of loss and self-consciousness is most readily apparent in the phrase "I am lost").[14] This loss is therefore no threat since to be "halted without an effort to break through"—and this is referred to immediately after the declaration "I was lost"—is to demarcate a halting in which the subject comes to know itself as halted. This stated inability to break through would repeat on the level of the subject what occurs when the "sad incompetence of human speech" is understood as an inadequacy of language with respect to meaning. This inability again operates as the sign of something unattainable in order to force the subject back upon itself, in order to reflect itself and, in that reflection, see what it was and is like. Consequently, for the subject to speak, what has to break through in the lines that state, "I was lost; / Halted without an effort to break through," is a relation of "now" to "then" that seeks to recognize loss as something posited as well as recognized by the operation of recollection. In other words, what is unfolding in the apostrophe to the imagination is a sequence that defines the possibility of historical knowledge and, above all, the possibility of a passage from language to history. This sequence may be discerned in the apostrophe as it runs from name to naming, from naming to simile, from simile to self-consciousness, from self-consciousness to history and, ultimately, as figured in the last lines of the apostrophe, from history to apocalypse.[15] Through this sequence (language, figure, self-consciousness, history, and apocalypse) and the interrelated steps it presumes in order to arrive at a history for its language, a subject can only arise if language can be determined as the incompetent, inadequate expression of its existence. While such an incompetence would arise from a historical subject, the language named by this incompetence cannot arise from the same source for there can be no historical subject until there is a language in which the subject may both posit and address its historicity or even language's stated inadequacy.

What the historical subject rests upon is stated explicitly when the consciousness which can (only) be said to be present all along is described immediately following the statement of loss and the halting of the poet. In these lines, the inability to "break through" leads to the emergence of a conscious subject by means of a conjunction whose role reiterates the "like" through which the "unfathered vapour" is introduced. Moreover, this emergence takes place within a conspicuous invitation to cross and ascend, an invitation to cross from here and now to an invisible there:

> I was lost;
> Halted without an effort to break through;
> *But* to my conscious soul I now can say—
> 'I recognise thy glory': in such strength
> Of usurpation, when the light of sense
> Goes out, *but* with a flash that has revealed
> The invisible world, doth greatness make abode,
> There harbours, whether we be young or old.
> (1850, 6:598–603; emphasis mine)[16]

Through the conjunction formed by the first "but," the previously apostrophized imagination is turned away from as the poet addresses his conscious soul. This turning away would establish what is, in effect, a border between an imagination that was incompetently addressed in the form of an apostrophe and the speech of a poet now able to address this incompetency. The border established here not only allows this speech to take place but also presents it at a time different from that in which the poet was halted without an effort to break through. The text reads, "I *now* can say." To speak from within this "now" is to reiterate the passage between "Imagination" and "here" which occurs in the opening line of the apostrophe ("Imagination—here the Power so called"). By speaking in a here and now, the poet would again speak of what is passed. And indeed, the very act of speaking introduced by this "but" would demand that what is spoken about be regarded as something already passed over—just as the words "I was lost" would speak of a loss that remains thoroughly historical. What is then at stake in this passage (and what therefore supports the notions of subject and history it implies) is a crossing that must always be recognized as having been missed. To recognize that a crossing has been missed is to recognize a loss and, above all, one's own loss ("*I* was lost") in such a way that this act of self-reflection articulates and contains a difference between past and present. So crucial is this difference that the very possibility of a relation between event or act and historical discourse depends on it. Indeed, so close is the relation of self-reflection to history that one is unthinkable without the other—the tendency to speak of self-reflection as an act underlines this collaboration. Consequently, despite the association of self-reflection (and the concept of self-reflexivity it is based upon) with a deemphasizing of the historical, such a deemphasis, in fact, marks the most forceful and radical assertion of history: the history of language's relation to itself. Without such an assertion, no historical writing could lay claim to the title of history. This collaboration between self-reflection and the historical would not only ground the possibility of historical discourse, but it would do so by attempting to regulate the relation of language to meaning at the expense of language. The preoccupation with history or the subject in the interpretation of literature cannot avoid a collaboration of this kind, a collaboration that views the incompetence of interpretation in terms of a pathos arising from a difference between language and meaning. In these lines from the apostrophe, the price to be paid by such collaboration is spelled out only too clearly if attention is given to the precise nature of the crossings or conjunctions that articulate each part of the sequence already outlined above (naming, simile, consciousness, and history and the figure of its apocalypse).

In the case of the passage just referred to, "but" is the conjunction that ought to permit the crossing from loss to consciousness and recognition. Yet, for this recognition to occur, the conjunction "but" must be regarded as establishing a border as well as effecting its transgression—and it is never more effective in this role than when it is read as simply a grammatical conjunction, as a simple passage to the recognition of what (like the crossing of the Alps) could not formerly be brought to cognition in its historicity (that is, in the singularity of an actual occurrence). However, if the conjunction is to be so understood, one could well ask, why should there be any effort to break through when the very fact of being halted already enables a crossing over to take place? Why should there be any effort to break through when being halted is not the obstacle but the means of this transgression? The transgression enacted by the phrase "'I recognize thy glory'" would usurp both the prior halted state and the conjunction "but" through which the crossing to speech ("I now can say") becomes possible. Such an understanding of the conjunction takes for granted that it is possible to posit a difference within the syntax of these lines *as if* this difference were essentially historical in origin and in effect, that is, *as if* such a difference were able to replicate within language the difference between "actual" events *and* language. In other words, for this difference to exist, language must be able to establish a historical relation to itself, a relation that takes place in and through itself. Not only would such a relation regulate what language can say but, quite apart from speaking about any definite object, this relation, in its most essential form, would also presume that language can say that it speaks, can say that it is capable of speaking and, moreover, is able to know what *it* is saying when it speaks. But, does language know what it says when it says that it speaks? Could language ever be capable of saying "I now can say"? The question is crucial because the transgression undertaken in the apostrophe demands such an ability.

To be precise, the historical relation of language to itself involves what is, quite literally, a predicament. Such a relation involves a declaration ("I now can say") which requires that whatever follows be recognized as a speaking that possesses all the punctuality and singularity of an act. At the same time, the predicament ought to be subsumed within what it leads to, or, to use the terms employed by Wordsworth in this passage, it should be unfathered by the act of speaking to which it gives rise. How this unfathering occurs in the course of this passage may be traced from the way in which the apostrophe proceeds from being "halted without an effort to break through" and then arrives at the appearance of human speech in "'I recognise thy glory.'"

In following the path of this unfathering, it becomes quickly apparent that two crossings occur: the first entails a crossing from a seemingly historical event ("I was lost") to a statement about speaking ("I now can say—"); the second turns once again upon a dash ("I now can say— / 'I recognise thy glory'") which marks the crossing to a speaking that has already been introduced through speech.[17] Through this second crossing the first would be usurped. As a result of this usurpation, what initially caused the halting of the poet (the vapor which enwraps both the rising imagination and the apostrophizer of the imagination) would be overcome. Yet, this overcoming of the vapor which envelops both the imagination and the poet involves one further turn. The recognition spoken in these lines is given in a phrase set off within quotation marks: "I now can say— / 'I recognise thy glory.'" As such, the recognition is preceded by a phrase that introduces it as human speech. This introductory statement is not, however, usurped by the recognition it has fathered. For this usurpation to occur, it must be assumed that the second "I" is the property of a conscious subject. Only on condition of this assumption is it possible to dispel the difference made in these lines between a declaration about speaking ("I now can say") and the speech it gives rise to (" 'I recognise thy glory' "). The recognition of the imagination and its glory is incapable of usurping such a difference precisely because it is unable to perform what is announced in its own predicate (*prædicere:* what is spoken before). Given that the subject of this predicate could never have said " 'I recognise thy glory,' " it must be effaced if the recognition it is followed by is to possess any competency. For this effacement to occur, what the phrase "I now can say" introduces must be more than *like* human speech.

Through these effacements and usurpations, the apostrophe would unfold as a chain of usurpations whose possibility (the poet being lost) would no longer need to be accounted for since it would be concealed by this chain: the saying of "I recognise thy glory" would usurp the "now" of "I now can say," the "now" would usurp the halting of the traveler (and thereby translate this halting into speech), this halting would usurp the declaration "I was lost," and then, the very making of this declaration would usurp the state of being lost from which it is derived. The assertion that one is lost is the self-deception that sustains this whole sequence. But, what gets in the way or, rather, what always remains at each juncture in this sequence is the conjunction, the "but," the "like," the "dash."[18] Within such a sequence, the apostrophe would also figure as a conjunction whose address would be obscured, veiled, even enwrapped in an unfathered vapor as soon as this apostrophe, this "like," and this "but" are read as being preceded by a gap, a loss, a vacancy, or a missed experience which is recognized *as if* it were a gap, a loss, a vacancy, or a missed experience. It is such a recognition that the apostrophe to the imagination would itself perform through an act of speaking after, an act of speaking about a pass which has not only been passed over but which needs to be unfathered if it is ever to rise to consciousness. Such gaps and losses are precisely the predicaments which establish the border so necessary to any crossing over as well as to any breaking through "Under . . . banners militant." Here, the larger pattern of the episode's structure is repeated in a passage that purports to have moved beyond the loss that occasioned its appearance. Yet, it remains to be seen whether such gaps and losses are not the effects of a voluntary or self-inflicted double crossing whose purpose is to efface the passage preceding the apostrophe to the imagination by reducing it to a merely "external scene."

To question this reduction is to question not only the lines that precede the apostrophe to the imagination but also the historical occasion and indeed the historical knowledge which separates the "external" scene from the apostrophe. Only by means of such a separation would it be possible to address the imagination as a mode of interrelation which allows a subject to recover from a lost or missing experience by taking the place of that loss or missed experience. By positing this separation or border between the "external" scene and apostrophe, this episode would affirm a movement from the historical to the imagination. The frequent recurrence of such a movement would indicate a dialectical complicity between history and what is called imagination in Romanticism. However, the status of the history that fuels this complicity remains to be made known. Consequently, the questions that will remain to be asked concern the place of this "external" historical scene in the course of this passage. To what does the apostrophe respond in this scene? History? But, if history, why does the apostrophe follow a sequence that runs from the naming of language to the apocalyptic flooding of the Nile? Why does such a sequence have to be undergone after the external scene and its account of a historical moment such as crossing the Alps? And why does the sequence unfolded in the apostrophe derive itself from a self-reflexive origin more usually invoked in the context of self-consciousness? But, first and foremost, what is it *like* to cross the Alps according to the notion of history elaborated by this passage from *The Prelude?*

The Way Up and the Way Down

whither shall I turn
By road or pathway, or through trackless field,
Up hill or down, or shall some floating thing
Upon the river point me out my course?

—Wordsworth, *The Prelude*

To return to the pass which has been the site of so much critical haste is to confront the difficulty that necessitated not only this haste but also the apostrophe to the imagination. At the same time, this return demands that one also confront the sadness associated with the incompetence of human speech in the apostrophe. The demand is made by the passage that describes the ascent to the pass. Wordsworth writes:

Yet still in me with those soft luxuries
Mixed something of stern mood, an under-thirst
Of vigour seldom utterly allayed.
And from that source how different a sadness
Would issue, let one incident make known.

(1850, 6:558–62)

The sadness referred to in these lines is utterly different from the "Dejection taken up for pleasure's sake" as well as the "gilded sympathies" and "sober posies of funereal flowers" (1850, 6:551–53) which appear in the lines immediately preceding the description of the climb to the Simplon Pass. This difference is most pronounced in the formal characterization of the source of dejection and its accompanying images of sadness in the lines preceding the ascent. The "dejection," "gilded sympathies," and "sober posies" of these lines are all said to be gathered from the "formal gardens of the lady Sorrow" (1850, 6:555). Such a formality at the source of dejection and sadness in this passage would appear to be precisely what permits the alleviation of that sadness: "Gathered . . . / From formal gardens . . . / Did sweeten many a meditative hour" (1850, 6:554–56). The sadness expressed before the description of the climb to the Simplon Pass is thus tempered by the pleasure derived from formal arrangement.

The formal, however, has more to fulfill than an aesthetic function. Here, as always, the formal sustains the mode of figuration that presents sadness as being emblematic of pleasure and it does so by providing the substitutive pattern through which sadness and pleasure may be exchanged for one another. The recourse to a formal context is hardly accidental since the exchange of sense whereby sadness becomes an emblem of pleasure is inconceivable without the guidance established within a formal structure of opposition and exchange. Here, as in the *Poetics,* a formal arrangement is called upon in order to assure that sense will be preserved whenever one thing follows in the steps of another. Without this formalism, the Aristotelian mimesis which understands "this" in the place of "that" could not even be conceived.[19] Moreover, without this formalism, there could be no pleasure to oppose to and then put in the place of sadness. Yet, even though the lines preceding the description of the poet's ascent to the Simplon Pass (6:551–56) dissolve their sadness in the pleasures of formal arrangement, what follows tells a different story, a story in which the unavoidable formalism of any historical knowledge must be faced. It is in these lines that Wordsworth takes up the issue of historical knowledge in terms of the essential formal structuring that governs historical causation. It should also be remarked that this formalism is no less essential even when history is reduced to incontrovertible facts such as, for example, the passage of Napoleon through the Alps. Indeed, to grant facts like this one the power of determining literary significance is to adopt a mimetic pattern described by Aristotle: οἷον ὅτι οὗτος ἐκεῖνος (this [the apostrophe to the imagination] because of that [Napoleon, for example]).[20]

The lines through which a critique of the formal structure of historical knowledge is presented take up the question of the sadness announced in the opening sentence of Wordsworth's description of the ascent to the Simplon Pass. These lines do not simply oppose another kind of sadness over and against the pleasurable sadness of this dejection. Rather, they speak of a sadness that may only be known through the attempt to record the history of an incident. This sadness comes from a source, "an underthirst of vigour" which is "mixed" with the soft luxuries and emblematic sadness inseparable from the production of pleasure. This different sadness cannot be construed as external to the balanced and symmetrical relations required by "Dejection taken up for pleasure's sake." Even though the source of this different sadness cannot be divorced from such a symmetrical relation, this does not mean that its presence is determined by such a symmetry. Indeed, within this formal symmetrical relation, Wordsworth writes that this different sadness is "seldom utterly allayed"—"allayed" indicating a lessening or neutralization which occurs by means of a mixing in. The use of "seldom" in this phrase might suggest the hope that an utter allaying of the source of this different sadness can in fact take place. The expression of this hope marks a departure from the 1805 text where "something of stern mood" is said to be "never utterly asleep" (1805, 6:490), that is, never without utterance, never silent. The hope expressed by the revision in the 1850 text would imply that this utterance be neutralized by its absorption within the substitutive and, ultimately, soporific exchange which finds pleasure in the place of sadness. Indeed, if the source of this different sadness were to be utterly allayed or mixed in, one would have to be, to adopt the language of the 1805 text, in a state of sleep but, even then, one would have to be *utterly* asleep. Such an utter loss of consciousness is precisely what cannot be sustained—as if it were possible to state "I now can say, 'I am utterly asleep'" without remarking an utter discontinuity between language and the state in which its presumed subject is to be found.[21] Through this discontinuity, a difference would be made known and it is in the name of such a difference that the Simplon Pass episode unfolds as it records the passage of a difference whose inability to substitute pleasure for sadness resists the formal, emblematizing activity that supports such a substitution.

The emphasis this different sadness receives in the opening lines of the ascent promotes the anticipation of something about to be unveiled, something climactic, something secret, as if the passage through the Alps were comparable to the search for the source of the Nile.[22] Accordingly, something of the apocalyptic character frequently associated with the rise of the imagination may be discerned—at least in the Greek sense of the word *apocalypse* as that which is uncovered, disclosed, revealed (ἀποκάλυψις). It would indeed be difficult to resist the seductive force of this anticipation especially since these lines on the Simplon Pass are explicitly introduced in anticipation of an incident that will "make known." In this respect, the lines that precede the apostrophe to the imagination cannot be considered an "external scene." Rather, they are situated within an epistemological question that prefaces any reading of the apostrophe to the imagination and, hence, must precede the unfathering through which the imagination is made known. Not only does this question turn upon the possibility of making something known, but it arises in the form of an imperative ("let one incident make known") addressed to the relation between event and history. In short, it is addressed to the knowledge of an event (which is not the same thing as addressing that event itself). The promise of knowledge made through this imperative would thus function as a guide to the reading of this passage. Here, the imperative would join with a sense of apocalypse to the extent that both promise a knowledge that would have no likeness precisely because each is predicated upon the unrepeatability of a single incident.

Although the promise made by the imperative ("let one incident make known") would serve as a guide through the pass, the events that take place in the course of this passage relate a parting of the ways between what guides and what is guided. This parting forms the possibility of an incident, that is, it forms the possibility of an event whose historicality is yet to be made known. The parting is recorded as follows:

> When from the Vallais we had turned, and clomb
> Along the Simplon's steep and rugged road,
> Following a band of muleteers, we reached
> A halting-place, where all together took
> Their noon-tide meal. Hastily rose our guide,
> Leaving *us* at the board . . .
>
> (1850, 6:562–67)

Wordsworth and his companion begin their climb following the band of muleteers which functions as their guide. They reach a halting-place which serves as the place of their noon-tide meal: such is the place of parting out of which arises the incident that introduces the apostrophe to the imagination. Thus, the knowledge of a different sadness which this incident is to make known would appear to arise within a sequence whose ostensible function is to precipitate the imagination out of an inability to experience an anticipated event. From the unfathering of this anticipation, the imagination is to be made known. Such at least would be the pattern affirmed by a proleptic reading of this passage, a reading that fits the rise of the imagination into the vacancy generated by an anticipation (crossing the Alps) that could not be met at the place where its external and historical existence is meant to reside. With the departure of their guide, Wordsworth and his companion would appear to be already part of this sequence since, to the extent that the guide acted as the father of their steps, they would now, in effect, be unfathered. A parting of this nature is not, however, to be confused with the cause of their missing the point at which the Alps ought to be crossed. Indeed, this parting makes explicit the figurative role played by a guide who stands in the place of a future. In other words, such a guide promises to lead to a synthesis of anticipation and incident, that is, the guide promises to realize the meaning anticipated by every figure. This does not mean that the departure of the guide is synonymous with the departure of something literal. Rather, it is the departure of what sustains anticipation. From this departure, there arises that mode of figuration from which the literal is derived.

In the Simplon Pass passage, this structure of guidance would allow whatever comes afterward to be recognized as occupying the place of whatever went before. As such, this passage is organized around a structural relation from which no historical writing can claim exception. However, with the departure of the guides this structure undergoes an unbinding. As a result of this unbinding, Wordsworth and his companion arrive at a torrent that effectively thwarts the possibility of experiencing the event they so anticipate. From this summary, it can be seen that the passage to this torrent is no mere descriptive narrative but rather a movement toward the unavoidable necessity of reading the landscape in Wordsworth, a necessity that is the immediate consequence of the departure of a guide:

> Hastily rose our guide,
> Leaving *us* at the board; awhile we lingered,
> Then paced the beaten downward way that led
> Right to a rough stream's edge, and there broke off;
> The only track now visible was one
> That from the torrent's brink held forth

> Conspicuous invitation to ascend
> A lofty mountain.
>
> (1850, 6:566–73)

Both the downward slope and the tracks beaten into the landscape now serve as a guide which leads to a breaking off formed by the edge of a stream whose roughness would indicate the uncertainty of its course. It is the roughness of this edge that not only brings to a halt the "beaten downward way" but also, this edge halts the mode of reading that leads Wordsworth and his companion to the stream in the first place. In order to proceed without a guide, Wordsworth and his companion must distinguish the course of their future steps from the landscape that faces them. In the absence of their guide, this distinction involves reading, not the landscape itself, but rather, the path which cuts across that landscape.

Since the discernment of this path is based on a marking beaten into the ground by the feet of those who have already passed, what Wordsworth and his companion read at this moment would be the traces of history. These traces, written into the landscape, are now read as promising an overcoming of their first "halting" as well as an overcoming of the departure of their guide. At the same time, this promise transforms the marks made in this landscape in order to produce a place from which a knowledge of history can be originated. Since this transformation takes place in the name of history, the path or line through which it is enabled would also anticipate the role played by a border in establishing the historical knowledge so crucial to the sense of anticlimax that precipitates the sudden rise of the imagination. Thus, the border and the path are alike in their effect; both would facilitate a passage through the Simplon Pass since both are predicated upon a knowledge of the difference between what comes (or goes) before and what goes (or comes) after. In the case of the "beaten downward way," this knowledge is only produced once the marking on the face of the landscape is read as possessing a linearity from which the knowledge that something went before is derived. By means of this linearity, and despite the departure of their guide, Wordsworth and his companion still retain a form of guidance. However, since this marking of the "beaten downward way" is effectively an inscription on the landscape, it belongs, first and foremost, to the mode of articulation shared by both writing and human speech. As such, this marking participates in the sadness that underscores this whole episode. Hence, what sustains the prospect of history in the linearity of this path is an understanding of both writing and human speech *as* marking the very difference that grounds the possibility of historical knowledge. Not only would this understanding of writing and human speech relate past and present (as in the case of this "beaten downward way") but it would assert the difference between language and the historical in such a way that language (as an incompetent vehicle of meaning) would always be history's figure for itself.

The temporal ordering of before and after which the linear reading of the "beaten downward way" reinstates is halted by the torrent. This halting occurs in such a way that the notion of linearity or path which promises the attainment of history is unable to sustain that promise whether it be understood as an event (crossing the Alps) or as the tracing of a past through the footsteps of the departed guide. This inability arises precisely because the torrent is indifferent to the relation between what went before (the guide) and what comes after (Wordsworth and his companion). As a result, if they are not to be "halted without an effort to break through," then, the kind of reading of the landscape which led Wordsworth and his companion to the "rough stream's edge" is once more demanded. In this instance, the border produced by the torrent's brink hardly marks the loss of their way but rather signals the possibility of their continued anticipation of an ascent: across the border of the torrent, "from the torrent's brink" a track is perceived, "the only track now visible." This track which again cuts across the landscape is, however, read as more than a simple track, it is read as a "conspicuous invitation to ascend / A lofty mountain." The track is addressed as if it were inviting Wordsworth and his companion with the promise of a site at which a border and a crossing may be recognized. As such, it would appear to continue the temporal ordering of before and after through which the historical event anticipated by this episode is maintained.[23]

To accept the invitation of the "only track now visible" requires, however, that the difference between before and after can no longer be derived from a temporal source. To continue along the path visible on the other side of the torrent is to reverse the positions occupied by, on the one hand, what went before (the guides), and, on the other, what is guided or comes after (Wordsworth and his companion). This reversal appears in a rather banal way when Wordsworth and his companion read the invitation of the ascending track as offering the possibility of "overtak[ing] / Our comrades gone before" (1850, 6:576–77). Through such a reading, Wordsworth and his companion envisage that they will effectively take the place of their guides since, by overtaking them, they would actually occupy the place of guidance. However, as this episode makes clear, Wordsworth and his companion will not overtake their guides. As a result, the formal arrangement that allowed sadness to be substituted for pleasure is also halted with this crossing. Accordingly, what occurs in this passage cannot be restricted to a simple game in which one position is exchanged or substituted (even arbitrarily) for another. As will become clear, a more complex understanding is unfolding within these lines from *The Prelude*. Such an understanding does not require the divorce of language and history nor does it enlist a formal understanding of language as a means of deconstructing an equally formal model of history. To trace this understanding, one must recall why the ascending path on the other side of the torrent is taken.

To this point, Wordsworth and his companion appear to act in accordance to a historical model based on linear continuity. This model demands that they should continue to ascend yet, when confronted by the torrent, the decision to cross and ascend has nothing to do with either this expectation or with the expressed hope of overtaking their departed guides. Here, it is important to remember what is stated first in the sentence which describes the situation in which Wordsworth and his companion have arrived. They take the path that ascends because it is "the only track now visible." The fact that this path ascends (and so meets their expectation) occupies a place of secondary importance:

> *The only* track now visible was one
> That from the torrent's brink held forth
> Conspicuous invitation to ascend
> A lofty mountain.
>
> (1850, 6:570–73; my emphasis)

Not only is the ascent secondary but this path is not related in any explicit way to the anticipated event that guides this episode: it leads to *a* lofty mountain but not necessarily *the* border whose crossing overshadows this episode. Moreover, they proceed along this track because it is the only path available to them. As a result, the historical event envisaged by their intention of "overtak[ing] / [Their] comrades" is derived from a crossing which by itself gives no reason for such historical optimism. The path is taken simply because it is there. Accordingly, when they cross the torrent, Wordsworth and his companion depart from the sequence that had served as their guide and they do so by attempting to continue that sequence. For this sequence to be possible, they must place a bridge where there is in fact no bridge but only the hope that the figurative bridge they have built will be justified by their subsequent arrival at a border. However, such a hope as well as the model of history it espouses are discounted in the language used to describe this scene.

The words adopted by this passage emphasize a landscape that affords no physical relation between the path taken and the path about to be taken—even after noting the "conspicuous invitation," that is, the bridge on which this continuation hangs, the joining of the two paths is described as "crossing the unbridged stream" (1850, 6:574). Since the relation that sustains the future promise of a border has no correlation in nature, any continuation of the path already taken will be predicated upon the inability to know whether or not there is a necessary relation between what came before and what is supposed to happen after the crossing. Consequently, the sole justification for persisting with the historical model that guides their steps prior to the torrent lies in a future that holds out the promise of a place where the border, its crossing, and, therefore, historical knowledge may all coincide. But, because this promise cannot be derived from what occasioned it, there arises another model of history. This second model derives its knowledge from what would negate the former's continuity. Rather than close the gap between itself and the event or events it would overtake, this latter model effectively seeks to preserve such a gap as its own reward. Through this gap it becomes possible to regard the landscape as a competent form of human speech (it offers a "conspicuous invitation") since such a gap preserves the possibility (and only the possibility) of a historical relation between language and event. In this respect, Wordsworth and his companion proceed by adopting a model of history which is strictly analogous to that negativity which controls the figurative usurpation of human speech in the apostrophe to the imagination. Yet, prior to the apostrophe, this model preserves less a historical experience (crossing the Alps) than a language whose history is drowned by the apocalyptic claims of the apostrophe. Instead of permitting Wordsworth and his companion to overtake the "comrades" who had gone before, the "only track now visible" leads to the origin of all address and all invitation: instead of mounting a lofty mountain, never mind mounting to a border, Wordsworth and his companion mount to the mouth of a peasant.

Where Three Paths Meet

> *An ancient servant of my father's house*
> *Was with me, my encourager and guide.*
>
> —Wordsworth, *The Prelude*

Following the noon-tide meal, this episode involves a movement which progresses from guides who remain mute (the muleteers, the "beaten downward way," the "only track now visible" and its "conspicuous invitation") to a source of guidance that finally speaks. Through this speech Wordsworth and his companion come to know that the crossing they had sought is not to be experienced as an event. Accordingly, the words of the peasant will demand particular attention since it is in such a "human speech" that their relation to history will be exemplified. It is reported:

> A peasant met us, from whose mouth we learned
> That to the spot which had perplexed us first
> We must descend, and there should find the road,
> Which in the stony channel of the stream
> Lay a few a steps, and then along its banks;
> And that our future course, all plain to sight,
> Was downwards, with the current of that stream.
>
> (1850, 6:579–85)

From this mouth, Wordsworth and his companion learn that by returning to where they have just been they may reassume their place on the path already taken by their guides. It would now appear that their recovery from error is solely a matter of recognizing a landscape that had been concealed by the rising of the stream. Here, again, the downward course of the landscape is instrumental in the recognizing that their previous reading of the landscape (first as a "beaten downward way" and then as an "invitation") had led them into error. In this instance, the return of the landscape as a guide suggests that their previous error may be attributed to something hidden or otherwise missed. The error in this example does not, however, arise because something is hidden or missing. Nor does it arise "like some unfathered vapour." Rather, it arises from a mode of reading which proceeds as if the paths crossing the surface of the landscape could now be linked to a meaning that was not in error. This mode of reading is reasserted with such assurance that it is easy to forget the swollen stream and "conspicuous invitation" which had prevented Wordsworth and his companion from recognizing that their future course was downward. Like the "misreading" that offers so conspicuous an invitation, this recognition still takes as its reference the anticipated crossing that has so far guided their every step. Now, as before, the physical inclination of a landscape serves as the means to posit the difference associated with a border: after meeting the peasant, what is seen (a way down—"with the current of that stream") promises a site for what was not seen (a border already missed) and, prior to this meeting when they stand perplexed at the "rough stream's edge," what is seen (a way up—across the torrent to the peasant's mouth) promises both a site as well as the sight of what is not yet seen. Each instance involves a mode of reading that relates what is seen to what *is* not seen. However, in the language used after meeting with the peasant, this relation takes the form of equating what is *now* seen with what *was* not seen. What sanctions this shift in tense? What in fact is now seen that could not be seen before?

Within the overall course of this episode, what can now be seen should be the place of the missed crossing. Consequently, what is essential to the relation between a path that now proceeds unambiguously downward and the place of the missed crossing is the uncovering of the torrent as a place of connection. In other words the stream must be returned to its borders if the missed crossing is not only going to be uncovered but be uncovered as something that was missed. What must then be obtained is an ability to distinguish between error and history. Since history can only be said to have a past as a result of its knowledge of error, the crucial question that history must answer is a question about its ability to know error. In the context of this episode, the question is directed at how Wordsworth and his companion trace a path through the torrent.

While the recognition of the site of the torrent as a place of error asserts the possibility of arriving at the knowledge of a border which *was* missed and therefore continues to be unseen, this possibility may only be asserted by means of what *is* also unseen: the conjunction of paths concealed by the torrent. One unseen (the conjunction of paths) leads to another (the border). In this respect, to know the crossing of the Alps as a historical moment (rather than, say, a place to have lunch) is to define history according to an understanding that not only views language as naming something absent from sight but also makes the recognition of an absence the precondition of any historical knowledge. As the course of this meeting with the peasant makes clear, such a language-based model of history permits the future (which would also be absent if it were not for language) to be spoken of as if it were the past. And, indeed, it is such a possibility that allows what is described as a "future course . . . all plain to sight" to become the source of a knowledge of error. The future must be known as history if the missed crossing is going to have any historical existence. But, if this future is to be known as if it were history, Wordsworth and his companion would have to be already in sight of the road that proceeds "with the current of that stream." The only thing which is "all plain to sight" to Wordsworth and his companion at this juncture is the future learned from the words of the peasant since, what the peasant says cannot yet be seen. The peasant, we are told, says that the road may only be found, that is, seen, once Wordsworth and his companion descend to the site of their perplexity. But in the words of the peasant, the very fact of descending is no guarantee of finding or seeing the road. The peasant is reported as saying that they "*should* find the road." This use of what is *formally* the past tense of shall as an auxiliary for "find" is not simply a substitute for "would." Here, "should" does not indicate that the road will be found on condition of having descended to the site of perplexity but rather it may express the expectation that they *ought to be able* to find the road. The necessity of descending (they are told they "*must* descend") is thus qualified with an uncertainty about whether or not this descent can alone assure that the road will be seen and that a spot which had perplexed them first will be prevented from perplexing them a second time. What then is the necessity of the descent?

The descent to the site of their perplexity demands the exact retracing of their detour. Inasmuch as this meeting with the peasant causes Wordsworth and his companion to turn back upon themselves, it would produce a reflexive turn. The effect of this reflexive movement is to return Wordsworth and his companion to a path structured according to a mimetic understanding—in two senses; first, the course of the descent mirrors exactly the course of the ascent to the peasant's mouth, and second, the words of the peasant come to be regarded as a reflection of the past. At the same time, this reflexive turn is itself dependent upon a mimetic understanding of what the peasant says even though what the words of the peasant imitate cannot be known at the time of the meeting. Consequently, in these lines, a mimetic understanding is recovered by means of a reflexive turn occasioned by a speaking which could not yet be known as either mimetic or non-mimetic. This return to the mimetic is thus occasioned by a return to what *ought to have happened* and, as such, it marks a return to a path whose course would be controlled by its past (this course being the reflection of what ought to have happened as the imitation of what happened). The reflexive role assigned to the peasant is crucial in producing this return to the mimetic course. Yet, more than just a return to the mimetic is implicated here. Since any return to a mimetic understanding is predicated upon a knowledge of error (telling the difference between true and false imitation), it will also involve a return to the possibility of historical knowledge (to know what mimesis presents is to know what precedes or could precede this mimesis).[24] Consequently, the response of Wordsworth and his companion to the words of the peasant must give rise to an ability to distinguish between a figurative and a literal use of language.

When Wordsworth and his companion retrace their steps back to the place of their former perplexity, they do so because they can now read the torrent as if it were a veil, a figure whose literal significance is known even though it still remains hidden by the swelling of the waters. Thanks to this unveiling which amounts to a virtual receding of these swollen waters, the torrent is subsequently referred to as a "stream," or "brook." Although the word "torrent" will be used once more in the course of this episode (but only after Wordsworth and his companion have crossed out of the Simplon Pass), this use reasserts the identity of the stream over and above the swelling that produced a torrent. Accordingly, the torrent is now looked upon as if it were merely a perversion arising from an external source which belongs to the past—as the tense of the following phrase confirms: "a torrent swelled / The rapid stream" (1850, 6:643–44).[25] This substitution through which the stream is recovered is absolutely necessary if history is to remain a form of knowledge since, if one were to wait for the event which would reveal what the torrent veils then one must endure an apocalypse and its attendant erasure of not just history but, more important, the possibility of history. Lest this comment be understood apocalyptically, it should be made clear that the "end of history" does not bring history to an end. Like "the mighty flood of the Nile" and its discourse upon the landscape, an apocalypse marks the advent of history as an erasure of the past: the receding of the flood which marks such an event also erases how the landscape would have been marked.[26] What the discourse of history knows about and refers to as (its) past is yet to be known and this is as true in the case of an actual apocalypse as it is in the case of a figurative one "occurring" in the linguistic substitution of word for event. The possibility of history would thus center upon the question of how history may attain a knowledge of what ought to happen, that is, how it may attain knowledge of a past which cannot yet be said to have occurred. For such a knowledge to occur, it now appears that the advent of history must be preceded by not only the return of the mimetic but also, this return must be grounded in a reflexive structure which is derived from the error of the mimetic understanding it gives rise to.

As the account of what is learned from the peasant unfolds, the relation of historical knowledge and mimesis to a reflexive moment would be located in the recognition of a difference which the landscape is now understood as both pointing toward and reflecting, namely, the site of the Simplon Pass. On the strength of this recognition, the reflexive turn taken by Wordsworth and his companion may be viewed as providing the source as well as confirmation of the mimetic understanding that now leads them back to the torrent. The ability of this reflexive turn to be a source of mimetic understanding relies less upon the way in which "stream" and "road" are defined in relation to one another within the language used to recall the peasant's words. Instead of a difference that allows stream and path to go in separate directions, the "future course" defines a path that parallels exactly the course of the "stream" or "brook." Hence, from a track that cuts across the course of a torrent ("*Right* to a rough stream's edge"), the passage moves to a road that is most like the course of a stream (the road to be taken is "with the current of that stream" and "along its banks"). The emergence of this parallel follows immediately upon the renaming of what was previously known as a "rough stream" and then as a "torrent." This renaming finds its justification in the emergence of a relation between the road and the stream in which one is seen to determine the course of the other. This reflection of the road by the stream and vice versa is crucial since, without it, their subsequent course, although downward, would lack any specific guidance and would therefore repeat the perplexity occasioned by the torrent. Consequently, this episode emphasizes that the source of the knowledge that the crossing of the border was missed is to be found in a landscape that has been invested with both mimetic and reflexive properties.

The channeling of this passage toward such a relation indicates the extent to which the knowledge of having crossed the Alps relies upon a difference determined within an exclusive parallelism. Indeed, this parallelism is so constrained that it would understand the mimetic and the reflexive in terms of one another, that is, as capable of being substituted for each other (the self-reflexive being the movement through which the self imitates itself as itself). What is at stake in this "future course" is therefore not just the chiasmatic relation of the road to the stream but the chiasmatic definition of the very terms used to describe this relation. Since the whole passage to the historical knowledge that Wordsworth and his companion "had crossed the Alps" depends on the interrelation of a reflexive moment and a mimetic sequence, then, the configuration of path and road within what is referred to after the apostrophe to the imagination as first a "narrow chasm" (1850, 6:621), and, second, as a "narrow rent" (1850, 6:627) becomes the crucial moment that enables this historical knowledge to arise. It is precisely the placing of this chiasmatic relation in the "chasm" which produces an understanding of difference, albeit a difference restricted to the determination of parallelism and analogy. Not only does this difference enable the discourse of the torrent to be crossed with the course of a path *and* a stream, but, through the determination of this difference, the figurative model of a border, now recognized as having been missed, *will have been* produced.

That such a border is to be recognized through this relation of road to stream is clearly stated in a passage following the apostrophe to the imagination. Here, the difference between "road" and "stream" is named a margin:

> That night our lodging was a house that stood
> Alone within the valley, at a point
> Where, tumbling from aloft, a torrent swelled
> The rapid stream whose margin we had trod . . .
>
> (1850, 6:641–44)

Through the repetition of this difference, this margin, at the site of perplexity and then at the place of the "noon-tide meal," Wordsworth and his companion would cross out the conjunction that produced a "conspicuous invitation to ascend" and, in so doing, they would cross the perplexity of a torrent in which no distinction of path and stream, before and after, what was and what will be, could be discerned. The difference repeated through this sequence is constitutive of historical discourse; it is a difference that belongs to this discourse and, as such, would constantly remark an analogy between what it says and what it is about: what came after understood as what came before.

Still, it should not be overlooked that, in the course of this passage, the chiasmus of path and road, reflection and mimesis, which grounds such a difference results from what is called a "narrow rent" (what is referred to as the "narrow chasm" serves as the entrance to this "rent"). The analogy of road to path on which so much depends is thus the product of a rent, of a place where a tearing has given rise to a difference. Moreover, the analogy located in the place of this tearing is precisely what leads to the possibility of apostrophizing the imagination: not only is the sought-after border recognized as having been missed through such an analogy but the apostrophe rises in the place produced by the knowledge of such an absence. In this way, one border (formed by the stream and the path) produces the figurative path leading to the recognition of the border that will mark the crossing of the Alps and the rise of the imagination. Yet, for this crossing to be known in its absence, that is, for history to arise, the conjunction that gives rise to the relation of reflection to mimesis must be concealed in the interest of uncovering such a "border" path.[27]

As the description of the path down the Gondo Gorge indicates, any concealment of this conjunction requires that it will always be "rent" by an analogy. However, the analogy which produces this path leading to the knowledge that the Alps had been crossed is not simply the difference between a path and a road. Rather, the conjunction of paths which connects the "future course" to the site of a border would be like a place where three paths meet and, as such, would be like that exemplary place where unfathering and usurpation are so closely interrelated: the paths at Phocis. Without this conjunction, the passage in the "narrow rent" would remain an accident of nature and, accordingly, could not give rise to any knowledge of a border—it is not enough that this passage is downward as the course taken after the noon-tide meal makes clear (a "beaten downward way"). A course that was downward must be joined to a path that will continue downward if any knowledge of a border and hence of its crossing is to be arrived at. Indeed, without the knowledge of a third path different from the one up to the peasant's mouth and thus different from the path taken after the "noon-tide meal," then, to all intents and purposes, the Alps have not yet been crossed. The possibility of a place where three paths meet is therefore essential to this crossing. Whether or not this meeting actually occurs beneath the torrent is irrelevant. It is the possibility as well as the thought of such a meeting that is crucial.

As this passage indicates, historical knowledge of the border and its crossing requires a place that is *like* a place of unfathering and it does so in order to relate what came before to what comes after and thereby possess a history. The *Oedipus* of Sophocles is no exception to this requirement. Oedipus can only have a history after eradicating the perplexity of the past through the figure of a father. Yet, as in this passage, the recognition of such a place and such a usurpation is linked to a knowledge of error. To posit a place where three paths meet is to assert that what precedes the torrent is the meaning which allows the site of perplexity to be read as a site of error. Here, meaning would reside in a place of unfathering through which the past is joined to the present even though there is no certainty that the site of perplexity can or cannot be known as such a place. Indeed, to read this site as a place of unfathering rather than like a place where three paths meet is to usurp the torrent with a history, in this case, a literary history whose preference for parricide would avoid the question of whether or not Laius is the father of Oedipus.[28] At every juncture of this kind, it would seem preferable to recognize the murder of a "father" and have a knowable error to claim than to face the randomness of a discursive account whose conjunctions make it impossible to know whether or not an unfathering took place. To recognize an unfathering is thus to assert a continuity by substituting a misreading which can at least be known as a misreading in the place of this randomness. The whole possibility of this continuity rests upon the ability to know that the parricide where three paths meet as well as the crossing of the "rough stream" may be excused as errors. In addition, to recognize this conjunction as a misreading or error, is to insist upon a means of recognizing a knowledge that existed prior to this misreading, a knowledge that would not be in error. For this recognition to take place, what is discerned in such a prior position must now appear as what ought to have been known. Yet, if the recognition of what ought to have been known is to be called history then whatever has the status of an event or occurrence must be constantly usurped by a future if it is to have any existence at all. Such is the condition of historicity: history is what will have happened in order to know what was not known as an occurrence.

In the case of the Simplon Pass episode, what is unfathered as a result of recognizing a site where three paths are said to meet is the misreading which makes such a recognition possible, a misreading that is unfathered by the reading it gives rise to. Error is, in effect, unfathered in order to produce knowledge of itself as error as well as knowledge of what was concealed in this error. By virtue of this usurpation, there arises a crossing through which the border is recovered as if it were something that belonged to the past, that is, as if it were to be understood as possessing the same kind of existence as a physical or natural object in the landscape. Yet, this "crossing" remains unable to verify that the border it leads to can be derived from or even attain the status of a natural object that exists prior to the discourse in which it is recognized. As the climb to the

Simplon Pass makes abundantly clear, there is no necessary connection between the landscape and a border (if there were such a relation, the border could always be known at the moment it is crossed). In this respect, the border will always be the effect of a geography (*geo-graphein*). What is spoken or written about as having taken place before (i.e., what was) can have no past significance except as the result of this inscription.

In order to bypass this "before" which was never historically prior, the link to the past is produced as a relation that ought not to be inquired into. It is at this point that the topos of unfathering plays its most crucial role because what is unfathered—in the sense of possessing no antecedent—is precisely what cannot be inquired into. The interdiction that sustains this bypass is most clearly figured in the apostrophe to the imagination when the conjunction "like," which introduces the simile "like an unfathered vapour," is preceded by the phrase "rose from the mind's abyss." Here, the "unfathered vapour" is given a place from which it can derive a likeness, a place that is figured as an abyss. The crucial crossing of the torrent is described similarly. Wordsworth and his companion not only pursue a "beaten downward way" that "*broke off*" at the torrent but the continuation of their path is said to proceed from the "torrent's further *brink*." To speak of the origin of likeness and analogy in these terms is to ground these forms of mimesis in a physical feature that would force a halting to take place. Yet, instead of producing a halting, the abyss described in these lines is what bridges the torrent despite the latent threat, sublime or otherwise, that would accompany the presence of either an abyss or a chasm in this context. Abyss or chasm, what would be without ground belongs, in this way, to the place where knowledge rises—as the apostrophe to the imagination makes clear when it attributes such an abyss to the mind ("That awful Power rose from the mind's abyss / Like an unfathered vapour"). In its interdiction of further progress, the abyss, as a place of unfathering, would give rise to a reflexive turning back which necessitates that any further progression take place under the guidance of a mode of figuration that would now know the abyss as a place of interrelation. In this respect, the reflexive turn occasioned by an abyss is, strictly speaking, the return *of* mimesis, that is, it is the means through which mimesis simultaneously turns away from and guards the question of its own origin. Such a turn determines the possibility of this questioning as a path that cannot be taken. The interdiction of the abyss would thus become an unfathering produced by the very mimesis it is said to originate. At the same time, this interdiction would give rise to the possibility as well as the necessity of a mode of figuration which would act as the transport *of* meaning. What was an interdiction now appears as the origin of a mode of interrelation through which the past and the future are connected to one another. Yet, if this interdiction is to become such a mode of interruption then the abyss would have to be understood as an effect of the reflexive turn it gives rise to. Only by positing such an abyss can the turning back performed by this reflexive movement be justified. However, what is in fact posited at this moment is not an abyss but the figure of an abyss. Consequently, the abyss arises from the very mimesis it is supposed to give rise to. The characterization of the abyss as a figure without origin serves as a means of concealment for a mimesis only too willing to avoid inquiring into its own origin, its own historicity.

Echo and the Incidence of History

> *I was left alone*
> *Seeking the visible world, nor knowing why.*
> —Wordsworth, *The Prelude*

> In der Einsamkeit.—*Wenn man allein lebt, so spricht man nicht zu laut, man schreibt auch nicht zu laut: denn man fürchtet den hohlen Widerhall—die Kritik der Nymph Echo.—Und alle Stimmen klingen anders in der Einsamkeit!*
> —Nietzsche, *Die fröhliche Wissenschaft*

The production of an abyss or even a chasm through which a knowledge of the border is arrived at is itself a prefiguring of the movement that allows the rising of the imagination to be recognized in the apostrophe (the movement from "I was lost" to "I now can say"). While such a movement would mark a recovery from the rise of the imagination, its occurrence in Wordsworth's recounting of why the torrent was crossed indicates the necessity of a break between the apostrophe and the descriptive passage that precedes it.

Only through such a break can the imagination and the recognition of its glory even begin to assume the critical significance it has received. The break would excuse the apostrophe from any explicit relation to or repetition of a history of missed events. In the passage from "I was lost" to "I now can say," however, the apostrophe adopts the very same juxtaposition of "now" and "was" that was instrumental in giving a historical sense to an event that could not otherwise have had a history: the crossing of the Alps. The prior occurrence of this juxtaposition in the passage describing the ascent of Wordsworth and his companion to the peasant emphasizes that the apostrophe should be read in conjunction with the external scene that it seems to interrupt and leave behind so successfully. Indeed, through this conjunction, the recognition of the glory of the imagination is taken back to the torrent whose interruption of the path first elicits the temporal juxtaposition of "now" and "was." The lines in which this juxtaposition first occurs are the very lines which, thanks to the peasant's words, were subsequently recognized as a source of error: "The only track *now* visible *was* one / That from the torrent's further brink held forth / Conspicuous invitation to ascend / A lofty mountain" (1850, 6:570–73; emphasis mine). The pivotal importance of the conjunction of "was" and "now" to this whole episode is underlined by the unchanged recurrence, in both the 1805 and 1850 texts as well as the intervening manuscripts, of this line ("The only track now visible was one") which recalls a visible reason for such a crossing. This conjunction of a past tense and a temporal adverb specifying the present occurs in a passage written as if it were providing a narrative account of past events. At the same time, this juxtaposition of an adverb that speaks of the present and a verb that speaks of the past indicates the presence of a predicament which prompts this temporal disjunction. This predicament could easily have been concealed and the phrase "The only track now visible was one" rendered with greater narrative and temporal consistency if the text were simply a recounting of history. If this were so, then the line ought to read "The only track *then* visible was one" or even "The only track visible was one." Since this concealment does not in fact occur, there arises the question of why Wordsworth consistently writes "now" if the line really ought to mean "then" whether or not this word actually appears? What does it mean to say that something was now?

The presence of this "now" insists that this "external" passage in the Simplon Pass episode should not be read as a narrative whose historical status can be taken for granted—to do so would be to set the stage for the imagination to arise in the wake of an anticlimax whose occurrence would affirm the attainment of historical knowledge. Nor can this "now" be spirited away by protesting that it is a residue arising from the time at which this episode is written since then Wordsworth would have to write as if what had been learned from the peasant's mouth could be irretrievably forgotten. To assert that the "now" results from the time of composition is therefore to assert that the meeting with the peasant need never have taken place despite the fact that this meeting is absolutely necessary if any return to the path of mimesis and history is to be entertained. Nor can this passage be disposed of by making the absence of such a distinction become the means to locate the whole passage within the conscious, that is, the recollecting self of a poet who would now say "the only track visible was one." The difficulty repeated in each of these readings arises, first of all, from the failure of what would stand as the empirical source of historical knowledge (the landscape) and, second, from the inability of experience to take the place of that failure. Indeed, as even the phrasing of the line "The *only* track *now* visible was *one*" makes clear, the resort to experience (such as that possessed by the poet in hindsight or even by the reader of *The Prelude*) will not go very far in this episode. The use of "now" in this description of why the torrent was crossed can only be accounted for by resorting to an external source. (Even if the words of the peasant had not yet been reached, the phrasing of this line would indicate knowledge of another track and thereby a source for such knowledge at a time different from the meeting with the torrent—this indication of an external source may be remarked most clearly if a merely descriptive and recollective version of this line [i.e., "The only track . . . visible was one / That from the torrent's further brink held forth"] is again compared to what Wordsworth writes.) Thus, it is again to the peasant's mouth that one is led, a mouth that must be questioned again and again if the relation of "now" to "was" which consistently articulates this episode (not to mention *The Prelude*) is not to be unfathered in a reflexive structure whose temporal source cannot be seen.

While Wordsworth's narrative account of this episode enlists a peasant as an external source, what the peasant is reported to say does little to alleviate the temporal disjunction that demanded such a source. In Wordsworth's account, the peasant speaks of the future as if it were the past. The text reads: "A peasant met us, from whose mouth we learned . . . our *future* course . . . / *Was* downwards" (1850, 6:579–85; emphasis mine). The employment of this past tense in conjunction with a future may be accounted for by referring, once again, to the time of writing (that is, it arises merely because Wordsworth is looking back upon what is now known as the future). However, this account effectively ignores why this episode recounts an attempt to speak of a past (the passage down the Gondo Gorge) not only as if it *were* the future but also to speak of the past by recounting an incident in which this future could not yet have the status of a historical event or occurrence. Such an elision depends wholly upon deriving this passage from a future which is recognized as the (now past) time of its writing. Only through this recourse to the time of writing can the historicity of what is written be guaranteed. In other words, only by substituting a historical subject for a written text is it possible to speak of a future at the time of this incident, a future which has not yet happened but which, because of this association, becomes the guarantee of a past that ought to have happened (crossing the Alps and proceeding down the Gondo Gorge).

This recourse to a historical subject possesses considerable interpretive power; however, this power may only be bought at the price of asserting that the true significance of *The Prelude* lies in a constant recall of its own writing, its own production. Such a *Prelude* would always remember that it remembers and, accordingly, it would always remember that, in the last instance, its writing was (and is) about its writing (as if every perplexity could be avoided, concealed, missed by enwrapping it in some self-reflexive relation, as if every example of writing *were* known to be about its writing). Indeed, this recourse to the time of writing as a key to interpreting this passage demands nothing less than the positing of a self-reflexive relation as the condition of arriving at any historically coherent account of a "future course [which] . . . / Was downwards." This account would be as descriptive of the temporal relation of Wordsworth to the subject of *The Prelude* as it would be of the critical discourse eager to discover its own history, never mind affirm its ability to recognize history in such a work. But, what this positing of a self-reflexive relation turns away from as it seeks to learn its own history is in fact the question of learning. In particular, the question of what *is* learned from the mouth of the peasant as well as the question of what can be learned from the writing that records this learning. In the context of these questions, the conjunction of "future course" with "was" is crucial since to speak of this course in the past tense is to speak of a future that can only be recognized as the future because it would already be known in terms of the past. To know that some event or act may be referred to in the name of the future is to speak of the future as if it were already history: as the past would be known the future will always be known. But, if the future is to be known in the same way as the past, is the past any better a historical guide than the future? What Wordsworth reflects most explicitly at this point in the Simplon Pass episode is that the future is always the source of historical knowledge. As such, the future is less a temporal category than a general name for the possibility of history.

If historical knowledge is derived from the future, then, as this episode unfolds, the *Alps* could never have been crossed at the time of the noon-tide meal; the Alps are only crossed through the words of a peasant which are *then* recognized as taking the place of such a crossing. Not only does this substitution produce what is called history but, at the same time, it defines the present as a temporal or spatial gap. In the terms of the Simplon Pass episode, this gap is synonymous with the sense of anticlimax which offers a conspicuous invitation to transcend history in the form of an apostrophe to the imagination. As long as this apostrophe is read as a response to the historical knowledge of crossing the Alps, it can only rise from a gap marked as the past (even though its existence is an effect of a present that must be displaced into the past). In other words, history is to be produced by literalizing "now" in the place of "was." Since this literalization occurs through a substitution, what is known as the literal is derived from the figuration of the future.[29] Thus, what is at stake in this recounting of a passage across the Alps is not simply the possibility of deriving the difference of past and present but the possibility of history as a mode of figuration. As we have already seen, knowledge of a missed crossing is the most crucial element in establishing history as a figure for the past. As we have also seen, this episode's account of what the peasant says is instrumental in uncovering a missed crossing as the source of historical knowledge in this episode. But is the peasant really the source of this uncovering?

More than anything else, the instances of unfathering repeated in the course of this episode (both in the discovery of a place where three paths meet and in the description of the imagination's rising) take for granted what can be learned from the peasant's mouth. They also ignore the question of learning posed in and through this mouth. The necessity of learning is crucial here since without it there could be no history, never mind mimesis. This does not mean that without learning all would be a mere metaphor without a past (and hence not even a metaphor since, at the very least, a metaphor requires something in whose place it may stand if it is even to be recognized as a metaphor). To assert that this mere figuration is the only possible alternative would be to unfather "human speech" in the name of a nominalism that would evade the question of reference by denying that it is even a question—a denial practiced equally by those who would assert reference as the means through which language and meaning meet. It is to the question of learning that the "external scene" of the Simplon Pass episode leads, and, as the encounter with the peasant's mouth teaches, the difficulty that arises in the attempt to arrive at a genuinely authentic knowledge of history cannot be so easily evaded or even so "utterly allayed."

The encounter with the peasant's mouth occurs as a meeting neither foreseen nor sought after ("A peasant met us"). This meeting has no recognizable place within the sequence of likeness and analogy which leads Wordsworth and his companion from the "only track now visible" to the conspicuous invitation that beckons from across the torrent. Yet, instead of fulfilling this invitation with the anticipated incident (arriving at the address of a border) this episode rises to the site of all address in the mouth of the peasant. At this point, there is no direct reference to human speech, language is figured as a mouth from which they "learned" what was "all plain to sight," a mouth that is not only visible but makes known something they were unable to see. The peasant's mouth, like the torrent, is a place that must be looked at as well as looked over if a "future course" is to be translated at all. But what is overlooked in such a translation is not only the human speech of this mouth but also the fact that this mouth marks the high point of this whole episode. Accordingly, it is a mouth, or, more precisely, the place from which human speech proceeds, that one must look for at the end of this episode's anticipatory structure (and therefore its figurative structure since anticipation is always a figuring of what cannot yet have literal meaning). As such, the peasant's mouth becomes, in effect, the pass that Wordsworth and his companion must traverse if the imagination is to arise at all. Still, this is not a pass that one may cross over or even through but rather a pass that one must turn away from. At the same time, this pass, like the torrent before it, is also a place of perplexity that one cannot break through but only pass over. Here, translation would effect a crossing over and out of a mouth that is made to speak across a twisting and turning, an interlacing of languages. Yet, the peasant's mouth is not a pass which would permit a like crossing unless what is said through turns (*per plexi*) is repeated across turns (*trans plexi*). A translation thus stands as the means to ground the mimetic consequences of the peasant's reflexive role. In this respect, reflexivity and mimesis, like the stream and road in the "narrow rent" become translations of one another. But, if this translation is to take place, what comes out of the peasant's mouth must be regarded as the place in which a former literal pass may be recognized. While this mouth may become a figurative pass that allows Wordsworth and his companion to follow the narrow path that leads out of this passage, the physical turn which follows the production of such a pass is hardly coincident with the linguistic turns of this incident, in particular, with the perplexity of the translation on which this whole passage turns.

The perplexity and the question of likeness from which this mouth is inseparable is posed in the following lines:

> Loth to believe what we so grieved to hear,
> For still we had hopes that pointed to the clouds,
> We questioned him again and again;
> But every word that from the peasant's lips
> Came in reply, translated by our feelings,
> Ended in this,—*that we had crossed the Alps.*
>
> (1850, 6:586–91)

Hopes that pointed to the clouds end in a mouth which is now no longer seen but heard, a mouth which is given voice only after they have learned that their future course lies before them and only after they have realigned their reading of the landscape and its "beaten downward" ways. While the visual translation that precedes these lines could stand in the place of every word that came in reply to their repeated questioning, and, in so doing, act as its affirmation, the unfolding of this passage makes it clear that this is not the case. Instead of rushing to such a correlation between the landscape and what is heard, the visual gives way to what is grievous to hear, gives way to a hearing that had been effaced and would now be effaced again if the prior reading of the landscape were left to stand as that which is "all plain to sight," and, as if the words of the peasant were indeed to be more than like the landscape. In this conjunction of the visual with the heard, there would be more than an effacement of the speech that rises from the peasant's mouth; there would also be the effacement of a perplexity of likeness, the perplexity of a "like" that has been carried away in the constant return of an analogy between what comes before and what came after. And, nowhere would this return be more insistent than in the repeated acts of readdressing the landscape in order to facilitate a passage through this pass, acts which would replace what is grievous to hear with the discernible site of a border that can now be perceived as belonging to a past. Such a border ought to mark the missed high point—this point being an invitation to anticipate an ascent which was not met, an invitation to ascend to an address which could not be arrived at except by being addressed, that is, given an address by translating the actual high point of this episode (the "peasant's mouth") into its figurative high point (crossing the Alps).[30]

Through this transposition of language, the essential predicament articulating this episode would be forgotten as the peasant's mouth becomes secondary to the attraction of remembering a physical address. Yet, the location of this address can only be determined by asserting that what the peasant says not only gives a proper name to the "halting-place" of the "noon-tide meal" but also makes each of these names interchangeable with a border. From this sequence of substitutions, one border would emerge and upon this emergence the subsequent rise of the apostrophe to the imagination depends. To account for all this, what must arise in the mouth of the peasant is the origin of figuration. For this accounting to occur, such an origin must also posit a difference that corrects error, or, which amounts to the same thing, it must grant a knowledge of figurative language. Since this knowledge depends upon the discovery of an address for the "Simplon Pass" it would originate in a linguistic recrossing of what had never been crossed before. This recrossing and the prior crossing it anticipates are to occur through the same human speech, the speech of the peasant. But is this speech competent of such an occurrence? Does this speech possess no different sadness, a sadness which, devoid of pathos, cannot be *utterly* allayed? Does it produce, like an unfathered vapor, the coincidence which gives rise to a historical event or is it an incident which is only able to make known the necessity of history's imperative? "Let one incident make known. . . ."

The crossing-over produced through the peasant's mouth is termed a translation and as such it would be performed within a relation of likeness, a relation of before to after. Moreover, the regulation of address implied by this translation would be articulated according to a border, but this border can only be established through the very fact of a translation having taken place. But what is translated by Wordsworth and his companion? "*That we had crossed the Alps*"? For these words to say what the peasant said, they must be understood as one kind of crossing (translation) which speaks of another crossing (the particular historical event of crossing the border). Nonetheless, the crossing established by this translation is not a border in the sense of physical, historical division. Rather, it is the crossing of one address with another. Furthermore, this crossing takes place within a repetition that carries no necessary connection: an address (the peasant's words) is addressed (translated) to an address (the physical site of the Simplon Pass) which, at the very moment when it ought to have been a historical event, could not be recognized as like its address. Then and now, Wordsworth and his companion did not know how to address the address they sought and, as with the ascent to the peasant's mouth, this incompetence of address again marks a halting-place. The so-called external scene is thereby articulated by two halting-places: the first occurs in a disjunction between language and landscape, and, the second, in the disjunction between one language and another. There is, however, no essential difference between these two "halting-places" since they both arise from a disjunction which is proper to language. Also, the second "halting-place" cannot be regarded as if it were a singular definitive moment that may be attributed all the characteristics of a historical event. Instead, this latter halting occurs in the repetition of a questioning whose inability to address what the peasant says is reiterated by this very repetition ("We questioned him *again, and yet again*" [1850, 6:588; emphasis mine]).

What is repeated in this account of their meeting with the peasant is not simply ignorance of another language. Rather, what occurs is an unbridgeable halting that invites historical resolution. The repetition of this halting indicates, however, that language can only repeat its origin as an invitation to history which takes the form of an invitation to where three paths meet. Because of this halting, Wordsworth and the peasant address one another in words that do not know how to find their address either before the ascent to the pass, during the noon-tide meal, or, in the peasant's mouth. The halting that defines the speech of the peasant can hardly arise from a lack of meaning or even from an incompetency that dooms language to always miss what it means. Indeed, such a halting is the condition that allows a missed or missing meaning to be thinkable in the first place. Yet, even though this missed meaning would take the place of such a halting, it can only repeat this halting as the price that must be paid for a history that amounts to nothing more than a thinly disguised theory of how language may possess meaning. Consequently, rather than articulate a difference between language and some non-linguistic realm of event or act as the source of meaning, this passage is articulated by a halting which remains intralinguistic. It is to such a halting that the apostrophe is addressed, but not before the difficulty posed by this halting is brought to an unavoidable pass—if this pass were avoidable then one would have reached the point at which language is meant to be equivalent to the singularity of a historical act, which is to say, without reference of its own.

But, as this passage so amply indicates, the progress toward historical understanding, and, above all, the application of such an understanding to the lines preceding the apostrophe comes at a cost. In this episode, the cost of such understanding requires that the halting speech which gives rise to the repeated questioning by Wordsworth and his companion be brought to a close by nothing less than a deprivation of human speech effected through the closing of the peasant's mouth. This closing occurs at precisely the point that this passage moves from what was "all plain to sight" and turns to "every word that [came] from the peasant's lips." The passage proceeds by a movement from mouth to lips, the very movement that closes the mouth and, in so doing, focuses upon speech as the act of one lip bordering on to the other. In this way, there would arise a borderline in the place of address. An address that cannot be addressed is halted within the place from which it arises. This halting is not simply an act that closes the peasant's mouth, but, simultaneously, it allows whatever the peasant said to be sent to another address which, in this instance, is to be located in the feelings of Wordsworth and his companion. From this location, the address of the peasant is redirected yet again and placed in the mouth that did not know how to address the peasant's mouth except by closing it off and usurping the site of address. Yet, this halting of the peasant's halting speech is itself halted—which does not mean brought to an end—by its very emphasis on closing and ending.

The words of the peasant that are translated by feelings are only the endings of what the peasant is felt to say: "every word that from the peasant's lips / Came in reply, translated by our feelings, / Ended in this,—*that we had crossed the Alps*." Translated by these feelings, every word that the peasant utters ends in the same subordinate clause and it is only this subordinate ending which is repeated through this means of translation. What is removed is the speaking or saying of the peasant: the mouth is closed, the site of address unfathered so that the Alps may have been crossed. The Alps are crossed in a predicate whose source has been closed to questioning so that its subject may be posited. But, nowhere is it written that the peasant said "*that* [Wordsworth and his companion] *had crossed the Alps*." The repetition of an end emphasized by an unfathering of the peasant's mouth does not take place within a sequence that establishes this "translated" phrase as a predicate of the peasant. Rather, as this passage's repetition of the speech of Echo and Narcissus (the would-be subject of a repeated predicate) indicates, such a predicate belongs to a sequence of repetitions unable to affirm the semantic content of their conjunctions. In the case of this episode, it is not Wordsworth and his companion who would be the exact figures of Echo but rather the peasant. The peasant is the one who would be given speech as if he were speaking in his own words, however, he only attains such speech through the translation of Wordsworth and his companion. The peasant thus speaks as the echo of the words that Wordsworth and his companion say he said. However, these words are not the echo of something the peasant said nor, strictly speaking, are they the echo of what the peasant did not say. The words of Wordsworth and his companion would be an echo whose relation to what the peasant may or may not have said remains unknown. In other words, they are not even an echo despite the mythical narrative that one could find reworked here. Indeed, one cannot speak of an echo here since we do not know what the peasant's words are or were like, we are only given knowledge of what their likeness is like and it is precisely such a knowledge that would give an address to the border in the Simplon Pass. Yet, this is an address that would substitute a (visual) sight which is plain to see for a site which *was* not and which *is* not plain to see, the site of an address which again, through the sad incompetence of inadequate human speech, is made to be like what it addresses through translation. What such inadequacy conceals is its inability to know if there is indeed a relation, never mind a historical relation, between what it says and what was said. A historical discourse rests upon the possibility of there being such a relation since, within this discourse, what is said to be the past is a saying that ought to know what (it says) was. Or, to put this another way, it ought to know what was is. To echo the past or to echo what is said to be the past is no guarantee that such a knowledge does in fact arise—as if this knowledge could possess the singularity or punctuality of an event or act. The discourse of history cannot repeat the singularity of an event, rather it writes about the determined absence of its own subject. Without this absence being posited, no writing could unfold in the guise of history since, *then,* there is nothing for history to be about. Such a history would be in the position of a Narcissus who listens to an echo as if it were the voice of another. Rather than listen to an echo, history would listen to Echo; history would know the difference between Echo and echo.[31] Such a difference is no more decidable than the assumption that the words of Narcissus, once repeated, are addressed back to Narcissus. To know this difference would be to die in the pool of water with Narcissus (and without the benefit of ever knowing if what is heard were a repetition of one's own speech or the voice of another). It is the utter indestructibility of such a difference that would be overcome in an event which, like the crossing of the Alps, will always have been recognized. Such an indestructibility has a halting effect that thwarts the possibility of breaking through to where history was. And what is more indestructible here than language? Not even language can overcome its own indestructibility and arrive at history. Nor can Narcissus survive the piercing of reflection. For, what comes between Narcissus and (Narcissus? his echo? his history?) is a death, not an actual death but the death of an address, of somewhere to send (his? Wordsworth's? history's?) words. In this passage from *The Prelude,* the apostrophe to the imagination is already the address that the apostrophe would, but can never, address. Such is the sad incompetence of human speech and such is the sad difference that cannot be utterly allayed, cannot be allayed either *through* its uttering, or even in the pathos of sadness and its unfathered mourning—"there, there it is that sadness finds its fuel." There, there?

CHAPTER FOUR

History and the Primitive Theater
George Eliot

. . . un salon superbe tout resplendissant de lumière, dans lequel on ne peut parvenir qu'en passant par une longue et affreuse cuisine.

—Claude Bernard, *Introduction à l'étude de la médecine expérimentale*

By focusing on a work such as George Eliot's *Middlemarch,* this chapter would appear to turn from the context in which the critical questions posed by Aristotle, Coleridge, and Wordsworth can be so readily discerned. *Middlemarch* is not, after all, a text likely to follow Romanticism as a critical or theoretical proving ground.[1] The social, political, historical, and even scientific concerns of this novel do not seem to offer a friendly, or even conspicuous, invitation to the questions analyzed in the preceding chapters. Why would *Middlemarch* ever want to concern itself with the question of literary history, never mind how Aristotle develops such a question in the *Poetics?* Why would Eliot ever need to write a letter to herself to produce a deduction that no critical ventriloquy could justify? And why would Eliot ever need to develop a sense of history from a mouth whose intelligibility is restricted to its audibility? If Eliot had resorted to one or all of these examples in *Middlemarch,* there would be no need to read this novel in the context of the preceding chapters, since it would already be possible to conclude this study by repeating what has already been said. In such a case, *Middlemarch* would become the mimetic example, the mouth that speaks the truth of what has already been written, as well as an echo quite different from the one that can be heard at the end of the Simplon Pass. The turn to *Middlemarch* has quite a different motivation.

In the end, there is one evasion that can never be avoided: the evasion of narrative. Not simply the narrative that one could extract from a novel such as *Middlemarch,* but the narrative that has been adopted since the introduction to this study. For, clearly, the progression that leads from Aristotle to Coleridge, from Coleridge to Wordsworth, from Wordsworth to Eliot must appear to take the form of a narrative written by literary history and tied together by the thematic consistency of a mimesis unable to account for language as the performance of an act or event. It is in order to examine the historical and narrative claims of such a thematic history that this book now turns to *Middlemarch.* To be more precise, to chapter 15 of *Middlemarch* and its adoption of a metaphor whose presence in literature, philosophy, history, politics, and even science suggests a thematic consistency over and beyond its claims to historical knowledge. The metaphor of weaving.

The Prelude to History

> Mezozeugma *or the Middlemarcher.*
>
> —Puttenham, *The Arte of English Poesie* (1589)
>
> μεσόζευγμα: *a word which belongs equally to what precedes and to what follows.*
>
> —Liddell and Scott, *Greek-English Lexicon*

The frequency with which the metaphor of weaving is evoked in the course of *Middlemarch,* as well as in the critical literature of this novel, would seem to be entirely in keeping with a narrative whose expansiveness invites the attempt to bring it within the contraction offered by this metaphor and its derivatives.[2] The invitation to effect such a contraction is always difficult to resist, and never more so than when, in the "Prelude" to *Middlemarch,* the narrator describes the passing away of the very elements which have, historically speaking, offered focus as well as guidance. The narrator conveys the awareness of this passing away in the form of a comparison between the historical conditions governing the life of Saint Theresa and the conditions governing the history about to be unfolded in *Middlemarch.* The comparison begins by describing the life of Saint Theresa as an exemplary subject for those who would seek to gain what is, in effect, a knowledge of history, a goal normally regarded as one of the central concerns of this novel. The opening sentence of *Middlemarch* begins:

> Who that cares much to know the history of man, and how the mysterious mixture behaves under the varying experiments of Time, has not dwelt, at least briefly, on the life of Saint Theresa.[3]

Important though this comparison may be for an understanding of one of the principal characters in *Middlemarch,* Dorothea Brooke, the significance of this opening sentence also lies in the way that experimentation, variation, and temporality are understood in relation to the "mysterious mixture" that each of these elements acts upon. In this opening sentence, history is the result of the experiments of time, experiments that would seem to vary from one another while representing an underlying and unchanging conception. According to such an understanding, the life of Saint Theresa, which the narrator describes as "soar[ing] after some illimitable satisfaction, some object which would never justify weariness, which would reconcile self-despair with the rapturous consciousness of life beyond self" ("Prelude," 25), is only a variation, an experiment issuing from the movement of a progressive temporality. At the same time, the subject upon whom this temporality acts is a mixture—as if the subject were a chemical combination whose elements, not to mention its essence, may be discovered through closer examination, through an ever more radical line of inquiry such as that adopted by Lydgate in the course of this novel. The mixture that forms "the history of man" is, however, also mysterious; it cannot speak for itself even though it appears to speak a truth for which it seems to have been made. In the case of Saint Theresa, such a truth is reflected in what the narrator terms her *epos,* namely, "the reform of a religious order" ("Prelude," 25). Nonetheless, this *epos* is viewed as less the property of Saint Theresa than the product of her historical situation. This distinction is confirmed by the narrator when the lot of "later-born Theresas" is described: [they] were helped by no coherent social faith and order which could perform the function of knowledge for the ardently willing soul" ("Prelude," 25). In contrast to "later-born Theresas," the life of Saint Theresa is tied to the idea of a "coherent social faith and order," her *epos,* the song or utterance of her life, finds its author and therefore its voice in a center located outside the self. Despite its external location, such a center may intervene in order to grant wholeness and purposiveness to that same self. The situation of "later-born Theresas" would differ inasmuch as this kind of center can no longer exert such an exclusive influence.

Although the self may no longer receive coherency from such an external source, the narrator's underscoring of such a historical shift cannot be subsumed into the radical realignment of the concept of self so often perceived as the distinguishing characteristic of Romanticism: the sense that selfhood and coherency may be derived from an internal rather than an external resource. As if to discount any Romantic sense of a guiding light coming from within, the narrator describes the fate of those no longer in possession of an exterior focus in the following terms:

> With dim lights and tangled circumstance they [later-born Theresas] tried to shape their thought and deed in noble agreement; but after all, to common eyes their struggles seemed mere inconsistency and formlessness. ("Prelude," 25)

According to this experiment of time, thought cannot be shaped into agreement with deed, that is, thought cannot produce a lamp strong enough to enable sight nor can it disentangle itself from the circumstance in which it takes place. The consequences of this failure to follow the path frequently associated with Romanticism is clearly given in the final sentence of the "Prelude":

> Here and there is born a Saint Theresa, foundress of nothing, whose loving heart-beats and sobs after an unattained goodness tremble off and are dispersed among hindrances, instead of centering in some long-recognizable deed. ("Prelude," 26)

Faced with the difficulty of making thought enter into "noble agreement" with deed, the intentions of a latter-day Theresa not only tremble off but are dispersed just as at the end of *Middlemarch* when the "finely touched spirit" of such a Theresa (in the person of Dorothea Brooke) is compared to "that river of which Cyrus broke the strength, [and which] spent itself in channels which had no great name on earth" ("Finale," 896).[4] While the dispersing of the waters of the river Gyndes is an act of revenge for Cyrus, no such motive is attributable here.[5] Dispersal would appear to be what results once a single center, whether inside or outside, no longer exerts its influence *as* a center but rather meets a hindrance which had always been present even though concealed by the notion of a shift, the guarantor that a historical progression has, in fact, taken place.

The metaphor of weaving and its product, the web, would offer a means of retaining some kind of order and coherence which, despite being neither within nor without the self, would offer the possibility of allowing dispersed elements to be related to one another. As a metaphorical device, such a web serves a recuperative purpose to the extent that it threads together what might otherwise appear to be heterogeneous. Indeed, the greater the heterogeneity or dispersal, the more powerful this activity can become since, by its very nature, it thrives upon what is divided or differentiated—the metaphorical use of weaving is, in effect, a form of dialectical understanding. By virtue of its dialectical character, weaving is an art that does not seek any homogeneity based upon a single unified center. Furthermore, because this art does not require generically similar elements, it has the capacity to relate contradictory threads without in any way being affected by the contradiction. As such, the metaphor of weaving may be defined as an interlacing of differences. Consequently, to argue that weaving is only a metaphor binding together other metaphors whose individual claims to represent a totality must ultimately undermine that of weaving, is to misconstrue the relation of weaving to these same competing claims.[6]

Weaving is not simply *another* metaphor for the kind of totality which is capable of being deconstructed *as if* it represented a single entity, as if it were the narrative equivalent of Casaubon's "key to all mythologies."[7] Rather, it is the *relative* failure of such limited totalities which provides the materials for the metaphorical application of the art of weaving. This being the case, the question of whether anything may exceed the reach of this art becomes a redundant question since what threatens unity, and above all, semantic unity, is already suitable for inclusion within an ever expanding network of relations. Indeed, nothing may exceed the grasp of this art—precisely because whatever may be beyond its reach can only be determined in accordance to what has already been related, what has already been woven. In other words, what would exceed the relation produced by the art of weaving can always be placed in relation to it. It is a self-induced evasion to look toward an ever illusionary outside as the harbinger of what exceeds the grasp of this art.

The task to be undertaken is rather what Heidegger describes in the following reflection on the web of language:

> Ein Geflecht drängt zusammen, verengt und verwehrt die gerade Durchsicht im Verflochtenen. Zugleich aber ist das Geflecht, das die Wegformel [Die Sprache als die Sprache zur Sprache bringen] nennt, die eigene Sache der Sprache. Darum dürfen wir von diesem Geflecht, das dem Anschein nach alles ins Unentwirrbare zusammendrängt, nicht wegsehen. Die Formel muß unserer Nachdenken eher bedrängen, damit es versuche, das Geflecht zwar nicht zu beseitigen, aber so zu lösen, daß es den Blick in das freie Zusammengehören der durch die Formel genannten Bezüge gewährt. Vielleicht ist das Geflecht von einem Band durchzogen, das auf eine stets befremdende Weise die Sprache in ihr Eigentümliches entbindet. Es gilt, im Geflecht der Sprache das entbindende Band zu erfahren.
>
> A web compresses, narrows, and obstructs the straight clear view inside its mesh. At the same time, however, the web which the guiding formula [To bring language to language as language] names is the particular concern of language. Therefore, we may not disregard the web which seems to compress everything into a hopeless tangle. Rather, the formula must urge our reflection so that it attempts, not to remove the web, of course, but to loosen it so that it allows a view into the open togetherness of the relations named in the formula. Perhaps there is a bond running through the web which, in a constantly strange way, unbinds language into its own. What matters is to experience the unbinding bond within the web of language.[8]

Rather than unravel the web, the task of reflection is to think language as language—a formula that binds one ever more resolutely to language even as one attempts to find an analogy for language within language. While this binding is unavoidable, the matter it provides for reflection cannot be evaded merely on account of its unavoidability. To practice such an evasion would be to assert a state of linguistic purity which requires a formal purity already contradicted by the demand that it be meaningfully pure. To such an assertion nothing could ever be strange. Neither language nor history, despite their best-laid designs, can ever avoid this strangeness since, in such an avoidance, their strangeness will find its constant echo.

Even when language and history are thematized as a web, and, in this way, compressed, they must yet face an "unbinding bond" that has little to do with the unraveling of a web. To unravel a web is to apply one metaphor to another in the hope that something less (or more) than a metaphor will be produced. Since such an approach is destined to reproduce itself constantly (as metaphor), it is hardly surprising that it should fail to grasp the task that Heidegger's reflection spells out. There is no bond to be unbound for the bond is itself this unbinding. The task before us is then the question of how to experience such a bond within a web *and* its unraveling within a word that belongs equally to what precedes (weaving) and to what follows (unraveling). The question of a *middlemarcher* or *mezozeugma*.

Despite the historical chance that links the name of *Middlemarch* to a rhetorical term, Eliot's novel will seem a strange place to inquire into this "unbinding bond" which has been occluded so easily by the thematization of history and language as a web. Strange, because the occlusion is so pervasive; it even pervades the point at which the narrator of *Middlemarch* appears to reflect upon and restrict the metaphor of the web. In the "Finale," we are told: "The fragment of a life, however typical, is not the sample of an even web" (891). But, is this really a restriction? Is it even a critique of the metaphor that informs the narrating of *Middlemarch?* Has this metaphor been anything except uneven since the outset? Is not the pervasiveness of this metaphor directly attributable to its unevenness, that is, to a difference produced by the unraveling practiced by weaving? This unevenness is already an effect of weaving. Through this unevenness, the metaphor takes on historical credibility since it effectively counters the formal evenness or completeness that would threaten the historical relations it seeks to compress within its range. Consequently, through its inability to be synonymous with history, this metaphor appears to reflect history in an ever more exact relation.

It has been important to clarify the relation of this metaphor to history so that its unevenness, its inability to reflect history will not be taken as a deconstruction of this novel's narrative. To adopt such unevenness as if it were the sign of a deconstruction does no more than adopt a model of history which originates in an even web and then progresses to an uneven one. There is nothing strange about this model of history. Not only is the bind always unbound in this model but history is itself denied as it becomes what never happened. As historians will constantly remind us, Cyrus, for example, did exist. Mere existence, however, is not historical and that is where the question of history begins as a question of language. For what we call history would be as strange to Cyrus as language would be to an act or an event. While this question of history and language could be traced at many points in the course of *Middlemarch*'s narration, it takes on particular emphasis in chapter 15. This chapter not only contains the infamous and widely quoted remark about "unravelling certain human lots" that form "this particular web," but the narrative instances that follow this remark each recount a history that turns upon a word.

The Design of History

> *But the great Parmenides, my dear boy, beginning when we were young and to the end protested this, saying constantly in prose and meter, "Never shall this be forcibly maintained that things that are not are but you must hold your thought back from this path of inquiry."*
>
> —The Stranger (Plato, *Sophist*)

In an oft-cited passage from chapter 15 of *Middlemarch,* the narrator refers to the task of narrative in terms which make it clear that, in the present case, such a task involves neither spinning nor weaving a web but rather an unraveling of what is already woven and interwoven. While this passage is important with respect to *Middlemarch* as a whole (and is commonly treated as such), it also bears a direct relation to what will unfold in the course of this chapter, namely, the history of Tertius Lydgate's scientific researches into a common factor present in every part of a living organism and the performance of the actress whose husband will die on stage.[9] The narrator, after commenting upon the leisurely narrative practice of Fielding, makes the following statement:

> We belated historians must not linger after his example; and if we did so it is probable that our chat would be thin and eager, as if delivered from a camp-stool in a parrot-house. I at least have so much to do in unravelling certain human lots, and seeing how they were woven and interwoven, that all the light I can command must be concentrated on this particular web, and not dispersed over that tempting range of relevancies called the universe. (15.170)

How all the light commanded by the narrator will compare to the dim light of a later-born Theresa remains to be seen. Yet it would appear from this declaration that the narrator occupies a different position, one that resists dispersal by virtue of an ability to concentrate or focus upon a particular web and not be distracted by any desire to play the role of a Fielding who, the narrator comments, "seems to bring his arm-chair to the proscenium and chat with us in all the lusty ease of his fine English" (15.170). To place Fielding beneath the proscenium is hardly accidental in a chapter that will move toward a murder which may or may not have taken place under a proscenium in Paris. At this point, the narrator of *Middlemarch* seems far removed from such a theatrical representation. Instead, the narrator prefers the more modest role of an observer engaged in a patient study of what is described as having already taken place, of what has already been woven. The task the narrator takes on would thus be one of unfolding in the present the fabric of a history, the fabric of a set of relations for which the narrator is not responsible and could not in any way be viewed as its author.

In *Middlemarch,* the relations that form the subject of its history are concerned above all else with marriage, that is, they are concerned with an entering into relation, an interlacing of what the narrator refers to as "human lots." Viewed from this perspective, *Middlemarch* would be, in essence, a study of how relation may be represented and therefore of how the web or weaving through which this novel is so frequently perceived may be realized. Paradoxically though, this study must proceed, if the narrator's words are to be believed, by means of unraveling a web which can only come into existence through that same act of unraveling. As such, the narrator's unraveling would have to be, at the same time, a form of weaving. The presentation of how this weaving takes place in *Middlemarch* is thus the presentation of how the history and the lots the narrator seeks to unravel become woven in the first place. The novel is therefore, in a sense, a theater in which the production of history is to take place.

The first explicit reference to the action of weaving in this novel occurs when Rosamond Vincy's designs upon the newcomer to Middlemarch, Tertius Lydgate, are described in a way that repeats the traditional association between weaving and plot.[10] The narrator informs us that at the close of their first meeting

> their eyes met with that peculiar meeting which is never arrived at by effort, but seems like a sudden divine clearance of haze. . . . This result, which she took to be a mutual impression, called falling in love, was just what Rosamond had contemplated beforehand. Ever since that important new arrival in Middlemarch she had woven a little future, of which something like this scene was the necessary beginning. (12.145)

Between the arrival of Lydgate and this scene, Rosamond's weaving has taken place. Since such a weaving looks toward what has not yet happened, it cannot be associated with the creation of a past as it would have to be if the narrator's unraveling were simultaneously the weaving of the web that this unraveling pretends to undo. In this instance, weaving is presented as the plotting of the course of events that Rosamond wishes will become historical. What is woven by Rosamond has only the status of a scenario that may or may not be acted out. Thus, in this example, the actual history would be dependent upon the weaving of a cloth which will fit a situation not necessarily within its control but which may attain such a control by seeing actual events reflected in accordance to its script.

The representative and, indeed, the theatrical character that Rosamond's weaving gives to actual events is not an isolated aspect of her character or indeed of the novel. Immediately before the incident just cited, Rosamond, while being observed by Lydgate, is described in the following words:

> Every nerve and muscle in Rosamond was adjusted to the consciousness that she was being looked at. She was by nature an actress of parts that entered into her *physique:* she even acted her character, and so well, that she did not know it to be precisely her own. (12.144)

Rosamond, the weaver of scenes to be performed, is herself a performer and never more so than when she is being just herself. Already a play within a play can be discerned, a play within which the action of weaving has an important role. How this role is to be understood is conveyed when Rosamond's design upon Lydgate is depicted in terms of a desire to bring within her web "a man of talent, whom it would be especially delightful to ensnare" (12.145).[11] Yet, the weaving is not only designed to ensnare the man of talent but also to ensnare "connections which offered vistas of that middle-class heaven: rank" (12.145). Rosamond's web, itself a tissue of connection, is to lead to other relations through which a position of hierarchical significance is to be attained. At the same time, Rosamond will achieve a measure of authority and not as a result of what she becomes connected to by means of marriage but rather as a result of the fact that it is she who does the weaving and thereby produces the relation.[12] In this respect, the weaving of Rosamond is analogous to that of one who is attempting to unravel a history according to the web she has spun. In short, Rosamond is the author of a web upon which her future, interlaced with that of Lydgate, would be represented.

If Rosamond's activity may stand as an example of how weaving is to be understood in this novel, then one must also set against this example the narrator's reflection on the activity of Mrs. Cadwallader, an inveterate matchmaker who, unlike Rosamond, does not weave, but rather creates a vacuum which serves to devour its victim. In the following lines, the narrator first describes the nature of Mrs. Cadwallader's "plotting":

> Now, why on earth should Mrs. Cadwallader have been at all busy about Miss Brooke's marriage; and why, when one match that she liked to have a hand in was frustrated, should she have straightway contrived the preliminaries of another? Was there any ingenious plot, any hide-and-seek course of action, which might be detected by a careful telescopic watch? Not at all: a telescope might have swept the parishes of Tipton and Freshitt, the whole area visited by Mrs. Cadwallader in her phaeton, without witnessing any interview that could excite suspicion, or any scene from which she did not return with the same unperturbed keenness of eye and the same high natural colour. (6.83)

The narrator's emphatic answer, willing as it is to submit to the scrutiny of a telescope, does not however, quite explain Mrs. Cadwallader's activity which resembles that of Rosamond even though it is not presented as a "scene." Indeed, a telescope would not be strong enough or, as the older word for this instrument suggests, one does not have the right perspective (in the sense of a telescope or other viewing glass) if the nature of Cadwallader's matchmaking is to be perceived at all.

As the narrator explains in the following example, a different and a stronger kind of lens is required:

> Even with a microscope directed on a water-drop we find ourselves making interpretations which turn out to be rather coarse; for whereas under a weak lens you may seem to see a creature exhibiting an active voracity into which other smaller creatures actively play as if they were so many animated tax-pennies, a stronger lens reveals to you certain tiniest hairlets which make vortices for these victims while the swallower waits passively at his receipt of custom. In this way, metaphorically speaking, a strong lens applied to Mrs. Cadwallader's matchmaking will show a play of minute causes producing what may be called speech and thought vortices to bring her the sort of food she needed. (6.83)

Under a weak lens the observer may entertain the illusion that the "smaller creatures" actively play into the mouth of a creature which, in its voracity, is equally active. The illusion resides in the perception of this very activity, a perception that suggests that each creature determines its fate as well as the fate of others. In each instance, a single active cause is perceived to be at work, yet, by changing perspective, this causality is unraveled, that is, it is unveiled as being composed of a "play of minute causes" or "vortices" that may or may not ensnare a victim for the passive swallower. This closer observation, through its focus on single causality, offers at the same time a perspective on the relation at the heart of the kind of weaving practiced by Rosamond and which finds itself scrutinized in this example. Such a weaving, which is referred to in Cadwallader's case as identical to plotting, is composed of multiple vortices each of which turn upon a center, but a center that consists entirely of a vacuum. The plotting or weaving effected in this manner is so barely perceptible that the swallower may even appear to wait passively for "his receipt of custom," that is, wait passively to receive what seems to arrive through custom but which is actively determined by "certain tiniest hairlets which *make* vortices." What appears to occur as custom is in effect the result of a voracity which only seems to take place independently of its beneficiary. It is in this sense that Cadwallader "has a hand in" or at least attempts to have a hand in the interlacing of the eligible characters in this novel.[13] But the control, or indeed the authoring of plots, which forms the subject of these passages operates by dissimulating itself in the guise of a passivity, as if the victim to be swallowed or otherwise ensnared were the victim of an unavoidable destiny, in short, the victim of a relation that was already predetermined and only requires to be acted out in order to become historical. In the examples of both Cadwallader and Rosamond, authority emerges as being conditional upon either swallowing or ensnaring its intended victim in such a way as to produce a new set of relations between heterogeneous elements.

At this point, one could conclude, however provisionally, that the narrator's unraveling focuses upon the conditions that make possible the very existence of the web as well as the weaving which this unraveling takes as its subject. In such a case, the narrator would be simply fulfilling the role of an interpreter carefully observing a representation in which "equivalent centers" such as Rosamond and Cadwallader act the parts they know best, parts that are dissected in detail before our eyes as if we were the audience for this theatrical performance. It may be disquieting to this conclusion to emphasize what appears to be only a secondary detail (that such centers of activity can only act by virtue of centers that are essentially vacuums—a detail reinforced by the description of Rosamond as an "actress of parts that entered into her *physique*" [12.144]). Yet, in what follows, such a conclusion is unsettled further by the history of Lydgate, who, in this novel, would be the exemplary unraveler, the unraveler of the primary web to which all weaving and unraveling would be indebted.

Of Lydgate, it must first be remarked that he did not intend to play the part prepared for him in the scene woven by Rosamond. As we are told shortly after their initial meeting, "Each lived in a world of which the other knew nothing" (16.195). In fact, Lydgate is completely unaware that "he had been a subject of eager meditation to Rosamond, who had neither any reason for throwing her marriage into distant perspective, nor any pathological studies to divert her mind from that ruminating habit, that inward repetition of looks, words, and phrases" (16.195). Indeed, only by means of this ruminating habit can Rosamond form a relation to Lydgate and only then by digesting the "looks, words, and phrases" she has swallowed. This process of digestion is essentially a form of repetition through which Rosamond attaches to herself the image she has created of Lydgate. In effect, Rosamond only sees what she weaves, that is, the image represented on the surface of her weaving only serves the appetite of her design. Lydgate's failure to see Rosamond's weaving and the process it takes place within could already be considered a reflection upon his ability to unravel the primary web that stands at the center of his researches. As the example of Rosamond suggests, Lydgate may lack the ability to recognize the object of his research. If this were the only conclusion to be drawn from this comparison of the weaver and the unraveler, then Lydgate would be nothing more than the Casaubon of science. Should we then assume that the account of Lydgate's researches as well as the story of their origin is placed by mere chance in the chapter that describes the narrator as an unraveler? More specifically, why is the history of Lydgate placed immediately after the description of the narrator as an unraveler and immediately before the description of his scientific attempts to unravel a primitive tissue?

The cause of Lydgate's devotion is recounted as the discovery of a vocation which, we are told, arose from the "novelty" of looking into "the volumes of an old Cyclopaedia which he had never disturbed" (15.172–73). The scene is described as follows:

> They were on the highest shelf, and he stood on a chair to get them down. But he opened the volume which he first took from the shelf: somehow, one is apt to read in a makeshift attitude, just where it might seem inconvenient to do so. The page he opened on was under the heading of Anatomy, and the first passage that drew his eyes was on the valves of the heart. He was not much acquainted with valves of any sort, but he knew that *valvae* were folding doors, and through this crevice came a sudden light startling him with his

> first vivid notion of finely adjusted mechanism in the human frame. (15.173)

Anatomy, the science that defines the structure and relation of parts, reveals itself to the young Lydgate as the result of a manner of reading directed by inconvenience. Although this primary relation between Lydgate and his vocation involves no suggestion of being predetermined, another relation which contains a greater sense of determination soon takes its place. The page Lydgate begins to read describes the working of the valves of the heart and it is this description that leads to Lydgate's sense of vocation. The kind of connection from which this vocation evolves requires careful consideration, particularly since, like the source of historical knowledge in Wordsworth's Simplon Pass episode, it is dependent upon a relation within language and between languages.

The passage on the valves of the heart (and what other metaphor could be of such central relevance here?) confronts Lydgate with words he cannot understand. As the narrator remarks, Lydgate "was not much acquainted with valves of any sort." Because such valves are unknown to him, Lydgate remains ignorant of how the heart and the system of circulation it commands may be regulated. This deficiency is remedied by means of an intermediary: Lydgate "knew that *valvae* were folding doors." *Valvae,* the intermediary, provides the relation necessary if Lydgate is to understand the passage he has just read. Yet, this relation, facilitated by the resemblance of the Latin word to its English derivative, is supported by other relations based upon a specific understanding of language and its referentiality. Above all else, Lydgate's comprehension of this passage depends upon the Latin word's denotation of a device of separation and closure to be found in passageways. This device, having been recognized, subsequently provides the basis for understanding the valves described in the passage he reads from the Cyclopaedia. The folding door becomes a metaphor explaining the operation of the heart's valves. Lydgate's understanding depends less on the object described by *valvae* than on the formal similarity between the Latin word and its English cognate. One wonders what Lydgate would have understood if some philosopher had got to the heart first and called its regulatory mechanism *mensae*. This formal congruence from which Lydgate derives his understanding implies a historical continuity within language: that valve will refer to something similar to what *valvae* designates to a Roman. Here, metaphorical understanding becomes an index of historical continuity.

Thus etymology, language as the mediation of a historical past, and the extension of this mediation into metaphor, are all involved in Lydgate's deciphering of a passage that he could not immediately understand. This example of Lydgate's deciphering of a "finely adjusted mechanism in the human frame" consequently depends upon what may be referred to as a web of interrelations. These interrelations are derived from a particular understanding of the nature of language as a vehicle capable of conveying perception or, more precisely, of arriving at a perception which will, in retrospect, dissipate Lydgate's initial inability to comprehend. In the passage just cited, this dissipation is described as the result of a "sudden light." The presence of such a "sudden light" within the process of perception defines a moment of separation, a moment without apparent relation but after which coherence and understanding will have become possible. As such, light provides the necessary moment of interruption that separates Lydgate's understanding from its source. The separation is necessary if one recalls the formal character of the relation between *valvae* and valve. This relation makes it possible for one historically unknown referent (*valvae*) to become, in Lydgate's case, the source of another historically unknown referent (the operation of the valves of the heart). This understanding escapes, as it were, through the "crevice" opened by Lydgate's knowledge of Latin. It is precisely this crevice which allows such an understanding to lodge itself within the passage which had previously eluded his comprehension.[14] Aided by this crevice, the light of insight permits one "fact" to escape its origin in a formal relation. This fact subsequently becomes known as if it represented the logic of this same chain. Thus, the chain of facts underlying Lydgate's interpretation of the passage from the Cyclopaedia ("valve" resembles *valvae, valvae* means folding door, this meaning describes the operation of the valves of the heart) is made to reflect the circular movement of the system it serves to explain. Through this reflection, the merely formal is assured its place not only as a metaphor for historical relation but also as a metaphor of a history, namely, Lydgate's. In this episode, such a history may be traced to the opening of a book at a passage which contains a word that cannot be understood *immediately*. From this word, the history of Lydgate, the unraveler of the primary tissue, becomes possible. It is to the condition of such a possibility (which is also the condition of the chain of relations already discussed) that the subsequent narration of chapter 15 is now concerned: a history that turns upon a word.

Following upon the recounting of Lydgate's discovery of a vocation, chapter 15 presents, first of all, a description of Lydgate's medical ambitions. These ambitions, once set in motion, are reinforced by Lydgate's "conviction that the medical profession as it might be was the finest in the world; offering the most perfect interchange between science and art; offering the most direct alliance between intellectual conquest and the social good" (15.174). The medical profession as it *might be* emphasizes the potentiality of a most perfect interchange, a most perfect alliance. Here, Lydgate's vocation as well as the historical importance he assigns to the medical profession is guided by a potentiality that recalls the way in which Aristotle protects literary history and literary theory from is own historical tendency. However, as we are told, Lydgate gravitates toward a profession defined in terms of interchange and alliance in order to "work out the proof of an anatomical conception and make a link in the chain of discovery" (15.175). The project is reminiscent of Coleridge's in the *Biographia* to the extent that Lydgate directs his attention toward a link that Aristotle deemed necessary to set aside. And, again, like Coleridge, Lydgate's research is guided by the hope that "two purposes would illuminate one another: the careful observation and inference which was his daily work, the use of the lens to further his judgment in special cases would further his thought as an instrument of larger inquiry" (15.176). From this interchange and alliance, Lydgate's research is to proceed. At the same time, it cannot be forgotten that this research is an inquiry into the basis of all interchange and alliance. As such, Lydgate not only inquires into the possibility of his own method of inquiry as well as the possibility of his own profession (not to mention the profession of the narrator to be an unraveler) but also into the possibility of a totality of interrelations, a totality of interrelated differences—whose mode of interrelation is difference.

The possibility of such a totality, we are told, depends upon the ability to surpass the limit established in the researches of François Bichat, the late eighteenth-century physiologist who is referred to in this chapter's account of Lydgate's past. According to the narrator, Bichat held that "living bodies . . . must be regarded as consisting of certain primary webs or tissues, out of which the various organs—brain, heart, lungs, and so on—are compacted, as the various accommodations of a house are built up in various proportions of wood, iron, stone, brick, zinc and the rest, each material having its peculiar composition and proportions" (15.177). Bichat's theory rests upon a combination of primary elements which, according to the given analogy, do not need to be broken down further in order to arrive at the complete structure under investigation whether this be a living body or a house. What is required is an understanding of their interchange and alliance. For Bichat, this understanding takes as its starting point the impossibility of going beyond the tissues which, in this theory, are accorded the status of "ultimate facts in the living organism" (15.177). The theory is predicated upon phenomena into which it is not necessary to inquire if one is to obtain knowledge about the organism under examination. The primary webs or tissues are not in themselves a fit subject for inquiry, rather it is their relation which forms such a subject. Consequently, these phenomena mark the boundary of possible knowledge. As boundaries, they also serve to circumscribe the field of inquiry with the result that a certain understanding becomes conceivable on condition of this encircling. This approach, we are told, "acted necessarily on medical questions as the turning of gas-light would act on a dim, oil-lit street, showing new connections and hitherto hidden facts of structure" (15.177). The understanding that becomes possible is one of new facts and new connections within an already known passageway, but, a passageway known only by means of an inferior light. With Bichat, the light is superior and, because the field of inquiry is effectively circumscribed, it is all the more concentrated.

But, as the narrator recounts, "there would be another light, as of oxy-hydrogen, showing the very grain of things, and revising all former explanations" (15.178). This other light is presented in the form of a questioning of Bichat's ultimate facts, a questioning of the tissues themselves. Again, the narrator voices the question: "Have not these structures some common basis from which they have all started, as your sarsnet, gauze, net, satin and velvet from the raw cocoon?" (15.178). The role of analogy in formulating the question is decisive. Whereas Bichat had been content to inquire into the living organism as a system composed of ultimate yet individual facts that mark the limit of knowledge, Lydgate seeks to uncover the "raw cocoon" from which each of these facts has been derived. Of this research, we are told, Lydgate "was enamoured" (15.178). However, as this chapter unfolds, this relation between Lydgate and his research is defined in other terms, more precisely, in theatrical terms as Lydgate becomes enamored of an actress, a turn of events that precipitates the drama in which he has already begun to play a part, the drama of Rosamond. On this occasion, both drama and theater will be actually present, for the conclusion to this chapter concerns a theatrical representation during the course of which Lydgate will also find himself on stage. There is, however, an important sequence leading up to this conclusion that cannot be skipped over, a sequence that will relate in more precise detail the nature of Lydgate's unraveling of the "primitive tissue," the "raw cocoon" of the living organism.

Lydgate's research is described as a longing "to demonstrate the most intimate relations of living structure and help define men's thought more accurately after the true order" (15.178). The research involves representing with ever greater accuracy an order that is already woven, which is already, as Lydgate's framing of his guiding question implies, a structure of essential relation. Lydgate asks, "What was the primitive tissue?" (15.178). The narrator comments:

> In that way Lydgate put the question—not quite in the way required by the waiting answer; but such missing of the right word befalls many seekers. (15.178)

The answer that awaits depends on a word. But, if Lydgate's question misses the right word, which word is wrong in his formulation of the question? Any reformulation of the question faces a limited choice. If the "primitive tissue" is not to be known by another name, then, only two words could be wrong if this question is to remain a question about the "primitive tissue," namely, "what" and "was." The tense of Lydgate's question affirms that such tissue is already existent: "What *was* the primitive tissue?" The tense is crucial since it carries with it the inference of something that has already been completed, that is, of something whose essence can be known precisely because it is no longer in development.[15] In this case, the question contradicts what it is to inquire into, since such a tissue can no longer be living. According to the guiding question of Lydgate's researches, the intimate relations of the living organism are consequently regulated by what is already dead, by what has already achieved its essence.

In addition to the question of tense, there is the question of "what" and its determination of the primitive tissue as answerable to an inquiry that views such a tissue in terms of its substance, its quiddity. The method of research adopted by Lydgate gives further emphasis to this limitation of its object: "He counted on quiet intervals to be watchfully seized, for taking up the threads of investigation—on many hints to be won from diligent application, not only of the scalpel, but of the microscope, which research had begun to use again with new enthusiasm of reliance" (15.178). The method is one of dissection and ever closer observation of what has been dissected. For this reason, the intervals of research are to be watchfully seized, visual observation being the primary means of inquiry as well as the final arbiter of a tissue incapable of being divided further, incapable of further differentiation. Such a concentration upon the visual, while underlining an inquiry only able to perceive what can be seen or what can be rendered susceptible to visual perception reiterates the basis of Lydgate's discovery of a vocation. This discovery also turned upon a word, but a word that was already understood in relation to a visual object and could therefore be applied in order to understand what is not known. In the case of Lydgate's present research, an understanding similar to that which makes this vocation possible is also at work, yet, to this point, such an understanding has been unable to produce its foreseen result. Moreover, as far as the novel is concerned, Lydgate will make no further progress toward the discovery of this link. Lydgate's failure to achieve success in his researches, like Casaubon's failure to find the "key to all mythologies," may be attributed, as has frequently been the case, to mere individual inability, as if the difficulty were only traceable to subjective psychology. But, as the narrator has already suggested in reference to Lydgate's guiding question, there are other considerations. In the case of Lydgate, there is another story concerning his past, a story that is as instructive as the recounting of this exemplary unraveler's discovery of a vocation. Moreover, it is a story that turns upon a word—really.

The Success of Scandal and the Corpse of Aristotle

> *We take pleasure in looking at the most accurate images of things we find painful to see, such as the forms of the lowest animals and of corpses.*
>
> —Aristotle, *Poetics*

Like Lydgate's involvement with Rosamond Vincy in *Middlemarch,* the story of Lydgate recorded in chapter 15 is also the story of an actress whom Lydgate came to know while studying in Paris. The narrator presents this story "as an example of the fitful swerving of passion to which he [Lydgate] was prone, together with the chivalrous kindness which helped to make him morally lovable" (15.180). On the strength of this comment, the purpose of the story would appear to be directed toward unraveling the coexistence of two distinct tendencies in Lydgate, tendencies that later will be described in terms of "two selves" once the story of Lydgate's encounter with this actress moves toward its conclusion. Yet there is more to this incident than the mere unraveling of character. For the moment, it will be sufficient to recall the placing of this story immediately after the narrator's account of Lydgate's researches. As a result of this positioning, the chapter takes on the form of a threefold sequence: first of all, the description of the narrator's task as an unraveling as well as the description of where this unraveling is to take place (beneath the proscenium but without Fielding's armchair and above all without "the lusty ease of his fine English"—"belated historians" no longer possess such advantages); second, Lydgate's discovery of the vocation that leads to his subsequent research aimed at unraveling the "primitive tissue"; and, finally, the recounting of an episode from Lydgate's past which concentrates upon an actress whose behavior hinders the assumptions about language and representation that underpin his research as well as the narrator's guiding metaphor.

To emphasize, for the moment, only the relation between the last two parts of this sequence, it is to be noted that the narrator's account of the present state of Lydgate's researches leads into a story about the past and, in particular, about representation and the stage. That such a story should be recounted at this point becomes increasingly significant when it is remembered that Lydgate's own research will take no effective step beyond the stage which the narrator has just described. Indeed, the story of Lydgate's "research" into the primitive tissue can only progress by ignoring an incident in which the fate of this research is already decided.

The incident that arrests the course of Lydgate's research is introduced as follows:

> The story can be told without many words. It happened when he was studying in Paris, and just at the time when, over and above his other work, he was occupied with some galvanic experiments. One evening, tired with his experimenting, and not being able to elicit the facts he needed, he left his frogs and rabbits to some repose under their trying and mysterious dispensation of unexplained shocks, and went to finish his evening at the theatre of the Porte Saint Martin, where there was a melodrama which he had already seen several times; attracted, not by the ingenious work of the collaborating authors, but by an actress whose part it was to stab her lover, mistaking him for the evil-designing duke of the piece. Lydgate was in love with this woman, as a man is in love with a woman whom he never expects to speak to. (15.180)

The introduction to this piece of Lydgate's past repeats the movement of the chapter and also the unfolding of Lydgate's fate in the course of *Middlemarch:* the story of his research gives way to theatrical representation. Unable to "elicit the facts he *needed,*" Lydgate relinquishes his experiments for the evening and goes to see a melodrama which, we are told, is "the ingenious work of collaborating authors." This detail about the melodrama's composition is of considerable importance when set beside the history of Lydgate's researches. For what is Lydgate's research if not the work of several authors each succeeding one another? Certainly, such collaboration is not executed in the same manner as it is by those responsible for the melodrama Lydgate goes to see. Yet, with respect to the "primitive tissue," there is collaboration to the extent that it is the sum of Bichat's research, the work of his successors, and the researches of Lydgate which will demonstrate the "more intimate relations of the living structure" and thereby "define men's thought more accurately after the true order" (15.178). This parallelism is strengthened by the fact that Lydgate's knowledge of this play is derived from repetition, precisely the means adopted by the experimental method of his researches. As a result of such parallelism, what Lydgate goes to see this evening can be read as an unambiguous account of what impedes his research.

Despite assuming the position of the researcher who only needs to elicit certain preconceived facts in order to have his work recognized as authoritative, Lydgate is unable, in this example at least, to proceed beyond the "mysterious dispensation of unexplained shocks." However, on this occasion, Lydgate has enough wisdom to finish his evening with a melodrama he has already seen several times as if the repetition of something he already knows could compensate for the failure of facts to repeat the assumption of a theory:

> This evening the old drama had a new catastrophe. At the moment when the heroine was to act the stabbing of her lover, and he was to fall gracefully, the wife veritably stabbed her husband, who fell as death willed. A wild shriek pierced the house, and the Provençale [the actress] fell swooning: a shriek and a swoon were demanded by the play, but the swooning too was real this time. Lydgate leaped and climbed, he hardly knew how, on to the stage. (15.180–81)

As a piece of theater, this play would represent an action as if it were history. This is not to say that the play only depicts events known to have occurred but rather, it depicts, in an Aristotelian sense, what could have happened.[16] Nevertheless, in both the depiction of the actual and the possible, it is presumed that what takes place on stage is historically different from what is represented (whether or not the represented event actually took place is immaterial, what is important is this *historical* separation between what appears to take place on stage and what in effect can take place in history). This Aristotelian understanding would even account for any attempt to interpret a play as the act it represents. The logic of this interpretation is patently syllogistic and owes much of its currency to this characteristic: the play represents what is historically possible, only a possible history can take place on a stage, therefore the play represents itself. Even this interpretation is still thoroughly mimetic in the sense which literary history has attributed to this word since

Aristotle's *Poetics.* If the syllogism, so attractive to a postmodern sense of history as performance, can be resisted, this incident reveals a more complex relation to the history of mimesis. While this play may represent an action (possible or factual) which is historically different from itself (and the self-reflexive understanding is also dependent on this difference), it is only as a result of the meaning attributed to mimesis that such a historical distinction can arise in the first place. Accordingly, the action represented will always owe its existence to the fact of its being represented, to the fact of its being placed within a setting that suggests the possibility of its historicality but does so without itself ever being that history.

At this point, the question already raised in connection with the narrator, the question of how to unravel history, also makes its presence felt. The task of the narrator in *Middlemarch* is described as the task of unraveling what has already been woven but, in order to accomplish this unraveling, the narrator must perform a weaving that takes place in and through this same unraveling. What is to be present ought to be the product of its representation—in both the mimetic and self-reflexive senses. The mimetic structure of this representation (to which each of the previous performances of the melodrama witnessed by Lydgate adhered) undergoes a strange twist this evening. The action to be represented in the play is taken over by another action in which the actress Laure really stabs her actual husband who plays the role of her lover in the melodrama. The plot put together by the ingenious work of the collaborating authors would appear to add yet another collaborator and yet another author. If Laure were regarded as a collaborating author who adds to the melodrama already written, then, this passage would affirm the notion of history that Schelling elaborates using the example of a play:

> Wenn wir uns die Geschichte als ein Schauspiel denken, in welchem jeder, der daran Teil hat, ganz frei und nach Gutdünken seine Rolle spielt, so läßt sich eine vernünftige Entwicklung dieses verworrenen Spiels nur dadurch denken, daß es Ein Geist ist, der in allen dichtet, und daß der Dichter, dessen bloßen Bruchstücke (*disjecti membra poetae*) die einzelnen Schauspieler sind, den objektiven Erfolg des Ganzen mit dem freien Speil aller einzelnen schon zum voraus so in Harmonie gesetzt hat, daß am Ende wirklich

> etwas Vernünftiges herauskommen muß. *Wäre* nun aber der Dichter unabhängig von seinem Drama, so wären wir nur die Schauspieler, die ausführen, was er gedichtet hat. Ist er nicht unabhängig von uns, sondern offenbart und enthüllt er sich nur successiv durch das Spiel unserer Freiheit selbst, so daß ohne diese Freiheit auch er selbst nicht *wäre*, so sind wir Mitdichter des Ganzen, uns Selbsterfinder der besonderen Rolle, die wir spielen. (*System, SW* 3:602)
>
> If we think of history as a play in which everyone who has a part plays their role quite freely and according to their inclination, then a rational development of this muddled drama can only be thought if there is one spirit who speaks in everyone, and if the playwright, whose mere fragments (*disjecti membra poetae*) are the individual actors, has already, in advance, placed the objective outcome of the whole into harmony with the free play of every individual, so that, in the end, something rational must emerge. However, if the playwright *were* independent of his drama, we should be merely the actors who carry out what he has written. If he is not independent of us, but reveals and discloses himself only successively through the play of our own freedom so that without this freedom he himself *would not be*, then, we are collaborators of the whole and are ourselves the self-discoverers of the particular roles we play.

Here, the historical existence and authority of the playwright does not reside in the mere repetition of what that playwright has written but rather in the independent discovery of what was written. This notion of history would be affirmed by regarding Laure's acting as both independent of and yet the same as the script of the melodrama. Such an independence (spoken of by Schelling as the play of the actor's freedom) is, in effect, the attempt to account for a historical relation between, on the one hand, "the objective outcome of the whole" and "the free play of every individual" which is placed into harmony beforehand (*zum voraus*) and, on the other, the play in which this relation is realized. In the context of chapter 15 of *Middlemarch*, such a relation would demand that Laure's stabbing is essentially a free act. But, what if it is impossible to determine it as a free act or even recognize it within the set of relations defined by the terms history and freedom?

When she stabs her husband, Madame Laure, the actress, appears to execute quite simply the play's demands. The stabbing is accomplished without the least deviation from what the action is meant to represent. In this respect, Laure's stabbing of her husband/lover may be said to *perform* that perfect imitation spoken of by Schelling, an imitation which, until it happens, is effectively concealed as if it were merely a representation of something which only appears to take place in the present. In this instance, the moment this performance fails to live up to its representative promise is the moment when the denouement of this evening's performance unveils itself as no longer being a surrogate appearance. Confronted with this outcome, the audience receives an unexplained shock: what the audience sees is not what seems to take place (the appearance of a stabbing) but, at the same time, it can only be what it seems. To describe this as an unveiling might suggest a sleight of hand as if there were a cloth behind which something might be hidden. What appears to have been concealed was not concealed at all, the stabbing takes place as it was meant to happen but with a literalness that is deadly. The figurative performance is murdered by being enacted. The corpse which Aristotle only admits into the *Poetics* as an imitation now finds itself literally onstage. It is precisely this concealing which conceals nothing that so affronts the association of theatricality with representation. It is also the concealing of nothing that makes possible the question subsequently voiced by the narrator when recounting the reaction to this incident:

> Paris rang with the story of this death: —was it a murder? Some of the actress's warmest admirers were inclined to believe in her guilt, and liked her the better for it (such was the taste of those times); but Lydgate was not one of these. (15.181)

In the eyes of the actress's warmest admirers, this incident achieves a *succès de scandale,* yet it is only scandalous to the extent that it is also a trap or, to use one of this narrative's most frequent metaphors, it is an entanglement into which Lydgate cannot help but fall.[17] The admirers do not quite fall into the same predicament, they are only *inclined* to attribute guilt and its implication of a premeditated intention. To go beyond inclination would be to murder the scandal by denying the possibility of a cause. It is only by being *inclined* to believe in the guilt of the actress that this incident may become a story, that is, a story capable of being repeated and circulated.

Within this passage, the end of the scandal, as well as the end of the story in which it is told, depends upon the discovery or unraveling of a cause. Such an end is offered when the narrator states (and this comment can only be taken at its face value for the present): "The notion of murder was absurd; no motive was discoverable, the young couple being understood to dote on each other; and it was not unprecedented that an accidental slip of the foot should have brought these grave circumstances" (15.181). Legally, there ought to be no scandal, since the whole incident has been determined an accident. To support this judgment, a needed fact has been elicited, but a fact whose only ground is that such an accidental slip of the foot "was not unprecedented," that is, the law interprets in accordance with the condition of Aristotelian *mimesis:* "Things that might happen" (*Poetics* 51^{b}5). In the eyes of the legal investigation, the actual stabbing is reduced to mimetic effect: what the audience was meant to see at the melodrama was in fact what it saw. Madame Laure, in both instances, acts according to an exterior cause, one produced by the work of collaborating authors, the work of an unfortunate accident. If the legal investigation were not to give a ruling of this kind (and a guilty verdict is of the same kind), it would be faced, as indeed we still are, with the bare description, "the wife veritably stabbed her husband." "Veritably" does not admit any cause whether accidental or premeditated. The only evidence is the fact of a deceased corpse in the place of an actor performing as a corpse.

As the inability to decide the actress's guilt makes possible her acquittal from the charge of murder, this inability also allows the story, the scandal, to circulate around Paris. At the same time, it is in the interest of this inability to decide that the narration continues. We are told that, despite being all the more popular for the fatal episode, Laure does not continue her engagement in the melodrama but disappears without warning. Lydgate, whose love for this actress has grown (as a result of this episode) to such a pitch that he is "jealous lest any other man than himself should win [her affection] and ask her to marry him" (15.181), is the only admirer affected by this disappearance. Thus, enamored of this actress, the unraveler of the primitive tissue sets off in a pursuit which the narrator describes in the following terms:

> Perhaps no one carried inquiry far except Lydgate, who felt that all science had come to a stand-still while he imagined an unhappy Laure, stricken by ever-wandering sorrow, herself wandering, and finding no faithful comforter. Hidden actresses, however, are not so difficult to find as some other hidden facts, and it was not long before Lydgate gathered indications that Laure had taken the route to Lyons. He found her at last acting with great success at Avignon under the same name. (15.181)

Lydgate, ever one to carry his inquiries as far as he can, interrupts his scientific researches in order to uncover the location of a hidden actress. Applied science, however, offers less of an obstacle to the successful elicitation of the required fact since there is, in this instance, an object of inquiry that will answer to its own name (Laure is found acting under the same name she used in Paris). The relation of a word to what it designates has not been corrupted and all Lydgate must do is to follow the path traced by this relation. Yet, the path Lydgate takes will not lead him toward something hidden but to something he has been looking at all along both in the theater of the Porte Saint Martin and in his own researches: the performance of facts.

After discovering Laure in Avignon, Lydgate speaks to her after the performance (in which she plays "a forsaken wife carrying her child in her arms" [15.181]) and obtains permission to visit her the next day when, we are informed, "he was bent on telling her that he adored her, and on asking her to marry him" (15.181). Having uncovered the actress of whom he is enamored, Lydgate desires to marry her. The discovery of the actress is thus preliminary to an interlacing, a weaving together of "human lots." There is, however, something untoward about Lydgate's plan which even he is aware of albeit only with respect to hidden actresses.[18]

> He knew that this was like the sudden impulse of a madman—incongruous even with his habitual foibles. No matter! It was the one thing which he was resolved to do. He had two selves within him apparently, and they must learn to accommodate each other and bear reciprocal impediments. (15.181–82)

The narrator's introductory remarks to the story of this incident in Lydgate's life had referred to this pursuit and subsequent proposal of marriage to the actress as an example of "the fitful swerving of passion to which he [Lydgate] was prone, together with the chivalrous kindness which helped to make him morally lovable" (15.180). The swerving to which Lydgate is prone, is, on this earlier occasion, described as exemplifying an act of "impetuous folly" (15.180). Now, this same act is referred to as the "sudden impulse of a madman—incongruous even with his habitual foibles" (15.181–82). On the first occasion, the act is accommodated as an example of a habitual tendency in Lydgate, but, on the second, this act can no longer be accommodated since it is incongruous with what it is meant to exemplify. This act is now viewed as the portrayal of a kind of madness whose consequences Lydgate is resolved to accept in order to bring into relation two selves that "must learn to accommodate each other."

Lydgate's "selves" are not the only selves that must accommodate each other as a result of his resolution. Lydgate's double self must, in order to reconcile this doubleness, accommodate the self of the actress, and vice versa. This accommodation depends upon the interlacing represented by marriage, that is, it depends upon another form of accommodation, another form of interlacing "reciprocal impediments." But why should Lydgate's seeking of this accommodation with Laure be viewed as if it represented the actions of a madman? For the narrator, the reason behind Lydgate's madness is the failure of a "persistent self." The narrator observes that it is "strange, that some of us, with quick alternate vision, see beyond our infatuations, and even while we rave on the heights, behold the wide plain where our persistent self pauses and awaits us" (15.182).[19] To the narrator, Lydgate lacks the "alternate vision" that would pierce the veil of his infatuation and thereby allow him to observe the earthbound, the grounded, and persistent self. But does Lydgate even have such a self? In Lydgate's case, does not such a self depend upon uncovering the primitive tissue, the tissue that persists in different forms and which is the possibility of all differentiation including its own? By uncovering this tissue, Lydgate becomes what he wishes to be. His self is, in fact, tied to his longing "to demonstrate the more intimate relations of living structure" (15.178). The demonstration still not performed, Lydgate does not yet have a persistent and grounded self such as the one described by the narrator and is thus subject to "reciprocal impediments." In Lydgate's proposal to Laure, the question of this self is preeminently present in a scene that involves the very nature of Lydgate's research, for, what does this proposal seek as its conclusion if not an intimate living structure? Hidden facts and hidden actresses are not so far apart, indeed, it may be impossible to find one without running into the other.

The next day having arrived, Lydgate goes to Laure. Their dialogue begins as follows:

> "You have come all the way from Paris to find me?" she said to him the next day, sitting before him with folded arms, and looking at him with eyes that seemed to wonder as an untamed ruminating animal wonders. "Are all Englishmen like that?"
>
> "I came because I could not live without trying to see you. You are lonely; I love you; I want you to consent to be my wife: I will wait, but I want you to promise that you will marry me—no one else."
>
> Laure looked at him in silence with a melancholy radiance from under her grand eyelids, until he was full of rapturous certainty, and knelt close to her knees. (15.182)

The persistent self pauses and awaits. Lydgate pauses and awaits a word, the word that will bind Laure to him, and, in so doing, allow him to return to the researches which, we were told earlier, were brought to a standstill while he "imagined the unhappy Laure, stricken by ever-wandering sorrow, herself wandering, and finding no faithful comforter" (15.181). Lydgate's proposal seeks to put an end to the wandering of Laure and at the same time end his wandering pursuit of her. To effect such an end, Lydgate proposes himself as the persistent self, the persistent center that will give both a focus and an aim to her life. But the end offered is hardly so persistent. Lydgate has not yet come face to face with the primary relation whose demonstration would seem to offer him the possibility of such a self. In this scene, Lydgate persists only because, unlike the "eyes that seemed to wonder as an untamed ruminating animal wonders," he practices the ruminating habit of Rosamond Vincy, that "inward repetition of looks, words, and phrases" (16.195), but without the conscious digestion of a skilled weaver of webs and plots such as Rosamond. Lydgate will be entangled by his own weaving. When Laure responds to his demand, his blindness to this weaving becomes all too obvious:

> "I will tell you something," she said, in her cooing way, keeping her arms folded. "My foot really slipped."
>
> "I know, I know," said Lydgate, deprecatingly. "It was a fatal accident—a dreadful stroke of calamity that bound me to you the more." (15.182)

What does Lydgate know? He knows that Laure's foot really slipped but had interpreted this slip as unintentional, "a fatal accident." Laure's reply confirms what he already knows. But what Laure says is not what he hears nor is it what he believes he saw on that evening at the theater of the Porte Saint Martin. The "dreadful stroke of calamity" that binds Lydgate to Laure is being unraveled:

> Again Laure paused a little and then said, slowly, "*I meant to do it.*"
>
> Lydgate, strong man as he was, turned pale and trembled: moments seemed to pass before he rose and stood at a distance from her. (15.182)

The intimate relation sought by Lydgate receives an unexplained shock as Laure offers this confession. The words Lydgate had just heard ("My foot really slipped") do not mean what he thought they meant and it is this meaning which Laure unravels when she states, "*I meant to do it.*"

The denouement of the melodrama takes place as Lydgate, having distanced himself from Laure, seeks to understand what he hears:

> "There was a secret, then," he said at last, even vehemently. "He was brutal to you: you hated him."
>
> "No! he wearied me; he was too fond: he would live in Paris, and not in my country; that was not agreeable to me."
>
> "Great God!" said Lydgate, in a groan of horror. "And you planned to murder him?" (15.182)

Before, the slip of Laure's foot was seen to be purely an accident, now, in Lydgate's eyes, it has become an intended act, it is planned, and, on account of this, it must have a cause. Accordingly, Lydgate declares that there is something secret, something hidden: the hidden actress has a hidden fact. Lydgate first explains what this fact is by theorizing that Laure's husband was brutal to her. Here, a sufficient cause would be sought. But such was not the case, Laure was merely tired of her husband and she did not, as he wished, want to live in Paris. Her disavowal of brutality is of no effect on Lydgate's inquiring mind. Convinced of her guilt, he can only utter the question, "And you planned to murder him?" To have planned the murder would satisfy Lydgate's understanding since there would be no loose ends: all is unraveled and tied together in the finality of a planned murder. As before, when the stabbing was believed to be accidental, Lydgate holds fast to what guides his understanding. In each instance, the result is the same, something which actually took place has been represented. Both explanations elicit the same fact: Laure's foot *really* slipped. But, as much as one explanation is flawed, so is the other. In Laure's reply to Lydgate's question, it turns out that the play may also be the murderer:

> "I did not plan: it came to me in the play—I meant to do it." (15.182)

It would be horrific enough for Lydgate if Laure had planned this act in advance. The murder was, however, accomplished without any preconceived design. It is in this fact that its horror would lie, a horror that is not without its effect on Lydgate who now stands as "mute" as the matter on which his researches had been focused. What Lydgate faces in his muteness is an act made possible by what the play was supposed to represent. Without the melodrama there would have been no murder. The same may be said of Laure since without her there would also be no murder. Consequently, when Laure says, "*I meant to do it,*" this intention has to be considered within the context that allows it to take place.

Without the unveiling of the "hidden fact" of her intention, it is impossible to elicit the actuality of her guilt from mere observation of the play and, at the same time, it is equally impossible for the law to interpret what actually happened. Both must decide in the absence of a fact they cannot elicit. Yet the admission of an intention is no resolution. The murder takes place as an act that should have only been its counterfeit, a counterfeit that ought to have preceded the actual occurrence of the stabbing. Laure's twice-repeated statement, "I meant to do it," unravels the kind of relation between what is intended and what is represented which supports the very motion of a representative act. In this unraveling, the literal usurps the figurative in order to render what the figurative would have concealed. It is this kind of figuration which supports and makes bearable the reciprocal impediment of Lydgate's two selves as well as his desire to marry Laure. Faced with what Laure unveils, Lydgate confronts the impediment of the figurative understanding he is guided by and it is this impediment which finds expression at the end of this scene—not just when Lydgate "stood mute" after hearing Laure say that she did not plan the murder but also when, "three days afterwards,"

> Lydgate was at his galvanism again in his Paris chambers, believing that illusions were at an end for him. He was saved from hardening effects by the abundant kindness of his heart and his belief that human life might be made better. But he had more reason than ever for trusting his judgement, now that it was so experienced; and henceforth he would take a strictly scientific view of woman, entertaining no expectations, but such as were justified beforehand. (15.183)

Lydgate recoils from Laure in order to return to the very experiments whose failure resulted in his attendance at the fateful performance of the melodrama. In effect, if what Lydgate returns to is not a persistent self, it is nonetheless a self that would seek persistence in scientific researches from which all performances such as that enacted through the melodrama are excluded.

From the profession of love, Lydgate retreats to the profession which, for him, presents "the most perfect interchange between science and art" (15.174), yet, he does so without any recognition of the interchange between science and language effected in this chapter of *Middlemarch.* Oblivious to such a recognition, Lydgate may believe that illusions are at an end for him, and that, accordingly, he may look to the rewards of an experienced judgment. As a result, Lydgate retreats from the art of the stage but does so by concealing its protagonist beneath another art, the art of his researches. By this concealment, Lydgate differentiates his subsequent life from the incident with Laure while, at the same time, dividing the art of the stage from the art of scientific inquiry. These distinctions are made in the name of science but, above all, in the name of a scientific method "entertaining no expectations, but such as were justified beforehand." Here, Lydgate not only returns to his situation prior to the fateful performance, when he sought to "elicit the facts he needed," he is also, once again, on the road to Avignon since the method to be adopted is already the method at work on that evening at the theater of the Porte Saint Martin and afterward when he sought to marry Laure. In the latter case, it is only because Lydgate is convinced of Laure's innocence that he pursues her. Thus, already "bound" to her as a result of her innocent act, Lydgate seeks the person to whom he has tied himself in order to elicit the word that would finally bind her to him: a mutual binding. Laure is, in effect, the "fact" needed to justify expectations which had apparently been justified beforehand (both by his own eyes and even legally). Consequently, Lydgate approaches Laure entertaining the expectation justified by the legal fact of her innocence as well as his own belief in what he has seen. But what happens denies this expectation by denying what had been justified beforehand. The return to eliciting hidden facts is a return to hidden actresses: hidden facts and hidden actresses are equal and reciprocal impediments even though, to this point, Lydgate only experiences the latter as an impediment ("Lydgate stood mute").

The impediment prompted by the actress is soon forgotten as Lydgate falls in love once again. On this occasion, he is "enamoured of that arduous invention which is the very eye of research, provisionally framing its object and correcting it to more and more exactness of relation" (16.194). The terms describing the research Lydgate undertakes in the wake of his experience of "hidden actresses" could hardly be more telling. In both cases, he is enamored, he invents according to what he sees, and what is seen serves as a frame which may be corrected in order to yield an ever greater exactness of relation. Such exactness justifies the frame while confirming its expectations. At the same time, the exactness of relation represented within this frame is meant to conceal any return of a hidden actress: the hidden fact, the primitive tissue is not allowed, in the name of science, to *appear as if* it were hidden behind something else (unlike the slip of Laure's foot which was not in any way hidden but takes place on stage for all to see). Consequently, it is such a slip that the hidden fact would cover up by means of a representation structured so as to unravel the object of its inquiry before the object can itself appear. Such is the condition of possibility of the primitive tissue, the primitive *textus*. As a result of this condition, the unraveling can only unveil itself as a weaving—a conclusion that emerges with the utmost clarity when the two threads of Lydgate's life, science and marriage, are considered as examples of the same predicament and not, as Lydgate would have them, in their separation, their difference.

As the eliciting of needed facts (the unraveling of a theory woven in advance) gives way to the desire to effect an interlacing, and as this interlacing is followed by the attempt to unravel the tissue that commands all weaving and unraveling, so, in the course of the novel, unraveling is succeeded by yet another weaving:

> Young love-making—that gossamer web! Even the points it clings to—the things whence its subtle interlacing are hung—are scarcely perceptible; momentary touches of finger tips, meetings of rays from dark orbs, unfinished phrases, lightest changes of cheek and lip, faintest tremors. The web is itself made of spontaneous beliefs and indefinable joys, yearnings of one life towards another, visions of completeness, indefinite trust. And Lydgate fell to spinning that web from his inward self with wonderful rapidity, in spite of experience supposed to be finished off with the drama of Laure—in spite too of medicine and biology. (36.380)

Now, Lydgate explicitly becomes a weaver engaged in the work of "subtle interlacings." In this work, he mirrors the weaving practiced by Rosamond, that is, the weaving through which she had represented to herself "a little future" in which Lydgate had no small part. In their mutual spinning, this future is realized to the extent that the resulting web represents what is to happen but which has not yet come into the present. Nevertheless, while this spinning is represented as mutually reciprocal (without impediments), this mutuality is also the result of an art similar to the one adopted by Lydgate in his attempt at "framing an object and correcting it to more and more exactness of relation" (16.194). The description of the "gossamer web" recounts the result of Rosamond's framing, her weaving, her ruminating and, above all, her acting. Because of these skills, Lydgate does not even recognize her as an actress. Furthermore, by contributing to the web she has been spinning, he conceals the fact that he is now "onstage" playing a part created for him in a history woven by Rosamond. Yet, such is his blindness and such his "arduous invention" ("the very eye of research") that he cannot see and, therefore, cannot know he is indeed playing this part. With this spinning (which effectively spells the end of his research), Lydgate has become an actor whose acting remains hidden from him and precisely because he does not draw to their conclusion the consequences of the drama represented by Laure but rather interrupted these consequences by a return to medicine and biology which takes the form of a return to the realm of apparently justifiable expectations. The drama performed at the theater of the Porte Saint Martin continues. In this scene, Lydgate would appear, and in particular would appear to himself, to be engaged in a spinning that is intentional and therefore not determined by a representation. The text, however, is Rosamond's. As a result of her weaving, both now act in accordance to what has been represented by this text, both in fact pursue what it ought to represent and only what it ought to represent.

If Lydgate becomes ensnared by Rosamond as the result of a drama that is not yet finished, two questions must be asked: the question of why this drama is unfinished as well as the related question of why his researches will always remain unfinished. Concerning the former, it could be said that such incompletion arises because the drama of Laure resists his interlacing (both with respect to his interpretation of what was represented on stage and with respect to his desire to be married, interlaced with her). Concerning the latter, it could be said that the primitive tissue itself resists his unraveling. One resists because it will not be bound together and the other resists because it will not be unbound. This binding and unbinding (as they appear in the forms of interlacing, weaving, and unraveling) are, however, closely related in the same activity: the activity that holds to the possibility of uncovering a fact in its actuality and not merely in a representation. Lydgate's collaboration in the weaving practiced by Rosamond is therefore no different from the weaving that underlies the pursuit of Laure and the continuance of his researches. Indeed, this weaving is constitutive of both this pursuit and his studies. Yet, to Lydgate, interlacing and unraveling remain separate activities and, because of this, they form a sequence of alternating movements, research/interlacing, unraveling/weaving. Within this sequence, each pair repeats the previous pair and, between each pair, another pair is created. Since the unfolding of this sequence is the history of Lydgate, such a history now appears as a weaving that accommodates or, more precisely, conceals reciprocal impediments at the center of each one of these pairings. Moreover, the alternation and differentiation between each part and each term of this sequence maintains a separation which is precisely what makes the unfolding of history possible (a consequence of this differentiation is that weaving and unraveling are represented as alternate activities—a necessary result if the history related by the narrator of this novel is even to appear historical).

At this point, the interlacing of *Middlemarch* and its narrator may be brought into view. As a result of the differentiation produced by the alternation between weaving and unraveling, the narrative also adopts the movement it has sought to unravel.[20] Through this differentiation, the narrative would still be woven together even as it appears to be unraveled. The story of Lydgate is, in this respect, the example of the narrator: Lydgate's story unfolds because he does not see that the part he acts (unraveler) is in fact the acting (out) of a representation (weaving) which effectively determines his actions. The mutual web of Rosamond and Lydgate is also such a representation, which is to say, they are only what they weave: their actions are the actions they represent to themselves and are in no way different from this representation. Accordingly, their weaving as well as the interlacing of their respective histories is an art of concealment, it conceals the fact to be elicited, it conceals what happens on the stage at the theater of the Porte Saint Martin, it conceals the primitive tissue, and it conceals what happens on both their stage and the stage on which the narrator sits (albeit without the comforts or the language of Fielding). But what are all these hidden facts?

Before considering the narrator's unraveling as a mode of concealing, let us first ask this question in a more particular way. What does this weaving conceal with respect to Rosamond and Lydgate? Two things: the nature of research into the primitive tissue and the reciprocal impediments that accompany such weaving whether they take place with respect to science or marriage. As the primitive tissue would be the product of Lydgate's weaving, so the future of Rosamond and Lydgate would be the product of a weaving that represents "visions of completeness" (the primitive tissue represents such a completeness since all tissue and all relation of whatever lives is to be derived from it, that is, all relation turns upon a vision ["the eye of research"] which does not see the condition of its visibility). The fate of Lydgate's history—and of Rosamond's—is that whatever they represent to themselves is at best a provisional framing that can never be actualized or demonstrated, their "visions of completeness" are a veil concealing a reciprocal impediment.[21] This impediment and its resultant muteness surfaces in the figure of the actress whose words do not permit a decision about whether or not she conceals an intention. Here, the sense in which Laure performs what is written or woven by the collaborating authors is different from the sense in which Rosamond and Lydgate perform their parts. They can never see themselves as their representation; to do so would be akin to committing a murder, the murder of the possibility of their narration. In short, this would be the murder of the difference that constitutes both the narratable and the representable, not to mention the logic of alternation (mutual reciprocation rather than reciprocal impediments) which assures their continuance. But, from within the weaving of Lydgate and Rosamond, such a murder would be impossible to produce, just as the primitive tissue, for the sake of missing a word, cannot be produced and all because the unraveling that takes place is guided by the structure of a representation that must first see what it presents to itself as something already different from itself. Only in the drama of Laure could this word be said to really exist, but, as we already know, when Laure responds to Lydgate's question, such a "word" is far from simple and precisely because it is so simple: "My foot *really* slipped." Does this "really" belong to the melodrama or to what happens on the stage that night? Does the slip belong to what precedes (the work of the collaborating authors) or to what follows (the performance of this collaboration)?

Rather than face what really happens in this word "really," Lydgate would murder this performance (of the melodrama or of *Middlemarch?*) and thereby decide the guilt of Laure while missing the textual arrest of this scene, its mezozeugma. To adhere to such a decision, Lydgate in fact murders the performance he would inquire into by determining it as only a mode of representation or repetition. In this way, Lydgate differentiates between actor and what is to be acted, or to use Austin's terms, Lydgate would differentiate between the performative and the constative—a distinction Laure's words do not affirm or deny. By means of this differentiation, Lydgate's weaving, interlacing, and unraveling (all activities of representing to oneself) manage to conceal the real performance of that evening as if it were behind a veil, and above all, behind a narrative. It is such a differentiation which makes history possible as the history of something, even though, as represented on the stage at the center of chapter 15 of *Middlemarch,* the historical is restricted to the actuality of a future perfect, the actuality of what appears is that which will have been: quod erat imitandum imitatio fuerit.

The Form of Difference

> *His mind glancing back to Laure while he [Lydgate] looked at Rosamond, he said inwardly, "Would* she *kill me because I wearied her?" and then, "It is this way with all women." But this power of generalizing which gives men so much the superiority in mistake over the dumb animals . . .*
>
> —Eliot, *Middlemarch*

Inasmuch as the narrator would be a historian, one can already discern, thanks to the history of Lydgate as it is recorded in chapter 15 of *Middlemarch,* that the actual unraveling of human lots practices an interlacing more complex than that ever attempted by Lydgate in his search for the primitive tissue. To trace the nature of this interlacing, one must first return to that point in chapter 15 when the narrator suggests that the failure of Lydgate's research is already determined since he succumbs to that "missing of the right word [which] befalls many seekers." As a result of this failing, Lydgate becomes the victim of a relation he cannot unravel (his ensnaring by Rosamond being the conclusive comment on this failing), or, which amounts to the same, he is the victim of a relation he can neither interlace nor weave, the very relation he would subsequently discover as if he had never been performing such an interlacing or weaving. It is this performance that the structure of representation (understood as the repetition of a present) effectively frames as if it were concealed, anterior, hidden.

At the same time, this concealing is contingent upon the possibility of a difference, the possibility of placing one thing (if not one foot) in front of another. Lydgate's project to discover the primitive tissue, rather than uncover the tissue from which all other tissue is derived, and therefore related, is in fact a project which, if it could ever be completed, would discover a tissue that can no longer be differentiated, in effect the discovery of what kills the possibility of making such a discovery as well as the possibility of discovery itself. The completion of Lydgate's research would be the end of the means through which the primitive tissue may possess a relation to all other tissue. But such an end is purely hypothetical and it would be utterly naive to assume that the philosophical tradition to which this search for an undifferentiated origin is frequently associated in contemporary literary theory as well as literary history can be set aside so easily. If anything, such a tradition is eminently capable of knowing and analyzing this end as its hypothesis. The point is rather that this end cannot be seen as anything but a hypothesis which holds the possibility of losing its hiddenness (ὑπό: under, below, beneath), of moving from proposition (ὑπόθεσις) and into position (θέσις)—in the sense that what is proposed or hypothesized underlies and determines what is to appear in its place. Consequently, to say that this tradition as well as Lydgate's research is doomed from the start is to misread the necessity of this failure in constituting, on the one hand, its possibility, and, on the other, its persistence. It is the nature and logic of this necessity and the interlacing it gives rise to that must now be observed on the stage where the narrator is positioned.

The story of Lydgate's history is, to a certain extent, the story of the narrator: both would unravel what has already been woven. In the case of Lydgate, one might say that the fate of such an unraveling is itself unraveled. It is this primary unraveling (of Lydgate's history) we will now be concerned with and, in particular, with its relation to the narrator's task. In the context of this concern, it is worth recalling the narrator's description of this task even though it would now appear in a different light:

> I at least have so much to do in unravelling certain human lots, and seeing how they were woven and interwoven, that all the light I can command must be concentrated on this particular web, and not

> dispersed over that tempting range of relevancies called the universe. (15.170)

This unraveler, in the attempt to *see* how human lots *were* woven and interwoven, does not seek a primitive tissue such as that sought by Lydgate, yet this task is nonetheless related to such a project. As Lydgate and Rosamond weave their desired denouements, the web they produce serves as an image. The unraveling of this image is the coming into history of what the web represents. In this instance, history replaces its representation, that is, history follows upon an arrangement of different threads which have been made to enter into relation with one another. History is therefore the result of a relation that is not in itself historical but rather theoretical in nature. Consequently, if what this arrangement portrays is to become historical it must be dissolved by what it represents: from the viewpoint of imitation, what is seen in the mirror is no longer the effect of a mirror or an image and neither is this a reversion of one for the other. For the moment, this process of dissolution, as it occurs in the sequence of episodes which culminates in the mutual spinning of Lydgate and Rosamond, allows us to see the concealing of the awareness that what the web portrays is in fact the denouement of the historical within and not outside of its representation.

This concealing is, however, not confined to Lydgate but may be observed as the lives of each of the principal characters in *Middlemarch* are unfolded. To pursue these other "Scenes of Provincial Life," as *Middlemarch* is subtitled, one would run the risk of becoming entangled in a "tempting range of relevancies" which enact and reenact in different forms the fate of, first, representing a scenario to oneself, and, second, acting upon the strength of that representation as if this acting were its hidden, anterior presence. What is of concern at this point is the relation of these forms, that is, the relation of their differences. It is this relation that is to be found at its most concentrated and yet most far-reaching in the figure of the narrator. Indeed, the very existence of these different forms depends upon the relations wrought by the narrator even though within their individual spheres they would constitute what Bichat considers "certain primary webs or tissues." Viewed from this perspective, the activity of the narrator would appear to perform the role written for the primitive tissue in the melodrama of Lydgate's research inasmuch as the narrator's task encompasses the spinning of these primary webs as well as the possibility of their interrelation. To this extent, the history of Lydgate would reflect the unraveling of the narrator both in the organization of its sequence and in the way that this history is itself an examination of unraveling.

At the same time, Lydgate's reflection of the narrator plays a part in a drama in which the narrator is also a performer. This part becomes especially clear if one recalls that, in this novel's description of the narrator's task, the act of unraveling is described first. It precedes both observation and knowledge of how certain human lots are woven and interwoven. The unraveling thus serves to bring the relation of whatever is woven and interwoven into the realm of what can be seen while presenting these relations as if they belonged to the already woven past. As such, this relation cannot precede the unraveling even though it may be represented as so doing. The unraveling causes the relation of what has already been woven and interwoven.[22] Without this relation there could have been no anterior weaving, no primary web or tissue. From this fact, which the historical necessarily hides from itself by means of what it weaves or interlaces, one can begin to discern how the web of narration is being spun: it proceeds from its own inability to relate what had been represented to itself as being possible to relate. In other words, it proceeds from a weaving only too aware of the difference from which it is spun. It is this inability of the web to coincide with what it ought to represent which provides the basis for the interlacing practiced by the narrator under the name of unraveling. The history of Lydgate is the story of the possibility of this kind of interlacing and, in a sense, the narrator achieves what Lydgate fails to realize. Yet this success cannot be confused with Lydgate's search for a primitive tissue. To finish what Lydgate attempts would have turned the narrator into a murderer of the possibility of history (but not history; like stones, history can never be murdered). The question of how the narrator unravels the history of this novel thus becomes the question of how such a murder is avoided. To return to the example of Lydgate, this is the question of how a word may be missed.

In an unpublished essay thought to have been written in 1868 (*Middlemarch* was begun the following year as a story which was, at that point, concerned solely with Lydgate), Eliot speaks of form in a way that is of particular significance to the activity of unraveling in this novel. Although the passage in which this occurs is of considerable length, it requires to be quoted in full if Eliot's understanding of the relation between form and difference is to be adequately presented:

> Plain people, though indisposed to metaphysical subtleties, can yet understand that Form, as an element of human experience, must begin with the perception of separateness, derived principally from touch [of which the other senses are modifications]; & that things must be recognized as separate wholes before they can be recognized as wholes composed of parts, or before these wholes again can be regarded as relatively parts of a larger whole.
>
> Form, then, as distinguished from merely massive impression, must first depend on the discrimination of wholes & then on the discrimination of parts. Fundamentally, form is unlikeness, as is seen in the philosophic use of the word Form in distinction from Matter; & in consistency with this fundamental meaning, every difference is form. Thus, sweetness is a form of sensibility, rage is a form of passion, green is a form both of light & of sensibility. But with this fundamental discrimination is born in necessary antithesis the sense of wholeness or unbroken connexion in space & time: a flash of light is a whole compared with the darkness which precedes & follows it; the taste of sourness is a whole & includes parts or degrees as it subsides. And as knowledge continues to grow by its alternating processes of distinction & combination, seeing smaller & smaller unlikenesses & grouping or associating these under a common likeness, it arrives at the conception of wholes composed of parts more & more multiplied & highly differenced, yet more & more absolutely bound together by various conditions of common likeness or mutual dependence. And the fullest example of such a whole is the highest example of Form: in other words, the relation of multiplex interdependent parts to a whole which is itself in the most varied & therefore the fullest relation to other wholes. Thus, the human organism comprises things as diverse as the finger-nails & tooth-ache, as the nervous stimulus of muscle manifested in a shout, & the discernment of a red spot on a field of snow; but all its different elements or parts of experience are bound together in a more necessary wholeness or more inseparable group of common

> conditions than can be found in any other existence known to us. The highest Form, then, is the highest organism, that is to say, the most varied group of relations bound together in a wholeness which again has the most varied relations with all other phenomena.[23]

Quite apart from its intrinsic significance, Eliot's discussion of form and difference in this passage could be read as a commentary upon the history of Lydgate as it has already been traced, as well as the explanation of the narrator's relation to that history. Eliot begins with the perception of separateness as it is derived from touch, and then goes on to state that the other senses (such as the sight employed by Lydgate in his research) are modifications of this sense which offers an essential experience of difference, an experience that takes place through contact and proximity. At the same time, Eliot's discussion is derived from a sequential logic which recognizes, first of all, separate wholes before wholes composed of parts may be perceived and then, as a result of this latter perception, even larger wholes may be recognized. The whole is first discriminated before it is seen to be part of another whole. Through this sequence, form yields to further complexity as each successive whole enters into relation with another in order to become parts of yet another whole. The principle fueling this growth is first called unlikeness and later difference. Eliot's deliberate use of these two terms is no mere stylistic variation, it articulates a relation between two interdependent and intimately connected senses of form, each of which is contributing to the other. First, we are told that form is unlikeness and then that every difference is form. Even though this formulation appears to be chiasmatic (as if Eliot had said, "form is difference, difference is form") one must also emphasize that the actual formulation ("form is unlikeness, . . . and every difference is form") already implies a relation that is not simply what one would associate with the reversibility and inversion of a self-including and self-concluding totality. The form produced by difference would be, at its most essential, single. Such a "single" form provides the basis for a more complex form composed of unlikeness. Here, the question of how a more complex whole composed of forms related by difference can be thought becomes crucial to an understanding of how the unraveled or differentiated threads of *Middlemarch* ought to be considered.

According to Eliot, such a complex whole is a process of knowledge that involves an alternating process of distinction and combination, or, in the terms of the present context, difference and relation. The two elements that form this alternation are mutually connected in their result, yet both this result and its alternation depend upon difference as their antecedent and motivating principle: "smaller & smaller unlikenesses" precede their "grouping & associating . . . under a common likeness," and "wholes composed of parts more & more multiplied & highly differenced, yet more & more absolutely bound together by various conditions of common likeness or mutual dependence." There would appear to be no boundary to a logic so inexhaustibly capable of reproducing itself and precisely because it turns upon the *relation* of difference: the only limit is difference itself and that is already a relation, already the integration of yet another part to an ever increasing whole. What might exceed this relation has only the appearance of doing so since the "highest Form . . . is the highest organism, that is to say, the most varied group of relations bound together in a wholeness which again has the most varied relations with *all other phenomena*" [emphasis mine]. In each case, the relation is articulated by a difference that separates in order to bind together. Such a difference is far from being a deconstructive formulation since it clearly sees heterogeneity as a cause of totality.

As already suggested, the work of this difference is the radical root of a metaphysics which, recognizing its inability to overcome the difference it makes, thematizes that very difference as the form of its knowledge. There are, in fact, two levels of metaphysical thought at work in this relation and they may be, for our present purposes, referred to in the name of Lydgate and in the name of the narrator. To say that the Lydgatean metaphysics (not to mention Casaubon's) is "deconstructed" in the course of this novel is to have already participated in the more intricate weaving that the unraveling of this so-called deconstruction would use to undermine a simplified metaphysics. What arises through this weaving is rather a relation that governs the aesthetic elaboration of metaphysics into narrative and in no way does this weaving or *its* unraveling lead to a deconstruction. This activity governs the possibility of a metaphysics *beyond* the monological and singularly unified understanding which only forms part of the story and part of the history it relates. Indeed, without the failure of the monological, there could be no metaphysical concept of history. It is precisely such a concept that informs Eliot's discussion of form.

Reading *Middlemarch* in the light of this discussion allows the complexity and intricacy of its parts to be seen. The reference to light as the condition of this seeing is no accident. In her discussion, Eliot's sole mention of light serves as an example of the definition of a whole (and in this "flash of light," the "sudden light" leading to Lydgate's discovery of a vocation is also implicated). Moreover, it describes the minimal articulation of the difference to which the "highest Form . . . [or] highest organism" and the narration of *Middlemarch* all belong. This articulation is given in the following manner: "A flash of light is a whole compared with the darkness which precedes & follows it." The logic through which this comparison becomes possible is crucial. The flash of light as a whole is defined in distinction to what it is surrounded by: darkness, night. The light breaks in upon the dark and it is the time and space in which it breaks that would appear to constitute its wholeness. But light separates and becomes whole through this separation as well as in the place of this separation.[24] Thus, as that which renders, this light has in its wholeness a differentiating effect: its wholeness is the difference it establishes. Light brings difference and within this difference its wholeness resides. Why light should be afforded so exemplary a status in explaining a differentiating wholeness is attributable to the fact that the relation it initiates may, by virtue of the essential simplicity of the example, stand as the most primitive and the most essential image for the beginning of history. Before light there is no genesis of relation, no genealogy of creation and procreation, no narrative and history. Thus, the whole imaged in this flash of light is more than a mere example but a "whole" that inaugurates the possibility of a differentiating wholeness. Yet this whole is not and cannot be complete by itself. It cannot be complete without the difference through which it is marked off from darkness. This "failing" is precisely what leads to "the most varied group of relations bound together in a wholeness which again has the most varied relations with all other phenomena." The flash of light rend-ing the darkness is the primitive form of the wholeness composed of the most varied relations and it becomes such because it is not in itself or by itself whole. Already in its very appearance, the flash of light takes place in "alternating processes of distinction and combination": it both joins and separates darkness. This process is far from seeking a translucence whereby darkness is overcome or rendered into light. Such an achievement *would have been* its end if only this flash of light had been whole in itself to begin with (then there would be no need for this process of entering into relation). This end being impossible, the best such a metaphysics can hope for is the tautology in which its continuance is assured: light is light. This tautology *is* the interlace *of* difference, the copula that also flashes in the middle of darkness but, as such, it can never be merely empty since this tautology is the guarantor of ever more varied relation, of ever increasing "wholeness" and thus of ever increasing difference at the very point where difference ought to have found itself. This failure is far from invalidating the whole process, on the contrary, it is the hidden fact of its affirmation.

Where, one might ask, does this leave the narrator of *Middlemarch* and, in particular, the task envisioned by its narrator? If history can only begin with relation, then the web to be unraveled by the narrator will have been the result of this differentiating activity. In the case of Lydgate, both his research and his pursuit of Laure were informed by such an activity: his research through its differentiation of tissue and his differentiation of what takes place on stage the evening Laure stabs her lover/husband. On each occasion, Lydgate misses the word that would complete the interlacing and weaving he seeks to unfold, in short, the word that neither affirms nor denies the deception he has represented to himself in order to become tied to an object. The narrator, when describing the nature of Lydgate's inquiry, is as emphatic about the failure of this inquiry as about an "awaiting answer" ("What was the primitive tissue? In that way Lydgate put the question—not quite in the way required by the awaiting answer; but such missing of the right word befalls many seekers" [15.178]). As already noted, this failure in the way the question is put turns upon its interrogative and its tense. "What was" anticipates a substance already defined, in essence, a wholeness resting in its singularity. Thus, to view the narrator solely through the perspective of Lydgate's unraveling would demand that the history to be unraveled in this novel is in the subject of "was"—whether this subject be fictional or actual is immaterial since both answer to a representational structure derived from a grammar. Lydgate's failure thus becomes the possibility of a history which arises out of the impossibility of either discovering or recovering something that never *was* but which happens in the attempt to recognize history. Rather than belonging to the past or to some origin, the primitive tissue *is* the relation of the "primary webs of tissues," which is to say that a primitive tissue is already at work ensuring the denial of its discovery as well as the possibility of a history in which the attempt to achieve its discovery will be unfolded.

The Primitive Theater

> γράμματα *are called* φάρμακα λήθης
>
> —George Eliot, *Folger Notebook* [Euripides]

> *There is the danger that not-being has got twisted up with being in an interlacing of this sort and it is very strange* [ἄτοπος: out of place].
>
> —Plato, *The Sophist*

As the emphasis upon a word in Lydgate's history makes clear, the weaving and unraveling practiced by both Lydgate and the narrator involves, first, a question of how discourse and language are to be understood, and second, a question of the relation between such an understanding and what appears to be heterogeneous to language. In pointing to these two questions, the emphasis upon a word places the narrative of this chapter within a philosopheme which also appears in Eliot's immediate intellectual context:

> En effet, les lettres ne sont rien par elles-mêmes, elles ne signifient quelque chose que par leur groupement sous telle ou telle forme qui donne un mot de telle ou telle signification. Le mot lui-même est un élément composé qui prend une signification spéciale par son mode de groupement dans la phrase, et la phrase, à son tour, doit concourir avec d'autres à l'expression complète de l'idée totale du sujet. Dans les matières organiques, il y a des éléments simples,

> communs, qui ne prennent une signification spéciale que par leur mode de groupement.[25]
>
> In effect, letters are nothing by themselves, they signify something only by their grouping in such and such a form which gives a word such and such a meaning. The word itself is a composed unit which takes on a special significance from the way in which it is combined in a sentence, and the sentence, in its turn, must agree with others in the complete expression of the total idea of its subject. Concerning organic materials, there are simple, common elements which take on a special significance only by the way in which they are grouped.

The passage is from Claude Bernard's *Leçons de physiologie expérimentale appliquée à la médecine* (1855–56), and not only does it reflect a tendency to resort to a linguistic paradigm as a means of interpreting the organic and biological but also it evokes the example of the formation of words as a means of evading the path Parmenides cautioned against taking, the path that leads into a discourse on nothing. Clearly a discourse on and of the letter ought to be avoided. However, as a commentary on Lydgate, this passage could well be rewritten in order to read: "The primitive tissue is, as a letter, nothing by itself," or, "the element capable of no further differentiation would be nothing (not even nothing) since, if isolated, any meaning or significance it might possess would have been erased by and in this isolation." It is thus in a word that the primitive tissue is to be found but a word already understood as a *textus,* that is, as a grouping of letters already understood as a semantic unit. Here, the starting point and goal of Lydgate's project ("the most perfect interchange of science and art") would be explicitly present in a word, in a *textus* of letters which marks the common ground of science and art. But, as in all interchanges of this kind, a perfect imitation is required. In other words, if there is to be such an interchange, science must be knowable as language. Such is the essential assumption of Claude Bernard in the passage just cited.

In this context, the hidden fact sought by Lydgate would require nothing more than the discovery and completion of a hidden grammar. Yet, as G. H. Lewes (who read and marked the passage by Bernard)[26] is witness to, this grammar can only assert, at its limit and as its limit, a theory of position, the position occupied by already recognizable words: "It is through the manifold ideal constructions of the Possible that we learn to appreciate the Actual. Facts are mere letters which have their meaning only in the words they form; and these words again have their meaning, not in themselves alone but in their positions in the sentence."[27] If "facts are mere letters," they would have no intrinsic significance, since without relation, without arrangement, they could possess no meaning but also, now, Lewes extends to words what Bernard restricted to letters. Is it the word or the letter which is nothing by itself? Predictably, the all too familiar failing of a one-to-one correspondence between sign and signified would raise its head here. But, what is less familiar and less recognized in this all too recognizable trope of arbitrariness is the role this failing plays in an ever more pervasive principle of meaning whose expression is less concerned with reference to a substance or an object than with the possibility of entering into ever increasing sets of relations—in a way that recalls Eliot's reflection on form and difference. Indeed, what Lewes describes as "the Actual" is constituted by such relations rather than by something already existing. Accordingly, the function of a scientist can no longer be one of simply transcribing the real. In any case, the mirror is defective and recognized as such. Such a defect does not, however, arise from any failure in the mirror's ability to reflect: the defect lies in the fact that the mirror can reflect an event without that event having become an object for reflection. The mirror, like the recourse to the grammatical paradigm of language is blind to what would be called history as well as to the meaning bestowed upon a group of events or even a grouping of words or letters. In both cases, what is obscured may be posed in the question, "Why this grouping rather than another?" Or, more specifically in relation to language, "Why these letters rather than those to produce the sign that it is said to mean . . . ?"

Prior to either Eliot, Lewes, or Bernard, the question of a linguistic paradigm and its relation to a primary interlacing or primitive tissue may be traced to the concluding section of Plato's *Sophist*. In the context of an inquiry into the nature of discourse, the Stranger gives the following account of the origin of discourse:

> STRANGER: . . . when "lion," "stag," "horse" are spoken and all the other names of those who perform these actions, such a succession

> does not yet make discourse (λόγος), for in neither case does the voicing (φωνηθέντα) of the words indicate action or inaction or the existence of what is or is not, until the verbs (ῥήματα) are mingled (κεράσῃ), then the words fit, and their first combination (πρώτη συμπλοκή) becomes a sentence (λόγος), about the first and shortest form of discourse (λόγων). (*Soph.* 262ᵇ9–ᶜ7)[28]

According to the Stranger, it is from a πρώτη συμπλοκή, or more precisely, from a "primary interlacing" which mingles verbs with names that a discourse or sentence may arise. Συμπλήκειν, to plait or weave together, is both the condition and the effect of language.[29] Why this example should occur at this point in the *Sophist* is made clear in a short statement that closely precedes this Platonic reference to a "primitive tissue":

> STRANGER: The separation (διαλύειν) of each thing from all is the utterly final obliteration of all discourse (τελεωτάτη πάντων λόγων . . . ἀφάνισις). For our power of discourse is derived from the interweaving (συμπλοκὴν) of the forms (εἰδῶν). (*Soph.* 259ᵉ4–6)[30]

The separation described by the Stranger would also be an unraveling to the extent that the word used for separation in this passage contains the verb that refers to the act of untying or loosening.[31] As such, this separation ought to be the undoing of the primary interlacing on which all discourse is supposed to rest. Yet, this separation would hardly lead to a philosophic tragedy, that is, to a philosophy obliterated by its own hand. This *katharsis* is, as it were, only entertained since the threat it poses is always blunted by the ability to discourse about such an obliteration.

For the Stranger and his philosophy, what threatens most is only thinkable in terms of what is at stake, namely, philosophy. Consequently, what constitutes a threat is thought in terms of an intermixture of philosophy and *its* obliteration.[32] What is really at stake then is an intermixture that allows philosophy to think and thereby control (which in the present case means deny) its own end.

The crucial threat posed by intermixture becomes explicit in the exchange that comes directly after the foregoing quotation:

> STRANGER: Well, consider how we were struggling at just the right moment against that sort [of separation] and were proving (προ-

> σηναγκάζομεν [also "forcing"]) that one mingles (μείγνυσθαι) with another.
>
> THEAETETUS: To what purpose?
>
> STRANGER: Our purpose was to establish discourse as one of the kinds of things that exist. If we were deprived of this, we should be deprived of philosophy, which would be the greatest deprivation; but at the present moment we must come to an agreement about what discourse is; if we were robbed of it by its absolute non-existence, we could no longer discourse (λέγειν) and we should be robbed of it if we agreed that there is no mixture (μεῖξιν) of anything with anything. (*Soph.* 260a1–b260b2)

The possibility of discourse is to rest upon an agreement as the difference which separates one thing from another is allayed through mixture. What this agreement aims at is spelled out by a return to the question of not-being which lies at the center of the argument between philosopher and sophist in the course of this dialogue (there can be no theory of language without the resolution of this question since a theory of language is at the same time always a theory of meaning). At this point, the Stranger states the conclusion reached in this earlier argument, namely, "We found that not-being was one of the classes of being scattered throughout all being" (*Soph.* 260b7–8). Now, it is such a discovery which is to be looked for in discourse, that is, whether not-being "mingles (μείγνυται) with opinion and discourse" (260b10–11). As the Stranger goes on to say, the reason behind this inquiry is to find out if false discourse is possible (260c1–4), because, if it is, then deception is possible, and if deception is possible, then the discourse of the sophist (predicated upon the denial of any existence for not-being) will have been shown to be a mere juggling of words, a sleight of hand.

In the following passage, the Stranger outlines the attempt to relate not-being to being through otherness, an attempt that clearly demonstrates that one cannot simply oppose difference to a philosophical tradition whose thematization of unity has always been accompanied by a constant effort to think difference in analogy to what already exists:

> STRANGER: We have not only pointed out that things which are not are, but we have also shown what the form (εἶδος) of not-being is;

> for we have pointed out that the nature of the other (τὴν θατέρον φύσιν) exists and is cut into pieces throughout all existing things in their relations to one another, and we have dared to say that precisely each part of the other which is contrasted with being, really is not-being. . . . as for what we have now said not-being to be, someone, must either refute us and show that we are wrong, or so long as he cannot do that, he too must say, as we do, that the classes [of being] mix together (συμμείγνυται) with one another, and being and the other pervade all things and pervade one another, and the other since it participates in being, is [has existence], by reason of this participation, yet is not that in which it participates, but other, and since it is other than being, it belongs out of necessity to not-being. (*Soph.* 258d5–c3, 259a2–b1)

That the other is already understood in these terms by Plato points to the caution with which one must approach the belief that a literary text is, and cannot help but be, traversed by an otherness which turns out to be, all too frequently, nothing less than *its* otherness. In this passage, such an otherness, or not-being, performs the role of a difference within being. This difference, as the Stranger emphasizes, is neither the contrary nor the opposite of being but rather the relation of all that is, of all the forms of being (*Soph.* 255c–e). Here, Eliot's "every difference is form" should again be kept in mind and not only because of this Platonic determination of otherness but also because this determination occurs in the context of an argument concerning the interlacing of language as the reproduction of meaning. The thematization of this otherness as *something* that traverses the literary text would also be traceable to this attempt to maintain the thought of a totality that has already incorporated otherness within itself and does so through a theoretical understanding of language. Yet, in the case of both Plato and Eliot, more is involved than the mere tracing of an analogy between language and being which would, in the last instance, only affirm what it reflects into itself. It is at this point that the Stranger's transition from the relation between being and not-being to the question of deception in language becomes crucially important.

After recalling that not-being is or has existence, the Stranger moves to the demonstration that the interlacing which relates nouns and verbs into a statement of reference and meaning also reflects the existence of not-being. As the sequence of this argument indicates, knowledge of the existence of not-being is the prerequisite to a theory of language. In the context of the *Sophist,* such a demonstration of the interlacing of not-being within language will seek to drive the sophist from the cover under which he is said to have taken refuge, namely, the denial of false speech on which rests the sophist's argument that not-being cannot exist because what does not exist cannot have any kind of existence (*Soph.* 260^{b}11–^{d}3). The demonstration proceeds by way of two grammatically indistinguishable statements. The first, "Theaetetus sits," is agreed by both Theaetetus and the Stranger to belong to and to be about Theaetetus. The second, "Theaetetus, whom I am talking to at this moment, flies," it is also agreed meets the same conditions. Yet, one is to be true and the other false. Concerning the first, the Stranger comments, "The true one (ἀληθὴς) states about you that the things that are are" (*Soph.* 263^{b}4–5), and concerning the second, "the false statement states about you things other than the things that are. . . . and accordingly states things that are not as being" (*Soph.* 263^{b}7–12). From this, there arises "a combination (σύνθεσις) of verbs and names of that kind [which] seems to be in its being truly a false statement (λόγος ψευδής)" (*Soph.* 263^{d}2–4). The demonstration of falsity answers to the necessity that "imitations of real things" should be possible. At the same time and from the same argument, the Stranger would account for the existence of "a fallacious art (τέχνην . . . ἀπατητικήν)" (*Soph.* 264^{d}4–5). Through this art, the sophist would always speak of not-being as if it has no existence at all. What emerges as absolutely crucial, then, is to know this difference, that is, to know nothing as something—what amounts to a difference between what is and what is (not). By means of the Stranger's arguments, the fallacious art of the sophist would be located within the discourse it appears to oppose and even threaten with obliteration. Nevertheless, this threat is only conceivable within the horizon of the Stranger's understanding of discourse, hence the impossibility of attributing to it any power of escaping the interlacing to which it owes its existence.

Thanks to this interlacing, the Stranger may assert a definition of language which ought to permit him to ensnare a sophist within philosophic discourse. To be tracked down, the sophist must practice a discourse of true falsity in the sense that it imitates the form of truth while speaking falsely. Without this difference and without a knowledge of deception through which the discourse of the sophist is distinguished from the discourse of the philosopher, there could never be imitation: the possibility of imitation is contingent upon a knowledge of deception which is itself contingent upon a knowledge of imitation (the definition of deception is an imitation that does not present what it is). Consequently, by determining the possibility of falsity in language, the sophist's discourse could be nothing other than truly deceptive—without this distinction there would be no determinable difference between sophist and philosopher, between truth and falsehood. But, for this distinction to be tenable, the difference it assumes will demand the interlacing of imitation and deception as a dialectically differentiated yet inseparable pair.

In Plato, the necessity of such an interlace is given its most radical expression in the course of the dialogue that takes place on the day following that of the *Sophist*. In this dialogue, *The Statesman,* the primitive tissue of the *Sophist* again makes its appearance. On this occasion it occurs within an extended analysis of the art of weaving. The position this discussion holds in *The Statesman* is of considerable importance to the situation of both the Stranger and the sophist elaborated in the previous day's arguments. In the *Statesman,* the analysis of weaving intervenes when it is discovered that an example (and the paradigm of language in the *Sophist* cannot be forgotten here) has been found to require another example. This failing first leads to the necessity of giving an example of what example is. The example chosen at this point is again concerned with language—such is the example that paves the way for the discussion of weaving, the discussion of an example that will not fail. And again, the "primary interlacing" (πρώτη συμπλοκή) is involved although on a more radical level than when it appeared in the *Sophist.* Here, it is concerned with letters:

> STRANGER: . . . We know that children, when they are just getting some knowledge of letters . . . recognize particular letters well enough in the shortest and simplest syllables, and can make correct statements about them. . . . But, in other syllables they are once more in doubt about those same letters, and err in opinion and speech about them. . . . Wouldn't this be the easiest and best way to lead them to the letters they do not know? . . . To lead them first to

> the syllables in which they had correct opinions about those same letters and then to set the groups they did not yet recognize beside the syllables they recognize and by comparing them to show that their nature is the same in both combinations (συμπλοκαῖς), and to continue until the letters about which their opinions are correct have been shown alongside all those about which they are doubtful. Being shown in this way, the known letters become examples (παραδείγματα) and bring it about that every letter is in all syllables always called by the same name, either by differentiation from other letters, in case it is different, or because it is the same. (*Statesman* 277e3–278c1)

Following upon the failure of a chosen example, the Stranger offers a theory of example in the form of a method for teaching children to recognize letters. But, why, above all else, should language be chosen to exemplify the nature of example? What can language be an example of? Language?

In an earlier dialogue, *Phaedrus,* Socrates recalls the claim of Theuth that his invention of letters "will make the Egyptians wiser and will improve their memories; it is a medicine for wisdom and knowledge that I have discovered (μνήμης τε γὰρ καὶ σοφίας φάρμακον ηὑρέθη)" (*Phaedrus* 274e5–7). In reply, Socrates repeats the Egyptian king's objection to Theuth's claim: "You, who are the father of letters, have been led by your affection to ascribe to them a power opposite to that which they really possess. For this invention will produce forgetfulness in the minds of those who learn to use it, because they will not practice their memory. Their trust in writing, produced by external characters which are no part of themselves, will discourage the use of their own memory within them" (*Phaedrus* 274e9–275a5).[33] In the conclusion to this criticism of Theuth's invention, the Egyptian king accuses Theuth of having in fact only invented "an elixir, not of memory but of reminding (οὔκουν μνήμης ἀλλὰ ὑπομνήσεως φάρμακον νῦρες)" (*Phaedrus* 275a5–6), the latter being the effect of a writing which can only offer the semblance of wisdom. This kind of distinction repeats the argument employed by the Stranger against the sophist: like the sophist, writing and letters deal with the "semblance of wisdom" and, as such, they cause a forgetting of true wisdom and, indeed, of truth. Is the example used at this point in the *Statesman* exempt from such a forgetting? Is the example of the nature of example not a form of recollection, not a form of memory but rather a mere reminder itself incapable of recalling what it is supposed to recollect? If it is a form of memory, then this example of the learning of a primary interlacing serves to reiterate the nature of discourse (and therefore of philosophy) as the possibility of recollection.

Earlier in the *Phaedrus,* Plato refers to this activity of recollecting as the attempt to remember "those things which our soul once beheld, when it journeyed with the god and, lifting its vision above the things which we now say exist, rose up into real being" (*Phaedrus* 249ᶜ1–3). Moreover, Socrates continues, "it is just that the thought of the philosopher alone has wings, for he is always, through the potentiality of memory (μνήμῃ κατὰ δύναμιν) close to the very thing which is the godliness of the god. . . . A man who employs such memories (ὑπομνήμασιν) rightly is always being initiated into perfect mysteries and he alone becomes truly perfect" (*Phaedrus* 249ᶜ4–8). What was formerly distinguished from true memory (reminder or ὑπόμνημα), is viewed in this passage as providing the means through which recollection may perform the task of recovering what has been forgotten. Memory (μνήμη) is tied to what recalls (ὑπόμνημα), as the philosopher is tied to the sophist, as being is tied to not-being: one would always *be* beneath (ὑπό) the other. Moreover, as becomes clear in the dialogue immediately following Socrates' account of the Egyptian king's criticism of Theuth's invention of letters, the ability to come close to the godliness of the god involves a knowledge written in the soul (γράφεται ἐν τῇ . . . ψυχῇ [276ᵃ5–7]), an involvement that presupposes both discourse and the writing of letters. However, it is only the writing in the soul that is to be granted legitimacy. Consequently, in order to conceal, that is, cover and thereby protect such a writing from the threat of irreversible forgetfulness, its interlacing must, in the last instance, be about something, it must be imitative. For this reason, the sophist cannot be allowed to escape the conditions of discourse set by the Stranger but only, as it were, play within the rules of a philosophic game played with the letters of the alphabet. It is precisely the rules of this game that children learn when they are taught to recognize letters, syllables, nouns, verbs, and the first and shortest form of discourse, the primary interlacing (πρώτη συμπλοκή) which says little about what Theaetetus does ("Theaetetus sits. . . . Theaetetus flies") but plenty about the rules of an essentially dialectical interlace.

At the same time as the example of the nature of example gathers together the threads of the Platonic discourse, it establishes the need for an art of weaving. But, the manner in which this art is to be understood is determined in advance by means of an exemplary example (language) which intervenes after the failure of one example and does so in order to assure the success of another. To the extent that this intervention recalls the "primary interlace" that neither the sophist nor the philosopher can evade, it points to what the art of weaving is itself predicated upon: a play of truth and falsity in which neither may obliterate the other, or, to put this another way, the philosopher cannot murder the sophist since, as the Stranger rightly points out in the *Sophist,* to do so would be to obliterate all discourse and therefore all philosophy. Such a murder, such a self-destruction, would be the perfect imitation: a philosophy whose forgetfulness causes it to entertain the possibility of becoming what it represents to itself as its *telos,* an undifferentiated oneness, a primitive tissue no longer requiring the art of weaving to protect itself. But, inasmuch as this perfection is the denouement of the representation of philosophy as well as the melodrama narrated in chapter 15 of *Middlemarch,* it would be the end of a knowledge of deception and therefore it would make the recollection it is predicated upon impossible.

For philosophy, the end of knowledge (and therefore deception) would indeed be a dream, a phantasm whose substantiation or demonstration would force it to commit the act it cannot do if philosophy is to be possible, that is, philosophy would be forced to have a hand in its own murder. Philosophy murdered as a result of acting on the strength of what it represents to itself as possible. To avoid such a tragedy—or is it a melodrama?—the Stranger, at the end of the dialogue entitled the *Sophist,* will grant both blood and lineage (*Sophist* 268^{d}3) to the sophist.[34] The sophist must be a real threat, the sophist must have a history even if it is in the form of a history of nothing. This history is necessary because the philosopher requires that there be a language of deception (what the Stranger calls the juggling of the sophist) in order to philosophize. But does the juggler need a discourse of so-called absolute truth in order to juggle?

Hardly, for the philosopher is already a juggler although the philosopher's juggling has been given another name, the art of weaving, the art of spinning the "cloathes" that Coleridge could not produce in his attempt to demonstrate the absolute principle adopted in the *Biographia*—not to mention the clothes which, for Hegel, go hand in hand with the beginning of reflection.[35] Nevertheless, although it may be to Coleridge's credit that he could not adequately perform such a spinning, the same cannot be said of Plato, who, by incorporating the sophist, not only produced the philosopher's new clothes but also the necessity of continually renewing these clothes. From Plato we may derive the theoretical fashions in which even the question of theory is ignored—*les théories de la dernière mode*. As the *Statesman* underlines, such clothes are spun from the assurance that one can know what an art of deception really is. What is then at stake for philosophy, theory, and history if they are to be discourses of knowledge is a knowledge of deception and what this knowledge is itself dependent upon is nothing more and nothing less than an ability to make (a) difference. The difference produced through the pretense to know deception is the difference that not only permeates what the Stranger calls being, but also distinguishes between being and not-being. The possibility of narrative and history is derived from this same pretense to know deception since, without it, there could be nothing to recollect except those rem(a)inders whose collection can neither affirm nor deny what they are said to recollect. But, by what weaving is this pretense possible?

As the Stranger comments after defining the art of weaving, this example was not chosen merely for its own sake ("no reasonable person would want to pursue the definition of weaving for its own sake" [*Statesman* 285d8–9]). For what sake was it pursued? For the same reason the sophist was pursued? Not quite. Where the sophist was pursued in order to establish the discourse in which the pursuit was conducted, the pursuit of the art of weaving aims more explicitly at a dissection guided by a logic of cutting (τμῆσις).[36] The nature of this logic appears in the Stranger's introduction to the art of weaving:

> STRANGER: . . . just as we divided each subject before by cutting off parts from parts (τέμνοντες μέρε μερῶν), why not now apply the

> same process to weaving (ὑφαντικὴν) and, by going through each step as briefly as we possibly can, arrive quickly what concerns our present purpose? (*Statesman* 279^{b}7–^{c}3)

The first series of incisions are made as the Stranger seeks to define the nature of clothes. The definition begins with the statement that "all things that we make or acquire are for the sake of doing something or else to prevent something from being done" (*Statesman* 279^{c}7–9). The preventative class is now focused upon since this is obviously the class to which clothes belong. In order to proceed, this class is divided into two, "spells and antidotes" and "material defenses," the former being the category that is cut off at this point. Subsequently, a whole chain of incisions takes place, material defenses are split into equipment for war or protection, equipment for protection is divided according to its function of providing either a shelter or a covering, coverings are separated into those placed underneath or else wrapped around someone, wrappings are split into those composed of one piece or of many, the latter are divided according to whether they are stitched or unstitched, the unstitched are separated into those made of plant fiber and those made of hair, and finally, those made of hair are defined according to whether or not any other matter such as glue has been used in their manufacture.

After the sequence of division through which one element is excluded at each stage, a definition is arrived at: only those items which have been combined in and through themselves are given the name of clothes (*Statesman* 279^{e}4). Having defined the nature of clothes, the Stranger concludes this deduction by stating that the art of weaving (since the greatest part of it is concerned with the making of clothes, that is, defenses) differs only in name from the art of clothes-making. From this it can be seen that the art of weaving is understood as the example of whatever is united or joined together in and through itself. Such an understanding is made explicit when, after pointing out that the process of weaving is preceded by a process of separation, the Stranger states that "the web is certainly a joining together I suppose (Τὸ μὲν τῆς ὑφῆς συμπλοκή τίς ἐστί που)" (*Statesman* 281^{a}3). By making this distinction, the Stranger avoids the eventuality that the art of weaving would be confused with the art that prepares the threads, the art of carding (281^{a}8). By means of this distinction, weaving will be cut off from the arts of separation.

Through this and several subsequent distinctions, the Stranger moves to the definition of the example, that is, to the precise nature of the art without which all the other subsidiary arts (cut off during the development of the Stranger's argument) can have no meaning or purpose. At the center of the Stranger's argument, the following definition occurs:

> STRANGER: . . . when that part of the art of composition which is included in the art of weaving forms a web by the right intertwining (εὐθυπλοκιᾴ: straight weaving or evenness of texture) of woof and warp, we call the entire web (πλεχθὲν) a woolen garment, and the art which directs this process we call weaving (ὑφαντικήν). (*Statesman* 283ᵃ4–8)[37]

The example of weaving becomes, in these words, the example of a straight and unswerving art whose end is to provide protection other than the protection that may be received from the "antidotes" (ἀλεξιφάρμακα) against which the tmetic method of this argument develops. That the argument is to be set against precisely this kind of protection is made clear when, after recapitulating his definition of clothes, the Stranger comments that "at the very beginning we separated the art of magic which is concerned with antidotes" (*Statesman* 280ᵉ1–2). From the setting aside of magic, the discourse of the Stranger moves to the sought-after art which, in his words, "manufactures a defense of wool . . . called the art of weaving" (*Statesman* 280ᵉ3–4). This defense is referred to by the word πρόβλημα, that is, by a word that describes something put forward as a defense or as a barrier. What the Stranger is aiming at in this section of the *Statesman* thus becomes the definition of an essential art capable of producing barriers that are held together by means of the straight weaving, obstacles produced by the art of weaving which are destined to be reproduced upon unraveling.

The point where this art of the barrier would come to an end is precisely the point where example will not need another example—the reason given by the Stranger for the introduction of the discussion of weaving as well as for the example involving the recognition of letters by children. This is also the point where example and what it is supposed to represent ought to be joined in a straight or even weaving. In the case of the *Sophist* as well as of the narrator of *Middlemarch,* this weaving *was* not to be found in the discovery of a substance, a Lydgatean primitive tissue. And it is not a question of a substance in the *Statesman* either, since the example that is presented as not failing is the example that does not represent anything except the means through which it has been produced. This means, tmetic in essence, is a form of separation, division, and distinction such as that which first appears with the flash of light in the darkness. In the definition of language and weaving, such a separation would always be strung together precisely because separation and difference are understood as prior moments whose historical purpose is to be joined or woven together (in this respect the art of carding can only be invented for weaving). As such, separation would only be understood in terms of the joining it makes possible and which has been substituted in its place. To point to another meaning of the word used to describe this cutting (τμῆσις), a wound or incision is made as the place of a difference. Subsequent acts of joining, interlacing, and weaving represent the attempt to close this incision but without completely doing so. To erase it would destroy the memorial (ὑπόμνημα) without which recollection could not take place. Thus the attempt to close posits the necessity of repeating the τμῆσις, the wounding which makes recollection always remember that it must repeat this wounding. But can recollection remember even this? Does it wound something anterior to itself? If so, then, it is in the repetition of this self-inflicted wound that the subsequent weaving would assert that it may in fact represent something (if only this wounding). In such a self-reflexive act, the art of this weaving would disappear from view because all there is to be seen would be what has been presented. But, if not, then recollection could offer no better knowledge of history than those inscriptions on a headstone that could also be referred to by the word used for memory (μνήμη).[38] (Is this why Pallas Athene rends the web of Arachne? Unable to find a flaw which tells of the incision and wounding that is the condition of the web, does Athene make her incision in order to ensure that the web of Arachne will henceforth always be known as being about this incision?)

It is in the belief that an incision such as that made by Athene decides what the interlacing or weaving of the primitive tissue is about that Lydgate is ensnared. Despite judicious use of the microscope, he cannot see that the difference he seeks is neither visible nor invisible. Lydgate demands a headstone that would say and mean "here lies the primitive tissue," a demand as conceivable as an inscription that reads "Lydgate flies." Yet, while Lydgate's unraveling comes to an end in his inability to relate difference to a tissue (and ipso facto to a body), the narrator's unraveling would be predicated upon this very inability and, accordingly, it becomes the narrative of such impediments. Consequently, to the extent that the narrative of Lydgate's researches into the essence of relation can be read as an inquiry into the very possibility of history, the narrator's unraveling may be read as the narrative of the impossibility of such a history, which is to say, the impossibility of the narrative of history is the point at which theory and history become possible as the theory and history of literature. The unraveling of one would spin the web of the other. Here, the barrier or defense (πρόβλημα) that structures the argument of Plato's *Statesman* provides the basis of another kind of history: the exemplary history of the failure of history (for example). Nevertheless, the exemplary history of such a barrier may only repeat Lydgate's return to his studies after the meeting with Laure. In Lydgate's case, the deception offered by causation trips on a foot that cannot hold its ground and it is on the same foot (that *really* slipped) that the narrator's exemplary history will repeatedly trip as long as the failing it narrates is attributed to a self-deceived Lydgate. The recognition that such a failing arises from deception would still hold to the possibility of a crime having been committed on the stage at the Porte Saint Martin, to the possibility of a murder caused by a mirror. Saying that it came to me in the play would amount to saying that it came to me in a mirror if the text of the play is granted the ability to determine a historical act. Such an act would now become the history of its representation as it posits a difference within itself and then proceeds to narrate the history of this difference (in, for example, the impediment of Lydgate). Indeed, the historical in *Middlemarch* demands such a difference; it constitutes the activity of weaving and unraveling in each of their forms even though this activity which gives rise to a sense of history is plainly the result of a present cause, a present defect. For this reason the narrator is always a "belated historian" (15.170), a historian who is always *after* a history that has not yet gone before and, accordingly, is always *after* a past written in words that have no memory. As such, the presentation of the narrative as the unraveling of a preexistent web becomes the attempt to give pastness to a history composed of not yet present relations, a history that may not be narrated except by means of performing a wounding of these relations. Unraveling is in effect the barrier of weaving and interlacing, as well as the barrier of a belatedness which already assumes there is something to come after(ward). But, then, what does weaving and its history ever go after but the problem of their (own) invention? περὶ τῆς προβλημάτων ποιητικῆς . . . λέγωμεν ἀπολαβόντες. . . . About the production of barriers . . . let us speak setting apart. . . .

Notes

Preface

1. The question and these remarks occur in an essay Benjamin published in 1931 under the title "Literaturgeschichte und Literaturwissenschaft" [Literary History and Literary Scholarship] in *Gesammelte Schriften,* ed. Rolf Tiedemann and Hermann Schweppenhäuser, 7 vols. (Frankfurt: Suhrkamp, 1974–89), 3.1:283–90.

2. The current interest in the topic of literary history may be gauged from essays recently collected by Marshall Brown (*PMLA* 107 [1992]: 13–104), David Perkins (*Theoretical Issues in Literary History,* Harvard English Studies 16 [Cambridge: Harvard U. P., 1991]). The volume of essays collected by Ralph Cohen in 1974 should also be mentioned in this context (*New Directions in Literary History* [Baltimore: Johns Hopkins U. P., 1974]). Recent books on this subject include Perkins's *Is Literary History Possible?* (Baltimore: Johns Hopkins U. P., 1992) and Timothy Bahti's study *Allegories of History: Literary Historiography after Hegel* (Baltimore: Johns Hopkins U. P., 1992).

3. Thus Perkins: "There is a very real question whether postmodernist literary history . . . can serve the purposes for which histories were written if these purposes are still to organize the past, to make it comprehensible, to explain why it had the character and tendency it did, and to bring it to bear on our own concerns. . . . Thus literary history is in a state of ferment and crisis, not for the first time" (Introduction, *Theoretical Issues in Literary History,* 6). The tendency to blame postmodernism or poststructuralism for this crisis is not, however, universal. As René Wellek already confessed in 1982, critical history, the twin of literary history, is not a convincing form of history: "The attempts at evolutionary history have failed. I myself have failed in *The History of Modern Criticism* to construe a convincing scheme of development. I discovered by experience that there is no evolution in the history of critical argument" (*The Attack on Literature and Other Essays* [Chapel Hill: U. of North Carolina P., 1982], 77). It should not go unnoticed that it is the essential material of history, experience, which teaches that there is no convincing scheme of development to explain what the character and tendency of critical history might be, never mind "why it had the character and tendency it did."

4. For instance, one could mention the conference entitled "The Lan-

guages of Criticism and the Sciences of Man" held at the Johns Hopkins Humanities Center, October 18–21, 1966, and the subsequent publication of its proceedings (1970; *The Structuralist Controversy,* ed. Richard Macksey and Eugenio Donato [Baltimore: Johns Hopkins U. P., 1972]).

5. In the sense given to interpretation when Paul de Man wrote that "to become good literary historians, we must remember that what we usually call literary history has little or nothing to do with literature and that what we call literary interpretation—provided only that it is good interpretation—is in fact literary history" ("Literary History and Literary Modernity," in *Blindness and Insight,* 2d ed. [Minneapolis: U. of Minnesota P., 1983], 165). This sentence has had a considerable currency in the return to literary history documented in note 2 above, in particular, it occurs as a refrain across the essays collected by Brown and Perkins.

6. Benjamin, *Gesammelte Schriften,* 3.1:283. One might also add that the first poetics of literature had a similar origin: Aristotle kept lists of the plays performed at Athens.

7. On the relation between this phrase from Yeats's introduction to the *Oxford Book of Modern Verse* (1936) and M. H. Abrams's *The Mirror and the Lamp* (New York: Oxford U. P., 1953), see also Jonathan Culler, "The Mirror Stage," in *The Pursuit of Signs* (Ithaca: Cornell U. P., 1981), 162–63.

8. Is it a coincidence that the emergence of a "new" history could date the moment from which it would be possible to pronounce that for us theory is a thing of the past? This gesture toward the past has displayed a significant historical persistence whenever the possibility of interpreting literature, and, as in Hegel's case, overcoming literature is at stake. Such a gesture may also be found in the course of Aristotle's *Poetics* when Aristotle speaks of tragedy having come to a "standstill" (ἐπαύσατο [$49^{a}15$]).

9. In approaching the question of literary history and literary theory through the opening of the question of mimesis, this book owes a particular debt to the broaching of this question in the work of Philippe Lacoue-Labarthe, in particular, the essays collected under the titles *Le sujet de la philosophie* (Typographies I) (Paris: Aubier-Flammarion, 1979) and *L'imitation des modernes* (Typographies II) (Paris: Galilée, 1986).

10. Nietzsche also describes the recognition of a new historical epoch in terms of a transfiguration: "*Transfiguration:* Die ratlos Leidenden, die verworren Träumenden, die überirdisch Entzückten,—dies sind die *drei Grade,* in welche Raffael die Menschen einteilt. So blicken wir nicht mehr in die Welt—und auch Raffael *dürfte* es jetzt nicht mehr: er würde eine neue Transfiguration mit Augen sehen" [The helpless sufferers, the confused dreamers, the supernaturally entranced—these are the three divisions into which Raphael divided mankind. We no longer look on the world this way—and Raphael too would no longer be able to see this way now: he would see a new transfiguration with his eyes]. *Morgenröte, Werke,* ed. Karl Schlechta, 5 vols. (Frankfurt: Ullstein, 1969), 2:18, § 8, my translation.

11. In this respect, translation may be read in terms of one of its Latin cognates: *translaticius* (handed down from one's ancestors, traditional).

12. Puttenham's definition of mezozeugma is as follows: "And if such word of supplie be placed in the middle of all such clauses as he serves: it is by the Greeks called *Mezozeugma,* by us the [Middlemarcher]." As Puttenham states, the verb may be missing from the first or successive clauses of a sentence. Puttenham gives this example for the former: "*Either the troth or talke nothing at all.*" *The Arte of English Poesie* (1589; Kent: Kent State U. P., 1970), 176.

13. The bearing of this fragment on my readings of Aristotle, Coleridge, Wordsworth, and Eliot may be discerned in the verb used by Democritus to say "give a form" (ἐπιρρυσμίζω); one of the words that makes up this verb is ῥυθμός as a more frequent form of this verb makes clear: ἐπιρρυθμίζω.

14. Arthur Lovejoy, "Coleridge and Kant's Two Worlds," in *Essays in the History of Ideas* (Baltimore: Johns Hopkins U. P., 1948), 254. This essay was first published in *English Literary History* in 1940.

Chapter One
The Possibility of Literary History

1. Paul Cantor's essay, "Aristotle and the History of Tragedy" (in *Theoretical Issues in Literary History,* ed. David Perkins [Cambridge: Harvard U. P., 1991], 60–84) also argues for a more sophisticated relation to literary history in Aristotle's *Poetics.* While Cantor's account emphasizes that the *Poetics* has more in common with modern literary history, the following reading will be concerned with the *Poetics* as *an* example of literary history rather than with the *Poetics* as *the* example of literary history (which would include its subsequent treatment as an example of that history).

2. In this aspect, Aristotle's *Poetics* possesses a level of insight into the writing of history that the subsequent development of literary history as a "consciousness of definitely distinguishable periods" (E. R. Curtius, *European Literature and the Latin Middle Ages* [Princeton: Princeton U. P., 1953], 252) can no longer access. D. A. Russell, after emphatically repeating Curtius's observation that "antiquity had no historic sense in our meaning of the phrase" (Russell writes "total absence"), goes on to speak more truly than he perhaps realized when he describes Aristotle as a "potential historian" (*Criticism in Antiquity* [Berkeley: U. of California P., 1981], 166). It is precisely potentiality that forms the determining influence of not just classical literary criticism but also classical philosophy on the rise of literary history. This concept of potentiality is treated at length in sections 1 and 3 of this chapter.

3. Such an understanding of the *Poetics* would be in accord with René Wellek's understanding of critical history in the wake of its failed evolutionary model: "The history of criticism is . . . a series of debates on recurrent concepts, on 'essentially contested concepts'" (*The Attack on Literature and Other Essays* [Chapel Hill, U. of North Carolina P., 1982], 77).

4. The avoidance of this denial is more commonly referred to in a theoretical context as deferral. As will become evident in what follows, deferral

is hardly the property of non-metaphysical or deconstructive reading. Indeed, extreme care needs to be taken if the topos of deferral is to do anything other than affirm the tendency of literary criticism to resort to privileged thematic terms as the means of defining one approach among others. The location of such a deferral or non-closure as a structuring principle of Romantic literature (see, for example, Alice Kuzniar's *Delayed Endings* [Athens: U. of Georgia P., 1987]) is also of particular relevance here since it clearly indicates the persistence of a historical intent, namely, to define the advent of our modernity. However, the explicit location of this avoidance within Romanticism reflects less the defining moment of a new epoch. Rather, it underlines the extent to which evasion became a structuring device of what is to be interpreted rather than remain restricted to the practice of interpretation. As a result, Romanticism would have to be read as an extension of the critical understanding produced by the *Poetics*. In this case, instead of discarding an Aristotelian model of literature, Romanticism generalized the mode of production that generated this model so that it became a principle of literary *and* interpretative production.

5. Even M. H. Abrams, in his influential book *The Mirror and the Lamp* (New York: Oxford U. P., 1953), maintains the crucial importance of formal techniques in the practice of critical interpretation. Abrams writes: "Aristotle bequeathed an arsenal of instruments for technical analysis of poetic forms and their elements which have proved indispensable to critics ever since, however diverse the uses to which these instruments have been put" (10). It is hardly a coincidence that Abrams should preserve the formal contribution of Aristotle's *Poetics* since the historical emphasis of his interpretation of Romanticism would be unthinkable without it. In this respect, Abrams's understanding of a shift in critical sensibility owes more to the historical model which was bequeathed by the *Poetics* than it does to subsequent critical history.

6. Hegel, *Vorlesungen über die Philosophie der Geschichte, Werke in Zwanzig Bänden* (Frankfurt: Suhrkamp, 1970), 12:18; translation mine.

7. In particular, see $48^{b}15$–17 (*Poetics*) where Aristotle recounts the origin of mimesis and then goes on to state a relation between learning and the viewing of images.

8. Here, the reception of deconstruction into literary criticism is a case in point. This reception can effect no fundamental change as long as it remains trapped within a rhetoric which merely asserts the impossibility of a critical discourse. To argue that literary criticism becomes a rigorous mode of interpretation by articulating, for example, the impossibility of literary criticism or history, is to perpetuate a critical paradigm that is fundamental to Aristotle's *Poetics* as well as to Coleridge's *Biographia Literaria*. Through such a reception the whole question of a deconstructive literary criticism is implicated. Indeed, it would need to be asked if literary criticism could have assimilated deconstruction as anything other than the repetition of its own founding problematic, that is, the very problematic whose definition is at stake in the *Poetics*. On the topic of a deconstructive criticism, see

Rodolphe Gasché, "Deconstruction as Criticism," *Glyph* 6 (Baltimore: Johns Hopkins U. P., 1979), 177–215, and *The Tain of the Mirror* (Cambridge: Harvard U. P., 1986), 255–318.

9. The translations are my own and they err deliberately on the side of the "literal" in order to emphasize both the syntax and figuration of Aristotle's argumentation. Rather than translate μίμησις and its various forms by representation and represent, I have retained the words *mimesis, mimetic,* and have either adopted the paraphrase "produce mimesis" or used the derivative "imitate" for the verbal form. Line references, given in parentheses, are to the text presented by Roselyne Dupont-Roc and Jean Lallot, *La Poétique* (Paris: Seuil, 1980).

10. This logic, as Derrida has remarked, implies a kind of historicity that differs from history as an event or occurrence: "toute méthode, tout concept de méthode, dans le noyau minimale de ses prédicats, implique une espèce d'historicité. . . . Si toute méthode, tout comportement, toute opération, toute règle méthodique implique de l'historicité, ce n'est pas de n'importe quelle historicité qu'il s'agit. . . . La méthode a une histoire originale; je ne parle pas ici encore du *concept* de méthode qui a lui aussi son histoire et son historicité, mais de l'historicité propre de la méthode elle-même; cette historicité originale tient aussi au statut de la *répétition* qui instruit toute méthode. L'histoire, c'est ce qui ne se répète pas, dit-on, c'est la singularité de l'événement. Mais aucune histoire ne se constituterait comme telle sans une certaine itérabilité, sans itérativité, récurrence, sans la possibilité de former une tradition, de se livrer, de se garder, de se rassembler ou de s'accumuler, autant de formes de répétition, au sens le plus divers de ce mot" [Every method, every concept of method, even in the least significant kernel of its predicates, implies a form of historicity. . . . if every method, every procedure, every operation, every rule of method implies historicity, it is not any historicity. . . . Method has an original history; I do not speak here about the *concept* of method which has its own history and its own historicity, but about the historicity proper to method itself; this original historicity adheres to the law of *repetition* that instructs every method. History, one says, is what does not repeat itself, it is the singularity of an event. But no history could constitute itself as such without a certain iterability, without iterativity, recurrence, without the possibility of forming a tradition, of surrendering itself, of preserving itself, of gathering itself together and amassing itself, all forms of repetition in the most varied sense of the word]. "La langue et le discours de la méthode," *Recherches sur la philosphie et le langage,* Groupe de Recherches sur la Philosophie et le Langage, Cahier no. 3 (Paris: Vrin, 1983), 36–37; my translation.

11. Δύναμις is translated as "potentiality" throughout this chapter although "possibility" would also be an acceptable substitute. The δύναμις of something defines what it is possible for that thing to become, that is, its potential. This sense of potentiality may be understood by means of an example given by Aristotle in Book Theta of the *Metaphysics:* "We say that a thing is not something else, but of something else; for example, a chest is,

not wood, but wooden, and wood is, not earth, but earthen. If earth, in turn, is likewise not something else, but is of something, then the former is always potentially the latter. That is, a chest is not earth or earthen, but wooden, and wooden denotes what is potentially a chest and the material of a chest: the wood specifically of a chest, or this wood of this chest" (*Metaphysics,* trans. Richard Hope [Ann Arbor: U. of Michigan P., 1960], $1049^{a}18$–24; translation modified).

12. Contrary to the tendency prevalent in both the translation and interpretation of this text, this repetition reinforces the relation between the *Poetics* and the philosophical discourse from which it emerges. The tendency to distance Aristotle's use of δύναμις in the *Poetics* from the use of this term in more properly philosophical texts most frequently occurs as part of the attempt to distance the *Poetics,* and, ultimately, literary criticism, from its philosophical provenance. The commentary of Gerald F. Else is especially protective of this disassociation when he refers to this occurrence of δύναμις in the *Poetics:* "*Our* passage does not seem to have anything in common with either the identification or the distinction [of τέχνη and δύναμις] (certainly it does not *in any way* evoke the 'Aristotelian' distinction ἐνέργεια-δύναμις). . . . Rather it casts back to the sort of untechnical use we find in Plato . . . that is, the 'power' or 'capability' of the art, what it can do. Under the circumstances it is *natural* to associate δύναμιν in *our* passage with the concept of tragic pleasure and or catharsis" (*Aristotle's Poetics: the Argument* [Cambridge: Harvard U. P., 1957], 8; emphasis mine). D. W. Lucas, in a note to his edition of the *Poetics* (Oxford: Oxford U. P., 1968), suggests that δύναμις should be translated as "effect" (53) thereby affirming in a most economical manner what Else's disregard for the philosophical provenance of the *Poetics* also strives to attain. To see δύναμις as such an effect is to assert that this word only refers to the experience of a spectator, an assertion that underlines the role of the spectator in preserving a subject for criticism, a subject who would preserve the history of criticism and thereby maintain its debts.

13. "What is potential in the primary sense is potential because it can become actual: what has the potential to build means what can build; what has the potential to see means what can see; and what is visible means what can be seen. And the same reasoning applies to other cases; so that the reason or knowledge of the actual must be present before there is knowledge of the potential." *Metaphysics,* trans. Richard Hope, $1049^{b}13$–17; translation modified.

14. A passage from Hegel's 1825/26 introduction to his *Lectures on the History of Philosophy* clearly sets out the relation between potentiality (*Ansich*) and the formal difference which determines the development of critical history. After referring to Aristotle's concept of potentiality, Hegel goes on to state that "the potential, the simple, and the hidden develops itself and unfolds itself. Developing itself means positing itself, entering existence, becoming something different. At first it is differentiated only in itself and it exists only in this simplicity or neutrality. . . . What happens next is that it

acquires existence in relation to other things, it exists as differentiated. It is one and the same thing, or rather one and the same content, whether it is concealed in itself or whether it is unfolded, it exists as unfolded. Here there is only a difference of form (*ein Unterschied der Form*), but everything depends on this difference" (*Vorlesungen über die Geschichte der Philosophie,* ed. J. Hoffmeister, *Sämtliche Werke* [Leipzig: Meiner, 1940], Band 15[a], 103; translation mine).

15. Such an eventuality is, as Hegel points out, the product of "empty understanding," yet this has hardly prevented its adoption as a determining principle as well as a defense of critical history and all its possibilities. A paragraph from Part 1 of Hegel's *Encyclopaedia of the Philosophical Sciences* succinctly describes the discursive practice of this understanding and its unreflecting relation to potentiality or possibility: "Because possibility (*Möglichkeit*) is, in the first instance, the mere form of *identity-with-itself* (as against the concrete which is actual), the rule for it is only that a thing must not contradict itself. Thus, *everything is possible* since through abstraction every content can be given this form of identity. *Everything* however is just as *impossible* since in every content—because it is concrete—determination (*Bestimmtheit*) can be grasped as determined opposition (*als bestimmter Gegensatz*) and thereby as a contradiction. For this reason, there is no emptier expression than the statement of such possibility and impossibility. In philosophy, in particular, there should be no talk of showing *that something is possible* or *that something else is still also possible* or, as it is also expressed, that something is *conceivable*. The writer of history is just as directly warned not to employ a category which has already been explained as untrue by itself (*für sich*), however, the shrewdness of the empty understanding (*des leeren Verstandes*) pleases itself most in the shallow contrivance of possibilities and many more possibilities." *Enzyklopädie der philosophischen Wissenschaften* I, § 143, *Werke in Zwanzig Bänden* (Frankfurt: Suhrkamp, 1970), 8:282; translation mine.

16. A more general sense of sound would be conveyed by the word ψόφος whose usage describes noise or sound not produced by the larynx even though it may still describe articulated sound such as that produced by musical instruments as well as that produced by insects or the mere striking of one object against another. For a similar distinction made again with respect to articulation see *Poetics* 56[b]22–24.

17. In a less abstract sense, ἁρμονία names the art of the carpenter, the art of joinery.

18. For a history of the word ῥυθμός and its development from a spatial to a temporal term, see Émile Benveniste, "La notion du 'rhythme' dans son expression linguistique" (Paris: Gallimard, 1966), 327–35. On the relation of rhythm to mimesis, see also Philippe Lacoue-Labarthe's "L'echo du sujet" (in *Le sujet de la philosophie* (Typographies I) [Paris: Aubier-Flammarion, 1979], 217–303), and "La césure du spéculatif" (in *L'imitation des modernes* (Typographies II) [Paris: Galilée, 1986], 39–70). As will be recognized later, in the second chapter, the subsequent distinction of two senses associated with the same word (ῥυθμός and the modern senses of form and rhythm)

belongs to what Coleridge refers to as a process of desynonymization. This kind of distinction is not only characteristic of the attempt to define a critical approach but its appearance within the *Biographia* suggests its crucial importance in developing a critical vocabulary. Its contemporary counterpart may be found in any attempt to make what Derrida has written under the name of *différance* become a theory of reading based on difference. Indeed, this theory demands that the difference between deferral and difference be produced as the basis as well as the form (εἶδος) of a critical approach. But such an approach can, in fact, make no difference to the critical history it appears to deconstruct; rather, this approach affirms such a history as the formalization of difference. Through this formalization, critical history may continue as it has always continued.

19. The initial example of a mimesis that takes place through the use of colors and the making of images (ἀπεικάζοντες [47^a19]) would ultimately have to be included as part of this sequence. An examination of the place occupied by the visual arts in the argument of the *Poetics* is, however, outside the scope of this chapter, although the structure of "setting apart" which relates human sound (φωνή) to the making of images and which is also at work within this sequence will be analyzed later.

20. It is not until German Romanticism that any attempt is made to take up the question posed by Aristotle's lack of a common name for the work of a poet on the one hand and, a dialogue of Plato's on the other. The Romantic response to this question was to recognize the novel as the genre of a general mimesis. For example, Friedrich Schlegel writes in the *Kritische Fragmente,* "Die Romane sind die Sokratischen Dialoge unserere Zeit" [Novels are the Socratic dialogues of our time] (26). On the novel as the form of a general mimesis see Philippe Lacoue-Labarthe and Jean-Luc Nancy, *L'absolu littéraire* (Paris: Seuil, 1978) and Walter Benjamin, *Der Begriff der Kunstkritik in der deutschen Romantik,* in *Gesammelte Schriften,* ed. Rolf Tiedemann and Hermann Schweppenhäuser, 7 vols. (Frankfurt: Suhrkamp, 1974–1989), 1.1:7–122). Aristotle may lack a common name for Socratic dialogues and epic poetry as well as a name to distinguish poetic mimesis from the mimesis of philosophical or scientific work, however, the *Poetics* will find an adequate substitute for the latter in the figure of Oedipus. For Aristotle, Sophocles' *Oedipus the King* is nothing less than *the* example of literature in the *Poetics*. Oedipus names the possibility of critical reflection as well as the history in which this reflection perpetuates itself. It should also be noted that the *Poetics* would sanction this substitution in the chapter devoted to metaphor: "In certain cases, there is no already existing name for what the analogy describes, nonetheless it will be spoken about in the same way" (57^b25–26). As this passage indicates, the question to be posed does not at all concern what is substituted but rather the concept of analogy which authorizes this substitution. On the relation of Oedipus to Aristotle, see Paul Fry's "Aristotle as Oedipus: Form and Recognition in the *Poetics,*" in *The Reach of Criticism* (New Haven: Yale U. P., 1983).

21. The reliance of Aristotle's argument on this kind of analogy should help point out that modernism is not that new. Indeed, the exchanges between different artistic media fostered by modernism and, above all, by the critical concept of modernism, hardly mark a break with the analogy adopted by the *Poetics* in its attempt to define literature.

22. It would be easy to account for such changes, and at the same time ignore them, by evoking the transmission of the text of the *Poetics* as a factor determining the inconsistency between each combination of this set of three terms. Yet, to do so would be to determine this text in relation to the accidents *of* history and thereby avoid the very necessity at work within the *Poetics,* the same necessity from which the possibility of a discourse on the *Poetics* also arises. Neither Ingram Bywater's edition (*Aristotle on the Art of Poetry* [Oxford: Clarendon Press, 1909]), nor Lucas's (*Poetics,* 1968), nor the French edition by Dupont-Roc and Lallot (*La Poétique,* 1980) record any variant readings for the terms in this sequence. As will be seen, this sequence exhibits a logic that would also discount any explanation of the changes and replacements of the last two elements as being stylistic in nature.

23. On this aspect, Lucas comments, "μέλος denotes words sung and therefore includes ἁρμονία. But the words are nowhere treated as a significant part of the μέλος which appears to depend for its effect on ῥυθμός and ἁρμονία" (*Poetics* [1968], p. 61, note to 47^b25).

24. For an extensive application of such a line of argument to the *Poetics,* see Stephen Halliwell, *Aristotle's Poetics: A Study of Philosophical Criticism* (London: Duckworth, 1986). Halliwell, by stating that "Aristotle's guiding notion of mimesis is implicitly one of enactment" (128), accurately describes the direction that the argument of the *Poetics* is compelled to follow. Yet, despite his recognition of significant inconsistencies in Aristotle's argument, Halliwell does not explore these inconsistencies as an unavoidable consequence of any attempt to define language as a mode of mimesis. In this context, Halliwell's separation of a mimesis of enactment from what he calls "formal mimesis" (a mimesis that "entails or presupposes a direct correspondence between the mimetic subject and its model, a use of visual means to represent a visual object" [112]) is particularly telling. Above all else, this separation, by repeating the movement within the argument of the *Poetics* analyzed within this chapter, adopts Aristotle's mode of argumentation in order to overcome inconsistencies in that same mode of argument. In the case of Aristotle and Halliwell, this separation allows the general question of mimesis as a mode of repetition to be evaded. Such a general question cannot be channeled into an answer that traces "a number of distinguishable types of subject-object relationship" (123); nor does it presuppose a unitary answer or definition of mimesis which Halliwell's argument seems to entertain as the only alternative to his discernment of subject-object relationships (concerning Halliwell's argument, suffice it to add that to define mimesis as a number of distinguishable types of subject-

object relationship is to have already defined mimesis unilaterally as such a relationship); it is, rather, a question about this relationship and its historical dominance in the interpretation of literature.

25. Dupont-Roc and Lallot emphasize the figurative nature of this employment of ἔδυσμα: "Unknown to us before Aristotle, the sense we have here is certainly no worn-out metaphor: in the *Rhetoric* (III, 1406a19), Aristotle, when criticizing the style of Alcidamas as surcharged with epithets, plays on words by saying that Alcidamas uses epithets not as seasoning—ἔδυσμα—but as meat—ἔδεσμα" (*La Poétique* [1980], pp. 194–95; translation mine). In his commentary, Lucas also points to the metaphoric use of ἔδυσμα (Aristotle, *Poetics* [1968], p. 97).

26. Following the edition of the *Poetics* by Dupont-Roc and Lallot (*La Poétique,* 1980), the manuscript reading ἀπολαβόντες is accepted in place of the more frequently used emendation ἀναλαβόντες. The emendation to ἀναλαβόντες dates from the edition of Martin Bernays published in 1880 (see Dupont-Roc and Lallot, 186, n. 2) and is the accepted reading in the texts presented by both Bywater (1909) and Lucas (1968). In defense of their return to the reading in the manuscripts, Dupont-Roc and Lallot outline the difference between ἀπολαβόντες and ἀναλαβόντες as follows: "The verbal prefix *apo-* indicates that the elements in the definition are less a simple summarizing 'retake' (this is precisely the meaning of *ana-*)—than a 'setting apart,' an indication that the definition is a detached statement which will in its turn be taken up and analyzed in detail by the rest of the text" (186, n. 2). The only edition to retain ἀπολαβόντες since Bernays is that of Else (*Aristotle's Poetics: The Argument* [1957]). Else, however, does not question the relation of the definition of tragedy to what precedes it in the *Poetics,* preferring to conceal this question within a process of becoming that has already been stated in the *Poetics*. For Else, this process "avoids assuming a hyperbaton (ἐκ τῶν εἰρημένων τὸν γινόμενον ὅρον for τὸν ἐκ τ[ῶν] ε[ἰρημένων] γ[ινόμενον] ὅρον) and an awkward catechresis of γινόμενον." Both this hyperbaton and catechresis would be necessary if the syntax of the phrase in which ἀπολαβόντες occurs is to reflect the interpretation demanded by ἀναλαβόντες. Moreover, this process, Else states, "not only clarifies the present construction but supplies the proof that the 'history' in chapter 4 was intended as a record of tragedy's γένεσις εἰς οὐσίαν [generation out of its essence]. And this in turn facilitates our review of the items in the definition: they are in fact taken both from the systematic chapters 1–3 and from the 'history' [of tragedy]" (222). The setting apart of Aristotle's "review" facilitates Else's review of the empirical history of tragedy. Despite Else's return to ἀπολαβόντες, his interpretation of this word affirms the significance more readily facilitated by Bernays's emendation. Both Else's interpretation and the emendation legitimize the distinctly literary understanding of history that belongs to criticism. This understanding is most forcefully reflected in a principle of textual development which demands the meaningful relation of part to part, a principle which, as will become apparent, must assert itself in the discourse of the *Poetics*. It is the

possibility of this assertion, that is, the possibility that allows this assertion to take place which is paramount here.

27. At this point in the *Poetics,* one could talk of a recognition scene as Paul Fry has done (see *The Reach of Criticism,* 12–13 and 41). The movement involved in ἀπολαβόντες suggests that Aristotle already recognizes the predicament produced by the critical intention of the *Poetics.*

28. The verb εἴρω used by Aristotle at $47^{b}23$ is philologically distinct from εἴρω: fasten together in rows, string together (uses listed by Liddell and Scott, eds., *A Greek-English Lexicon,* 9th ed. [Oxford: Oxford U. P., 1940]). My thanks to Haun Saussy for clarifying this homonymy. It should be added, however, that despite the philological distinction of εἴρω (say) and εἴρω (fasten together) speaking and interlacing or binding together are consistently evoked together in the context of language and how it possesses meaning. In the *Sophist,* Plato uses such a fastening together as a metaphor for meaningful language (see $262^{b}9$–$^{c}7$). This passage from the *Sophist* as well as this metaphor of weaving or interlacing will be discussed further in chapter 4.

29. This sense of binding would however have to be distinguished from the sense of gathering that Heidegger gives to language in his essay "Λόγος," in *Vorträge und Aufsätze,* 3d ed. (Pfullingen: Neske, 1967).

30. One may note Derrida's reservations with regard to the endless mirroring of this *mise en abyme:* "I have never wished to overuse the abyss, nor above all the abyss structure [*mise en abyme*]. I have no strong belief in it, I distrust the confidence that it, at bottom, inspires, and I find it too representational to go far enough, not to *avoid* the very thing into which it pretends to plunge us" ("Coming into One's Own," *Psychoanalysis and the Question of the Text,* ed. Geoffrey Hartman [Baltimore: Johns Hopkins U. P., 1978], 120). On the place of the *mise en abyme* within the concept of the semantic, see Rodolphe Gasché, "Nontotalization without Spuriousness: Hegel and Derrida on the Infinite," *Journal of the British Society for Phenomenology* 17.3 (1986): 289–307.

31. This difference would be differentiated from all else and, as such, it would belong to "*unmittelbarer* Unterschied, *die Verschiedenheit* [*immediate* difference, *diversity*]" (Hegel, *Enzyklopädie* I, § 117, *Werke in Zwanzig Bänden,* 8:239). The form in which this difference would be expressed amounts to what Hegel refers to as the principle of identity: "*The principle of identity* [*Der Satz der Identität*] reads: '*Everything with itself is identical, A = A;* and negatively: *A cannot be at the same time A and not A.*' This principle, instead of being a true law of thought, is nothing but the law of *abstract understanding.* The *form of the proposition* itself already contradicts it; because a proposition also promises a distinction between subject and object this proposition does not fulfill what its form demands." *Enzyklopädie* I, § 115, *Werke in Zwanzig Bänden,* 8:237.

32. This passage is cited in full in note 14 above.

33. If Aristotle's definition of περί as a connecting word (ἄρθρον) without significance of its own ($57^{a}7$) is followed, then the *Poetics* would be about

the possibility of meaning in an articulation whose repetition has no decidable relation to meaning. In this case, the opening phrase of the *Poetics* could also be read as περὶ τοῦ περὶ τῆς ποιητικῆς λόγου . . . λέγωμεν. . . . [About the word about of the Poetics let us speak / About the phrase about the Poetics let us speak . . .].

Chapter Two
The Ghost of Aristotle

1. Although Coleridge's importance to the history of criticism cannot and should not be underestimated, one can yet ask why he should be persistently presented at the beginning of modern critical thought, that is, as either the formulator of the principles which stand behind New Criticism or, more recently, as the anticipator of an apparently deconstructive textuality. Historically, this former view has been informed by a much exaggerated reverence. In a textually more subtle way, the Coleridge-New Criticism genealogy has been criticized through the attempt to show that Coleridge has, in fact, more in common, whether inadvertently or intentionally, with what passes for the deconstructive tendencies of contemporary criticism. See, for example, J. C. Christensen, *Coleridge's Blessed Machine of Language* (Ithaca: Cornell U. P., 1981); Patricia S. Yeager, "Coleridge, Derrida and the Anguish of Writing," *Sub-Stance* 39 (1983): 89–102; C. M. Wallace, in *The Design of the* Biographia Literaria (London: Allen and Unwin, 1983), clearly identifies what is at stake in this deconstructive identification of Coleridge when she writes that the *Biographia*'s "design reveals a coherent and genuinely imaginative vision of the *necessary* character of *modern* discourse" (1; emphasis mine). In the end, the attempt to name Coleridge as the privileged and prior example of current theoretical insight indicates the extent to which the contemporary interpretation of literature is caught within the constant need to discover its modernity in a history no longer its own.

2. "Introduction," *Biographia Literaria,* ed. James Engell and W. Jackson Bate, 2 vols., in *Collected Works of Samuel Taylor Coleridge* 7 (Princeton: Princeton U. P., 1983), 1:xli. All parenthetical references given subsequently in this chapter are to this edition of the *Biographia.* Reference to other volumes in this edition of Coleridge's works will be preceded by the abbreviation *CC.*

3. *Collected Notebooks,* 3 vols. to date (Princeton: Princeton U. P., 1957–), 3:4400. This text will be referred to subsequently as *CN* followed by volume and notebook entry number. The note to this entry reports that "⟨S.T.C.⟩ is in the hand of Sara Coleridge, as far as one can make an assertion on so small a specimen."

4. With the deletion of chapters 5–12, this lack of a precedent became a physical act in George Sampson's edition of the *Biographia* (1920). However, critical uneasiness with these metaphysical chapters has not always been remedied in such an effective or obvious way. A recurrent remedy has been to assert a unity distinct from and despite an aberrant and confusing textual practice (of which chapters 5–12 are the prime example). All too often

this remedy is the prelude to asserting an "imaginative unity," an assertion which has become all too predictable in a critical practice that prefers to evade the textual evidence of its own history—preferring instead to characterize the *Biographia* as a site of critical confusion and, in so doing, interrupt any inquiry into the necessity as well as the productive role this confusion plays on behalf of critical insight. This assertion of an imaginative unity is plagued by a difficulty common to other interpretations that have sought to relate the *Biographia* to an external unifying source, for example, George Whalley, who locates this source in Wordsworth ("The Integrity of *Biographia Literaria*," *Essays and Studies* 6 [1953]: 85–101). More recently, the reader has come to take the place Whalley ascribes to Wordsworth as a unifying source for this work although this only makes more explicit what Whalley had already displaced onto the name of Wordsworth. This emphasis upon the reader is particularly marked in Kathleen Wheeler's assertion that the subject of the *Biographia* is the "reading process" (see *Sources, Processes and Methods in Coleridge's* Biographia Literaria [Cambridge: Cambridge U. P., 1980]). A variation on Wheeler may be found in C. M. Wallace's claim that the design of the *Biographia* may be derived from "Coleridge's desire to make his readers think, to make them engage genuine ideas. . . . to make [them] think things through for [themselves] under his tutelage" (*The Design of the* Biographia Literaria, 3–4). As with every assertion of a unifying subject, there remains the question broached by Coleridge in a fundamental way in the *Biographia:* the question of how such a subject or unity may be both present in and yet differentiated from a given work. It is this question that Coleridge scholarship, in particular, has failed to return to, but, more generally, it is a question all too frequently avoided in the name of critical insight into the form or structure of a given work. This avoidance is, however, hardly a weakness within critical practice but rather a reflection of its strength.

5. This may be discerned in two quite different attempts to preserve Coleridge's importance to the understanding of literature, Thomas McFarland's *Coleridge and the Pantheist Tradition* (Oxford: Clarendon Press, 1969) and Jerome Christensen's *Coleridge's Blessed Machine of Language*. Each proceeds by trying to account for the method of Coleridge's compositional practice—whether explicitly stated or not, any reading of the *Biographia* that seeks to determine its compositional method amounts to a defense against plagiarism (or at least an attempt to excuse it by accounting for its necessity). As Christensen has pointed out, McFarland's account of the *Biographia* as a mosaic fails to undertake any consideration of the formal relation that enables a compositional practice associated with the plastic arts to be applied to a linguistic work. In contrast, Christensen seeks to articulate the discursivity of the *Biographia* according to a model of writing that he refers to as "marginal exegesis." Given this language, the question of Coleridge's plagiarism would seem to be displaced into concerns commonly associated with deconstruction. Indeed, the influence of certain deconstructive themes becomes apparent when Christensen writes that Cole-

ridge's "marginal method" is to be characterized by "the profusion of the peripheral [which] *bears* upon the absence of the central" (96; emphasis mine). The logic of this method should not be overlooked: to bear upon an absent center is to be supported by absence as a center. A center may be absent but that makes no difference to its centering effect: an absent center still operates as a center. Such an account of Coleridge's discursive practice would still need to distinguish itself from the ease with which marginality, the absent center and its never distant twin, infinite regression, have been thematized as a significant source of critical insight in the literary and critical appropriation of deconstruction, an appropriation that has failed to recognize the complexity of the metaphysical thought in which deconstruction operates. The stake in such an appropriation is clearly expressed by Christensen when he writes: "Too close attention to the ground of freedom would lead to questions arising in an endless series, and freedom would be submitted to that ceaseless, discontinuous change from which Coleridge recoils. Such a closure of metaphysics is the terminal hazard that Coleridge's method constantly struggles to evade" (115), and later, "Coleridge acts out the dilemma. . . . by, in effect, giving up a quest that might open up an infinite and infinitely debilitating regress. For that search, however, Coleridge has *simply* substituted its *proper* metaphor, a *thoroughly* marginal method" (116; emphasis mine). To assume that the closure of metaphysics may be effected by an "endless series" does not explain why the notion of an endless series or infinite regress may be considered as anything other than a metaphysical determination. An infinite regress is fueled by the same logic employed by metaphysics in its quest for an unconditioned ground. Suffice it to add that only through metaphysics could such an endless series arise and only through metaphysics could it have a *proper* metaphor. Consequently, to argue that metaphysics is brought to a close by an endless series is far from being a hazard to metaphysics since it repeats and arises from the simplification which restricts metaphysics to a self-deceiving pursuit that contemplates closure as an attainable goal.

6. Coleridge's use of ventriloquy as a metaphor for the speaking of truth occurs with some frequency in his writings. These occurrences are not consistent in reserving ventriloquy for the speaking of truth. Coleridge also uses ventriloquy as a metaphor to describe how conscience and reason speak, however, these uses still associate ventriloquy with faculties that may be regarded as sources of truth. In Coleridge's literary criticism, and only in the criticism of drama, is ventriloquy used as a term of censure to indicate a weakness of composition whereby "the author, Acting like a Ventriloquist, distributed his own insipidity" ("Lectures on Shakespeare" [1811–12], *Lectures 1808–1819: On Literature,* ed. R. A. Foakes, *CC* 5, 1:351). In such an occurrence, the ventriloquy of truth is usurped but it is usurped by being too transparent. The association of ventriloquy with not just the speaking of truth but with the very structure of Romantic literature has been made by Edward Bostetter in *The Romantic Ventriloquists* (Seattle: U. of Washington P., 1963). For Bostetter, ventriloquy permits the Romantic poets to

transcend the particular and arrive at the expression of truth—"The poet became in reality the divine ventriloquist projecting his own voice as the ultimate voice of truth" (4) and, later, "To an increasing degree the poem has become the medium through which the ventriloquist poet attempts to release the unconscious, to give it voice and form apart from the conscious self" (306). Such an assumption demands at least some reflection on the passage from a metaphor to an interpretative model (that is, on how a metaphor may become an idea). In what follows, ventriloquy (provisionally understood as a projection of voice, *tout court,* or a projection into someone or something else, whether a dummy or an object) is discussed as presenting an essential problem that cannot be confined to Romanticism, but, properly speaking, is a problem that constitutes literary criticism itself.

7. This dependence on audibility as a primary condition is reflected in Coleridge's earlier and later references to ventriloquy: "TRUTH is of too divine and spiritual an essence to be susceptible of commixture with the foulness of its accidental vehicle. . . . If we could dissever from the ideas the ludicrous association, we would personify REASON as a ventriloquist; it is of inferior importance into what uncouth vessel she throws her voice, provided only that it is audible" (1800; *Essays on his Times, CC* 3, 1:120); "Reason which remains always the one and the same, whether it speaks through this or that person: like the voice of an external Ventriloquist, it is indifferent from whose lips it appears to come, if only it be audible" (1809, 1818; *The Friend, CC* 4, 1:192 and 4, 2:127). However, in 1816, the audible is again accompanied by the visual but in a way that points to an unquestioned relation of what is seen as what is to be heard: "When the nervous system is approaching to the waking state, a sort of under-consciousness blends with our dreams, that in all, we imagine as seen or heard, our own self is the ventriloquist, and moves the slides in the magic-lanthorn" ("The Statesman's Manual," *Lay Sermons, CC* 6:80). Here, what is said to be audible is originally a visual reference; what is seen is imagined as being heard. In other words, what is audible is what is seen to be audible. On this confusion of senses the possibility of a ventriloquistic practice rests, yet, to use the words of Coleridge from an 1819 letter in which he turns once again to the notion of ventriloquy, the difficulty of its practice lies in the witnessing of this passage between the eye and the ear (an eye which gives the ear something to listen to) as well as in the necessity of this witnessing: "From whatever dirty Corner, Straw Moppet, the Ventriloquist Truth causes her words to proceed, I not only listen but must bear witness that it is *Truth* talking" (*Collected Letters of Samuel Taylor Coleridge,* ed. E. L. Griggs, 6 vols. [Oxford: Clarendon, 1956–71], 4:979 [December 13, 1819]. This edition will subsequently be referred to in notes as *CL* followed by volume, page number, and, in parentheses, the date of the letter). While Coleridge's references to truth as a ventriloquist constantly rely upon a notion of language whose intelligibility is derived from audible speech, a quite different understanding of the relation between speech, language, and intelligibility is given by Ferdinand de Saussure: "La langue est nécessaire pour que la parole soit

intelligible et produise tous ses effets" [Language is necessary so that speech may become intelligible and produce all its effects]. (*Cours de linguistique générale* [Paris: Payot, 1972], 37).

8. By this relation what is hidden is always indicated, but this indication serves, at the same time, as a means of concealing the hiding place of truth. This relation is analyzed at length in a reading of Plato's *Sophist* by Jean-Luc Nancy. At one point in his reading, Nancy refers to the art of the ventriloquist as the art of hiding the hiding place while showing what is hidden ("cacher la cachette en montrant le caché, c'est l'art du ventriloque"), ("Le ventriloque," in *Mimesis des articulations* [Paris: Aubier-Flammarion, 1975], 271–338).

9. As Derrida has remarked, such a silence not only lies at the center of auto-affection but also marks a spacing without which neither auto-affection nor this silence could be thought. See *La voix et le phénomène* (Paris: PUF, 1967), especially "La voix qui garde le silence." As will become clearer in the course of the *Biographia,* there could be no critical project without assuming auto-affection or the *causa sui* as a basis for its relation to literature.

10. *CN* 1:1515.

11. *CL* 4, 584–85 (September 17, 1815); this same letter goes on to underline that "the Biographical Sketches are not a *Preface* or any thing in the Nature of a Preface, but a Work per se."

12. *CL* 4, 578–9 (July 29, 1815).

13. This function has been clearly described by Derrida in the following words: "Elle [une préface] énoncerait au futur ('vous allez lire ceci') le sens ou le contenu conceptuels de ce qui aurait *déjà* été *écrit.* Donc assez *lu* pour pouvoir être rassemblé en sa teneur sémantique et d'avance proposé. Pour l'avant-propos, reformant un vouloir-dire après le coup, le texte est un écrit—un passé—que, dans une fausse apparence de présent, un auteur caché et tout-puissant, en pleine maîtrise de son produit, présente au lecteur comme son avenir. . . . Le *pré* de la préface rend présent l'avenir, le représente, le rapproche, l'aspire et en le devançant le met devant. Il le réduit à la forme de présence manifeste" [The preface would announce in the future tense ("you are going to read this") the conceptual meaning or content of what would *already* have been *written.* And thus sufficiently *read* for it to be gathered in its semantic tenor and proposed in advance. For the fore-word, reconstituting after the fact an intention-to-say, the text is something written—a past—which, in a false appearance of the present, a hidden and all-powerful author in full mastery of his product, presents [the text] to the reader as his future. . . . The *pre* of the preface makes the future present, represents it, draws it closer, breathes it in and, in going ahead of it places it before. The *pre* reduces it [the future] to the form of manifest presence]. "Hors livre," *La dissémination* (Paris: Seuil, 1972), 13, translation mine.

14. Coleridge, *Aids to Reflection* (New York: Chelsea House, 1983), 136. The word *tautegorical* is also used by Coleridge to define the symbol in *The*

Statesman's Manual ("a symbol [ὁ ἔστιν ἄει ταυτηγόρικον] is characterized by a translucence of the Special in the Individual." [*Lay Sermons,* ed. R. J. White, *CC* 6:30) and in Coleridge's lecture "On the *Prometheus* of Aeschylus" ("the Prometheus is a *philosophema* ταυτηγορικὸν" [*Transactions of the Royal Society of Literature,* vol. 2 (1834), 391]. Little attention has been given to this word, or indeed to the role of neologism as a crucial discursive element in Coleridge. Philippe Beck and Éric Dayre both discuss *tautegory* in "Coleridge et l'écriture tautégorique" (*Digraphe* 48 [June 1989]: 9–12) yet do so only as a means to account for Coleridge's mode of writing in the "First Lay Sermon"—as if the mere definition of this word could account for a textual practice. The lack of attention given to this word is even more marked in the extensive literature on Coleridge's plagiarism of Schelling, a lack that is easily accounted for since the excerpts of Schelling cited or paraphrased in Coleridge's *Biographia* have tended to define critical interest in Schelling. Is this why a passage from Schelling's *Einleitung in die Philosophie der Mythologie* has never entered into this literature? In the following passage, Schelling picks up the word *tautegorical* from Coleridge and at the same time makes a remark that offers a comment on the excessive critical attention given to the question of Coleridge's plagiarisms: "Ich entlehne diese Ausdruck [tautegorisch] von dem bekannten Coleridge. . . . Für den erwähnten treffenden Ausdruck überlasse ich ihm gerne die von seinen eigenen Landsleuten scharf, ja zu scharf gerügten Entlehnungen aus meinen Schriften, bei welchen mein Name nicht genannt worden. Einem wirklich congenialen Mann sollte man dergleichen nicht anrechnen. Die Strenge solcher Censuren in England beweist jedoch, welcher Werth dort auf wissenschaftliche Eigentümlichkeit gelegt und wie streng das *suum cuique* in der Wissenschaft beobachtet wird" [I borrow this term (tautegorical) from the renowned Coleridge. . . . For this apt term I give up willingly his borrowings from my writings beside which my name was not mentioned and which his own countrymen severely, all too severely censured. One should not credit a truly congenial man in this way. The strength of such a censure in England shows the value placed on the propriety of scholarship over there as well as how strongly the *suum cuique* is observed]. *Sämmtliche Werke,* ed. K. F. A. Schelling, 14 vols. (Stuttgart and Augsburg, 1856–61), 11:196; translation mine. (Subsequent references to this edition will use *SW* followed by volume and page number; unless otherwise noted all translations are my own.) For a word, Coleridge may speak in the words of Schelling but this is also a word that Schelling needs if the words Coleridge borrows are to account for a critical project grounded in the necessity of tautegorical utterance. The only recognition of a relation between Coleridge and Schelling on the basis of this word has been R. J. White's reference to the conversation about Coleridge's plagiarism that took place between Benjamin Jowett and Schelling (recorded in *The Life and Letters of Benjamin Jowett, M. A.,* see *CC* 6:30, n. 3).

15. This statement runs counter to a large body of critical writing that unquestioningly assumes that the *Biographia* is an autobiography. Shaw-

cross's description of the *Biographia* as an autobiography may be singled out as decisive in this respect (see "Introduction," *Biographia Literaria,* ed. J. Shawcross [Oxford: Oxford U. P., 1907], lv), but an equally important factor would be the propensity of literary criticism to act as if the *Biographia* had in fact realized its critical project. Only on the basis of this assumption would it be possible to affirm the claims made by the genre of autobiography, yet this condition has not stopped criticism from regarding those claims as undeniable and then applying them to a work that could ground neither criticism nor, ipso facto, autobiography. In such an application, literary criticism projects *its* voice into the mouth of authority and listens to itself as if it were hearing the voice of another. To read the *Biographia* as an autobiography is to forget the double bind of the ventriloquy which allows such a reading to occur in the first place.

16. To assume that the discursive "I" is in fact Coleridge would amount to viewing this text and actually hearing Coleridge speak. Such a hearing of a present voice is the condition of not only assigning a discourse to a subject but also to the very concept of subjectivity. The relation of a discourse to a subject has been analyzed by Benveniste in these terms: "A quoi donc *je* réfère-t-il? A quelque chose de très singulier, qui est exclusivement linguistique: *je* se réfère à l'acte de discours individuel où il est prononcé, et il en désigne le locuteur. C'est un terme qui ne peut être identifié que dans ce que nous avons appelé ailleurs une instance de discours, et qui n'a de référence qu'actuelle. La réalité à laquelle il renvoie est la réalité du discours. C'est dans l'instance de discours où *je* désigne le locuteur que celui-ci s'énonce comme 'sujet.' Il est donc vrai à la lettre que le fondement de la subjectivité est dans l'exercice de la langue" [To what then does *I* refer? To something very singular that is exclusively linguistic: *I* refers to the individual discursive act in which it is pronounced and it designates the speaker of that discourse. It is a term that can only be identified in what we have called elsewhere an instance of discourse which has no reference except to its occurrence. The reality to which it refers is the reality of a discourse. It is in the instance of a discourse in which the *I* designates the speaker that the latter is expressed as a "subject." It is therefore literally true that the foundation of subjectivity is found in the exercise of language]. Emile Benveniste, "De la subjectivité dans le langage," *Problèmes de linguistique générale* (Paris: Gallimard, 1966), 261–62. On the formal condition of the identity associated with subjective consciousness, see also Immanuel Kant, *Kritik der reinen Vernunft, Werkausgabe,* ed. W. Weischedel, 12 Bände (Frankfurt: Suhrkamp, 1968), A 363. Subsequent references to the first *Kritik* will use *KRV* followed by edition and page number.

17. See, for example, *CL* 4, 584–85 (September 17, 1815).

18. Even at the point when criticism would declare itself to be the subject of its own understanding, this relation remains in force. The relation of criticism to literature has been merely interiorized—in the same way as ventriloquy would interiorize within the *Biographia* the relation of this text to its author. In each case, what is sought is a reflexive relation that would

allow one to stand for the other without being the other. The place of this relation within autobiography has been described by de Man as follows: "The autobiographical moment happens as an alignment between two subjects involved in the process of reading in which they determine each other by mutual reflexive substitution. The structure implies differentiation as well as similarity since both depend on a substitutive exchange that constitutes the subject. This specular exchange is interiorized in a text in which the author declares himself to be the subject of his own understanding." "Autobiography as De-Facement," in *The Rhetoric of Romanticism* (New York: Columbia U. P., 1984), 70.

19. Despite the importance of both synonyms and desynonymization to the critical project undertaken in the *Biographia,* these topics have been restricted to merely an aspect of Coleridge's thought on language. Desynonymization has received significant individual attention in Joel Weinsheimer's "Coleridge on the Synonymity and the Reorigination of Truth" (*Papers on Language and Literature* 14 [1978]: 269–83) and William Galperin's " 'Desynonymizing' the Self in Wordsworth and Coleridge" (*Studies in Romanticism* 26 [1987]: 513–26)—a brief and historical account of desynonymization may be found in James McCusick's *Coleridge's Philosophy of Language* (New Haven: Yale U. P., 1986), 91–92. Galperin is particularly suggestive about the link between ventriloquy and desynonymization when he writes that "the rhetoric of desynonymization . . . enables Coleridge to distinguish himself in the *Biographia* without finally doing so" (521). Such a rhetoric would offer Coleridge the ability to speak the truth without being disregarded and without having what is said undermined by his recognition. The question posed by Galperin's comment is whether such a distinction can be limited enough to know that it is not final or, to be precise, to know that it is a distinction at all. The question is crucial to a knowledge of both synonyms and desynonymization (and therefore the whole idea of a desynonymizing process). Galperin touches upon this question when he argues that "synonymity . . . deconstructs . . . mutual autonomy [desynonymization of Coleridge and Wordsworth]" (521), and, later, "Coleridge's 'I'-ness or *bios* is undone by his *Biographia,* which exposes the similarity, the identity, of which difference and selfhood are representations" (526). Weinsheimer's argument demands a similar privileging in the relation of difference to identity when he writes about synonymity as a "return of the same with a difference" (282). But, what Weinsheimer calls the same cannot clearly be the same since, if it returns with a difference, then he is talking about two separate things related by an identity. Given the presence of both Gadamer and the language of Heidegger as support for Weinsheimer's argument, it is worth alluding to Heidegger's clarification of the self-contradiction involved in a return of the same with a difference at the very beginning of Heidegger's "Der Satz der Identität": "Damit etwas das Selbe sein kann, genügt jeweils eines. Es bedarf nicht ihrer zwei wie bei der Gleichheit" [For something to be the same, one is enough at any given time. Two are not needed for the same as is the case with identity]. *Identität und*

Differenz (Pfullingen: Neske, 1957), 10, my translation. In each case, Galperin's and Weinsheimer's arguments would suggest that the question of synonymity might be best approached through Heidegger's attempt to think difference *as* difference rather than by any attempt to think synonymity as difference.

20. Coleridge, *Philosophical Lectures,* ed. K. Coburn (London: Pilot Press, 1949), 174.

21. What is here described as a synonymy of language is in fact the rhetorical figure of interpretation: "Interpretatio est quae non iterans idem redintegrat verbum sed id commutat quod positum est alio verbo, quod idem valeat" [While repeating, interpretation does not say the same word over again but that word changes position with another word which means the same]. *Rhetorica ad Herennium,* 4.38, my translation.

22. Since the 1983 edition of the *Biographia* signals no editorial change to the text of this footnote, punctuation and typography have been made consistent with prior editions, notably the 1847 edition.

23. See *Biographia* (1983), 1:84, n. 2.

24. That it is indeed indifference that makes possible the relation of "I" and "me" to a third term is indicated by Coleridge in a passage from *Aids to Reflection.* Despite its emphasis upon opposed terms, this passage uses an example whose opposition is no more apparent than that of "I" and "me" to one another: "When two subjects, that stand to each other in relation of *antithesis* or contradistinction, are connected by a middle term common to *both,* the sense of this middle term is indifferently determinable by *either.* . . . Thus, if I put hydrogen and oxygen gas, as opposite poles, the term *gas* is common to both; and it is a matter of indifference, by which of the two bodies I ascertain the sense of the term" (225). It is through such an indifference that the *Biographia* speaks of the imagination in chapter 7: "There are evidently two powers at work, which relatively to each other are active and passive; and this is not possible without an intermediate faculty, which is at once both active and passive. (In philosophical language, we must demonstrate this intermediate faculty in all its degrees and determination, the IMAGINATION)" (1:124–25).

25. This place of the autobiographical within criticism does not mean that criticism is a form of autobiography (for a discussion of criticism in terms of such a form see Jeffrey Plank's article "Literary Criticism as an Autobiographical Form" [*Wordsworth Circle* 13 (1982): 169–74]), but rather, that criticism, as a form of knowledge, would require the kind of self-relation commonly associated with the genre of autobiography if it is to avoid what de Man has called defacement (see "Autobiography as Defacement," 67–81). But, even if this relation were attained it would also enact the very defacement it sought to avoid. Indeed, this avoidance is precisely how such a defacement takes place.

26. *KRV* A xii.

27. Hegel, *Differenz des Fichteschen und Schellingschen Systems der Philosophie, Werke in zwanzig Bänden* (Frankfurt: Suhrkamp, 1970), 2:9–138. Cole-

ridge's relative neglect of Hegel does not prevent, however, the argument that one can become Hegelian without any sustained or direct knowledge of key Hegel works (see Kathleen Wheeler, "Coleridge's Theory of Imagination: A Hegelian Solution to Kant?" *The Interpretation of Belief: Coleridge, Schleiermacher, and Romanticism,* ed. David Jasper [Basingstoke, U.K.: Macmillan, 1986], 16–40). Direct evidence that Coleridge had read Hegel is given by a small number of annotations to a volume of Hegel's *Wissenschaft der Logik* [The Greater Logic]. These annotations are reprinted in *Marginalia, CC* 12, 2:988–97. As this volume points out, Coleridge's understanding of Hegel may be cursory at best.

28. Vorerinnerung, "Versuch einer neuen Darstellung der Wissenschaftslehre," *Sämmtliche Werke,* ed. I. H. Fichte, 8 Bände (Berlin: 1845–46), 1:420–21. All citations of the text of the *Wissenschaftslehre* and the introductions will be to this edition of Fichte's works. Subsequent references will be given in parenthesis in the text, using the abbreviation *WL* followed by volume and page number of this edition. Unless otherwise noted, translations are my own. The notion of *Darstellung,* which may be translated as "presentation" (literally: "a placing there") tended, in Fichte and Schelling, to denote an exposition through which the systematicity of knowledge attempts to unveil a self-grounding authenticity. On *Darstellung* and its place within philosophical discourse, see Philippe Lacoue-Labarthe, "Typographie" in *Mimesis des articulations* (Paris: Aubier-Flammarion, 1975), 166–270.

29. Schelling, *Abhandlungen, SW* 1:347; Hegel, *Differenz, Werke* 2:9. The consistent appeal to this difference indicates how necessary this unaccounted distinction between figurative language and the literal existence of a given text is to the development of speculative philosophy after Kant as well as to the critical methods that evolved in its wake. As Fichte also reveals, such a distinction is to be applied to his own philosophy: "Die Wissenschaftslehre ist von der Art, daß sie durch den bloßen Buchstaben gar nicht, sondern daß sie lediglich durch den Geist sich mittheilen läßt" [The science of knowledge is of a kind that does not allow itself to be communicated by the mere letter but solely by the spirit]. *WL* 1:278.

30. "Er soll diejenige *Tathandlung* ausdrücken: die unter den empirischen Bestimmungen unsers Bewußtseins nicht vorkommt, noch vorkommen kann, sondern vielmehr allem Bewußtsein zum Grunde liegt, und allein es möglich macht" [It is intended to express that *Act* which does not and cannot appear among the empirical states of consciousness, but rather lies at the basis of all consciousness and alone makes it possible]. *WL* 1:91.

31. For Fichte's full exposition of this principle, see *WL* 1:93–102.

32. "Er [Kant] redet *von einer Täuschung, die stets wiederkehre, unerachtet man wisse, daß sie Täuschung sei*" [He (Kant) speaks of a deception which constantly recurs, even though one knows it to be a deception]. *WL* 1:513. Fichte's misunderstanding of what Kant refers to as a deception may be gauged from the speed with which he attempts to determine such a deception as the sign of an "unstable inner conflict" and then asserts, "*Es kehrt,*

meiner Erfahrung nach, keine Täuschung zurück" [In my experience, no deception recurs]. *WL* 1:94. For the passage in which Kant describes the operation of such a deception, see *KRV* B 355.

33. On the crucial role of the imagination in Fichte's *Science of Knowledge,* see *WL* 1:216–17, 239, 241, and 243.

34. "Im konsequenten Stoicismus wird die unendliche Idee des Ich genommen für das wirkliche Ich: absolutes Sein, und wirkliches Dasein werden nicht unterschieden. Daher ist der stoische Weise allgenugsam, und unbeschränkt; es werden ihm alle Prädikate beigelegt, die dem reinen Ich, oder auch Gott zukommen. . . . Die Wissenschaftslehre unterscheidet sorgfältig absolutes Sein, und wirkliches Dasein, und legt das erstere bloß zum Grunde, um das leztere erklären zu können. Der Stoicismus wird dadurch widerlegt, daß gezeigt wird, er könne die Möglichkeit des Bewußtseins nicht erklären. Darum ist die Wissenschaftslehre auch nicht atheistisch, wie der Stoicismus notwendig sein muß, wenn er konsequent verfährt" [In a consistent stoicism, the infinite idea of the self is taken to be the real self; absolute being and real existence are not distinguished. Hence the stoic sage is all-sufficient and unconfined; all the predicates belonging to the pure self, or even to God are due to him. . . . The Science of Knowledge carefully distinguishes between absolute being and real existence, and employs the former merely as a basis to explain the latter. By this means, as will be seen, stoicism is refuted, it cannot account for the possibility of consciousness. Hence the Science of Knowledge is not atheistic either, as stoicism necessarily must be, if it is thoroughly worked out]. *WL* 1:278. In a passage occurring just before this statement, Fichte would also reject Coleridge's assertion. Fichte writes that a system built upon such an assertion would be unable to account for self-consciousness precisely because it could not distinguish "reflektirtes, und reflektirendes, das Bewußtsein selbst, und der Gegenstand desselben, sich nicht unterscheiden lassen" [the reflecting and the reflected, consciousness itself and the object of the same]. *WL* 1:275. Evidently, if Coleridge read this passage, he misunderstood or else forgot it in order to remember Schelling.

35. Fichte writes that the not-self "völlig unabhängig von dem Ich, und seinem Triebe ist, *ihren* Weg geht, und nach *ihren* Gesetzen sich richtet, wie dieser sich nach den seinigen richtet" [is wholly independent of the self and its drive, which goes *its own way,* and conforms to *its own* laws, as does the drive of the self]. *WL* 1:308–9. In so defining the not-self, Fichte accords to it precisely the attributes associated with nature in its relation to knowledge.

36. Hegel speaks of such principles as follows: "The principle of one is the subjective Subject-Object, and of the other the objective Subject-Object; hence the system of subjectivity also contains the objective, and the system of objectivity also contains the subjective." This remark occurs in the section entitled "Comparison of Principles of Philosophy" from *Differenz, Werke* 2:107.

37. This lack of emphasis does not mean that Coleridge will move toward a different conception of the imagination as Thomas McFarland ar-

gues in *Coleridge and the Pantheist Tradition:* "The function of the imagination in a system of absolute idealism is always constitutive and regulative, therefore, never, as in Coleridge, truly mediating and reconciling" (307). Not only does McFarland's argument not consider the different levels of the imagination in Kant, but Schelling, whose *System* is closest to what the *Biographia* argues at this point, does define the activity of the imagination as mediating: "Es muß also mit diesem Widerspruch eine Tätigkeit entstehen, die zwischen Unendlichkeit und Endlichkeit in der Mitte *schwebt.* Wir nennen diese Tätigkeit indeß Einbildungskraft bloß der Kürze halber, und ohne dadurch etwa ohne Beweis behaupten zu wollen, das, was man insgemein Einbildungskraft nennt, sei eine solche zwischen Endlichkeit und Unendlichkeit *schwebende,* oder, was dasselbe ist, eine Theoretisches und Kraftisches *vermittelnde* Tätigkeit" [With this opposition, there must also arise an activity which *wavers* in the middle between infinity and finitude. For the time being and for the sake of brevity, we will call this activity imagination, without wishing thereby to assert without proof that what is generally called imagination is such a *wavering* between finitude and infinity, or what is the same, an activity *mediating* the theoretical and practical]. *System des transcendentalen Idealismus, SW,* 3:558; emphasis mine. This work of Schelling's will be referred to subsequently as *System.*

38. The passage from Schelling translates as follows: "Philosophy acts upon objects of *inner sense* and cannot, as in mathematics, attach to every construction an outer intuition. Hence, if it is to be clear (*wenn sie evident werden soll*), philosophy must set out from the most original construction; the question is therefore, what *is* the most original act *for the inner sense?*" (*Abhandlungen, SW* 1:445). See also *System, SW* 3:350, for a similar statement.

39. Coleridge's immediate source for this quotation is Juvenal, *Satire* 11.27. The command itself is from one of the series reportedly engraved on the pillars of the temple at Delphi (see A. Bouché-Leclercq, *Histoire de la divination dans l'antiquité,* 4 vols. [Paris: 1880], 3:155). Curiously, the 1983 edition of *Biographia* describes this maxim as being "inscribed over the temple at Delphi" (1:252, n. 1). To place this command in such a crowning position reflects a claim for legitimacy that no existing account is able to provide. In Plato's *Phaedrus,* no such physical claim is made even though this command would also have a primary place when it is given as Socrates' reason for not inquiring into such things as "Gorgons or Pegasuses." Socrates states: "I am not yet able to know myself according to the Delphic inscription; this still unknown, it of course appears ludicrous to me to consider other things" (229^{e}5–230^{a}1). It is also the mythical that Coleridge would avoid in adopting a philosophy that would lift the cloak of Kant, the cloak that appears wherever Kant is "constrained to express himself mythically or equivocally" (1:157).

40. To my knowledge, the only reference to this command in Schelling occurs in the first of a series of public lectures dating from January 1821: "Also die ganze Bewegung ist nur Bewegung zur Selbsterkenntniß. Der

Imperativ, der Impuls der ganzen Bewegung, ist das Γνῶθι Σεαυτόν, Erkenne dich selbst, dessen Ausübung *allgemein* als Weisheit angesehen wird. Erkenne was du bist, *sei,* als was du dich erkannt hast, dieß ist die höchste Regel der Weisheit" [Accordingly, the whole movement is a movement toward self-knowledge. The imperative, the impulse of this whole movement is the Γνῶθι Σεαυτόν, Know Thyself, the practice of which is generally considered wisdom. Know what you are, *be* what you know yourself as, this is the highest rule of reason]. "Über die Natur der Philosophie als Wissenschaft," *SW* 9:226.

41. The difference is also remarked in the *Zusatz* to Hegel's introduction to the third part of the *Encyclopedia of the Philosophical Sciences.* Hegel also refers to the Delphic command but, unlike Coleridge distinguishes it sharply from any external source: "Die vom delphischen Apollo an die Griechen ergangene Aufforderung zur Selbsterkenntnis hat daher nicht den Sinn eines von einer fremden Macht äußerlich an den menschlichen Geist gerichteten Gebots; der zur Selbsterkenntnis treibende Gott ist vielmehr nichts anderes als das eigene absolute Gesetz des Geistes" [The summons to self-knowledge issuing from the Delphic oracle to the Greeks does not have the meaning of a command externally imposed on the human mind by an unknown authority; rather, the god who impels to self-knowledge is none other than the absolute law of the mind itself]. Hegel, *Enzyklopädie der philosophischen Wissenschaften,* III, *Werke* 10:9.

42. The same questions also apply to the current tendency to reduce reading to an act as in the phrase, "the act of reading." The aesthetics that makes such a reduction possible (but never articulated by that reduction) merely extends the activity of the self in Fichte and Schelling into a form of self-conscious identity which then serves as a principle of critical interpretation. In an extension of these questions, it could be asked, "Can reading ever be an act that does not have to be read?"

43. *CN* 3:4265 (September 1815).

44. As early as the opening sentences of the section dealing with Hartleian association (chapter 5 of the *Biographia*), Coleridge notes how the presence or absence of the will has been a guiding principle for those "men in all ages, who have been impelled as by an instinct to propose their own nature as a problem" (1:89). Subsequently, Coleridge comes to regard the absence of the will as an impossibility when he states that the will "is perhaps never wholly suspended" (1:112)—a position that makes any absence of the will serve as an affirmation of its presence.

45. Nietzsche, *Jenseits von Gut und Böse, Werke,* ed. Karl Schlechta (Frankfurt: Ullstein, 1984), 3:26–27, § 17.

46. *CN* 3:3708 (March 1810).

47. Nietzsche, *Jenseits von Gut und Böse, Werke* 3:28, § 19.

48. The connection between self-consciousness and the metaphor of light (as in the critical example of a lamp) is made explicitly by Schelling: "Das Selbstbewußtsein ist der lichte Punkt im ganzen System des Wissens, der aber nur vorwärts, nicht rückwärts leuchtet" [Self-consciousness is the

luminous point in the whole system of knowledge, however, it only shines its light forward and not backward]. *System, SW* 3:357.

49. The passage translated and modified by Coleridge is as follows: "Wenn das *Objektive* willkürlich als das Erste gesetzt wird, wir doch nie über das Selbstbewußtsein hinauskommen. Wir werden alsdann in unseren Erklärungen entweder ins Unendliche zurückgetrieben, vom Begründeten zu Grund, oder wir müssen die Reihe willkürlich abbrechen, dadurch, daß wir ein Absolutes, das *von sich selbst* die Ursache und die Wirkung—Subjekt und Objekt—ist, und da dieß ursprünglich nur durch Selbstbewußtsein möglich ist, dadurch, daß wir wieder ein *Selbstbewußtsein* als erste setzen; dieß geschieht in der Naturwissenschaft, für welche das Sein ebenso wenig ursprünglich ist wie für die Transcendental-Philosophie . . . , und welche das einzig Reelle in ein Absolutes setzt, das von sich selbst Ursache und Wirkung ist—in die absolute Identität des Subjektiven und Objektiven, die wir Natur nennen und die in der höchsten Potenz wieder nichts anderes als Selbstbewußtsein ist" [Whenever the objective is arbitrarily posited as the first, we are still never beyond self-consciousness. Our explanations are then either driven back endlessly from the grounded to the ground or we must arbitrarily break off the series, thereby we posit an absolute which is *by its own self* cause and effect—subject and object—and since this is originally only possible through self-consciousness, for this reason, we again posit self-consciousness as primary; this occurs in natural science, for which being is as little primary as it is for transcendental philosophy. . . . which posits its sole reality in an absolute—in the absolute identity of the subjective and objective which we call nature and which in its highest power is again nothing other than self-consciousness]. *System, SW* 3:356.

50. Coleridge, in fact, condenses Synesius at this point. In Synesius's Third Hymn the words cited by Coleridge form part of a series of attributes: "πατέρων πάντων / πάτερ, αὐτοπάτωρ, / προπάτωρ, ἀπάτωρ, / υἱὲ σεαυτοῦ" (*Hymni et Opuscula,* ed. N. Terzaghi, *Scriptores Graeci et Latini* [Rome, 1949], 1:145–48). Grammatically, the πατήρ of Coleridge's "πατὴρ αὐτοπάτωρ" belongs to the first phrase, "of all fathers / father." A literal translation of these lines from Synesius would read, "of all fathers / father, self-fathering, / forefather, without father, / son of himself." Coleridge's arrangement of these lines stresses even further his striving for a determination that will contain a principle of generation within itself—the self-enclosing character of an origin that would escape being "driven back from ground to ground."

51. Plato, *Cratylus* 432^{b}1–^{d}9; see also Derrida, "La Pharmacie de Platon," *La dissémination,* 159–60.

52. Hegel, *Wissenschaft der Logik, Werke* 5:290. This same section of the *Science of Logic* clearly relates the "infinite series" described by Coleridge (*Biographia,* 1:285) to not only such a superstition but also to what Hegel terms bad or spurious infinity: "Die *unendliche Reihe* enthält nämlich die schlechte Unendlichkeit" (*Werke* 5:289). On the distinction between this "bad infinity" and the notion of infinity in deconstruction, see Rodolphe

Gasché, "Nontotalization without Spuriousness: Hegel and Derrida on the Infinite," *Journal of the British Society for Phenomenology* 17 (1986): 289–307.

53. It should be noted at this point that Schelling will later account for freedom through a concept of indifference. See *Über das Wesen der menschlichen Freiheit, SW* 7:336–416.

54. See also the lecture from 1818 published as "On Poesy or Art" for an extended account of this distinction (*Biographia* [1807] 2:253–63). An exhaustive list of Coleridge's use of copy and imitation is given by Frederick Burwick in "Coleridge and Schelling on Mimesis" in *The Coleridge Connection,* ed. Richard Gravil and Molly Lefebure (London: Macmillan, 1990), 178–99.

55. Schelling, *Philosophische Schriften,* Landshut: Krüll, 1809. Indeed, in the case of Coleridge's reference to Raphael, two passages from Schelling's *Abhandlungen* are alluded to but not cited by the 1983 edition of the *Biographia* as sources for what Coleridge expresses in his reference to Raphael's *Transfiguration.* Both of these passages use the word *Copie* and not the word *Nachahmung* (which is used in the *System* to describe philosophy's free and perfect imitation of an original series). The second of the two is as follows: "In unserer Erkenntniß ist nichts unmittelbares (eben deßwegen nichts Gewisses) wofern nicht die Vorstellung zugleich Original und Copie, und unser Wissen ursprünglich und durch ein ideal und real zugleich ist. Der Gegenstand ist nichts anderes als unsere selbsteigne Synthesis, und der Geist schaut in ihm nichts an als sein eignes Produkt. Die *Anschauung ist völlig tätig, eben deßwegen produktive und unmittelbar*" [In our explanations nothing is immediate (precisely for this reason nothing is certain) unless representation is at the same time original and copy, and our knowledge is original and thoroughly real and ideal at the same time. The object is nothing other than our very own synthesis, and the mind intuits in it nothing but its own product. *Intuition is totally active, in this way productive and immediate*]. *SW* 1:379. The mere occurrence of *Original* and *Copie* in this passage as well as the earlier one may be cause enough for the 1983 edition of the *Biographia* to refer to them even though Schelling makes no attempt to distinguish copy from either original or imitation unlike Coleridge in his critique of materialism.

56. "Über das Verhältniß der bildenden Künste zur Natur" [Concerning the Relation of the Plastic Arts to Nature] (1807), *SW* 7:328.

57. One should also note at this point that Raphael's *Transfiguration* may be read as double interruption. For such a reading, see Louis Marin, *La voix excommuniée* (Paris: Galilée, 1981), 73.

58. On the inseparability of history from philosophy understood as metaphysics, see Heidegger, "Entwürfe zur Geschichte des Seins als Metaphysik," *Nietzsche* (Pfullingen: Neske, 1961), 2:458–80.

59. "Das ganze System zwischen zwei Extreme fällt, deren eines durch die intellektuelle, das andere durch die ästhetische Anschauung bezeichnet ist. Was die intellektuelle Anschauung für den Philosophen ist, das ist die ästhetische für sein Objekt. Die erste, da sie bloß zum Behuf der beson-

deren Richtung des Geistes, welche er im Philosophiren nimmt, notwendig ist, kommt im gemeinen Bewußtsein überhaupt nicht vor; die andere, da sie nichts anderes als die allgemeingültig oder objektiv gewordene intellektuelle ist, *kann* wenigstens in jedem Bewußtsein vorkommen. Es läßt sich aber eben daraus auch einsehen, daß und warum Philosophie *als* Philosophie nie allgemeingültig werden kann. Das eine, welchem die absolute Objektivität gegeben ist, ist die Kunst. Nehmt, kann man sagen, der Kunst die Objektivität, so hört sie auf zu sein, was sie ist, und wird Philosophie; gebt der Philosophie die Objektivität, so hört sie auf Philosophie zu sein, und wird Kunst" [The whole system falls between two extremes of which one is represented by intellectual and the other by aesthetic intuition. What intellectual intuition is for the philosopher, aesthetic intuition is for his object. The former, since it is necessary purely for the purpose of that particular direction which the mind takes in philosophizing, cannot be found at all in ordinary consciousness; the latter, since it is nothing other than intellectual intuition given universal validity, or become objective, *can* be found at least in every consciousness. From this very fact it may be seen that, and why, philosophy *as* philosophy can never become universally valid. The one thing to which absolute objectivity is given is art. Take, it could be said, objectivity away from art and it ceases to be what it is and becomes philosophy; give objectivity to philosophy and it ceases to be philosophy and becomes art]. *System, SW,* 3:630.

60. Indeed, Coleridge, by espousing the higher absoluteness asserted through this inclusivity would be open to the criticism that Schelling levels at those who would distinguish philosophy and religion by maintaining an empty space outside philosophy which philosophy cannot fill but which may be filled by faith. Schelling states: "Das Absolute kann aber nicht vom Absoluten . . . verschieden kann. . . . Es folgt daher notwendig, daß jenem, welcher über dem Absoluten der Vernunft noch ein anderes als Gott setzt, jenes nicht wahrhaft als solches erscheinen, und daß es bloß eine Täuschung sei, wenn er ihm gleichwohl diese Bezeichnung noch läßt, die ihrer Natur nach nur Eines bezeichnen kann" [The absolute cannot be differentiated from the absolute. . . . It necessarily follows from this that whoever, above the absolute of reason, places, as God, another absolute, the former (absolute of reason) is not truly absolute, and it is a naked deception whenever this designation, which by its nature can only designate a single concept, is left to it]. *Philosophie und Religion, SW* 6:21. As Schelling also argues in this work, there is no difference between the absolute thought within philosophy and religion.

61. To bring philosophy to an end by substituting literature or even literary criticism in its place does nothing more than make literature speak on behalf of philosophy—as Schelling's *System* clearly demonstrates when the aesthetic is given the mantle of universal validity. To bring philosophy to such an end is to continue it by another name.

62. A denial explicitly repeated by Coleridge: "Were it in my power, my works should be confined to the second volume of my 'Literary Life,' the

essays of the third volume of "The Friend" . . . and some half dozen of my poems." *CL* 4, 925 (February 28, 1819).

63. Is it for this reason that Coleridge returns to Synesius of Cyrene at this point in the *Biographia?* The following lines are cited in the middle of the final paragraph of the last thesis: "Μάκαρ, ἵλαθί μοι! / Πάτερ, ἵλαθί μοι / Εἰ παρὰ κόσμον, / Εἰ παρὰ μοῖραν / Τῶν σῶν ἔθιγον!" [Blessed one, be gracious to me, / Father, be gracious to me, / If beyond what is ordered, / If beyond what is destined, / I touch upon that which is thine] 1:286; Hymn 3, lines 113–17. Although in the *Biographia* these lines are cited after Coleridge's description of the will as πατὴρ αὐτοπάτωρ, υἱὸς ἑαυτοῦ [father self-fathering, son of himself] (1:285; Hymn 3, lines 145–48), they precede these phrases in Synesius's Third Hymn. Moreover, the context of these lines in Synesius's Third Hymn is not without significance to the path taken by the *Biographia:* "Let the sinuous trend of serpents sink beneath the earth, and that winged serpent also, the demon of matter, he who clouds the soul, rejoicing in images and urging on his brood of whelps against my supplications. Do Thou, O Father, O Blessed One, keep away from my soul these soul-devouring hounds, from my prayer, from my life, from my works. May our heart's libation be a care to Thy august messengers, wise bearers to Thee of holy hymns. Now am I borne back to the starting-point of sacred poesy (Ἤδη φέρομαι ἐπὶ βαλβῖδας ἱερῶν ἐπέων). Already does the oracle echo in my mind (ἤδη καναχεῖ ὀμφὰ περὶ νοῦν). Be full of goodness. . . ." Hymn 3, lines 86–113; *The Essays and Hymns of Synesius of Cyrene,* trans. A. Fitzgerald, 2 vols. (London: Oxford U. P., 1930), 1:376. As in Schelling, one returns to a starting point but here, Synesius expresses this point as a voice (ὀμφή refers to oracle in the sense of a voice that is heard and not simply to the site of an oracle), which "rings" or "resounds" in the mind of the poet (in addition to "echo," the verb καναχέω suggests a sharp sound, particularly the ringing sound of something metallic). Thus, with Synesius, one returns to the starting point in order to hear the authoritative voice, whereas with Schelling, and with Coleridge too, the return to such a point ought to be the engendering of one's own authoritative voice.

64. C. M. Wallace in *The Design of the Biographia Literaria* (London: Allen & Unwin, 1983) is the first to observe that the missing deduction of the imagination is secondary to what she describes as a "gap" in Coleridge's philosophical argument "between Thesis VI and its Scholium, between the one force or single ground and the personal triune God" (81). Wallace then goes on to state that "autobiographical resolution takes its [philosophical resolution's] place 'temporarily'" (81). Such an argument actually preserves the idea of a missing deduction on another level and, in this way, it repeats an appeal to what is missing as the possibility of a valid argument.

65. Schelling already gives voice to such a question early in the *System:* "Allein was Philosophie *sei,* ist eben die bis jetzt unausgemachte Frage, deren Beantwortung nur das Resultat der Philosophie selbst sein kann. *Daß* die Auflösung dieser Aufgabe Philosophie sei, kann nur durch die Tat selbst beantwortet werden, *dadurch, daß man zugleich mit dieser Aufgabe alle die*

Probleme auflöst, die man von jeher in der Philosophie aufzulösen suchte" [But what philosophy *may be,* is precisely the up till now undecided question, whose answer can only be the result of philosophy itself. *That* the resolution of this task is philosophy can only be answered through the achievement itself, *by this means, one simultaneously resolves with this task all the problems which, hitherto, one sought to resolve in philosophy*]. *System, SW* 3:358. According to this passage, the task of philosophy is to resolve precisely those problems which constitute such a task, yet, philosophy so viewed must aim at nothing more than the annulment of philosophy. The completion of philosophy *as* philosophy would suggest, however, that the practical task of philosophy is to prevent any such annulment.

66. Kant, *KRV* B 705–6.

67. Ibid., B 854.

68. Ibid., B 597.

69. Ibid., B 598.

70. Here, the sense of wonder invoked by both Plato and Aristotle as the origin of philosophy would become philosophy's amazement with its own powers of interruption. See Plato, *Theaetetus* 155^{d}2–4, and Aristotle, *Metaphysics* 982^{b}12–17.

71. Plotinus, *Enneads* 3.8.4; Synesius, Hymn 3, lines 226–27. The Greek text that Coleridge translates in this footnote is incorrectly cited in the 1983 edition, an irony Coleridge could hardly have anticipated when he introduced the passage from Plotinus with the words "The passage, that follows . . . appears to me evidently corrupt . . . no writer more wants, . . . or is less likely to obtain, a new and more correct edition" (1:240n.). Coleridge's rendering of the lines from Synesius are cited from Sara Coleridge's edition of the *Biographia* (1847, 1:248); the Terzaghi edition of Synesius reads ἄρρητε (Hymn 3, line 228) for Coleridge's Ἄρρητα.

72. See *Biographia,* 1:72–73 and section 2 of this chapter.

73. Plotinus, *Enneads* 3.8.4. This continues the passage cited previously by Coleridge.

74. "That letter addressed to myself as from a friend, at the close of the first volume of the Literary Life, which was written without taking my pen off the paper except to dip it in the inkstand." *CL* 4, 728 (April 29, 1817). Given the importance of this letter in the *Biographia,* the context of the preceding remark is worthy of note as it concerns Coleridge's preference to publish a volume of letters which, he believes, would be "thrice the value of my set publications." *CL* 4, 730 (May [20], 1817). The letter from April 1817 has drawn more attention as literary criticism has attempted to assimilate and reflect deconstruction. There have been two significant attempts at tackling this letter as the reflection of philosophical and rhetorically deconstructive exigencies. In the first, G. V. Spivak ("The Letter as Cutting Edge," in *Literature and Psychoanalysis,* ed. S. Felman [Baltimore: Johns Hopkins U. P., 1982], 208–26) analyzes the letter as a necessity of the philosopher's desire for coherence, a necessity that marks the impossibility of such coherence. To avoid philosophy's continual deferral of its own com-

pletion, the letter is said to "occlude" the resulting gap in order to father the "Law of the imagination." This is achieved by means of a cut made by the letter in the philosophical argument. Spivak concludes, "All images of a cutting that gives access to the Law is a mark of castration. It is the cut in Coleridge's discourse that allows the Law to spring forth full-fledged. The removal of the phallus allows the phallus to emerge as the signifier of desire" (220–21). To state that the Law springs forth full-fledged oversimplifies the difficulties of this section of the *Biographia*—and nor can philosophy be so easily reduced to a thematic desire for coherence. This reduction indicates a desire for coherence no different from that attributed to philosophy. Jerome Christensen (*Coleridge's Blessed Machine of Language*) attempts a more textually subtle line of thought when he asserts that "the letter of the man is the man of the letter—a chiasmus" (172). Within, Christensen's argument, the occurrence of such a chiasmus serves as an interruption. Yet, it is only by considering this chiasmus as uninterrupted that one could affirm the substitution of man and letter or even religion and philosophy. The difficulty faced by Coleridge in the *Biographia* would be evaded by such an understanding of the chiasmus.

75. The friend is not the only one to experience this state of affairs. In a letter from April 1817 Coleridge writes about the composition of the *Biographia* in terms that repeat precisely the feelings of someone who discovers himself to be the perpetrator of a bull: "I became bewildered, wrote and wrote, and destroyed and erased, till I scarcely knew whether I was on my head or my heels." *CL* 4, 726 (April 29, 1817).

76. Milton, *Paradise Lost,* ed. Merrit Y. Hughes (New York: Macmillan, 1985), 2:666–70.

77. The role of chiasmatic relation is explicit in Schelling who, in the *System,* invokes it as the sign of the principle of philosophy: "*Das Princip der Philosophie muß also ein solches sein, in welchem der Inhalt durch die Form, und hinwiederum die Form durch den Inhalt bedingt ist,* und nicht eines das andere, sondern beide wechselseitig sich voraussetzen" [*The principle of philosophy must therefore be one in which content is determined by form, and form in return by content;* not one determining the other, but both mutually presupposing one another]. *System, SW* 3:360.

78. The text cited is that published by John Payne Collier as *Seven Lectures on Shakespeare and Milton* in 1856. This text is quoted from *Lectures 1808–1819: On Literature* (*CC* 5, 2:495–96; for Collier's earlier longhand transcription of this lecture see this same edition, 1:311).

79. Milton, *Paradise Lost,* 2:727–28.

80. This birth is recounted as follows: ". . . on the left side op'ning wide, / Likest to thee in shape and count'nance bright, / Then shining heav'nly fair a goddess armed / Out of thy head I sprung." Milton, *Paradise Lost,* 2:754–58.

81. Such a deduction is what Fichte refers to as a "beneficent deception." The passage in which Fichte speaks of this deception clarifies the philosophical role of the "missing deduction." Fichte writes: "Allerdings,

hätten wir auch alle bisherige Untersuchungen ohne eine wohlätige Täuschung der Einbildungskraft, die unvermerkt jenen bloß entgegengesezten ein Substrat unterschob, gar nicht vornehmen können; wir hätten über sie nicht denken können, denn sie waren absolut Nichts, und über Nichts kann man nicht reflektiren" [Certainly, we could not have undertaken all our previous inquiries without a beneficent deception by the imagination which unobserved placed a substrate under these mere oppositions; we should not have been able to think about them for they were absolutely nothing, and about nothing one cannot reflect]. *WL* 1:224.

82. On hovering (*Schweben*) as the anticipation of synthesis, see Peter Szondi, "Friedrich Schlegel und die romantische Ironie," *Schriften*, 2 vols. (Frankfurt: Suhrkamp, 1978), 2:22. Lacoue-Labarthe and Nancy also describe such a hovering when they refer to the motif of mixing within Romanticism as the approach to a limit: "Le motif du mélange, sans être ni produire le mélange lui-même (puisqu'il n'est rien), mène jusqu'au bord extrême de ce qu'il mêle: le genre, la littérature, la philosophie" [The motif of mixture, without either being or producing mixture itself (since it is nothing), leads right to the extreme edge of what mixes: genre, literature, philosophy]. (*L'absolu littéraire* [Paris: Seuil, 1978], 421). In each case, the motif of hovering or mixture takes the place of what is anticipated but does so in a way that turns away from the anticipated result in order to preserve it and its continued anticipation.

83. "Le chiasme, la réversibilité, c'est l'idée que toute perception est doublée d'une contre-perception (opposition réelle de Kant), est acte à deux faces, on ne sait plus qui parle et qui écoute" [The chiasmus, reversibility—this is the idea that every perception is doubled by a counter-perception (the real opposition of Kant)—is an act with two faces, one no longer knows who speaks and who listens]. Maurice Merleau-Ponty, "Notes de travail," *Le visible et l'invisible* (Paris: Gallimard, 1964), 318. For other discussions of the chiasmus and its structure, see Andrezj Warminski, "Prefatory Postscript," in *Readings in Interpretation: Hölderlin, Hegel, Heidegger* (Minneapolis: U. of Minnesota P., 1987) as well as Rodolphe Gasché's introduction to these readings; Derrida, "+ R (par-dessus le marché)," in *La verité en peinture* (Paris: Flammarion, 1978), in particular, 189–92. Although deconstruction involves reversal and dissymmetry as part of its intervention, it would be a hastily formed evasion to thematize deconstruction as only a play of reversal and dissymmetry represented by a chiasmus. Even in the period when Derrida makes use of the chiasmus, one should note the reservations expressed by tense as well as hasty thematization: "le χ (le chiasme) (qu'on *pourra toujours* considérer, *hâtivement*, comme le dessein *thématique* de la dissémination)" [The χ (the chiasmus) (which one *will always be able* to consider, *hastily*, as the thematic design of dissemination]. "Hors livre," La dissémination (Paris: Seuil, 1972), 52; emphasis mine. In the same essay, Derrida makes the following comment on the reversal of those classic philosophical oppositions which offer so easy a target for the reversals desired by a wide variety of literary criticism: "Ces oppositions ne constitu-

aient pas un système *donné,* une sorte de table anhistorique et foncièrement homogène, mais un espace dissymétrique et hiérarchisant, traversé par des forces et travaillée dans sa clôture par le dehors qu'il refoule: expulse et, ce qui revient au même, intériorise comme un de *ses* moments. C'est pourquoi la déconstruction comporte une phase indispensable de *renversement.* En rester au renversement, c'est opérer, certes, dans l'immanence du système à détruire. Mais s'en tenir, pour aller *plus loin,* être plus radical ou plus audacieux, à une attitude d'indifférence neutralisante à l'égard des oppositions classiques, ce serait laisser libre cours aux forces qui dominent effectivement et historiquement le champ. Ce serait, faute de s'emparer des moyens d'y *intervenir,* confirmer l'équilibre établi" [These oppositions have not constituted a *given* system, a kind of ahistorical and thoroughly homogeneous table, but a dyssymetrical and hierarchializing space traversed by the forces and, in its closure, worked over by the outside it drives back, expels and, which amounts to the same, interiorizes as one of *its* moments. This is why deconstruction includes an indispensable phase of *reversal.* To remain with this reversal is to operate, certainly, within the immanence of the system to be destroyed. But, to stick to an attitude of neutralizing indifference in regard to these classical oppositions in order to go *further,* in order to be more radical or more audacious, this would be to grant free rein to the forces that effectively and historically dominate the field. This would be, for want of taking possession of the means to *intervene,* to confirm the established equilibrium]. "Hors livre," 11–12.

84. Indeed, to see the letter of the friend as the unavoidable narrative of such a "missing" philosophical deduction is to maintain the critical project of the *Biographia* by asserting that this narrative interrupts the movement toward totality represented by the "missing" deduction. A remark by Derrida in "Edmond Jabès et la question du livre" succinctly indicates the misconstrual of language necessary to this privileging of narrative or a "missing" philosophical discourse at a point where a lapse in signification occurs: "Prétendre le [un *lapsus* essentiel entre les significations] réduire par le récit, le discours philosophique, l'ordre des raisons de la déduction, c'est méconnaître le langage, et qu'il est la rupture *même* de la totalité" [To pretend to reduce it (an essential *lapse* between one signification and another) by a narrative, by a philosophical discourse, by the order of reasons in a deduction, is to misconstrue language and to misconstrue that language is *itself* the rupture of totality]. *L'écriture et la différence* (Paris: Seuil, 1967), 107–8.

85. Nietzsche, *Jenseits von Gut und Böse,* 3:30.

86. Sara Coleridge points out in the 1847 edition of the *Biographia* that this phrase had been stroked out in copy of the *Biographia* containing some marginal notes of Coleridge (*Biographia* [1847], 297, n. 13). The crossing out of this phrase would effectively divorce the imagination more completely from the terms of the philosophical argument of the *Biographia.* The necessity of interruption in the *Biographia* would itself be interrupted in this case.

87. The candle metaphor is Coleridge's and appears in a letter from September 1818: "The inconsistency Schelling has contrived to hide from himself by the artifice of making all knowledge bi-polar . . . I myself was *taken in* by it . . . and adopted it in the metaphysical chapters of my Literary Life—not aware, that this was putting the candle horizontally and burning it at both ends." *CL* 4, 874 (September 30, 1818). Clearly, Coleridge would rather hold the candle by its end; then, at least, it could serve as a lamp rather than a reflection of itself.

Chapter Three
Where Three Paths Meet

1. All parenthetical references to *The Prelude* are to the 1850 text published in the Norton edition (*The Prelude 1799, 1805, 1850,* ed. J. Wordsworth, M. H. Abrams, and S. Gill [New York: Norton, 1979]). Departures from this edition are based on the manuscript materials published in the Cornell Wordsworth series (*The Fourteen Book Prelude,* ed. W. J. B. Owen [Ithaca: Cornell U. P., 1985]).

2. Not only is this passage evoked repeatedly in the interpretation of *The Prelude* but more significant than the fact of this repetition is the tendency to put aside the discursive position of this episode. In his extensive study, *Wordsworth's Poetry 1787–1814* (1964; New Haven: Yale U. P., 1971), Geoffrey Hartman emphasizes the compositional structure of *The Prelude* and, in so doing, positions the apostrophe to the imagination in Book 6 as the conclusive passage in the development of the imagination's relation to nature in *The Prelude* (see pp. 44–48, 54–55, 60–69). This tendency is even more marked in studies of the sublime. Both Thomas Weiskel (*The Romantic Sublime: Studies in the Structure and Psychology of Transcendence* [Baltimore: Johns Hopkins U. P., 1976], 195–204) and Paul Fry ("The Possession of the Sublime," *Studies in Romanticism* 26 [1987]: 189–207) position the Simplon Pass episode as the culminating example of their arguments. Weiskel's reading of this episode, although recognizing a "perplexity which *seems* to resist the light of interpretation" (195; my emphasis), sees no perplexity in retrieving the sense of an experience that the apostrophe to the imagination is said to "occlude." Hence, this passage only *seems* to resist; its ostensible subject is an appearance masking an actual subject it is unable to voice directly but which can be known negatively. More than Weiskel, Fry's reference to this passage is accompanied by a consciousness of his own repetitive gesture when he states that it "has become a tradition to end discussions of the sublime with a bow to Wordsworth's great interruptive apostrophe to Imagination in *The Prelude*" (205). However, such an awareness does not prevent the persistence of the dialectical understanding which dominates the interpretation of the apostrophe. Indeed, in this passage, alienation would be unthinkable without such a dialectical resolution through which this same alienation is overcome even as it is produced. In the case of literature, this alienation is *predicated* upon an understanding that defines language according to an inability to possess what it is said to name. Yet, if

such a definition is to be possible, a full knowledge of what it means to have possession would be required, otherwise, it would be impossible to know when and if any possession were alienated. In short, this definition demands the possession of possessing. Because an inability to arrive at an unalienated possession is built into such a dialectic, a future full of alienation (a possession evermore about to be) will always be assured, precisely because the initial production of the possibility of possession (how else could alienation arise?) remains unquestioned. The tendency to place this passage in a final position also occurs in Paul de Man's "The Intentional Structure of the Romantic Image" (1960, 1968; *The Rhetoric of Romanticism* [New York: Columbia U. P., 1984], 1–17). But the placing of this passage in de Man's essay would have to be read in the context of an analysis concerned less with the imagination as an intent of consciousness than with the relation of language to origination. Indeed, the tendency to place this passage in a culminating position without any consideration of such a relation indicates an argumentative structure that confidently assumes a historical progression toward a knowledge embodied by this very episode. De Man's "Time and History in Wordsworth" (lecture, Christian Gauss Seminar, Princeton University, 1967; *Diacritics* 17.4 [1987]: 4–17), in which the Simplon Pass episode is returned to, complicates further the exemplary status of this passage with respect to the reading of Wordsworth as well as the history of Romanticism. Indeed, de Man's analysis of the metaleptic movement through which history is named would already account for the frequency as well as the necessity of "bowing" before this passage in a critical discourse wishing to preserve a sense of history that is dialectical in origin. That history should be so consistently at stake—either as a means to structure critical interpretation or else as a means to ground this and similar passages in the singularity of historical events or facts (a recourse that is perhaps as far removed from any authentic experience of history as could be imagined)—whenever this passage is addressed has less to do with the thematics of this passage than it has to do with the possibility of thematic interpretation in general. But, what makes reference to this passage so necessary a conclusion either interpretively or actually would be the extent to which it seems to promise a passage to history rather than a reflection on any such passage.

3. My reading of this episode focuses primarily on the 1850 text despite the recent tendency to prefer the 1805 version of the Simplon Pass episode from *The Prelude* as affording more radical poetic insights (see Robert Brinkley, "The Incident in the Simplon Pass: A Note on Wordsworth's Revisions," *Wordsworth Circle* 12 [1981]: 122–25; Isobel Armstrong, "Wordsworth's Complexity: Repetition and Doubled Syntax in *The Prelude* Book VI," *Oxford Literary Review* 4.3 [1981]: 20–42; Weiskel also turns to the 1805 version at critical moments in his interpretation of this passage [*The Romantic Sublime,* 195–204]). The only other exception to this recent tendency has been Susan Luther's "Wordsworth's *Prelude,* VI, 592–616 (1850)" (*Wordsworth Circle* 12 [1981]: 253–61), and, as is the case here, Luther is not con-

cerned with the superiority of one version over another—as if one text could be thematized as being, from a theoretical point of view, "better" or more insightful than another. While Luther's reading focuses exclusively on the apostrophe and, to date, it represents the closest attention this passage has received with respect to its language and syntax, this reading tends to understand the questions raised by such a syntax only in semantic terms. This tendency leads to a conclusion that finally affirms experience at the expense of the language in which it arises: "The poet's coupling of ostensibly logical, argumentative surface discourse with semantic *and* syntactic ambiguity and striking tropes are what make it possible for readers generally to agree with him that the experience in VI. 592–616 is something important and original—even if we cannot assign it one or a final name" (259–60; emphasis mine). To speak of syntax in terms of naming is to shift the complexity of Wordsworth's "human speech" into a realm that defines language in relation to something external whether or not this object is an actual thing or an experience. Properly speaking, such a definition of language is restricted to semantic concerns.

4. The peculiar attraction of Romantic criticism to the line "Like an unfathered vapour" is particularly marked in Hartman's writings on Wordsworth. The emphasis Hartman already places on the apostrophe in *Wordsworth's Poetry 1787–1814* issues into an increased attraction for an "unfathered vapour" in his essay "Blessing the Torrent" (*The Unremarkable Wordsworth* [Minneapolis: U. of Minnesota P., 1987], 75–89). This essay, which is more richly concerned with the place of naming (it is actually a reading of the sonnet "To the Torrent at Devil's Bridge, North Wales, 1824"), refers to the apostrophe to the imagination in Book 6 of *The Prelude* on two occasions (84, 89). For Hartman, this apostrophe as well as the apostrophe of this sonnet are in effect intertwined with the "*radical* homelessness of the imagination" (84; emphasis mine). What this "radical homelessness" amounts to is described in the following sentences: "The [phrase] 'shall we . . . bend o'er the abyss' [from *Descriptive Sketches* (1793), 176–86] . . . is totally transformed in *Prelude* VI, where Imagination rises from the mind's abyss in a moment of *involuntary divination.* Also in the *perplexity* of 'How art thou named?' [from "To the Torrent . . ."] forced from a poet who is swept away by imagination, and who barely keeps a hold on reality via this beachhead or bridge. If there is an answer to 'How art thou named?' it might be, once more, 'Imagination!' " (89; emphasis mine). Some of the attributes attached to this passage in *The Prelude* may be discerned from such language as "involuntary divination" as if the imagination's rising were in fact "an unfathered vapour"—here indeed would be a beachhead, a bridge and, above all, a *radical* homelessness. The difficulty of this passage is to read the rising of the imagination which is *like* such a vapor. In the penultimate paragraph of his essay, Hartman addresses such a difficulty in the following words: "Let the interpreter take some responsibility. Let him venture the thought that 'How art thou named?' is *addressed* to the power of the imagination, or the place (home) it seeks. . . . But if the subject ad-

dressed is imagination, the predicate is an involved series of quotations" (89; emphasis mine). While a complexity is to be perceived in a predicate comprised of a whole series of quotations, the complexity of the relations embodied by these quotations would also require a return to the perplexity that marks the structure of the address as it is unfolded in this episode of *The Prelude.*

5. In the context of the "Drowned Man" episode from Book 5 of *The Prelude,* Cynthia Chase speaks of "a general predicament [for] the reader of Romantic texts: an erosion of the distinction between literal and figurative modes on which recovery of meaning depends" ("The Accidents of Disfiguration: The Limits to Literal and Rhetorical Reading in Book V of *The Prelude,*" *Decomposing Figures* [Baltimore: Johns Hopkins U. P., 1986], 14). Chase goes on to remark that a "text both requires to be read literally and thwarts attempts to fix its referential status" (14). In the present context, what is envisaged would take the form of a literal reading of the conjunction, a reading of what "like" is like in this passage rather than what it gives rise to. Within such a reading, it would be unwise to forget Benjamin's observation in "The Task of the Translator" that "die Forderung der Wörtlichkeit [ist] unableitbar aus dem Interesse der Erhaltung des Sinnes" [the demand for literalness is not derivable from an interest in the preservation of sense]. "Die Aufgabe der Übersetzers," *Gesammelte Schriften,* ed. Rolf Tiedemann and Hermann Schweppenhäuser, 7 vols. (Frankfurt am Main: Suhrkamp, 1974–89), 4.1, 18. Since this demand for literalness (discussed by Benjamin in a context concerned with the literality of translation) becomes first and foremost a question of syntax rather than a question exclusively restricted to sense or meaning, it would not be possible for a text to require a literal reading as long as this requirement is understood as only an attempt to recover meaning. Indeed, as Wordsworth's structuring of the Simplon Pass episode indicates, the thwarting of an anticipated meaning has an affirmative role to play in concealing the ground of a subsequently unquestioned historical knowledge.

6. While this land could also be referred to as a place where "The Child is Father of the Man" neither "My Heart Leaps Up" nor the "Immortality" Ode (to which this line forms part of the epigraph) would allow this mode of self-relation to remain unquestioned. Indeed, the two lines following the phrase "The Child is Father of the Man," that is, "And I could wish my days to be / Bound each to each by natural piety," not only make use of a conditional tense but do so in order to express how one day is related to the next. Thus, the relation of days that will lead from child to man (the relation that fathers the man) is a wish whose conditionality leaves room to doubt that the child will necessarily continue to be the father—"I could wish" is very different from either "I do wish" or "I wish." This binding has only the status of a wish, a desire for self-engenderment as well as a self-knowledge in which Man remains identical to his past. In this respect, the development of this poem in lines 3–6 ("So was it when my life began; / So is it now I am a Man; / So be it when I grow old, / Or let me die!") repeats the dialogue

between Oedipus and the Sphinx: both relate three stages of a life in which Man would not only know himself but become his own father. As will be clear, such an eventuality occurs through a figurative substitution which takes the place of a binding together which the poem, in the face of death, could only wish for.

7. A militant vocabulary is not only part of this passage's diction (Wordsworth's own introduction to this section on the Alps speaks of a "march of . . . military speed" [1850, 6:492]) but, as Andrzej Warminski has already remarked ("Missed Crossing: Wordsworth's Apocalypses," *Modern Language Notes* 99 [1984]: 988–89), M. H. Abrams also adopts such a vocabulary in order to characterize a perceived and recurrent pattern in *The Prelude* (see Abrams's "English Romanticism: The Spirit of the Age" in *Romanticism and Consciousness,* ed. H. Bloom [New York: Norton, 1970], 109). This vocabulary can hardly be restricted to Abrams, rather, it would seem to come into play whenever the critical discourse it is adopted by encounters difficulties in the relation between itself and the text it interprets. Hartman moderates this *via militaris* into a more "natural" *via luctationis* when, in "Blessing the Torrent," he speaks of the address "How art thou named?" as a "*beachhead*" that "keeps a *hold* on reality" (89; emphasis mine). The military diction (as well as the recourse to wrestling) indicates, perhaps, nothing more than a distinct aversion to being "Halted without an *effort* [1805: *struggle* (6:530)] to break through" (1850, 6:597; emphasis mine).

8. Although the exclamation mark following the word imagination is absent from the 1850 text, the dash occurs in both the 1805 and the 1850 editions. However, in the earlier text, "here" does not occur immediately following the dash: "Imagination!—lifting up itself / Before the eye and progress of my song / Like an unfathered vapour, *here* that power / In all the might of its endowments, came / Athwart me . . ." (1805, 6:525–29; emphasis mine). In his comparative analysis of these two versions of this passage, Robert Brinkley asserts that in the 1805 version "the referent of the deictic [here] is 'before . . . my song' while the referent in the 1850 edition is the Simplon Pass" ("The Incident in the Simplon Pass," 123). Although the 1805 text is thematically more explicit in its calling attention to the time of writing, the 1850 text does not lose this reference: its "here" points to the place in which the imagination is apostrophized, the place in which *The Prelude* is written or, to paraphrase the passage that originally came between the ascent to the pass and the apostrophe to the imagination, this place is the "scene before [us]" where *The Prelude* "lies in perfect view / Exposed, and lifeless as a written book" (1805, 8:726–27). As the Norton edition notes, this passage was "drafted late in March 1804, in an attempt to define Wordsworth's sense of anticlimax at having unknowingly crossed the Alps in August 1790. . . . In this original position [it] precede[s] drafts of the lines upon the imagination" (304). However, to emphasize that the only function of the "here" is to indicate the writing of *The Prelude* not only determines this writing in terms of an act but, at the same time, it demands complicity in a very determined negative knowledge which serves to con-

trast the passage through the Simplon Pass with the imagination. It is precisely this contrast that sustains the critical discourse on Romanticism and the historical understanding it proposes.

9. Such a dialectical recovery cannot be restricted to language. Indeed, if one reads what David Simpson calls the isolation of the imagination as the social and historical incompetence of the imagination, one has already recovered social and historical significance by means of this overdetermined incompetency. The dialectical nature of this relation of the imagination to social and historical concerns is expressed by Simpson in the following words: "As the Wordsworthian imagination is social, and defined even in its isolation by its relation to others, so it is also historical, defined in relation to particular others and at specific moments" (*Wordsworth's Historical Imagination: the Poetry of Displacement* [New York: Methuen, 1987], 1–2). The source of such a dialectic comes under scrutiny as the relation of the poet to the imagination is unfolded in the apostrophe.

10. This sequence whereby the apostrophe is followed by lines that are concerned more with the addressing subject than with the object of address would already indicate the extent to which the employment of an apostrophe requires that the addressing subject assert itself. The sequence is frequent enough to suggest that the apostrophe exerts a halting effect upon its user. See Paul de Man, *Allegories of Reading* (New Haven: Yale U. P., 1979), 29, for the occurrence of a similar pattern in a poem from Rilke's *The Book of Monastic Life*. For a reading of the figure of apostrophe in which it is linked to a "temporality of discourse," see Jonathan Culler, "Apostrophe," *The Pursuit of Signs* (Ithaca: Cornell U. P., 1981), 135–54. Although Culler would distinguish this temporality from the common sense of time, that is, a chronological sense, the retention of this term cannot avoid being afflicted with the same "sad incompetence of human speech" that makes the recourse to a temporality in and of writing an inevitable consequence of a context in which figurative language would be valorized. Two other studies of note with regard to the apostrophe are Mary Jacobus's "Apostrophe and Lyric Voice in *The Prelude*" (*Lyric Poetry*, ed. C. Hošek and P. Parker [Ithaca: Cornell U. P., 1985], and Barbara Johnson's "Apostrophe, Animation, and Abortion" (*Diacritics* 16.1 [1986]: 29–47).

11. This loss of the poet in the simile that enwraps is more directly stated in the 1805 version: "I was lost as in a cloud, / Halted without a struggle to break through" (1805, 6:529–30). Yet, despite this more direct statement, the later version indicates that the experience of being lost results explicitly from what the rising of the imagination is like. In both cases, loss arises from a simile.

12. To this sequence of substitutions, Abrams adds yet one more in order to be able to account for this sequence in terms of a particular consciousness: "Suddenly, in the process of reliving this experience while narrating it, Wordsworth is again lost within himself, as in a mist that rises from an abyss in the mind across his poetic path. The revised version [1850] of this passage makes clearer Wordsworth's double use of a journey, which is

literal for the tour he is describing and metaphorical for the process of composing the poem: 'Imagination. . . . / That awful Power rose from the mind's abyss / Like an unfathered vapour that enwraps / At once, some lonely traveller. I was lost; / Halted without an effort to break through'" (1850 ed.; 6:591–97). M. H. Abrams, *Natural Supernaturalism* (New York: Norton, 1973), 451–52. Not only does this reading require the evocation of a dramatic situation ("Suddenly . . . reliving this experience while narrating it") but it also requires that the lines "—here the Power so called / Through sad incompetence of human speech" be forgotten by being excluded from the revised version that Abrams cites as evidence.

13. Not only does the possibility of such an antecedent give rise to the father but also, as Derrida remarks in reference to Heidegger, it engenders the whole theoretical project in which a reflection on textuality is confused with metalinguistics: "Et le père? Ce qu'on appelle le père? Il tenterait d'occuper la place de la forme, de la langue formelle. Cette place est intenable et il ne peut donc *tenter* de l'occuper, parlant dans cette seule mesure la langue du père, que pour la forme. C'est en somme cette place et ce projet impossibles que Heidegger désignerait au début de *Das Wesen der Sprache* sous les noms de 'métalangage' (*Metasprache, Übersprache, Metalinguistik*)—ou de Métaphysique. Car finalement, l'un des noms dominants pour ce projet impossible et monstrueux du père, comme pour cette maîtrise de la forme pour la forme, c'est bien la métaphysique" [And the father? What is called the father? He would attempt to occupy the place of form, of formal language. This place is untenable, and he can therefore only *attempt* to occupy it, speaking in this way, for the sake of form, only the language of the father. In short, it is this place and this impossible project that Heidegger would designate at the beginning of "Das Wesen der Sprache" under the name of "metalanguage" (*Metasprache, Übersprache, Metalinguistik*)—or Metaphysics. Since, finally, one of the dominant names for this impossible and monstrous project of the father—as well as for this mastery of form for form's sake—is indeed Metaphysics]. Derrida, "Le retrait de la métaphore," *Psyché* (Paris: Galilée, 1987), 76–77; translation mine. Here, it cannot be stated forcefully enough that a critique of metaphysics which would take the form of merely asserting its impossibility is hardly a critique unless, of course, a critique has no other function than the affirmation of the metaphysical.

14. Through this denial of its own loss, the three designations of assertion (*Aussage*) described by Heidegger, namely, pointing out, predication, and communication (*Sein und Zeit* [Tübingen: Niemeyer, 1986], 154–55, § 33), would all be at work in this example of the subject's interpretation of itself as a subject.

15. An apocalypse is already anticipated at the end of the apostrophe when the flood of the Nile is evoked. These lines run as follows: ". . . blest in thoughts / That are their own perfection and reward, / Strong in herself and in beatitude / That hides her, like the mighty flood of the Nile / Poured from his fount of Abyssinian clouds / To fertilize the whole Egyptian plain"

(1850, 6:611–16). The receding of the waters of the Nile is known in Greek as an apocalypse (ἀποκάλυψις). In addition, the very last lines of this episode refer to the historical sense of the apocalyptic and, as in the case where the imagination is compared to an unfathered vapour, this reference takes place through the same conjunction: ". . . were all *like* workings of one mind, the features / Of the same face, blossoms upon one tree; / Characters of the great Apocalypse, / The types and symbols of Eternity, / Of first, and last, and midst, and without end" (1850, 6:636–40; emphasis mine).

16. In accordance to both MS.D and MS.E of *The Prelude,* the colon in the Norton edition (1850, 6:599) has been changed to a semicolon.

17. The reading text established in the Cornell Wordsworth edition of *The Fourteen Book Prelude* omits this dash, which only occurs in the 1850 text (the 1805 text, MS.D, and MS.E [which became the copy used to produce the 1850 text] all read: "I now can say"). To object to this analysis on the ground of an inability to know what the punctuation ought to be would amount to an avoidance of the question raised by a difference that is still made whether or not it is marked by a dash. On these terms, the dash may be read as simply the name indicating a space which would mark a break between what is meant to be present as a "speaking" and a writing about speaking: the omission of a dash does not lessen the need to read such a difference. Even if the version in the Cornell Wordsworth's reading text ["I now can say,"] reflected manuscript evidence rather than grammatical preference, it should not be forgotten that its comma would mark, once again, a halting-place.

18. What remains is precisely that part of human speech which Aristotle defines in the *Poetics* as a sound without meaning: σύνδεσμος δέ ἐστιν φωνὴ ἄσημος ἣ οὔτε κωλὺει οὔτε ποιεῖ φωνὴν μίαν σημαντικὴν [The conjunction is a sound without significance which neither hinders nor causes a single significant sound]. $1456^{b}38–57^{a}1$; translation mine. As Derrida recalls in "The Double Session," these words have always been said to possess no full meaning of their own, they form "une cheville syntaxique, non un catégorème, mais un syncatégorème, ce que les philosophes, du Moyen Age aux *Recherches Logiques* de Husserl, appellent une signification incomplète" [a syntactical plug, not a categorem but a syncategorem: what philosophers from the Middle Ages to Husserl's *Logical Investigations* have called an incomplete signification] (*La dissémination,* 250). The reference to such connectives as only "plugs" would threaten the syntactic complexity of these words which are continually unfathered in order to be assigned the grammatical function of connection, interrelation, and so on. In addition to its obvious indication of an articulating joint, the "ankle" (*cheville*) would also involve a more extended context which, as will become clear below, is hardly unrelated to this passage in *The Prelude*. "*Cheville,*" as an articulated joint, would also translate the Greek ἄρθρον—the very word used by the Messenger to indicate where Oedipus plunged the brooches after believing that he had unfathered himself: he "lifted up [the brooches] and dug them into the sockets of his eyes (ἄρας ἔπαισεν ἄρθρα τῶν αὐτοῦ κύκλων)"

(Sophocles, *The Plays and Fragments* I, ed. Lewis Campbell [Oxford: Clarendon Press, 1879], line 1270). Moreover, in the paragraph that follows Aristotle's statement about conjunctions in the *Poetics,* ἄρθρον is defined in precisely the same language: ἄρθρον δ' ἐστὶ φωνὴ ἄσημος ἣ λόγου ἀρχὴν ἢ τέλος ἢ διορισμὸν δηλοῖ οἷον τὸ ἀμφί καὶ τὸ περί καὶ τὰ ἄλλα. ἢ φωνὴ ἄσημος ἣ οὔτε κωλύειοὔτε ποιεῖ φωνὴν μίαν σημαντικὴν" [Articulation is sound without significance which indicates a beginning, end, or division, for example, *amphi, peri,* and so on. Or else a sound without significance which neither hinders nor causes a single significant sound] (1457a6–9; translation mine). Even though this passage on articulation may be a later interpolation, such a historical objection remains irrelevant since what is under examination here is not the integrity or authenticity of Aristotle's text but rather the question of why connectives are incessantly and thematically relegated to the status of incomplete significations. It would seem to be no mere accident that unfathering involves such a violent turning upon connectives, conjunctions, and the like. Indeed, blindness and unfathering would always seem to be preferable in the face of these incomplete significations whenever a single significant sound is at stake.

19. It should not be forgotten in this context that Aristotle defines mimesis in terms of pleasure in the *Poetics,* namely, the pleasure derived from recognizing "this" because of "that" (see *Poetics* 48b17).

20. Aristotle, *Poetics* 48b17. On the relation of Napoleon to the Simplon Pass and, in particular, the apostrophe to the imagination, see Alan Liu, "The History in 'Imagination,'" in *Wordsworth: The Sense of History* (Stanford: Stanford U. P., 1989), 3–31. While Liu would not reduce history to facts (as he confesses, there is no single piece of evidence that Napoleon stands in the background of the apostrophe to the imagination), this does not prevent "an alliance between text and context considered as wholes" (25). As will be seen, in the third section of this chapter, the condition of such an alliance may already be read in Wordsworth's description of the ascent that leads to the mouth of a peasant if one pays attention to the text "—that we had crossed the Alps" and a context that does not permit any easy acceptance of this crossing as a historical event (or even the apostrophe as veiled history). How one arrives at a knowledge of this crossing is paradigmatic for how one understands Wordsworth's sense of history. As I argue throughout this chapter, the first passage (frequently referred to as 6a) is the site where the possibility of historical knowledge will be decided in the guise of reading the landscape as a guide to past as well as anticipated events. And, as the sequence of readings undertaken in this chapter seeks to demonstrate, the apostrophe strives to recognize the imagination through a sequence which repeats the attempt to recognize history in the description of the ascent. In this sense, one could speak of an alliance between history and the imagination, but, it is not an alliance determined by historical events nor is it determined by what Liu describes as "originating absence." As will be seen, "originating absence" is as much a part of the ideological or philosophical sense of history that would explain away such

an absence. Where language is concerned, to tell the difference between presence and absence is to know a difference between ideology and history.

21. Before the revision to MS.D which results in the substitution of "allayed" (1850) for "asleep" (1805), the possibility of such a discontinuity is present: "Yet still in me mingled with these delights / Something of sterner mood, an under-thirst / Of vigour, *seldom utterly asleep*" (MS.D, lines 539–41; emphasis mine).

22. For such a comparison, see Alan Liu, "The History in 'Imagination,'" in *The Sense of History*, 3–4.

23. That the invitation is conspicuous indicates that it becomes an invitation by being looked at. In other words, this passage across the torrent requires that the landscape be regarded as if it were a printed document addressed to Wordsworth and his companion. This book of nature only arises, however, through the discoursing of nature in the torrent, that is, one gets to the book of nature by *crossing* its discourse.

24. The definition of mimesis as both a mode of repeating what already exists and as a mode of knowledge is most pronounced in chapter 4 of Aristotle's *Poetics*. In this chapter, history and knowledge are derived from an aesthetic relation (here, one of pleasure) which supports the possibility of learning: "If one takes delight in visual images (τὰς εἰκόνας ὁρῶντες), it is because, in looking at them, one learns and one concludes, this [image] because of that (οἷον ὅτι οὗτος ἐκεῖνος)" ($48^{b}15$–17; translation mine). The place of learning in this relation is explicitly stated in the *Rhetoric* (see $1371^{b}4$–10). Even though Aristotle will go on to assert in chapter 8 of the *Poetics* that the poet is concerned with what might happen rather than what has happened, this concern only extends the structure of historical understanding to the future—what might happen is only understandable in analogy to what has happened (see $51^{a}36$–$51^{b}5$). According to Aristotle, the poet's concern is more philosophic ($51^{b}5$–6). If this is the case, then, what Aristotle determines to be philosophic demands that what is not yet history be regarded as if it were like history.

25. The word "torrent" first appears in a revision to MS.D (see *The Fourteen Book Prelude*, pp. 708–9) where it replaces "streamlet" in the base copy of this manuscript. The change from "streamlet" to "torrent" is paralleled by an earlier revision to the 1805 text in which the phrase "Right to a rivulet's edge" (1805, 6:503) becomes "Right to a rough stream's edge" (MS.D and 1850, 6:569). Through these revisions, the passage is marked by a sequence of linguistic substitutions which would transform the course of the stream as it attempts to recover a knowledge of error.

26. It should not be forgotten here that a basic science of figuration in the form of what we now recognize as geometry was employed in ancient Egypt as the means to recover the past by calculating the place of the boundary markers erased by the flooding of the Nile. Geometry, as an instrument of inscribing boundaries would also be a form of writing. As such, writing would also be a threat to memory, precisely because, in the case of the Nile, it would be encoded in an infinitely repeatable form that

would avoid any need to recall the past. Without the need to recall the past, what is called the past can be, in effect, always present. It is this aspect of geometry that Husserl draws attention to when he states that "the Pythagorean theorem, [indeed] all of geometry, no matter how often or even in what language it may be expressed, exists only once. Geometry is identically the same in the 'original language' of Euclid and in all 'translations'; and within each language it is again the same, no matter how many times it has been sensibly uttered, from the original expression and writing-down to the innumerable oral utterances or written or other forms of documentation" ("*The Origin of Geometry,*" in Jacques Derrida, *Edmund Husserl's* Origin of Geometry: *An Introduction,* trans. John P. Leavey [Lincoln: U. of Nebraska P., 1989], 160; translation modified). To be so completely translatable would be to lack history and therefore any need for recollection. It is hardly surprising that such an inscription should be viewed so consistently as a threat since what it undercuts is not simply metaphysics but the concept of history which restricts philosophy to the metaphysical. In the sense in which Husserl speaks of geometry as being "identically the same," there remains however the question of whether each inscription of geometry could be said to possess a history or whether each inscription marks the advent of a history that, in the end, will and can only arise because of this inscription.

27. Indeed, this covering over occurs by means of likenesses, in particular the likeness between what belongs to nature (torrent, stream) and what belongs to the human (path). The attainment of this likeness or identity between nature and the human marks a return to the identity between the guided and their guide with which the ascent to the Simplon Pass began. Schematically, then, the recognition of a border (that is, of a line that cuts across their path) occurs through a substitution of the natural (stream) for the human (guide) and this substitution is only possible by returning the discourse of nature (which is also seen to cut across their path) to a course which reasserts likeness and analogy as the basis of its progression, that is, as the basis of a history in the future, a future that will always be known as something that "was." By reading the course of the stream in place of its discourse (which is, in effect, their discourse), Wordsworth and his companion would again confirm, as de Man has remarked in "Literary History and Literary Modernity" (*Blindness and Insight,* 2d ed. [Minneapolis: U. of Minnesota P., 1983]), that "the basis of historical knowledge"—and the future is radically historical—"are not empirical facts"—where the torrent resides as a stream—"but written texts" (165)—even if these texts masquerade in the guise of historical or natural occurrences.

28. For a reading of the textual instances relating to this question in Sophocles' *Oedipus* may be found in Sandor Goodhart's "Ληστὰς Ἔφασκε: Oedipus and Laius' Many Murderers," *Diacritics* 8.1 (1978): 55–71. See also Pietro Pucci, *Oedipus and the Fabrication of the Father* (Baltimore: Johns Hopkins U. P., 1992).

29. The substitution of "what is" for "what was" would underline what

has been concealed in the philosophical discourse on essence. Here, the terms employed in a substitution that aims at the production of historical knowledge recall those employed by Aristotle in a definition of essence. However, in Aristotle, the terms are reversed, what was precedes what something is: λέγω δὲ οὐσίαν ἄνευ ὕλης τὸ τί ἦν εἶναι [I speak of essence without substance as what it was to be (something)]. *Metaphysics*, 1032^{b}14; translation mine. Aristotle's use of an imperfect tense (ἦν) in this definition indicates that what is called essence is understood in terms of its presence throughout a completed period of time. Nevertheless, this understanding can only arise in a reflection taking place in the present (if it did not, how would it be possible to know what was?). The close relation between reflection and this understanding of essence is underlined by a remark in the "Zusatz" to § 112 of Hegel's "Logic": "Der Standpunkt des Wesens ist überhaupt der Standpunkt der Reflexion" [The standpoint of essence is above all the standpoint of reflection]. *Enzyklopädie der philosophischen Wissenschaften*, in *Werke in zwanzig Bänden* (Frankfurt am Main: Suhrkamp, 1970), 8:232. How such an essence is understood by Hegel becomes clearer in the following definition of reflection: "Der Ausdruck Reflexion wird zünachst vom Lichte gebraucht, insofern dasselbe in seinem geradlinigen Fortgange auf eine spiegelnde Fläche trifft und von dieser zurückgeworfen wird" [The term reflection is first used about light to the extent that light continuing in a straight line strikes a mirrored surface and is thrown back from it]. *Enzyklopädie*, § 112; *Werke* 8:232. In this definition, essence would repeat the operation of mimesis and, like it, draw an understanding of its operation from the metaphor of a mirror. Such an understanding of essence is not only mimetic but also historical to the extent that this essence, like history, mediates a source which, to all intents and purposes, does not exist without the relation established by this mediation. Yet, as Hegel pursues the question of an essence in the "Zusatz" to § 112, this mimetic understanding through which essence speaks of what is past is described in terms of an irregularity of language: "Was nunmehr die sonstige Bedeutung und den Gebrauch der Kategorie des Wesens anbetrifft, so kann hier zunächst daran erinnert werden, wie wir uns im Deutschen beim Hilfszeitwort *sein* zur Bezeichnung der Vergangenheit des Ausdrucks *Wesen* bedienen, indem wir das vergangene Sein als *gewesen* bezeichnen. Diese Irregularität des Sprachgebrauchs liegt insofern eine richtig Anschauung vom Verhältnis des Seins zum Wesen zugrunde" [What the other meanings and uses of the category of essence now refer to can be recalled in German by our use of the auxiliary verb, *sein,* to indicate the past of the term *Wesen;* we refer to past being as *gewesen*. This irregularity of linguistic usage underlies in this respect a correct perception of the relation of Being to essence]. *Enzyklopädie*, § 112; *Werke* 8:232. This definition not only recalls Aristotle's to the extent that, for Hegel, *Wesen ist was gewesen ist,* but it also indicates an underlying structure in the thought of essence, namely, essence or what it is to be something is known in terms of what it was. As such, the possibility of defining essence is predicated upon historical knowledge. Yet, as in Hegel's example, what is known in the present in the form of a history does not arise initially from the past but from an irregularity of language. This irregularity is subsequently regularized and mediated by making *Wesen* enter into a relation with *sein* and *gewesen* as if the latter were an inevitable *derivative* of *sein*. This relation is supported, in the first instance, by nothing less than the forms of this verb's conjugation. Suffice it to say that the possibility of history as well as literary theory also depends, in the first instance, upon such a formal relation and, in the second, upon the substitution of one form for another. Concerning the relation of formalization to the latter, one should remember, as Paul de Man has noted, that theory would be inconceivable without such a formal moment (see "Hypogram and Inscription," *The Resistance to Theory* [Minneapolis: U. of Minnesota P., 1986], esp. 30). However, a question remains. Can an irregular verb account for the substitution of what is and what was? Can such a formal substitution account for essence not to mention a history of essence?

30. And translation is no stranger to this change of address—the noun form being derived from the supine of *transferre*, a verb used to indicate both a change of address in the sense of a change of location (this sense is still present in the ecclesiastical use of the word, for example, the relocation of a bishop from one see to another would be called a translation) and a change in how something or someone is addressed linguistically (either within one language or from one national language to another).

31. In this aspect, the thematic presence of part of the myth of Narcissus and Echo in the Simplon Pass episode differs crucially from Michael Ragussis's reading of this myth in *The Subterfuge of Art* (Baltimore: Johns Hopkins U. P., 1978). Ragussis cites and follows part of the paragraph from Nietzsche's *Die fröhliche Wissenschaft* (the complete paragraph is cited as an epigraph to this section) when he argues that, since "Echo's own words are necessarily always another's" she is the "spirit of critique" (232). For Ragussis, Echo "prepares the way for a self-consciousness that is a healthy self-criticism" (232) and later, "echo is a restless verbal form that does not cease to reflect back upon itself; E. M. Forster explains that echoes engender echoes" (232). In each of these descriptions, echo has a clear salutary effect that may be compared to learning the lessons of history and thereby avoiding the errors of the past. Yet, for echo to have such an educational effect, it would be first necessary to know, as I argue here, the difference between Echo and echo. If we constantly refer to the narrative of Ovid, this difference seems easy to maintain. However, as Ragussis indicates, what Ovid relates cannot be restricted to Narcissus or this narrative. As a verbal form, echo could be extended to the whole of language but this does not mean that every word is the echo of another word (as if language were no more than the "jocund din" described in the "Boy of Winander" episode from *The Prelude*). In a phrase Ragussis omits to cite, Nietzsche writes: "Und alle Stimmen klingen anders in der Einsamkeit!" [And all voices sound different in solitude!]. *Die fröhliche Wissenschaft,* in *Werke,* ed. Karl Schlecta, 5 vols. (Frankfurt: Ullstein, 1984), 2:419, § 182. If every echo sounds different,

could any word ever be the echo of another, rather than the echo of a word's otherness? If always the echo of a word's otherness, no echo could engender another echo without lacking the means to know whether or not this echo is its own. In this case, it is hard to see how Echo can be restricted to a critique of Narcissism since Narcissism is already that same critique—all voices, even Narcissus's, sound different in the solitude of (their?) echo.

Chapter Four
History and the Primitive Theater

1. This is not to say that *Middlemarch* has been untouched by deconstructive criticism or even literary theory. In addition to the articles J. Hillis Miller has devoted to this work ("Narrative and History," *English Literary History* 61 [1974]: 466–67; "Optic and Semiotic in *Middlemarch*," in *The Worlds of Victorian Fiction,* ed. Jerome H. Buckley, Harvard English Studies 6 [Cambridge: Harvard U. P., 1975], 125–45; and, "*Teaching* Middlemarch: *Close Reading and Theory,* in *Approaches to Teaching Eliot's* Middlemarch [New York: MLA, 1990], 51–63), theoretical themes such as discontinuity have also received emphasis (see, for example, Alexander Welsh, *George Eliot and Blackmail* [Cambridge: Harvard U. P., 1985], 216–58). Mention should also be made of Neil Hertz's "Recognizing Casaubon," in *The End of the Line* (New York: Columbia U. P., 1985), 75–96.

2. Despite the prevalent use of this metaphor in the interpretation of Eliot's narrative practice, little attention has been given to the history of this metaphor, never mind its appearance in ostensibly less fictional contexts. The most notable exception to this adoption of weaving as a critical term has been Gillian Beer's *Darwin's Plots: Evolutionary Narrative in Darwin, George Eliot and Nineteenth-Century Fiction* (London: Routledge, 1983), and Sally K. Shuttleworth's *George Eliot and Nineteenth-Century Science* (Cambridge: Cambridge U. P., 1984). Beer actually traces the metaphor of the web through Darwin's description of a "web of affinities" (see Beer, 167) and does much to clarify the thematic extension of this metaphor in other discourses as well as in *Middlemarch.* Nevertheless, even in Beer, there remains a tendency to take the metaphor of weaving and its accompanying metaphor of unraveling as a structural principle of a narrative unwilling to question its most inviting interpretive instrument. Not only does the thematic recourse to this metaphor still need to be read in *Middlemarch* but, also, there is the question of why this metaphor should consistently appear in contexts concerned with language, and, in particular, with a grammatical model of meaning. Two examples of this combination of grammar and the metaphor of weaving, one from Claude Bernard and the other from Plato, will be discussed later.

3. George Eliot, *Middlemarch* (Harmondsworth: Penguin, 1965), "Prelude," 25. All subsequent references to this edition are given parenthetically in the text (page number preceded by chapter number).

4. See Herodotus, *Histories* 1.190–91.

5. Despite Gillian Beer's emphasis on this dispersal as a metaphor for

the narrative of *Middlemarch,* Eliot's own remark on Cyrus's act of revenge suggests that such dispersal may be attributed to a fetish: "Fetichism:—Cyrus breaking the power of the river Gyndes, which drowned one of the white sacred horses—by dispersing its waters in a multitude of small canals." "Folger Notebook," p. 12 (in *George Eliot's* Middlemarch *Notebooks: A Transcription,* ed. J. C. Pratt and V. A. Neufeldt [Los Angeles: U. of California P., 1979]). Dispersal: the fetish of the modern as well as the modernity of literary form?

6. For an interpretation of the mutual exclusion of such claims as they appear in the principal groups of metaphor in *Middlemarch,* see Hillis Miller, "Optic and Semiotic in *Middlemarch,*" in *The Worlds of Victorian Fiction,* Harvard English Studies 6 (Cambridge: Harvard U. P., 1975), 125–45.

7. On the relation of metaphysics to such an entity, see discussions in chapter 2.

8. Martin Heidegger, "Der Weg zur Sprache," in *Unterwegs zur Sprache, Gesamtausgabe* (Frankfurt: Klostermann, 1985), 1.12:231. The manuscript of this lecture contains an annotation in Heidegger's hand which clearly relates his remarks about the web of language to the Platonic notion of συμπλοκή (interlacing or interweaving) discussed at the end of this chapter. The annotation is cited in the *Gesamtausgabe* edition and is as follows: "flechten—plectere συμπλοκή."

9. The lack of critical attention paid to this last part of chapter 15 is remarkable particularly since this part has as much to say about the nature of Lydgate's scientific researches as it has about the narrator's adoption of the metaphor of weaving.

10. There is one earlier reference to the web of a spider: "Has anyone ever pinched into its pilulous smallness the cobweb of pre-matrimonial acquaintanceship?" (2.45).

11. Later such an ensnaring is described in more forceful terms: "She [Rosamond] was riveting the connection with [Lydgate's] family at Quallingham" (58.630).

12. Rosamond's concern with relation above all else is emphasized in chapter 16: "Rosamond, in fact, was entirely occupied not exactly with Tertius Lydgate as he was in himself, but with his relation to her" (16.196).

13. Having a hand in the plot becomes, as the novel progresses, the prerogative of the dead. Both Farebrother and Casaubon attempt to guide events subsequent to their deaths—the story of the latter's attempt is told in the section of *Middlemarch* entitled "The Dead Hand."

14. The existence of a crevice is also related to seeing in chapter 6: "And there must be a little crack in the Brooke family, else we should not see what we are to see" (6.81).

15. As such, Lydgate's inquiry is Aristotelian in nature to the extent that, for Aristotle, essence is defined as τὸ τί ἦν εἶναι [what it *was* to be something] (*Metaphysics,* 983^{a}27). On this definition of essence in Aristotle as well as its repetition in Hegel, see chapter 3, n. 29.

16. Thus, Aristotle's distinction between history and drama in chapter 9

of the *Poetics:* "One says what took place, the other what could have taken place" (51^b4–5).

17. In this context, the narrative trap laid by the scandal involves precisely that kind of entanglement which (for want of a missing word!) accounts for every utterance as a compulsion to narrative. This relation between scandal and narrative recalls the etymology of the word "scandal": σκάνδαλον in Greek also means a trap or snare. On the provenance of this recourse to narrative as a theoretical insight into literature, see the passage by Derrida cited in chapter 2, n. 84.

18. Lydgate's inability to relate the interlacing of science with the interlacing of marriage is commented upon as follows in chapter 16: "He went home and read into the smallest hour, bringing a much more testing vision of details and relations into this pathological study than he had ever thought necessary to apply to the complexities of love and marriage, these being subjects on which he felt himself amply informed by literature, and that traditional wisdom which is handed down in the genial conversation of men" (16.193).

19. In terms of Schelling, Lydgate, and in particular, *Tertius* Lydgate's failing may be viewed as an inability of the self to construct itself. Schelling writes: "Dieses dritte Gemeinschaftliche, wenn es fortdauerte, wäre in der Tat eine *Konstruktion des Ichs selbst,* nicht als *bloßen* Objekts, sondern als Subjekts und Objekts zugleich" [This third common factor, if it persisted, would in fact be a *construction of the self itself,* not as a *mere* object, but rather as subject and object at the same time]. *System, SW* 3:400. It may be added that the narrator's conception of a persistent self sees less difficulty than Lydgate in attaining the kind of relation that defines a "persistent self."

20. This differentiation marks what Derrida has described as "le *point* où le mouvement de la signification viendrait régulièrement *lier* le jeu de la trace en produisant ainsi l'histoire" [the *point* where the movement of signification would come regularly to *bind* the play of the trace while producing in this way history]. "Hors livre," in *La dissémination,* 33.

21. Later this impediment appears in the form of a fracture: "It was as if a fracture in delicate crystal had begun, and [Lydgate] was afraid of any movement that might make it *fatal.* His marriage would be a mere piece of bitter irony if they could not go on loving each other. . . . The first disappointment had been borne . . . and life must be taken up on a *lower stage of expectation,* as it is by men who have lost their limbs" (64.702; emphasis mine).

22. It is in this sense that one can speak of unraveling as a weaving: unraveling produces what is seen in the form of a web and, as the persistent application of this metaphor of weaving to language confirms, such an unraveling could only be possible in the context of language. Hillis Miller has also commented on raveling and unraveling as the same activity albeit Miller plays upon metaphorical senses of the phrases "to ravel up a story" and "to unravel a story" ("The Problematic of Ending in Narrative," *Nineteenth-Century Fiction* 33. 1 [1978]: 3–7). The linguistic context of weav-

ing and unraveling would make it meaningless to ask "in what craft the word 'unravel' became equivalent to 'ravel.'" Suffice it to ask, in what craft does one really weave words?

23. "Notes on Form in Art," *Essays of George Eliot,* ed. Thomas Pinney (New York: Columbia U. P., 1963), 432–33. If the idea at the base of this passage (form is unlikeness . . . and . . . every difference is form") is considered in conjunction with the narrator's outburst in chapter 10 of *Middlemarch* ("I protest against any absolute conclusion . . ."), one might well want to agree with Hillis Miller's statement that "*Middlemarch* itself is an example of form arising from unlikeness, a form governed by no absolute center, origin, or end. Its meaning is generated by the juxtaposition of its several plots. The three love stories, for example, are as much different from one another as they are similar" ("Narrative and History," 499). The quickness with which Miller moves to this conclusion suggests reason for caution if one is to avoid the appearance of what Neil Hertz has called a "poised, deconstructive formulation" (see "Recognizing Casaubon," *The End of the Line,* 78).

24. In this context, a fragment of Heraclitus cannot be overlooked, particularly since it emphasizes the differentiation to which the thought of unity is indebted: τὰ δὲ πάντα οἰακίζει κεραυνός [The thunderbolt guides all things]. In *The Presocratic Philosophers,* 2d ed., ed. G. S. Kirk, J. E. Raven, and M. Schofield (Cambridge: Cambridge U. P., 1983), 197–98.

25. Claude Bernard, *Leçons de physiologie expérimentale appliquée à la médecine,* 2 vols. (Paris: 1855–56), 2:12. Cited by Shuttleworth, *George Eliot and Nineteenth-Century Science,* 144, translation mine.

26. See Shuttleworth for a brief account of Lewes's reading of Bernard (*George Eliot,* 226, n. 5).

27. G. H. Lewes, *The Foundations of a Creed,* 1:296, cited by Shuttleworth, *George Eliot and Nineteenth-Century Science,* 144. Shuttleworth also notes that Eliot was writing *Middlemarch* while Lewes was working on this volume.

28. The passages cited from the *Sophist, Statesman,* and *Phaedrus* represent much-modified versions of the translations published in *Collected Dialogues,* ed. E. Hamilton and H. Cairns (Princeton: Princeton U. P., 1961). On the πρώτη συμπλοκή in Plato, see Henri Joly's study, *Le renversement platonicien: logos, episteme, polis* (Paris: Vrin, 1980). On the theory of grammar in antiquity, see Jean Lallot, "Les origines de la théorie grammaticale dans l'antiquité classique," in *Travaux d'Histoire des Théories Linguistique* 1, ed. Luce Giard (Paris: U. of Paris, 1983), 31–47.

29. See also the discussion of εἴρω and λέγω in chapter 1. In addition to being verbs of speaking both are related to the activity of binding or gathering together and, as such, represent a form of interlacing. Plato's use of συμπλοκή emphasizes a synthetic function that did not find explicit expression until συμπλοκή became known as a rhetorical figure (see Alexander, περὶ σχηάτων, in *Rhetores Graeci,* ed. L. Spengel [Leipzig: Teubner, 1856], 30).

30. As the *Theaetetus* also makes clear, the combination of names is re-

garded by Plato as the essence of reason: ὀνομάτων γὰρ συμπλοκὴν λόγου οὐσίαν ($202^{b}3$).

31. The activity described by διαλύειν (formed from the verb λύειν: to free, loosen, untie, destroy) would be in strict opposition to the activity described by the verb διαπλέκειν (based on the verb from which συμπλοκή is derived, πλέκειν: to weave, plait).

32. On the subject of obliteration in philosophy, see Philippe Lacoue-Labarthe, "L'obliteration," in *Le sujet de la philosophie* (Typographies I) (Paris: Aubier-Flammarion, 1979), 111–84.

33. On this passage from the *Phaedrus* and, on the logic of the φάρμακον in particular, see also Derrida, "La pharmacie de Platon," in *La dissémination* (Paris: Seuil, 1972), 69–197.

34. Similarly, the "bad" letters and writing of Theuth become the "brother" of the legitimate writing of the soul. See Derrida, "La pharmacie de Platon," 171–72.

35. "Die Kleidung überhaupt, abgesehen von künstlerischen Zwecken, findet ihren Grund einesteils in dem *Bedürfnis,* sich vor den Einflüssen der Witterung zu schützen, indem die Natur dem Menschen nicht wie dem Tiere, das mit Fell, Federn, Haaren, Schuppen usf. bedeckt ist, diese Sorge abgenommen, sondern ihm dieselbe im Gegenteil überlassen hat. Anderenteils ist es das Gefühl der Schamhaftigkeit, welche den Menschen antreibt, sich mit Kleidern zu bedecken. Scham, ganz allgemein genommen, ist ein Beginn des Zorns über etwas, was nicht sein soll. . . . Bei allen Völkern, bei denen ein Anfang der Reflexion gemacht ist, finden wir deshalb auch in stärkerem oder geringerem Grade das Gefühl der Scham und das Bedürfnis der Bekleidung" [In general clothing, apart from artistic purposes, finds its reason, for one thing, in the *need* for protection from the weather, since nature has given man this concern while exempting animals from it by covering them with fur, feathers, hair, scales, etc. For another thing, it is a sense of shame which drives men to cover themselves with clothes. Shame, considered quite generally, is the start of anger against something that should not be. . . . Among all peoples who have risen to the beginning of reflection we find therefore in a greater or lesser degree the sense of shame and the need for clothing]. Hegel, *Vorlesungen über die Ästhetik, Werke* 14.2:402–3).

36. In its rhetorical usage, τμῆσις also names the separation of a compound word into its parts (for example, Virgil's separation of *quaecumque* in the line "Quae me cumque vocant terrae"). As this example indicates, the cutting is usually performed by the intervention of another word.

37. This definition of weaving which is centered on the product of this activity is repeated by Aristotle in the *Metaphysics* at a point where the subject is again the concept of δύναμις or potentiality: "Weaving is in the textile being woven" (*Met.* $1050^{a}32$–33) and "in those cases in which something beyond the activity is produced, the action lies in the product" ($1050^{a}30$–31).

38. For the Doric and Aeolian form of this word (μνῆμα), Liddell and Scott also cite its use to designate the memorial of a person or thing, a mound or building in honor of the dead, and a coffin, alongside its general use to denote a monument.

Index

Theory and the Evasion of History

Designed by Ann Walston

Composed by Village Typographers, Inc.,
in Baskerville

Printed by Princeton University Press
on 50-lb. Glatfelter Natural
and bound in Holliston Roxite